S0-BGW-198

NATIONS OF THE MODERN WORLD

ARGENTINA	H. S. Ferns *Professor of Political Science, University of Birmingham*
AUSTRALIA	O. H. K. Spate *Director, Research School of Pacific Studies, Australian National University, Canberra*
AUSTRIA	Karl R. Stadler *Professor of Modern and Contemporary History, University of Linz*
BELGIUM	Vernon Mallinson *Professor of Comparative Education, University of Reading*
BURMA	F. S. V. Donnison, C.B.E. *Formerly Chief Secretary to the Government of Burma Historian, Cabinet Office, Historical Section 1949-66*
CHINA	Victor Purcell, C.M.G. *Late Lecturer in Far Eastern History, Cambridge*
CZECHOSLOVAKIA	William V. Wallace *Professor of History, New University of Ulster*
DENMARK	W. Glyn Jones *Professor of Scandinavian Studies, University of Newcastle-upon-Tyne*
MODERN EGYPT	Tom Little, M.B.E. *Former Managing Director and General Manager of Regional News Services (Middle East), Ltd, London*
EL SALVADOR	Alastair White *Lecturer in Sociology, University of Stirling*
EAST GERMANY	David Childs *Senior Lecturer in Politics, University of Nottingham*

MODERN GREECE — John Campbell
Fellow of St Antony's College, Oxford

Philip Sherrard
Lecturer in History of the Orthodox Church, King's College, London

HUNGARY — Paul Ignotus
Formerly Hungarian Press Counsellor, London, 1947-49, and Member, Presidential Board, Hungarian Writers' Association

INDONESIA — Donald W. Fryer
Professor of Geography University of Hawaii

James C. Jackson
Professor of Modern Asian Studies Griffith University, Brisbane

ITALY — Muriel Grindrod, O.B.E.
Formerly Editor of International Affairs *and* The World Today
Assistant Editor The Annual Register

MEXICO — Peter Calvert
Senior Lecturer in Politics, University of Southampton

NORWAY — Ronald G. Popperwell
Fellow of Clare Hall, and Lecturer in Norwegian, Cambridge

PAKISTAN — Ian Stephens, C.I.E.
Formerly Editor of The Statesman, *Calcutta and Delhi, 1942-51*
Fellow, King's College, Cambridge, 1952-58

PERU — Sir Robert Marett, K.C.M.G., O.B.E.
H.M. Ambassador in Lima, 1963-67

THE PHILIPPINES — Keith Lightfoot
Naval, Military, and Air Attaché, British Embassy, Manila, 1964-67

POLAND — Václav L. Beneš
Late Professor of Political Science, Indiana University

Norman J. G. Pounds
Professor of History and Geography, Indiana University

PORTUGAL	J. B. Trend *Late Fellow, Christ's College, and Emeritus Professor of Spanish, Cambridge*
SOUTH AFRICA	John Cope *Formerly Editor-in-Chief of* The Forum *and South Africa Correspondent of* The Guardian
THE SOVIET UNION	Elisabeth Koutaissoff *Formerly Professor of Russian, Victoria University, Wellington*
SPAIN	George Hills *Formerly Correspondent and Spanish Programme Organizer, British Broadcasting Corporation*
SWEDEN	Irene Scobbie *Senior Lecturer in Swedish, University of Aberdeen*
SWITZERLAND	Christopher Hughes *Professor of Politics, University of Leicester*
SYRIA	Tabitha Petran
MODERN TURKEY	Geoffrey Lewis *Senior Lecturer in Islamic Studies, Oxford*
YUGOSLAVIA	Stevan K. Pavlowitch *Lecturer in Balkan History, University of Southampton*

NATIONS OF THE MODERN WORLD

INDONESIA

INDONESIA

By DONALD W. FRYER
and
JAMES C. JACKSON

LONDON/ERNEST BENN LIMITED

BOULDER/WESTVIEW PRESS

First published 1977 by Ernest Benn Limited
25 New Street Square, Fleet Street, London, EC4A 3JA
& Sovereign Way, Tonbridge, Kent, TN9 1RW
and Westview Press
1898 Flatiron Court, Boulder, Colorado 80301

Distributed in Canada by
The General Publishing Company Limited, Toronto

Printed in the United States of America

ISBN 0 510-39003-X
ISBN 0 89158-028-X (USA)

Preface

TO SURVEY A COUNTRY as large and as diverse as Indonesia within small compass is a formidable undertaking, and any such treatment must be highly selective. This work is the product of two academic geographers, formerly colleagues in the Department of Geography of the University of Malaya, who, despite their subsequent wide separation, have continued for many years to work closely together on problems of national development in South-east Asia. Inevitably, the choice of material selected for description and analysis reflects the pattern of our own professional interests, and in the treatment of certain themes we have drawn substantially on our previous published work, and on research currently in progress. Nevertheless, the work is in no sense a geography of Indonesia, even if at times we have been drawn into a discussion of what an earlier school of geographers might have called the personality of Indonesia. Our primary objective has been to provide for the informed layman, or for the businessman or public servant whose responsibilities make some knowledge of the country highly desirable, an impression of the landscapes and ways of life of Indonesia and how they came to be what they are; we have also tried to identify the more urgent of the many pressing problems confronting the country, and we hope, modestly, to suggest how an approach to a solution may be explored. We cannot pretend to have found a solution itself; that discovery, if it comes at all, can only be made by Indonesians.

All Europeans who have the temerity to write about Third World countries must be prepared to meet the charge that their analysis is the product of an ethnocentric bias, and we concede that our knowledge of the country is highly particulate and that a deeper understanding of Indonesian character requires, among other things, a lifetime of work and residence there. But we trust that our bias, or pattern of value judgements as we would prefer to call it, is explicit. Some of our comments on present-day Indonesia are harsh, but we know that our strictures are shared by many

Indonesians, and that nothing is to be gained by mincing words. Our comments, moreover, are motivated by a profound sympathy with, and respect for, the ordinary Indonesian people, whose needs and aspirations have for so long been given little real cognizance by those in authority, notwithstanding all protestations to the contrary. And here we are on firm ground; we know from our own experience in the field and from our students what the daily round of the peasant is like, and how he comes to make the complex pattern of decisions that govern his working life. We make no apologies for placing problems of the rural economy in the very forefront of our study; they are the most enduring, the most intractable, and the most pressing of all Indonesia's difficulties, and we believe with many scholars that the country may not long survive unless some solutions acceptable to the great mass of its rural population are found, and quickly. We have tried to steer a course for the reader through the labyrinthine intricacies of Jakarta and national politics, and to assist the reader, if he so wishes, to explore the rich literature on this field. But it is essential to realise at all times that the capital, important though it is in many ways, is nevertheless utterly divorced from the experience of the great mass of the population, and that in the regions life goes on, as it must, in much the same way whatever happens. But it cannot go on for very much longer simply because the resources available to support it are not expanding rapidly enough to cope with population increases. In view of its current importance, both to Indonesia and the world, an extended treatment is given to the petroleum industry, currently regarded as the potential saviour of the country. It is regretted that considerations of space do not permit a similar discussion of both timber and fisheries, two other extractive industries experiencing boom conditions in recent years, and whose exploitation likewise seems to generate remarkably few new employment opportunities, and to enlarge the disparity between the few super-rich and the multitudinous poor.

Some practical difficulties require to be brought to the attention of the reader. In 1972 Indonesia and Malaysia, whose national languages are essentially similar, adopted a new and uniform spelling system (known in Indonesia as EYD, or improved spelling system) to replace the different systems that they had inherited from the Dutch and British administrations respectively. In Malaysia the transition was made very rapidly, and is now in universal use. In Indonesia, however, the resources for speedy implementation were just not available, and the changeover has been slower; new and old forms continue to be used, and the spellings of some common words still differ between the two countries, e.g., 'new' is *baru* in Indonesia, *baharu* in Malaysia, although the word is pronounced as the Indonesian version suggests. Generally, the new system employs the consonants of the English system for writing Romanised Malay languages, but the vowels are largely as in the Dutch system. One peculiarity, however, is the use of 'c' for the Dutch 'tj' and the English 'ch', so that the familiar Atjeh, or Acheh, becomes the odd-looking Aceh. The new 'c' thus has much the same sound as the Italian 'c' before 'e' and 'i'. Another is that 'sy' is pronounced as 'sh'. Those unfamiliar with Indonesian or Malay and in doubt as to the pronunciation of some words should remember that the accent generally falls on the last syllable, or on the last syllable of the root word in a compound word, and that a very short, or enclitic, 'e' is inserted to aid the Indonesian and Malay tongue in pronouncing a double consonant. Recent changes in the names of familiar places compound the difficulty; place-names are thus first identified by their English forms, with the modern name in parentheses, e.g., Makasar (Ujungpandang); thereafter, the current name is used throughout, except in the historical chapters where the use of modern forms would make for confusion, and where the name in use at the time is retained.

The difficulty also extends to personal names, and here the objections to the system have been understandably strong. In practice anybody who wishes to spell his name in the way he has been accustomed, as is the case with everybody of any importance, continues to do so. Those who are deceased, however, have no such privilege, and many names have been changed in accordance with the new system. We have tried to follow popular usage, and the names of the living are spelt in the old way. Indonesians, as with many other Asian peoples, are usually identified by their given names, and the use of family names is really an accommodation to the needs of a modern administration. Several such names are really titular, or denote positions of rank or affiliation in a formerly feudal society, but the omission of such names can give rise to confusion when the given name is common to more than one person of prominence. Names are thus generally given in full, but where there is no possibility of confusion, the usual practice is followed; thus the former Prime Minister Ir. Djuanda Kartawidjaja (Ir. is a Dutch abbreviation for a qualified engineer) is identified as Juanda (modern spelling, being deceased). The spelling of Javanese names presents difficulties in that Javanese orthographical conventions are inapplicable to modern Indonesian, and the reader can expect to encounter Javanese and Indonesian versions, e.g., Pakubawana (Javanese), Pakubuwono (Indonesian). The traditional Javanese romanisation may also include Dutch conventions, e.g., Trunadjaja (Indonesian, Trunojoyo). The romanisation of Javanese is a complex matter, and in practice Javanese and Indonesian usages are often interchanged; nevertheless, there is a tendency for Indonesian orthography to prevail over Javanese with the passage of time.

Apart from spelling, another major difficulty for the scholar and the general reader alike is Indonesia's extraordinary propensity for coining acronyms, a bureaucratic disease which unfortunately has been passed on to Malaysia. No complete list of these can be compiled, for such is the volume of current output that any such attempt is speedily rendered obsolete. New acronyms pass rapidly into both the written and spoken languages, and although some fall into disuse with the passage of time, the total in circulation continues to mount steadily. A glossary of those employed here is provided for the reader, but if at times he finds himself at a loss for understanding, so too does the specialist.

Several colleagues and students of the authors have provided valuable assistance and comment in the preparation of this work. We are particularly grateful to Professor Robert Van Niel of the Department of History, University of Hawaii, who kindly read large sections of the manuscript; at several points Dr Van Niel parts company with the views expressed here, but although we have felt ourselves unable to accommodate him on all these differences, we have greatly benefited from exposure to his penetrating comments, derived from a deep knowledge of the country. Others who have helped in a multiplicity of ways include Mr W. Soewarto, Dr Oey Hong Lee, Dr Ida Bowers, Miss Iris Shinohara, Professor Gerrit de Heer, and Dr Wade Edmundson. To Mr Peter Jennings of the Fluor Corporation we owe a special debt of gratitude. The authors, of course, accept full responsibility for all errors and shortcomings.

D. W. F.
J. C. J.

Contents

List of Illustrations

(All are inserted between pages 192 *and* 193 *)*

Acknowledgements

ACKNOWLEDGEMENTS are due to the following copyright-holders for permission to reproduce the illustrations:

Camera Press Limited: 3, 20, 21, 22, 23, 24, 25
Indonesian Embassy, London: 2, 8, 16
Dr James C. Jackson: 1, 4, 7, 9, 13, 14, 15, 16, 18

Numbers 10, 11, and 19 are taken from the *Batavia Handbook* and 5, 6, 12, and 17 from the *1930 Handbook of the Netherlands East Indies*

Map

THAILAND
MALACCA STRAIT
Banda Aceh
5°
ACEH
PENINSULAR MALAYSIA
Medan
Kuala Lumpur
Anambas Is.
NORTH SUMATRA
SINGAPORE
Bintan
RIAU
Pekanbaru
Riau Archipelago
0°
WEST SUMATRA
Singkep
Padang
Jambi
JAMBI
Bangka
Mentawai Is.
SOUTH SUMATRA
Palembang
BENGKULU
Bengkulu
LAMPUNG
5°
Tanjung Karang
Banten
0
Km
400
10°
Christmas Is
a.k.
100°
105°

SOUTH CHINA SEA
SABAH
BRUNEI
Natuna Is.
Tarakan
EAST
MALAYSIA
SARAWAK
EAST
KALIMANTAN
WEST
KALIMANTAN
Pontianak
Samarinda
Balikpapan
CENTRAL
KALIMANTAN
Karimata
Is.
Belitung
Palangkaraya
SOUTH
KALIMANTAN
Banjarmasin
JAVA SEA
Bawean
Jakarta
WEST JAVA
Cirebon
Semarang
Madura
Bandung
CENTRAL JAVA
Surabaya
WEST NUSA
TENGGARA
YOGYAKARTA
Yogyakarta
EAST JAVA
BALI
Lombok
Denpasar
Mataram
Sumbawa
110°
115°

MINDANAO
PHILIPPINES
Sulu Archipelago
Talaud Is.
Sangihe Is.
Manado
Ternate
Tidore
Halmahera
NORTH SULAWESI
CENTRAL SULAWESI
Palu
SOUTH SULAWESI
SOUTHEAST SULAWESI
Kendari
Seram
Buru
Ambon
MALUKU
Ujungpandang
BANDA SEA
EAST NUSA TENGGARA
Wetar
Atauro
Flores
Dili
Sumba
Timur (Port.)
Kupang
TIMUR SEA
120°
125°

International boundary
Provincial boundary
Medan Provincial capital
JAMBI Name of province

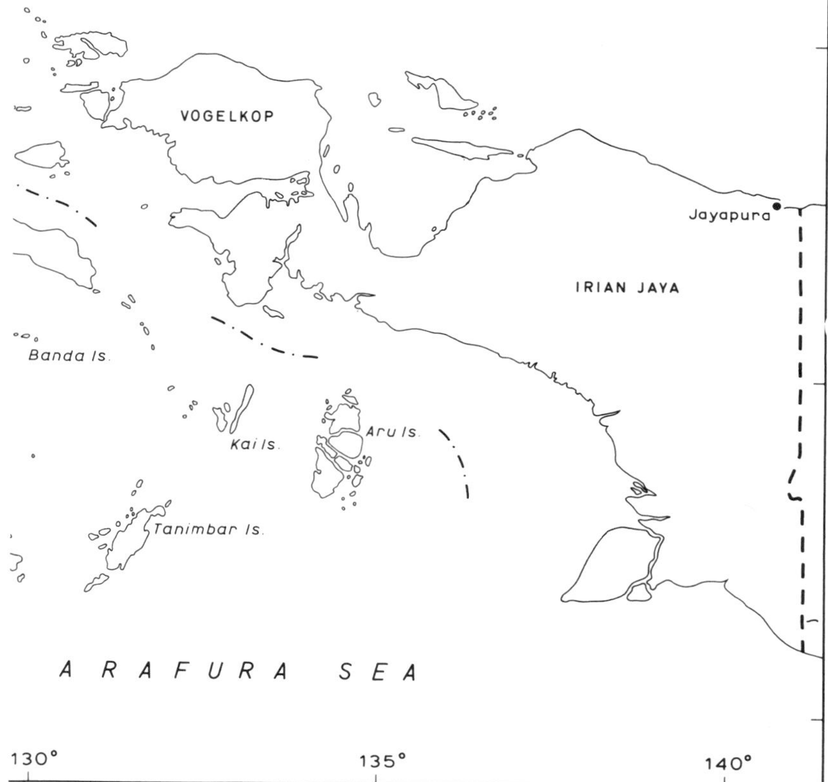

CHAPTER 1

The Land and the People

THE REPUBLIC OF INDONESIA ranks third among the six major countries of the Third World (China, India, Indonesia, Brazil, Bangladesh, and Nigeria) that between them account for half of world population, and among the independent states of Asia, only China and India possess a larger geographical area.[1] Indonesia contains some 40 percent of the total population of South-east Asia (that is, the Indochinese peninsula in the broadest sense together with the archipelagos of the Indonesian and Philippine republics), yet within this region it has never attained the position that its size and population would appear to command, and its attempt to establish such a hegemony brought the country to the verge of complete disaster. With the possible exception of North Vietnam, Indonesia is the poorest country in real terms in the whole of South-east Asia, and there is little evidence that living standards have shown any marked improvement for more than three decades.[2] Indonesia's economic record was long one of the most miserable in the entire Third World, and only since the fall of Sukarno in 1966 has economic development been accorded any real priority, as opposed to lip-service, in national goals.

The term Indonesia appears first to have been used by J.R. Logan, editor of the *Journal of the Indian Archipelago,* in 1850, and in 1884 it was adopted by the German ethnologist A. Bastian to designate all the island chains of the Indian and Pacific Oceans lying between Madagascar and Formosa. Since that date Indonesia has been widely used in scientific literature, and the name became increasingly attractive to Dutch writers as a substitute for the official Netherlands Indies. By the outbreak of World War II it had passed into widespread local use, and in 1948 the Dutch administration in Batavia (Jakarta) gave it official recognition. Independent Indonesia succeeded to all the territory of the Netherlands Indies with the exception of West New Guinea (Irian Barat, or, more commonly, Irian), which Indonesia did not gain *de jure* until 1969, when under a so-called 'act of free choice' a hand-picked delegation of Papuan chiefs and headmen gave an embarrassing 100 percent vote for continued adhesion of the territory to Indonesia, which had occupied it since 1963 under the terms of a United Nations agreement. Despite the attempts of 'Free Papua' leaders to enlist the support of the black African states in the U.N. in condemning the suppression of a 'one-man, one-vote' plebiscite, the decision was greeted with relief by the organisation, and any effective challenge to Indonesian rule will come only from the granting of independence to the Australian-administered territories of Papua and New Guinea, an event which took place in 1975.

The republic began its official existence on 17 August 1945, following the unexpected capitulation of the Japanese to the Allies, with a short proclamation of independence by Sukarno, who became the country's first President. There followed a long and confused struggle in which while the new republic fought for its life against the Dutch who were attempting to reoccupy their former colonial possession, the leaders of its fissiparous political parties fought ferociously for mastery. Although independence became effective in December 1949 when the Dutch formally transferred sovereignty to the new state, it was not until a year later, on the fifth anniversary of the declaration of independence, that a unitary Republic of Indonesia became a reality.

This long and exhausting struggle, in which the intervention of the United Nations was decisive, nevertheless left deep scars which time has so far been powerless to heal. Economically Indonesia began its existence at a most propitious time, with high prices for all of its products as a result of the Korean War. But these large windfall earnings, which were equated with the fruits of victory over the Dutch, were speedily frittered away by the incompetence and corruption of both ministers and officials. Political and economic instability has been extreme throughout the lifetime of the republic, and the attempt by President Sukarno after 1959 to restore national cohesion through a 'Guided Democracy' and a 'Guided Economy' merely accelerated the decay and disruption of economic and political life. To the traumatic experiences in the two decades preceding independence of acute economic depression, Japanese occupation, and the revolutionary war, Indonesia in the following two decades suffered a communist-led rebellion, inter-regional civil war, foreign war first against the Dutch in West New Guinea and then against the newly-formed federation of Malaysia (both euphemistically termed 'confrontations'), and a second communist revolt which produced a bloodbath reminiscent of the massacres that accompanied the partition of British India in 1947. Each succeeding political shock further aggravated the chronic inflationary pressure in Indonesia's stagnating economy, and with the runaway inflation brought on by the huge expenditure incurred in the confrontation of Malaysia, central budgetary control had virtually ceased to exist by the end of 1965, foreign exchange reserves were exhausted, exports had fallen to the lowest level in the republic's history necessitating default on the huge foreign debt, and complete economic collapse appeared imminent.

Much of this burden of indebtedness was the direct consequence of Sukarno's dream of establishing himself as the spokesman for the entire Third World, and building up *Indonesia Raya* (Greater Indonesia) as the foremost military power in South-east Asia. The first nation to owe its existence to the United Nations, Indonesia withdrew from the organisation and also from the World Bank and the International Monetary Fund early in 1965, and even planned a rival international body, *Conefo* (Conference of New Emerging Forces, that is, the new nations of the Third World), expenditure on which constituted a further drain on Indonesia's diminishing financial resources. After the fall of Sukarno a year later, Indonesia rejoined all three organisations, having established what could conceivably be an important principle, that secession from the United Nations is possible without penalty.

But there were more deep-seated reasons for Indonesia's travail than Sukarno's delusions of grandeur. After mid-1965 the government of General Suharto moved steadily towards the adoption of more pragmatic economic and foreign policies, and resumed cultural and economic contacts with the West which earlier had appeared likely to be replaced by links with the communist world. By 1972 the Indonesian economy had recovered in a way that scarcely seemed possible five years earlier, and the country was soon to receive enormous windfalls through the quadrupling of petroleum prices following the Yom Kippur War. But this has done very little to combat the basic economic and social shortcomings which the country inherited at birth, and whose resolution is essential to national survival. These problems take their origin in the great diversity of the physical environment, the maldistribution of resources within the national territory, the multiplicity of ethnic and cultural groups making use of these resources, and how such groups perceive themselves and their activities in relation to the Indonesian nation as a whole. This situation is epitomised in the inscription on the Indonesian Great Seal, *Bhinekka Tunggal Ika,* usually translated as Unity in Diversity.[3] But the islands that now constitute Indonesia never possessed any unity save that created by the Dutch, or forged in opposition to

Dutch rule, and with the achievement of independence it has been difficult for the several parts of Indonesia to agree on common goals. A unity that exists only in diversity does not appear a very positive one.

Rapid economic growth in some parts of the world has often greatly assisted national cohesion and stability. Not the least of Indonesia's misfortunes, a government policy aimed at promoting national integration has often impeded rather than stimulated economic growth. In relation to its large and rapidly growing population, Indonesia's resources are only meagre, and their geographical distribution is poorly related to national needs. Yet Indonesia's leaders and their many overseas admirers have long proclaimed the country's vast wealth of natural resources, which have often been pronounced as inferior only to those of the United States and the USSR. The concept that what is now Indonesia possesses vast untapped, yet easily exploitable, resources has existed for centuries. It is a myth; but unfortunately, it is a myth that dies hard, and 'until it is finally nailed, there is scant prospect of finding a way out of Indonesia's manifold difficulties'.[4] Even in 1964 an expert American body could write that

> the agricultural and industrial potential of Indonesia, developed and utilizing to the full its enormous reserves of manpower, could bring its citizens to a standard of living comparable with that of the world's most prosperous countries. Such were the prospects which lay ahead of the leaders of the triumphant Indonesian nationalist movement in 1950.[5]

Some broadly similar comment could be made about any of the more populous countries of the Third World. What is misleading about such statements is that they suggest the possibility of a large increase in living standards in the near future, when in fact no such possibility exists, and the political consequences of such optimism, reiterated *ad nauseam* since the birth of the republic, are likely to be severe. Even given a continuation of rational economic policies, the creation of a less corrupt and more dedicated public service, a high level of foreign aid, and a political and social climate favourable to the foreign investor, all conditions which are very far from being assured, Indonesia by the year 2000 might be able to raise its *per capita* GNP to perhaps $300, or rather more than double that of 1967 in terms of constant prices. Indonesia's oil bonanza notwithstanding, any serious world depression, or a failure of the world economy to grow at the pace of the post-war period, would delay attainment of such a goal.[6] It would, however, be no mean achievement in view of a present rate of population growth of not far short of 3 percent per annum, which gives an absolute addition of over 3 million each year. But even then the country would possess a *per capita* GNP less than two-thirds of that of Malaysia in 1970, and less than one-third that of Singapore in the same year. In absolute terms, the gap between living standards in Indonesia and its near neighbours appears likely to be far higher at the end of the century than at the present, by which time the greater part of Indonesia's present oil and gas resources will be exhausted.

Indonesia's principal resources, as with any country, are its land and its people, or more pertinently, the attitude to work and life of its population. It is true that the country's mineral wealth will almost certainly prove to be far larger than was believed in the past. Large additional oil-and gas-fields probably await discovery, particularly offshore, and although the geological structure is such that there is little chance of the discovery of the massive mineral deposits of the kind that are transforming the Australian economy, profitable discoveries of deposits of nickel and copper have already been made, and a more detailed search will almost certainly yield additional prizes. But most Indonesian soils are exceedingly poor in plant nutrients, and these are speedily exhausted in cultivation; areas of good soil are limited, and through centuries of monoculture have a low productivity. All are very densely populated. The forest area is certainly enormous, but its productivity is, and will long continue to be, very low. Vast areas of forest are being destroyed each year to permit an extension of the agricultural area, but which because of soil qualities and cultivation practices cannot long be maintained in cultivation. Indonesia's indigenous population is far from homogeneous, but few of its basically Malay peoples are strongly achievement motivated, and most economic activities outside food-producing agriculture are dominated by aliens, particularly the Chinese. Because of restrictions on alien enterprise designed to promote a national economy, that is, one owned and operated by indigenous Indoesians, many export industries operated at half-cock for many years, greatly impoverishing the whole country. Despite the adoption of more realistic economic policies since 1966, the rehabilitation of the traditional export industries is still far from complete.

Although over much of the archipelago an India-derived cultural heritage modified by an Islamic overlay of varying depths, an agrarian way of life based either on the *sawah* (the flooded rice-field) or on the *ladang* (a forest clearing devoted to subsistence cropping, but sometimes to export-oriented cash crops, particularly rubber), and languages of common Malay origin together provide some cohesive elements, geography and economic interests strongly pull the various parts of Indonesia in different directions. One such sundered part is the Malay peninsula, now shared by three sovereign states, but which has played almost as important a part in Indonesian history as any major island.

Geographic fragmentation is the most obvious architect of disunity. Indonesia extends over some 17° of latitude athwart the Equator, and over nearly 48° of longitude; the national territory is thus dispersed over some 8 million square kilometres (rather more than 3 million square miles) of the surface of the globe, an area as large as that of Australia or of the United States less Alaska. The total land area, however, is only some 2.03 million square kilometres (782,400 square miles), and is disseminated between nearly 14,000 islands.[7] The comminution of the national territory is not quite so extreme as it appears, as the five largest islands, Kalimantan (Indonesian Borneo), Sumatra, Irian, Sulawesi (Celebes), and Java (including Madura), account for nearly 92 percent of the land area and for nearly 94 percent of the population; discounting empty and isolated Irian, the four large western islands, occasionally called the Greater Sunda Islands in the past, form a compact group with more than 90 percent of the population and the country's physical resources. But while it is true that the distances separating the larger islands are not large, and the intervening seas are comparatively calm for most of the year and can be traversed from end to end by small sailing craft using the seasonal oscillations of wind systems over the archipelago, the operation of an efficient low-cost inter-island transport system has so far been beyond the country's capacity.[8] The high cost and capricious schedules of the national shipping lines, that is, those owned and operated by indigenous Indonesians as well as state-owned lines, contributed a large quota to the discontent of the *Tanah Seberang*, or Outer Islands (those parts of the country outside Java), which has been reinforced by the failure since independence to provide improvements or even minimum maintenance for the many small ports in outlying parts of the archipelago. The shortcomings of sea transport are reinforced by the fact that a large proportion of the total land area consists of mountains and swamps, so that apart from Java and Sumatra which have the best overland transport systems, contact between urban centres even on major islands is often only possible by sea. This shortcoming is in part offset by a proliferating network of air services, but the principal users of internal airlines are government servants, and there is no question that in the absence of greatly improved inter-island surface transport, national cohesion will remain weak, and economic growth will be slow.

Indonesia's peculiar physical geography is the product of its extremely complex geological structure. The arcuate alignment of islands, their intense volcanic activity, and frequent earthquakes are all evidence of great crustal instability. Volcanism is most active in Java, progressively less so in Sumatra (Indonesian, Sumatera), the Nusa Tenggara or Sunda Kecil (formerly Lesser Sunda Islands), Sulawesi, and Maluku (Moluccas), and entirely absent in Kalimantan and Irian. Volcanic ejactamenta help to replace the soluble minerals necessary for plant growth removed by downward percolating water, and in the hot and perpetually humid climate of the greater part of Indonesia such leaching is continuous throughout the year, thus producing soils of extremely low fertility. The plains surrounding the great volcanic cones of Java contain some of the densest rural populations in the world, but the relationship between volcanic activity and population density is complex; much depends on the chemical composition of the magmas generating the 'fall-out' and on the material culture of the people. Some intensely volcanic areas in eastern Indonesia support only a light population. The general poverty of the soils in the *Tanah Seberang* and the limited facilities for irrigation go far to explain their low overall population density, but even where as in the Padang highlands of West Sumatra or in the Minahasa peninsula of Sulawesi a benign volcanism has produced soils of above-average fertility, and hence in higher population densities, the latter never approach the average density for Java.

Java, which with Madura possesses nearly two-thirds of the total Indonesian population, appears always to have been the most populous island, for alone of the major islands it includes no disproportionately large area of mountains or swamps. The fertility of its plains, enriched by volcanic material carried by wind and water, and the ease with which irrigation could be practised with simple technologies, early encouraged their conversion into sawahs, and although the upland area is extensive, it is only exceptionally that it constitutes a major obstacle to movement or is repellent to settlement. Such negative areas are largely confined to parts of West Java (*Jawa Barat*), and to certain limestone areas, in particular the southern mountains, which border the Indian Ocean. The largest plains, such as the north-coast plain of West Java, and the south-coast plain of Central Java (*Jawa Tengah*) where the southern mountains are breached, are very densely populated; but some of the smaller plains of Central Java's north coast probably possess the highest rural densities of the globe.

The distinction between Java and the Outer Islands is the most fundamental division in every aspect of national life. It epitomises the contrast between the sawah and the ladang, or an inward-looking subsistence agriculture and an export-oriented one linked to the world economy; between a centralised bureaucracy deeply rooted in an old feudal aristocratic order, and an achievement-motivated regionalism; between mysticism and pragmatism. The Indonesian revolution under Sukarno gave a preponderance of political power to the Javanese, the country's dominant ethnic group; but the physical resources whose harnessing may eventually liberate Indonesia from the direst poverty, are overwhelmingly located in the *Tanah Seberang,* whose opposition to Javanese power has been a major theme in Indonesian history.

Yet Java itself possesses great variety, and in some ways is a miniature replica of the whole country. Much of the landscape is extremely attractive to the visitor. The vast expanses of bright green, or gold according to season, of the sawahs of the great plains resemble placid seas, from which the darker greens of the villages rise like islands, the dwellings invisible behind the thick plantings of coconuts, fruit trees, bamboos, and other perennials planted in the house lots. In Central and in East Java (*Jawa Timur*) sawahs may rise gently, tier upon tier, up the valley sides, and in the complex volcanic plateaux of West Java, or in Bali, plummet dramatically in great cascades of terraces, sometimes scarcely one metre in width, to deeply incised rock-strewn rivers. But it is a desperately poor and overcrowded land, and the sensitive traveller soon realises that the apparent beauty is bought at a heavy social cost. Nowhere is the face of poverty more strikingly obvious than in the limestone areas, where no sawahs are to be found; these are a patchwork of maize and tapioca cultivation with occasional teak plantations, and innumerable goats which steadily lay waste an already debased vegetation. Nor is any area as poverty-stricken or as depressing to the visitor as the karst-like Gunung Sewu (Thousand Mountains) south-east of Yogyakarta; yet even this desolate expanse, in which even drinking water is often in scarce supply in the dry season, is thickly populated by the standards of the Outer Islands.

Everywhere in Indonesia, and most strikingly in Java, there are swarms of children. Java's population growth is a demographic classic; from Raffles's estimate of 4.6 million in 1815 numbers had grown to 42 million by 1930, and even if the earlier figure is a gross underestimate, as appears probable, the change in a society which had remained almost entirely rural throughout, is forceful enough. But by 1970 Java's population surpassed 75 million, and

100 million will be attained before 1980. West Java, however, is somewhat less populous than are Central and East Java, and in some ways has closer affinities with the *Tanah Seberang* than with the rest of the island. Thus, although the North Java plain, in which is situated the national capital, Jakarta, is almost as densely populated and intensely cultivated as are any of the plains to the east, to the south and west, a mountain and plateau country presents very different patterns of land use. As in the Outer Islands, cash crops replace rice, which tends to be confined to the more fertile basins and irrigable valleys. On poorer soils at low elevations much land is planted to rubber, and in the Puncak (summit) district south of Jakarta, the capital's nearest hill-station and site of many week-end and holiday villas of the élite, and in the Priangan highlands south of Bandung, tea estates are numerous. At the junction of mountain and plain some 50 kilometres south of Jakarta, and in danger of being engulfed at no great future date by the capital's sprawl, is Bogor (formerly Buitenzorg), site of one of the world's most famous botanical gardens, and whose work was of fundamental importance in the establishment of a flourishing commercial tropical agriculture in the Netherlands Indies. The home of the Faculty of Agriculture of the University of Indonesia, Bogor is also a testament to Thomas Stamford Raffles, the remarkable Governor of Java during the period of British occupation in the early nineteenth century, and whose handiwork has proved so enduring in the island; his palace, for many years overlooking the lake in which grows the famous giant *Victoria regina* water-lily from the Amazon, was the official residence of the Governor-General of the Netherlands Indies, and since independence has been the home of the President.

West Java's Sundanese population, which is more akin to the Lampung people of South Sumatra than to the Javanese to the east, helps to reinforce a climatic and economic similarity with the larger island. West Java has no dry season; the sugar industry so important further east never developed, and typically equatorial crops such as rubber do well. Sundanese work on rubber and tea estates, and although rice-farmers in the lowlands, have not completely abandoned ladang cultivation in the remoter uplands. In West Java, but scarcely of it, Jakarta, with its swollen population fast approaching 5 million, is the most populous urban centre in South-east Asia. The focus of every aspect of national life and a home to large colonies of every indigenous group in the archipelago, to say nothing of the country's largest concentration of Chinese, Jakarta's physical appearance and pathetic attempts to provide its burgeoning population with employment, housing, and utilities of all kinds on a miniscule budget, recall the great cities of India rather than the opulent capitals of Singapore, Kuala Lumpur, and Bangkok in Indonesia's neighbours. West Java's own regional capital, Bandung, is a much more salubrious and attractive city, situated in an old lake basin at an elevation of some 700 metres (2,300 ft). A major manufacturing centre and with a population of more than one million, Bandung might well have become the national capital but for the intervention of World War II, for the Dutch administration had long planned an escape from the steamy heat of Batavia to this hill city.

West Java merges into Central Java in the great volcanic massif of Selamat. Eastwards to the Ijen massif in Besuki in the island's eastern extremity extends a series of great volcanic cones, nearly all of which exceed 3,000 metres in elevation (almost 10,000 ft), and rising in Semeru in East Java to 3,676 metres (12,060 ft), the highest point in the island. Their lower slopes and encircling plains are intensively cultivated, often with two crops in the year, and all are densely populated. A dry season becomes progressively more marked to the east, although there are great differences in the rainfall regime between north and south coasts. These circum-volcanic plains once supported an important sugar industry, whose allegedly baleful influence on Javanese rural society is examined in Chapter 4. At higher elevations are plantations of coffee or tea, above which extends the forest, or what remains of it, so important for the preservation of irrigation systems.

Under the pressure of mounting population, and peasant, or *petani,* land hunger, illegal cutting and clearing of the forest for fuel or for the planting of tapioca or other tuberous crops have now reduced the proportion of forest land far below the minimum for the preservation and maintenance of irrigation and drainage systems. By 1970 scarcely 15 percent of the area of Java was forested, as against a minimum of 30 percent deemed desirable by the Netherlands Indies Forestry Department before World War II. In the wake of this attack on the forest have come accelerated run-off, increased erosion, the progressive silting of drainage and irrigation channels, and increased susceptibility to flooding, in sum a continuous degradation of both land and man.

In the days of the Netherlands Indies, numerous hill-stations provided relief from the steamy heat of the plains for government servants and senior personnel of the great planting and trading companies. Though greatly run down, the stations still exist and the Indonesian government was overlong in ignoring their substantial tourist potential. Several of the volcanoes are exceedingly dangerous, and are thus under constant observation so that the population at risk can be evacuated in good time. But familiarity breeds an inevitable contempt; it is always extremely difficult to persuade villagers to leave their established homes and fields, and when danger is directly perceived, it is often too late to avoid. The splendid Netherlands Indies Vulcanological Service was an immediate casualty of independence, and as with many of the old colonial scientific services, creating an effective replacement was a long and arduous task. Gunung Merapi north of Yogyakarta, one of a great quadrilateral of volcanic peaks with Sumbing, Sindoro, and Merbabu, is probably the world's most restless volcano, and its ceaseless activity is frequently punctucated by more violent eruptions. Kelut, to the east of Kediri in East Java, and which over the past millennium has erupted in paroxysmal fury every 30 years on the average, is even more dangerous on account of its crater lake, the contents of which are expelled in eruptions, producing *lahar,* or hot mud flows. These not only cause loss of life but are extremely destructive of agricultural land, sweep away any houses, dams, or other obstacles in their path, and by blocking watercourses cause serious flooding on the Brantas river. After the disastrous eruption of 1919 which resulted in over 5,000 deaths, Dutch engineers constructed a system of siphons to drain the lake, but these became blocked in subsequent eruptions, and the *lahar* produced by the last great eruption of 1966 were just as devastating as any of the past, destroying part of the town of Blitar some 30 kilometres distant.

To the north and south of the volcanic massifs are belts of limestones, although in East Java the barren southern mountains are frequently breached by fertile valleys, where before World War II the Netherlands Indies sugar industry reached its apogee in the great mill and estate plantings of Lumajang. Madura, which has long formed an administrative unit with East Java, is a continuation of the limestone landforms of Rembang to the west. With its thin dry soils and sawahs confined to a narrow rim around the coasts, densely populated Madura well fits the Scots description of Fife, 'a beggar's mantle fringed with gold'. Large numbers of Madurese have migrated to the major island, and together with immigrant Balinese give East Java a more mixed population than that of Central Java, the cultural hearth of the Javanese people.

Densely populated Bali and Lombok closely resemble East Java, from which they have been separated by recent earth movements. Bali is renowned for the beauty of its landscape, and for the art and culture of its people, whose skill in tunnelling through the soft volcanic tuff of Gunung Agung has created some of the most intricate indigenous irrigation systems and rice terraces in Asia. The

Balinese are unique in largely retaining a Hindu-based religion, which was formerly more widespread in Indonesia before the coming of Islam, and the great volcano Gunung Agung is sacred to them as the focal point of the world, above which dwell the gods. Bali has acquired a reputation as a haven of peace and beauty, in which man and nature are in harmony. But in 1963, after some 200 years of quiescence, and at a time which coincided with the beginning of the greatest of all Balinese rituals of dedication and purification, the *Eki Dasa Rudra* held every 120 years, Agung exploded in a series of paroxysmal eruptions which caused over 1,500 deaths, and destroyed or damaged for some three decades to come nearly one-third of the island's cultivated land. Many villagers were asphyxiated by the incandescent *nuées ardentes* which rolled at high speed down the mountainside, but others who could have fled the rain of ash and the lava flows chose not to do so, and, stricken with the wrath of their gods, calmly awaited death as their priests, with banners flying, marched straight into the path of the advancing inferno, determined to propitiate the gods by the full and proper observance of the great ritual, which the government had in vain asked them to call off.[9] Nevertheless, this natural disaster caused far less loss of life and damage to the social structure than a man-made one two years later, when a murderous fury swept over the island in the wake of the *Gestapu* plot of 1965, and as in Java and parts of Sumatra, communists and their sympathisers (usually poor landless peasants whose ideological commitment was minimal) were butchered in thousands.[10] Clearly, the Western image of Bali needs revision.

Although densely populated Lombok reproduces the landscapes of Bali, this Islamic island lacks the cultural attractions of its neighbour. The naturalist Wallace, joint discoverer with Darwin of the Theory of Evolution, drew his line separating the fauna of Asia from that of the Australian region along the Lombok Strait, although it is now generally recognised that he placed this division too far to the west. East of Lombok, the Nusa Tenggara (South-east Islands), sometimes Sunda Kecil (Little Sunda Islands), present a different world. Both Sumbawa, where in 1815 Tambora burst forth in one of the most violent explosions in history, and Flores possess active volcanoes, but many of the smaller islands are non-volcanic, and the poverty of their soils is allied with a severe dry season, which becomes fiercer eastwards towards Australia. Limited opportunities for irrigation thus severely restrict the extent of sawahs, and although the overall density of population is light, the province is an area of net emigration. To the north Maluku (Moluccas) is drenched with rain throughout the year, and its small well-populated volcanic islands contrast with the much larger and more numerous non-volcanic ones just as they have throughout history. Although the spice islands of Banda, Ambon (Amboyna), Ternate, and Tidore constitute the part of Indonesia with the longest European contacts, the province is now a backwater in national life. Rugged and scantily populated Buru has been selected as a place of permanent banishment for the hard-core communists imprisoned in Java after *Gestapu*. Yet Maluku has long been a centre of resistance to a unitary Indonesia, and although its attempts at establishing independence were suppressed, *émigrés* in the Netherlands continue the struggle, and the desire for autonomy is still strong.

Sumatra and Kalimantan have a special importance in that they generate over 90 percent of Indonesia's income, so that the two islands carry a heavy responsibility for the financial resources for Indonesia's development plans. Dissatisfaction in Sumatra at its prolonged exploitation by the central government, which, Sumatrans claimed, granted to it totally inadequate funds in return for its large foreign-exchange earnings, boiled over in 1957-58 in the PRRI-*Permesta* rebellion.[11] Although provincial authorities now receive a direct share of any foreign exchange from any exports originating within their area, the sense of exploitation has by no means disappeared, nor has the smuggling trade to which it gives rise.

With a population of some 21 million in 1971, Sumatra is the next most populous island after Java, and on almost every test has the best balance of population to resources of the whole country. But even Sumatra has a large proportion of useless land. Its mountainous western rampart, the *Barisan* (range, or barrier), is punctuated by numerous volcanoes, among which Kerinci (3,805 metres, or 12,470 ft) is the highest point in Indonesia outside Irian. The Barisan presents a steep scarp to the Indian Ocean, and the great rivers draining the gentler eastern slope have created an enormous expanse of repellent swampland, much of it produced during historical times, which occupies almost one-third of the island. The Barisan, however, contains numerous fertile and densely populated basins, and on its eastern flanks are located many rich petroleum-bearing structures. Parts of this eastern zone possess soils enriched by volcanic ejactamenta, and particularly favoured is the northern extremity abutting on the Malacca Strait; here before World War II was located what was perhaps the most intensive concentration of large and highly efficient estates in the world, producing tobacco, rubber, palm-oil, tea, and sisal. Moreover, it is only in the highland basins of the Barisan, or where irrigation works have been provided for the new 'colonies' of Javanese immigrants, that sawahs are commonly to be found in Sumatra. Many indigenes have long practised a ladang agriculture, which in this century has become increasingly commercialised through plantings of pepper, coffee, and rubber, so that food production is frequently relegated to a subsidiary role. These peasant plantings in fact predated the establishment of European estates, but were greatly stimulated by them, and in the inter-war period an enormous extension of smallholder rubber production swiftly carried the Netherlands Indies to the verge of becoming the world's largest rubber-producer, threatening to displace Malaya, which had occupied that position since the beginnings of the plantation rubber industry early in this century.

Sumatra not only accounts for about 85 percent of Indonesia's petroleum production of some 70 million tons in 1974, but has other valuable mineral wealth. It contains the country's only commercially exploited coalfields, and the islands of Bangka, Belitung (Billiton), and Singkep to the east, and administratively part of Sumatra, have long been famous for their tin, of which the Netherlands Indies, and for a time in the early 1950s Indonesia also, was the world's second largest producer.

Kalimantan resembles Sumatra in its heavy year-round rainfall and dense forest cover. But the island's rugged core, the absence of active volcanoes and consequent poverty of the soil, and the vast areas of coastal swamps have protected much of the forest from the encroachments of agriculture, and with only a little over 4 million people in 1971, Kalimantan had the lowest population density outside empty Irian. Nevertheless, the island possesses substantial resources; it produced some 15 percent of Indonesia's petroleum in 1974, and large expansion programmes were in hand. In the eighteenth century western Kalimantan was one of the principal mining areas of South-east Asia, and its goldfields attracted many immigrant Chinese, whose descendants now grow pepper, rubber, and other cash crops. But its most obvious resource is its forest wealth, exploitation of which before 1966 was only fitful in comparison with that of neighbouring Sabah (North Borneo). Japanese interests have since been extremely active in developing the lumber industry, but all too often the interests of conservation and a sustained yield have been ignored, and the downturn in the industry at the end of 1974 consequent on the growing prospects of world depression may provide a much-needed respite from unregulated cutting. Although a few 'colonisation' schemes have been launched in South and East Kalimantan, mostly by veterans' associations, Kalimantan can never attract large numbers of land-hungry from Java. But with its mineral wealth, export-oriented agriculture, and developing forest industries, Kalimantan will continue to play an important role in national economic life.

Contorted and mountainous Sulawesi is almost twice as populous as Kalimantan, but lacks the larger island's strong external economic orientation. Its most favoured areas for settlement are the regions of active volcanism in the southern peninsula, and in the Minahasa, at the extremity of the northern peninsula. In the Ujungpandang (Makasar) area, sawah agriculture is combined with fishing and coconut cultivation in the traditional pattern of coastal Malay peoples, but the inhabitants of the southern peninsula have long sought a livelihood from the sea, and the Makasarese and Buginese have a reputation for piracy and trading; Buginese sailing craft still traverse the archipelago from end to end, in competition with modern shipping services. The Minahasans and Menadonese have perhaps been more heavily influenced by the West than any other indigenous group, and, as with the Ambonese of nearby Maluku, are largely Christian. In the Minahasa and in the Sangihe and Talaud islands to the north are found the most extensive coconut plantings in Indonesia, much of whose produce has for years been smuggled to Philippine ports to avoid the low prices paid by the Indonesian government, just as the rubber of Sumatra continues to be clandestinely shipped across the Malacca Strait. Mineral exploitation appears likely to become of increasing importance to Sulawesi and its offshore islands, which have long been known to possess deposits of both ferrous and nonferrous minerals. In the past, inaccessibility and technical difficulties in processing have discouraged the working of such deposits, but nickel-mining in the south-east peninsula is now well established through joint ventures of Japanese capital and the government.

In contrast, it is difficult to see much future for many decades to come for backward and isolated Irian, populated by some 800,000 of the world's most primitive people. The acquisition of this formidable wilderness of jagged mountains, whose highest points remain perpetually snow-covered (Puncak Jaya, formerly Puncak Sukarno and Carstensz Toppen in the Netherlands Indies, some 5,029 metres or 16,500 ft in elevation, is the highest point in Indonesia), and of the largest and most repellent swamps in the world by a poverty-stricken and bankrupt nation already oversupplied with such useless land, completed the creation of a free Indonesia 'from Sabang to Merauke', as ardent nationalists desired. But as with the Netherlands Indies, Irian will consume more resources than it can generate if Indonesia wishes to consolidate its hold and contain a nascent Papuan nationalism, and the long battle for its acquisition was primarily a device for maintaining a sense of national unity, as it was the only major issue on which most Indonesians thought alike. Since its effective occupation in 1963, flights of the native population across the border into the Australian-administered territories, and armed uprisings against Indonesian authorities by interior tribesmen, have indicated that all was not well with Irian. Indonesia's claim to the territory rests on its status as the legatee of the Netherlands Indies, and on the vague historic suzerainty exercised over part of the island's west coast by the sultanates of Ternate and Tidore; none of the leaders of Indonesia have ever expressed any nostalgia for the desolate landscapes bordering the Digul river, where many of them were incarcerated by the Dutch before World War II. Whatever the verdict of history, the geological, biological, and ethnological affinities of West New Guinea are all with the remainder of the island and with the Australian continent, and even before the transfer of power, the Dutch administration had established with its Australian counterpart a permanent joint committee for the resolution of common problems. This development was attacked by Indonesia as a device for perpetuating colonial rule.

Irian's resource base is slender in the extreme. Its Papuan and Melanesian population practises a ladang, or shifting, agriculture, in which roots and tubers almost entirely replace cereals, and there is little surplus available for sale. The development of a more commercialised agriculture is greatly impaired by the almost complete absence of overland transport, and given the formidable terrain, the costs of providing this would be extremely high. The biggest, and virtually the only, industry in the territory at the time of the handover was a little petroleum production from the Vogelkop (Bird's Head) peninsula, but prolonged exploration had brought little return, and the company was on the verge of withdrawing from production at the time of the transfer. Preparatory work was also in hand for the development of a suspected large copper-ore body on the southern slopes of Carstensz. Through good fortune, and the 1967 Foreign Investment Law, the hopes for a brighter future for the mineral industries of the territory were realised. But much ill-will was generated immediately after the handover by the removal to Java of everything mobile or in short supply in stagnating and inflation-racked Indonesia, and isolating the territory's own currency from the Indonesian rupiah was expensive and created many opportunities for fraud on the part of officials. Even the small proportion of the population that had been drawn into the miniscule modern economy of the Dutch administration largely returned to the traditional way of life, and most of the labour for the new mineral enterprises has had to be imported, a development certain to increase social tensions in the future. Irian, in sum, cannot expect any major public development expenditure for some time to come; but long before that time, the successor to Papua-New Guinea will have become a member of the United Nations, and Indonesia may face strange new problems.

Although in practice disposal outside the capital rested in large part with the panglimas (local military commanders), there is little doubt that in the decade after 1955 Javanese interests prevailed in the allocation of resources, and indeed in most aspects of national life. The Javanese account for little more than 40 percent of the country's total population, but they constitute by far the largest ethnic and cultural group. Sukarno, the country's first President, was half-Javanese and half-Balinese, but Suharto, his successor, is a Javanese, born and bred in a Central Java village. While Javanese are to be found throughout the country, and especially as officials, their homeland is Central and East Java; important concentrations of Javanese are, however, found in North Sumatra, where they constitute much of the labour force in the estate industries, and in South Sumatra and Lampung, where they have settled in planned 'transmigration' schemes, or as volunteer migrants. Despite post-war Indonesia's rapid urban growth, Javanese society is still overwhelmingly village oriented, and retains many of its old feudal roots. The *priyayi,* the Javanese aristocracy, occupied an important role in the Netherlands Indies between the senior Dutch administrators and the peasantry (*rakyat,* or in Javanese, *wong cilik,* the 'little people'), and although as a class the *priyayi* were discredited during the revolution for their subservience to the Dutch, and, with a single important exception, all the princely houses were swept away, their lower levels were catapulted into the topmost positions in government service with independence. Indonesia's chronic political instability augmented the power and influence of the permanent senior officials, and, to many peoples of the Outer Islands, the Javanese is identified as the upstart jack-in-office. In theory all feudal titles were abolished after the revolution, but a *Raden* (prince) is still respected, and although the most eminent of the hereditary aristocracy, the Sultan of Yogyakarta and the country's Vice President, has for long discarded all observance of feudal practices and ritual, he continues to command the solemn deference due to his rank, and in his own *daerah* (region) is still regarded as a demigod by the elderly and uneducated.

In contrast to coastal Malay peoples such as the Acehnese of northern Sumatra or the Makasarese of Sulawesi, both noted for their pugnacity and rigorous observance of the Muslim faith, which is held by perhaps as much as 90 percent of the Indonesian population, the Javanese are a docile people on whom the mantle of Islam rests but lightly. Vestiges of earlier Buddhist and Hindu beliefs, and a broad substratum of animism, clearly show through, and most rural Javanese are strong believers in fate, portents, and the spirit world. This Javanese tradition is epitomised as *abangan,* in contrast to the *santri,* whose lives are closely regulated by Islamic tenets, although the pressure of events as Indonesia slowly moves into the modern world steadily operates to obliterate such stereotypes. The life of the village is ordered by the *adat,* or customary law, and the practices of *musyarwarat* (discussion), *mufakat* (consensus), and *gotong-royong* (mutual help). Ideally, the decision-making process is a broad collective responsibility, in which a strongly expressed submission of a take-it-or-leave-it nature is grossly discourteous, as is also a direct refusal or negation; this traditional Javanese *adagio* was brilliantly employed by General Suharto, first in removing President Sukarno from office, and then in denying him any effective political influence. The Javanese is only really *senang* (contented) when in his own, usually rice-cultivating, village, and in different environments is a prey to melancholy; to leave the village is a confession of failure or social inadequacy, and although many Javanese have abandoned their ancestral homes to seek now economic opportunities in the towns or in the *Tanah Seberang,* the proverb *'mangan ora mangan, kumpul'* (eat or not eat, remain with me) reflects the strong pressure of forces binding the Javanese to the village of his birth. He is an indifferent estate-worker, less efficient and resourceful than his Tamil counterpart in the Malay peninsula, and forced by the government in Batavia upon a reluctant planting industry, which would have preferred imported Chinese labour, but which might well have obtained a higher productivity had it treated him better. The Javanese 'colonies' of southern Sumatra have no desire to compete with the native Lampungers as swidden (ladang) producers of dry-field food crops, coffee, or rubber; their sawah environment has to be reproduced through expensive government irrigation works, so that they live in 'little Javas'.

Although communism in Indonesia, as throughout South-east Asia, has always been particularly associated with the Chinese community, and has Peking rather than Moscow as its lodestar, for reasons which are discussed in Chapters 4 and 5, it grew to be a powerful force in the Javanese heartland during the Sukarno regime. To all dedicated Muslims in Indonesia, whether Javanese or non-Javanese, communism of course was anathema. But Javanese communists and their supporters were not prepared to abide by the traditions of society, to endure without complaint and with fortitude, even to starve if necessary, but demanded immediate and forceful action to improve the level of welfare, a course from which all good Javanese instinctively recoil, for their society possesses many methods of redistributing income; the rich man who ignores his social obligations is ostracised. Hence the traditional docility was replaced by an unparalleled ferocity as the custodians of *adat* and orthodox Muslims rounded on the trouble-makers after the collapse of the *Gestapu* revolt. Yet the situation in the longer run is clearly unstable; if Javanese or any traditional society cannot provide places for all of its growing numbers, the outcome can only be further outbursts of violence.

Of the 300 other linguistic or cultural groups distinguished in Indonesia, only the Sundanese of West Java number more than 10 million, and the great majority number less than one million. But several peoples of the Outer Islands have achieved a greater degree of success than the Javanese in adapting their societies to a changing world; Sumatrans were prominent in most Indonesian cabinets before the imposition of Sukarno's 'Guided Democracy', and it was hardly their fault that their efforts were largely unavailing. One of the best-known peoples of Sumatra is the Minangkabau, a Muslim group much studied because of its matriarchal-oriented society, and originally sawah farmers in the highland basins of the Barisan in Central Sumatra. But from this core the Minangkabau have expanded into the neighbouring lowlands, to become flourishing coffee, coconut, and rubber smallholders; they also migrated across the Malacca Strait, where their descendants now combine padi planting with rubber smallholdings in the valleys of Negri Sembilan. The traditional Minangkabau dwelling, with its soaring upswept roof, is very striking, and its style has been much copied, even in modern architecture, throughout the Malay world. The Minangkabau are also noted for their business acumen and for their shrewdness as traders, and are one of the few indigenous peoples able to compete with the Chinese.

The various Christian peoples have an importance out of all proportion to their small numbers, as they have become much more Westernised than other indigenous peoples, and have long enjoyed superior educational facilities through the mission schools. The Bataks, a group of half a dozen related tribes inhabiting the volcanic highlands bordering Lake Toba, were converted by Lutheran missionaries only in the latter half of last century.

Some Batak *marga* (clan), however, are predominantly Muslim, as is the case with the *marga* Nasution. Formerly swidden agriculturists, the Bataks have also become cash-crop farmers, and since the Japanese occupation have migrated in large numbers into the adjacent estate area of the Oostkust, as it was called in the Dutch days, now part of the province of North Sumatra. Bataks are found in white-collar jobs throughout the country; they are widely employed as office-workers on estates and in the administration, and as teachers. They are also well represented in the army, which, despite much non-professional deadwood, offers more opportunity for advancement based on merit than any other indigenous organisation.

The largely Lutheran Minahasans and Menadonese, already noted as prosperous owners of coconut estates or smallholdings, also owe much of their standing in the country to superior education. The Ambonese, who through long contact with Portuguese and Dutch are both Catholic and Lutheran, still cultivate nutmeg and clove gardens, the resources that first led Europeans into these Eastern seas, and found many employments in the service of Europeans. The Ambonese were particularly numerous in the armed forces of the Netherlands Indies, and many still serving in 1949 elected to emigrate to the Netherlands rather than accept life in an independent Indonesia. The uncompromising attitude of these Ambonese Dutch citizens, who had declared a government-in-exile of 'The Republic of the South Moluccas' in the Netherlands, became an embarrassment to the Dutch government as relations with Indonesia steadily improved under the Suharto administration, all the more so as Ambonese demonstrations, in conformity with world trends among dissident minorities and displaced peoples, became steadily more violent. That many in Maluku found a unitary Indonesia uncongenial has already been remarked; but as with the Sultan of Turkey who in his distant provinces ruled lightly so that he could rule at all, outside the towns, and sometimes even within them, the writ of Jakarta long counted for little in the more distant eastern islands.

However, all Indonesians are Javanese, Madurese, Balinese, Karo (Batak), Buginese, Boyanese (from Bawean Island) first, and Indonesians second; their primary allegiance is to their linguistic or ethnic group. In the cities peoples of the various groups, and especially new in-migrants, tend to congregate together in distinct colonies, and it is only to the educated élite that such communal ties have little appeal. To the young, schooled in the Malay-derived national language *Bahasa Indonesia,* even if speaking the local language at home, traditional ethnic values are also of less significance, and the fact that more than 40 percent of the population is below the age of 15 and less encumbered with the shibboleths of the past should be an enormous asset to Indonesia in adjusting to a changing world. After the remarkable educational achievements of the early post-independence years, the sharp decline in educational facilities and standards produced by the excesses of the later years of the Sukarno regime was thus a major tragedy.

The non-indigenous Chinese, Arabs, Indians, Eurasians, and Europeans, though in total less than 3 percent of the population, have a fundamental importance in economic life. Of these groups, the largest and most important is the Chinese, but as with all non-indigenous peoples, long residence and intermarriage with Indonesians have greatly modified its traditional values and allegiances. Peoples of Chinese and mixed Chinese-Indonesian ancestry have been variously estimated at between 2½ to 3 million, and are customarily divided between the *totok,* or China-born, whose value systems are still largely those of the homeland, and the *peranakan,* or locally born, who have been greatly influenced by Indonesian institutions, and who are often heavily Westernised. As throughout South-east Asia, the Chinese are mainly urban and engaged in trading and shopkeeping, but they are also important producers of cash crops, either as estate-owners or as smallholders; though seldom directly engaged in rice cultivation, they are very active in the rice industry as merchants and millers. They are also numerous in banking and finance, in processing and manufacturing, and in the learned professions. Long mistrusted, and occasionally massacred in both colonial and independence periods alike, the Chinese have nevertheless remained indispensable. Their future, however, is uncertain, and for an extended treatment of the Chinese problem in Indonesia and its background, the reader is referred to Chapter 9.

As with the Chinese, Arabs and Indians have lived in the archipelago since pre-European times. Most of Indonesia's 60,000 or so Arabs are from the Hadramaut, where most eventually return, or hope to do so when they have amassed enough for retirement. The Arabs are largely confined to the cities of Java, where they are petty traders or moneylenders, but some Arab enterprises are of surprisingly large size. Being orthodox Muslims, the Arabs are not considered an alien community, and intermarry freely with Indonesians; an Indonesian of exceptional business or financial acumen often proves to possess some Arab blood. The smaller Indian community is likewise mainly urban, although a few still live in north-east Sumatra, descendants of indentured estate labourers brought in during the latter half of the last century. Sukarno's estrangement from India in 1963 resulted in a sharp decline in the fortunes of the Indian community, and in the following years many returned home.

The Eurasians are now largely of historical interest, for few of the 150,000 or so resident in the country in 1949 now remain. These offspring of Dutch-Indonesian unions were legally and socially part of the European community in the Netherlands Indies, and their principal employment was in government service, but some were engaged in European business houses, and in the professions. Being largely dependent on the colonial administration for their livelihoods, the future of most *Indos,* as they were sometimes called, became bleak in the extreme with the transfer of sovereignty, and many chose to be repatriated to the Netherlands, a country few had ever seen. Of those who elected to remain, most were in effect driven out by the nationalisation of all Dutch assets in 1958, and these also were accepted as immigrants by the Netherlands.

The pre-war Dutch community was remarkable for the substantial numbers born in the Indies, and who seldom if ever visited the Netherlands. Many of these, sooner or later, had to leave the land they had called home for a distant one on the other side of the globe. Since 1950 Dutch citizens have accounted for all but a small proportion of the 30,000 or so Europeans normally resident in the country, but their numbers have fluctuated according to the state of Indonesia-Netherlands relations. Even American, British, and other European personnel were withdrawn from the country in the wake of the 1964 'sequestrations', but with the fall of Sukarno, the numbers of Dutch and other Europeans rose sharply after 1966. Prominent among these new elements were the Americans, most of whom were connected in one way or another with the booming petroleum industry; less conspicuous, but almost as numerous, were the Japanese, whose interests were rather more diverse. As throughout the Third World, however, all of these are now 'birds of passage', living and working in the country for a few years and then returning home; the days of permanent white settlement have in all probability vanished for ever.

NOTES

[1] For years before 1972, international organisations appeared divided over whether Indonesia or Pakistan had the larger population. The *Demographic Yearbook* of the United Nations and its Economic Commission for Asia and the Far East consistently recorded Indonesia's population as the larger. The World Bank, however, always preferred Pakistan, and its *World Bank Atlas 1969* quotes an estimated

mid-1967 population of 120 million for Pakistan and 110 million for Indonesia, as against 111 million for Indonesia and 107 for Pakistan recorded by the United Nations for the same year. The creation of independent Bangladesh from Pakistan's eastern wing finally put the matter beyond all doubt. Indonesia's 1971 census recorded a total population of some 119.2 million, which the United Nations estimated had grown to 126 million by mid-1973.

[2] The *World Bank Atlas 1970* tentatively estimated *per capita* GNP in Indonesia as only $80, the same as the figure for Burma. But *per capita* consumption of rice, one of the best tests of the level of wellbeing in Asia, was much higher in Burma.

[3] It is probable that Sukarno saw in this largely Sanskrit-derived motto an Indonesian equivalent of the American *E Pluribus Unum.* The concept of one from many can be rendered unequivocally in modern Indonesian, but the use of a classical form taken from a fourteenth century Javanese poem to correspond with the Latin of the West results in a loss of precision, and the translation given suggests a negative element. Most of the other symbols of independent Indonesia, including the national anthem and the flag, were adopted by an Indonesian Youth Conference of 1928.

[4] Charles A. Fisher, 'Economic Myth and Geographical Reality in Indonesia', *Modern Asian Studies,* vol. 1, 1967, 166.

[5] U.S. Army, *Area Handbook for Indonesia,* Government Printing Office, Washington, 1964, 1.

[6] In a speculative review of the world in the year 2000, the Hudson institute gives Indonesia a projected *per capita* GNP of only $123 in terms of 1965 dollars. But economic performance has improved since the fall of Sukarno. In 1974 Hanna calculated that 90 percent of the population received a *per capita* income of only $70 per annum; if gross national product doubled twice within a generation while population merely doubled, the ordinary Indonesian would receive a *per capita* income of scarcely more than $100 in the year 2000, assuming a continuation of the present highly inegalitarian distribution of income between the élite and the peasantry. See Herman Kahn and Anthony J. Wiener, *The Year 2000,* the Macmillan Company and Collier Macmillan Ltd, London and New York, 1967, 165, and Willard A. Hanna, *Indonesian Projections and the Arithmetic of Anxiety,* American Universities Field Service, Southeast Asia Series, vol. 22, no. 3, 1974.

[7] Including some 412,000 square kilometres (159,000 square miles) of Irian Barat. Of the 13,677 islands enumerated in Indonesia, 12,675 are uninhabited and only 6,044 are named. Nugroho, *Indonesia in Facts and Figures,* Djakarta, 1967, 4.

[8] Indonesia claims all inter-island seas as territorial waters, a claim that is not recognised by the major powers. There are, however, numerous precedents for national claims to mineral wealth on continental shelves beyond recognised territorial waters, and the nations of South-east Asia have divided up their marginal seas for oil and gas exploration. In late 1971 Indonesia and Malaysia jointly declared as territorial waters the important routeway of the Malacca Strait. See also p. 245.

[9] Virtually nothing from the large international aid received by Indonesia for disaster relief was ever disbursed to those affected. The pathetic inability and unwillingness of Sukarno's Indonesia to organise any effective relief and rehabilitation programme for those affected by volcanic eruptions, a potential disaster the country must be prepared to face at any time, was also demonstrated in the Kelut eruption of 1966. The Suharto government will be expected to perform substantially better in the event of any new eruption.

[10] On *Gestapu,* see pp. 97-100.

[11] See pp. 78-9, 82-5.

CHAPTER 2

Early Indonesian History

INDONESIAN HISTORY before the Dutch colonial era is largely devoid of detailed and reliable data. It is clear, however, that as the world's largest island complex, the sheer size, fragmentation, and ecological diversity of the archipelago have always fostered differential development, and this tendency has been augmented by the difficulties of travel overland and the dominating role of the sea as a medium for human movement and cultural diffusion.

Four basic threads run through the history of the region and go far to explain its intricate ethnic and cultural patterns. Firstly, its location athwart the sea links between the two great Asian culture realms has made Indonesia a frontier for influences stemming from both China and India. Secondly, since prehistoric times the archipelago has experienced a stream of cultural intrusions, each impinging initially only on random locations and each modified in terms of existing patterns to yield an 'Indonesianised' version which spread later to other parts of this island world. Thirdly, a persistent feature of the multitude of islands, large and small, is the sharp contrast between the peoples of the coasts and those of the forested hilly interiors. Finally, the rivalry for political and commercial supremacy between the centrally located, agriculturally based realms of Java and the trade-oriented thalassocracies astride the Strait of Malacca has provided a continuing theme since the dawn of recorded history.

Relatively few archaeological sites have been intensively excavated in Indonesia; moreover, most of the materials used by early man decompose rapidly in a humid tropical climate. In consequence, only the barest outline of prehistory is available and this is partly speculative, resting as it does on such indirect evidence as present-day ethnic, linguistic, and plant distributions. Skeletal remains found in the Brantas valley of eastern Java, dating from about 10,000 years ago, suggest that the original human population was of a proto-Australoid racial type, traces of which still exist in the eastern isles. In time, these first inhabitants were apparently succeeded by an inward movement of Negrito (dwarf Negroid) peoples thought to be represented today by a few scattered groups such as the Orang Akit of Sumatra. Without exception, this earliest human stratum was at a Palaeolithic culture stage, subsisting by food-gathering, hunting, and fishing.

Thereafter, it is usual to see the prehistory of the region in terms of a slow southward movement of peoples and cultures from the Asian mainland, which involved a general drift from west to east through the archipelago and occasionally far out into the Pacific so that only vestiges remained in Indonesia. It has been generally conjectured that successive arrivals in this movement occupied the better coastal and riverine lowlands of the islands, from which, after some ethnic and cultural mixing, they displaced the existing population. This is an attractive and superficially plausible hypothesis which provides an apparent explanation for the marked cultural boundary between coasts and interiors. As Sopher observes, however, 'the sharp contrasts which exist can only be adequately explained as the result of the juxtaposition of a sea-oriented culture and a traditionally land-oriented one'.[1] The cultures of most interior peoples do not suggest that they once occupied coastal locations.

Today, peoples with Melanesoid-Papuan characteristics become increasingly common towards the east of the archipelago. This distribution, together with skeletal remains identified as of a similar type, suggests an association with a once widespread Mesolithic culture of which archaeological traces occur in several parts of the region. These peoples relied on an economy in which food-collecting, hunting, fishing, and mollusc-gathering were of great importance. Some were possibly non-agricultural, sea-oriented nomads. On land, however, riverbanks, estuaries, and coastal margins were favoured localities for settlement, and probably in the vicinity of these a rudimentary cultivation began, in form essentially a 'jungle gardening' combining the periodic cutting and burning of small patches of forest for planting yam and taro and various fruits and such multiple-purpose palms as coconut and sago. Ethnobotanical data indicate that, with regional variations, this root-fruit-palm cropping complex came to characterise the greater part of the archipelago. Ever since, however, its western margin has slowly retreated in the face of the later intrusions, and currently yam, taro, and sago remain as food staples chiefly in the eastern islands.[2]

This Mesolithic culture persisted for several millennia, but approximately 5,000 years ago a Neolithic technology began to enter the island world from the north. It is customary to attribute this introduction to the seaborne migration of the ancestral Indonesians into and through the archipelago, a formative human movement which for long was interpreted as two major waves of migration widely separated in time. According to this view, the earliest arrivals termed Proto-Malays or Nesiots, occupied the coastal areas, displacing or absorbing the existing population; in turn, they too were pushed inland by the later Deutero-Malays, who continue to inhabit the principal coastal and riverine lowlands. This hypothesis fails to provide a fully satisfactory explanation of the evolution of Neolithic culture patterns in Indonesia. It is more probable that the intrusion of an Indonesian ethnic type with a Neolithic cultural heritage occurred not as distinct waves of migration, but as a gradual series of long-distance movements by small groups at intervals over a period of many centuries, as part of a continuous process apparently resembling the later migration of Malays to Madagascar. A long-continued drift of this nature would clearly include groups with slightly differing cultures; later arrivals, and those from specifically favoured home environments, would carry knowledge of newer techniques. Settling in different parts of the archipelago, attracted perhaps by differing ecological conditions, these incursions of Neolithic colonists generated the emergence of increasingly complex and differentiated culture patterns, which were subsequently modified by an immense amount of inter-island movement and exchange. These movements took place against, and in part were conditioned by, changes in the distribution of land and sea, which in a zone of great coastal instability were often rapid and profound.

Shrouded as it is in obscurity, undoubtedly the most significant outcome of these Neolithic movements was the introduction of rice into Indonesian agriculture.[3] In the absence of evidence, definitive statements on this intriguing question are impossible. Yet, the folk-tales of several groups of Indonesian shifting cultivators do refer to a time when they relied on root-crops, and contain symbolic renderings of how they first acquired rice-seed and a knowledge of how to cultivate this cereal. The implication is that rice, as a staple food crop, entered *existing* patterns of shifting cultivation. This may have occurred in certain areas in the early Neolithic; once introduced, the new crop spread, progressively displacing the previous staples, until rice eventually became a major crop of shifting cultivators virtually everywhere west of Sulawesi, and assumed a focal position in the developing cultures.

At present the shifting cultivation of rice shows a much wider distribution in Indonesia than does that of *sawah* or wet-rice. Many different techniques of sawah cultivation are practised in the archipelago and this form of agriculture was seemingly introduced to different areas at different times by different groups. Sawah cultivation was probably first carried to random parts of Indonesia, of which east-central Java is one of the likeliest contenders, at a relatively late stage of the Neolithic. In a few selected areas it became an established feature of the economy, ousting earlier agricultural systems, but it is improbable that irrigated rice cultivation was practised widely until very much later. Indeed, its adoption in many parts of Indonesia has occurred only in the last half-millennium, a development which, in a growing number of instances, can be dated fairly precisely.[4] The intrusion and subsequent diffusion of hill-rice and sawah cultivation, and the consequent evolution of regionally different agricultural systems, are but major examples of the manner in which cultural differentiations of lasting importance began to crystallise in the later prehistoric period. The use of metals, such as bronze and iron, was also intrusive; first introduced in the late centuries B.C., it too affected only selected areas, and the greater part of the region retained a basically Neolithic culture which persisted widely well into the Christian era. When exiguous documentary references to the archipelago first begin to appear, it was already the home of groups at markedly different cultural and economic levels.

During the early centuries of the Christian era commercial links developed between the archipelago, with its gold, aromatic woods, resins, and spices, and India and China. Ever since, the growth and fluctuating nature of trade both among the islands and with other regions has exerted a powerful influence on Indonesian history, and provides a key to the type of political unit which became characteristic almost everywhere except in Java. Throughout most of this island world virgin forest was abundant but largely empty and yielded little save 'jungle products' of interest to the outside world. In these circumstances, trade was the principal fount of wealth and political structures had an essentially commercial base. River-mouth settlements flanking the major sea routes grew into petty states whose rulers sought to exercise some control over the movement of products from the interior and who derived additional income from tolls on passing vessels, the more successful of them using force to direct international traffic to their ports. Where a loose control could be exerted over several neighbouring rivers, larger structures emerged, and, since these states rested on commerce and their maritime links, advantageously located rulers sometimes developed a superiority which permitted the creation of sea-based empires linking many of these smaller port principalities as tributaries. The foundation and maintenance of these structures depended entirely on the mastery of water-borne commerce; they were fragile spheres of influence, not clearly defined territorial units.

Small states of this type had probably begun to appear by the beginning of the Christian era. The first political units for which direct evidence exists, however, reveal that by the fifth century Indian cultural influences were well established, and that they became increasingly apparent in art and architecture, in the use of Indian scripts, in the acceptance of a mythology derived from Indian epics, in the attribution of divinity to rulers, and in the observance of the sacred laws of Hinduism. In the past, the introduction of these features was seen in terms of waves of Indian colonisation, but more recent research suggests that it resulted from a long-continued process of cultural diffusion whereby Indian elements gradually penetrated the relatively advanced cultures of the incipient state system and were there modified in accordance with existing customs, beliefs, and traditions, a process usually termed 'Indianisation'.

Trade links between India and the archipelago are of great antiquity, and by the early centuries A.D. small colonies of Indian merchants had appeared at key locations along the major sea routes. In time, the merchants were followed by priests and literati. In some instances at least, Brahmans, or Hindu priests, were probably welcomed by indigenous rulers, who came to recognise that Indian concepts could serve to strengthen their own political positions, and thus many Indian ideas and customs came to be accepted in courtly circles. The new cultural features had their greatest effects on the ruling élites and penetrated the lives of the ordinary population far less deeply, forming but the thinnest of veneers overlying continuing indigenous patterns. Indeed, even amongst the élites many of the older animistic beliefs persisted and showed a marked tendency to blend syncretically with Hinduism and with the Buddhism which entered the region later. This spread of Indian cultural influences had its strongest impact on the western half of the archipelago where south-east Sumatra and east-central Java were the outstanding hearths of the resultant 'Indianised' culture.

Srivijaya, the first empire known to have arisen on the basis of inter-island and international trade, developed from the south-east Sumatran kingdom of Palembang.[5] By extending its authority over the adjacent coasts and eliminating or neutralising rivals, Srivijaya acquired control of the Straits of Malacca and of Sunda and built up its prosperity and power by enforcing the use of its ports on the commerce passing through these crucial thoroughfares. The population of its hinterlands was sparse and the empire comprised little more than 'a confederation of trading ports on the fringe of the primeval forest',[6] but as a centre for the exchange of island produce and of the exports of India and China, Srivijaya retained its position as the dominant commercial power in the archipelago from the seventh to the twelfth centuries. Its capital, Palembang,also became a focus of Buddhist learning in the region and the expansion of its empire was accompanied, in certain directions at least, by the spread of this Indian religion.

For many reasons, not all of which are clear, by the twelfth century Srivijaya was losing significance as a power in the archipelago. It is likely that the continued seaward growth of the swampy coastal plains of south-east Sumatra had reduced the site advantages of its capital. Moreover, its attempts to monopolise commerce by using force to compel passing ships to use its ports, where heavy duties were exacted, began to provoke a response from others with interests in trade. Indeed, for this very reason in 1025 the Cholas of south India launched a series of attacks on many of its possessions which had weakening effects, and, as time passed, rivalry with the developing ports of north Java became more intense. By the later thirteenth century this remarkable early thalassocracy had disintegrated into a number of separate small Sumatran kingdoms, of which the most notable was Melayu (Jambi). In 1228 the Malay royal house of Palembang withdrew to the Minangkabau highlands of west Sumatra, and the erstwhile commercial heart of the empire fell into the hands of a band of Chinese corsairs.

Although very little is known about them, several Indianised states also emerged in Java in the early centuries A.D. Here, the principal focus of early cultural and political development was the central neck of the island where the Hindu kingdom of Kalinga held sway in the seventh century, and where the Buddhist Sailendra dynasty, builders of the magnificent monument of Borobudur, rose to prominence in the mid-eighth century. The subsequent emergence in this same area of the kingdom of Mataram is usually held to signify a revival of Hindu traditions and customs. Located initially in the central plains, the transfer of the seat of this kingdom to the interior of eastern Java heralded the opening of a long period in Javanese cultural history during which the vicissitudes of the realms in the east overshadowed the rest of the island.

For more than three centuries the story is dominated by the rise and fall of kingdoms in this part of Java, each establishing for itself a new *kraton,* or seat of power. 'This shifting of the main center of political strength', writes Vlekke,'suggests the existence, lying next to each other but not without many interconnections, of a number of small principalities, more or less in permanent competition with each other for the first place....'[7] Although equally as fragile and imprecise, these states in east and central Java differed fundamentally from the thalassocracy created by Srivijaya and from the smaller political units which, at various times, have appeared elsewhere in the island world, and in which the wealth generated by trade was the only basis for power. In contrast, the relatively dense, sedentary, and productive population engaged in sawah cultivation on the fertile volcanic soils of the eastern two-thirds of Java provided an agrarian foundation for state formation. Generally, part of the realm was set aside to support the court by means of taxes and services levied at village level, and the right to these sources of income in more distant regions was granted by the ruler to relatives and officials. According to tradition, the early Javanese rulers possessed divine authority and were the protectors of their realm and subjects, but in practice their position was precarious; the seeds of downfall were ever present in intrigue at court or in the ambition of one of these regional appanage-holders.

The last *kraton* of Mataram in central Java lay close to the early tenth-century Prambanan group of Hindu monuments on the Kedu plain, north-east of Jogjakarta (Yogyakarta). About 929 a new capital was founded much further east in the Brantas valley, and for the next half-millennium remained the crucible of Javanese history. This move was followed by 'a weakening of Hindu influence on government, religion and art and a corresponding increase in the importance of the native Javanese element'.[8] Close links were forged with Bali and some of the islands further east. But rising politico-commercial ambition apparently led to a rivalry with Srivijaya, which, according to some accounts, culminated in the destruction of Mataram's capital and the collapse of the kingdom at the beginning of the eleventh century. Shortly afterwards, a united kingdom was again created in eastern Java by Airlangga, one of the island's famous historical figures, and this new state acquired a significant share in trade with the eastern archipelago, which brought increasing prosperity to the ports of north-east Java. Presumably to forestall fraternal strife, in 1045 Airlangga divided his realm between his two sons, giving one the kingdom of Kediri to the west of the Kawi mountains and the other the kingdom of Janggala to the east. Despite a flowering of Old Javanese literature and a clear growth in the tide of commerce, historical records of the next century and a half are exceedingly sparse. It seems, however, that early in the twelfth century Kediri absorbed its neighbour Janggala, and became a commercially powerful well-organised state, with considerable influence in the eastern isles.

Whatever the cause, Kediri fell in 1222 and was succeeded as the major power in Java by the kingdom of Singhasari with its capital north-east of Malang. Oblique information on Singhasari occurs in the Javanese chronicle the *Pararaton,* or 'Book of Kings'. Culturally, it was characterised by an intricate blending of Hindu, Buddhist, and indigenous features, with the Javanese element dominant in many spheres. Economically, it derived wealth from the developing spice trade with the Moluccas, on which the north Java ports were beginning to thrive. Moreover, under its last ruler, Kertanegara (1268-92), the influence of Singhasari was extended in the archipelago; Madura and Bali were acquired and attempts were made to achieve a hold in Sumatra. In 1289 Kertanegara refused to render the customary homage to the Chinese emperor and rejected the imperial envoys who visited his court; three years later he died in an attack by neighbouring Kediri. Meanwhile, Kublai Khan had prepared a punitive expedition to avenge his insulted envoys. This arrived in Java after Kertanegara's death, and, holding the ruler of Kediri responsible for the earlier outrage, it defeated him. Kertanegara's son-in-law, Vijaya, who had survived these various troubles, successfully used this Chinese invasion to achieve power. In 1293 he established his *kraton* at Majapahit in the lower Brantas valley, and founded 'the last great dynasty in Javanese history which maintained the Hindu tradition'.[9]

The era of Majapahit rule has passed into popular legend as a 'golden age' of Indonesian history and served as a source of symbolism for many of Sukarno's ambitions. Nevertheless, although faded remnants of glory lingered for long thereafter, the state reached its apogee under the direction of its most famous *patih* (or chief minister), Gaja Mada, who held this office from 1330 to 1364. The royal family played some part in the administration, but at the height of Majapahit's renown power lay in the hands of this influential *patih* who codified its laws and customs and dictated its policy. Some impression of the splendour of its walled capital city may be had from the *Negarakertagama,* the epic composed by Prapanca in 1365. The poet also offers illuminating and entertaining vignettes of the life of the ruling élite, of its glories and debaucheries, and of regal peregrinations when local beauties and 'the choice of the virgins' were brought to the king's encampment. But, like most courtly chronicles, the *Negarakertagama* is an amalgam of fact and fiction. It assigns to Majapahit a huge empire comprising dependencies throughout present-day Indonesia and much of the Malay peninsula. Although Majapahit did pursue a policy of expansion under Gaja Mada and in the later fourteenth century launched expeditions against Tumasik (old Singapore) and Palembang, in reality, as Professor Berg has shown, its sphere of control was restricted to eastern Java, Madura, and Bali.[10]

From being one of the strongest powers in the archipelago, Majapahit began to lose this position late in the fourteenth century with the beginning of a long period of political confusion and intermittent civil war. It was already seriously weakened when the *kraton* at Majapahit was abandoned in 1468. At the same time, the rise of an international entrepôt at Malacca (Melaka) and the further development of inter-island commerce conferred increasing significance and wealth on the ports of north Java. Through them passed most of the island's agricultural exports, especially rice but also many other foodstuffs, and in return they sent salt and textiles to the interior capitals. Traders brought spices from the Moluccas for trans-shipment to Malacca and returned with cargoes of textiles and food. Through their contacts with Malacca, these flourishing coastal states fell under Muslim rule and by the end of the fifteenth century were undermining Majapahit's former supremacy. The final disintegration of this last Hindu-Javanese kingdom occurred under the pressures exerted by these Muslim potentates in 1513-14. The decisive blow was dealt by the Sultanate of Demak, which, with control over the northern rice-growing plains between Japara and Grisek and a major share of the island's trade, then became the most powerful Javanese state. The survivors of the Majapahit dynasty hung on precariously in the extreme east until 1639, when they moved to Bali.

Muslim Arab merchants had frequented local ports for several centuries before Islam gained its first converts in the archipelago late in the thirteenth century. Indian traders, particularly Gujeratis, played an important role in the introduction of the new faith, and its subsequent expansion owed much to the developing trade in pepper and spices. The pepper vine, an introduced plant for whose produce local demand was small but for which a ready market existed in China and India, was already widely cultivated on hill-slopes in north Sumatra. The growing trade in pepper at Sumatran ports attracted foreign merchants and, as Fisher observes, 'the prestige enjoyed by wealthy Indian Muslim traders probably explains the initial desire of local rulers to accept the new faith in much the same way as their ancestors had adopted Hinduism and Buddhism'.[11] The rulers of the north Sumatran states of Perlak and Pasai were converted before 1300. Islam penetrated nearby Acheh (Aceh) in the second half of the fifteenth century and as this state extended its control over the pepper-growing areas of north-west Sumatra, it drew new areas into the fold; although the Sultan of Acheh failed in his attempt to force the Bataks of the interior to become Muslim, the spread of his authority was instrumental in converting the peoples of the Minangkabau highlands. Meanwhile, Islam had spread from Pasai to the newly-founded emporium of Malacca, which soon emerged as a focal point for its further propagation in the island world. During the fifteenth century several of the east Sumatran states, such as Kampar, Siak, and Inderagiri, fell under Malaccan control and accepted Islam. Malacca also developed close commercial links with the ports of north Java; as a result, the indigenous royal house of Tuban was converted, whilst in the other ports power was assumed by Muslim merchants. These harbour principalities then became new centres of diffusion, and, together with Malacca, played an important part in the conversion of the home of spices, the Moluccas, where the rulers of Ternate and Tidore became Muslim in the later fifteenth century. The expansion of the new faith gathered momentum in the following century, partly as a reaction against the arrival and activities of the Catholic Portuguese. By 1535 almost the entire north coast of Java had become Muslim, and a century later most of the rest of the island had been won over, as had the coastal populations of most other islands, particularly those engaged in trade.

As with all major cultural intrusions into the region, therefore, Islam had its initial effects in the west and has achieved far less widespread acceptance in the islands east of Celebes and Sumbawa. Since Malays and Javanese were the principal carriers of inter-island commerce, Malay had long served as the *lingua franca* of trade; it became also the chief language of transmission for Islam and the two were so closely identified in the emerging Muslim culture of the Outer Islands that to embrace Islam was to 'become Malay' (*masuk Melayu*). Spreading along the sea-lanes of the archipelago, this Muslim culture gained its first footholds among coastal trading peoples and from these *points d'appui* it gradually made inroads in succeeding centuries into more isolated communities inland. Nevertheless, many interior groups, notably the Dayaks of Borneo and the Toraja of Celebes, resisted this process and have retained their animistic beliefs, so that religious differences highlight one of the outstanding cultural divides in modern Indonesia: that between what Hildred Geertz terms the *pasisir* culture of the littoral, characterised by Islam and an orientation to water-borne commercial activity, and the non-Muslim cultures of the interior, most of which 'remained at least until the present century in virtual isolation from the outside world, each developing its own distinctive patterns of life'.[12]

Even where Islam was accepted, however, many earlier beliefs and practices have persisted and while in areas such as Acheh or Banjarmasin conversion had profound effects, elsewhere non-Islamic features are often prominent. Nowhere is this more in evidence than in Java, where the Sundanese of the west are zealous Muslims, but in the rest of the island 'in accepting Islam the Javanese merely added it as yet another component to their syncretic system of beliefs, in which imported Hindu and Buddhist teachings were inextricably intermingled with still earlier elements'.[13] The neighbouring island of Bali has indeed retained its Hindu traditions to become a unique tourist attraction. Thus, although Indonesia is now the home of about a seventh of the world's Muslims, the differential impact of the new faith has created peculiarly complicated religious patterns.

The first Europeans to establish a presence in the archipelago, the Portuguese, entered the region as this diffusion of Islam was gathering force. After an abortive sortie two years earlier, they succeeded in capturing the emporium of Malacca in 1511. Malacca had long been the chief distributing centre for spices, brought from the Moluccas by Javanese traders, and the basic Portuguese objective was to obtain a monopoly of the almost legendary trade in these highly lucrative exports for which, as 'a chief ingredient in apothecary and kitchen alike', there was a growing demand in Europe.[14] Both cloves and nutmegs were the produce of plants native to the Moluccas, and when the Portuguese arrived, most of the output was controlled by the rival rulers of the two Muslim sea states of Ternate and Tidore.

An exploratory expedition to the Moluccas was followed by regular trading voyages before the Portuguese finally achieved a base in the home of spices with the erection of a fort in Ternate in 1522. A year earlier, Magellan's Spanish fleet had reached Tidore, and until 1529 there was a competitive struggle between the two potentates and their European associates. Subsequent Portuguese efforts to gain Christian converts in the islands, which achieved some success in the Moluccas and Lesser Sunda Islands, and their abrogation of his former profits from the spice trade, evoked militant opposition from the Sultan of Ternate. Following his murder in 1570, this provoked a revolt in Ternate, and the Portuguese fortress was captured in 1574. The Portuguese thereupon concluded a treaty with Tidore, where they established a new fort four years later.

As part of a maritime commercial empire comprising a string of far-flung and often undermanned garrisons, the relatively insecure Portuguese bases in the archipelago were menaced continuously by rivals and competitors. Despite their monopolistic aspirations, the Portuguese failed to obtain more than a fraction of the coveted spice trade and most of the archipelago's commerce was still handled by Malay, Javanese, Chinese, and Indian merchants. Indeed, the Portuguese merely penetrated a long-established and complex trade network which continued to retain many of its earlier characteristics. Nevertheless, their presence did produce certain displacements in existing patterns. The cultivation of both spices and pepper was extended in response to a growing demand for which they were in part responsible, and the tendency of Muslim merchants to move elsewhere after the seizure of Malacca contributed significantly to the rise of new commercial centres such as Acheh, Brunei, and Macassar. Acheh, now growing in prosperity and power on the basis of the flourishing pepper trade, was extending its authority in Sumatra and the Malay peninsula, and became a dangerously close focus of Muslim opposition. Moreover, permission to establish a post in the Banda Islands, the home of nutmegs, was refused and although the Portuguese obtained a share in the pepper trade of Bantam (Banten) in 1545, they were effectively excluded from the ports of north Java by their hostile Muslim rulers.

The relative profusion of Western-language sources concerned primarily with the activities of these European interlopers tends to hide the essential continuity of historical development in much of the region and directs attention to the main areas of Portuguese interest: Malacca and the Spice Islands. During the sixteenth century, however, significant changes occurred in Java where two new states rose to prominence. After the eclipse of Majapahit the Sultanate of Demak had become the main power in the island, extending its control to include Bantam in the west. Located on the commercially important narrow Strait of Sunda, Bantam emerged as an independent sultanate in 1568. Thereafter, its sphere of influence grew to include west Java and much of south Sumatra, and Bantam developed into a key centre of the archipelago's pepper trade. Concurrently, the ruler of Mataram, until then a district tributary to the Sultanate of Demak, also successfully proclaimed his independence. Quickly gaining in strength, he extended his authority over the greater part of interior central Java and created a new agriculturally based empire whose *kraton* became 'the centre of the political, cultural and economic life of much of the island'.[15] Muslim Mataram reached its peak under the rule of Sultan Agung (1613-45), when the northern harbour principalities were subjugated and the surviving Hindu kingdom of Balambangan in the east was conquered. Mataram also made a vain attempt to dislodge the Dutch from their newly founded settlement of Batavia (Jakarta). The arrival of these competitors from the Low Countries at the end of the sixteenth century heralded the final collapse of the precarious and largely peripheral Portuguese empire in the archipelago. It presaged the opening of a new era in Indonesian history.

NOTES

[1] David E. Sopher, *The Sea Nomads: A Study Based on the Literature of the Maritime Boat People of Southeast Asia,* Memoirs of the National Museum, Singapore, no. 5, 1965, 385.

[2] The pace of this retreat accelerated over the past four centuries. See J.E. Spencer, *Shifting Cultivation in Southeastern Asia,* University of California Publications in Geography vol. 19, University of California Press, Berkeley and Los Angeles, 1966, 110-114.

[3] See J.E. Spencer, 'The Migration of Rice from Mainland Southeast Asia into Indonesia' in J. Barrau (ed.), *Plants and the Migrations of Pacific Peoples,* Bishop Museum Press, Honolulu, 1966, 83-9, and Chang Kwang-chih, 'Major Problems in the Culture History of Southeast Asia', *Bulletin of the Institute of Ethnology, Academia Sinica,* vol. 13, 1962, 1-26.

[4] In the case of Java, for instance, sawah cultivation is a relatively recent introduction to the Sundanese territories and did not begin in northern Bantam until the sixteenth century. In Timor wet-rice cultivation using a simple irrigation system was initiated by Rotinese settlers on the plain to the north-east of Kupang between 1810 and 1820.

[5] For a detailed assessment of the evidence concerning this early empire see O.W. Wolters, *Early Indonesian Commerce: A Study of the Origins of Srivijaya,* Ithaca, Cornell University Press, 1967.

[6] P. Wheatley, *The Golden Khersonese,* Kuala Lumpur, University of Malaya Press, 1961, 298.

[7] B.H.M. Vlekke, *Nusantara: A History of Indonesia,* The Hague, W. van Hoeve, 1965, 53.

[8] D.G.E. Hall, *A History of South-East Asia,* London, Macmillan, 1960, 60.

[9] Hall, op. cit., 71.

[10] C.C. Berg, 'De Sadeng-oorlog en de Mythe van Groot-Majapahit', *Indonesie,* vol. V, 1951, 385-422.

[11] C.A. Fisher, *South-east Asia: a Social, Economic and Political Geography,* London, Methuen, 1964, 92.

[12] H. Geertz, 'Indonesian Cultures and Communities' in Ruth T. McVey (ed.), *Indonesia,* New Haven, Human Relations Area Files, 1963, 31.

[13] Fisher, op. cit., 251.

[14] B. Schrieke, *Indonesian Sociological Studies,* Part 1, The Hague, Van Hoeve, 1955, 11.

[15] Hall, op cit., 204.

CHAPTER 3

The Dutch in the Indies

THE DUTCH WERE THE CHIEF DISTRIBUTORS of Asian produce in sixteenth-century Europe. As adventurous traders and middlemen, they were experienced in maritime exploration, versed in sophisticated financial techniques, possessed of capital in quantity, and, through Netherlanders who had served the Portuguese, had access to knowledge of navigation in the Indian Ocean. Thus, when Philip II of Spain and Portugal closed the port of Lisbon to their vessels in 1594, the Dutch quickly ventured eastwards to the source of the coveted spices. Despatched by an Amsterdam trading company, the first expeditionary fleet under Cornelis de Houtman reached Bantam in June 1596, concluded a treaty of 'friendship and alliance' with its Sultan, sailed round Java, and returned home. This voyage was hardly a financial success, but it pioneered the way and five more fleets left for the Indies in 1598. Although most of these were disastrous failures, the enormous profits yielded by the return cargoes of one of them fired ambitions at home. New companies were formed to trade in the East and more fleets were despatched; Dutch ships began to visit all parts of the archipelago and several small trading posts were established.

Competition between these various Dutch companies, and between Netherlanders and Portuguese, caused costs to rise and in 1600 a movement began towards unification of Dutch interests. Under government aegis, this culminated in 1602 in the amalgamation of the separate trading organisations into the *Verenigde Oost-Indische Compagnie* (or United East India Company). Granted a monopoly of Dutch trade east of the Cape of Good Hope and empowered to conclude treaties, establish forts and factories, and to maintain armed forces, the Company took over the trading posts and commerce of its predecessors. Its prime objective was to maximise profits from trade; its characteristic method was to aim at the most complete monopoly possible of the archipelago's more lucrative products, especially spices. As the seventeenth century progressed, it achieved a remarkable degree of success, far overshadowing its European and Asian rivals. 'Whatever its defects', writes Meilink-Roelofsz., 'in the sphere of trade the Dutch East India Company represented a far more efficient and, above all, much more business-like system than the government undertaking of the Portuguese'.[1]

The nature of the extant sources, offering as they do but fleeting spectral glimpses of indigenous life and society, fosters an impression that the arrival of Europeans was a turning-point in Indonesian history and, of course, in one sense it was, since but for their advent the documentary record would in all probability be slender in the extreme. For long, however, the new Western interlopers merely found a place for themselves in existing politico-commercial patterns, and the early Dutch were no exception. But it is difficult not to view the creation of the United East India Company, a large, complex, and ruthless organisation which soon effectively monopolised much of the region's trade, disrupted indigenous political relations, and subsequently began to acquire territorial possessions, as the opening of a new era for the islands. The Portuguese were speedily evicted from the Moluccas where the erection of forts and trading posts marked the start of efforts to obtain complete mastery of the trade in spices; new factories were established in Java and Celebes, and in 1609 the first Governor-General was appointed to supervise the 'forts, places, factories, persons and business of the United Company'. Asian traders were displaced with relative ease, in part because Mataram's subjugation of north Java contributed to the decline of Javanese overseas trade, but European rivals, notably the English, proved a different proposition. The English had penetrated the archipelago earlier than the Dutch, Drake passing through in 1579 and Cavendish in 1586, but regular trading only began with the formation of the English East India Company in 1600. The English Company had far smaller resources than the Dutch, but managed to open a growing number of factories and a fierce competitive struggle developed for spices in the Moluccas, and for pepper in Bantam and Sumatra.

The appointment of Jan Pieterszoon Coen as Governor-General in 1618 signified the start of far more vigorous efforts to consolidate the commercial position of the Dutch Company. Control of archipelagic commerce and its centralisation at a major entrepôt were seen as cardinal requirements. Coen therefore established Batavia, founded on the site of the small port of Jacatra, as the headquarters of Dutch operations and every effort was made, including a blockade of Bantam, to siphon away the business of existing ports and to make Batavia a focus for the Chinese junk traffic. Although hard pressed by Bantam and Mataram, the new settlement prospered and began to fulfil its function. Mataram unsuccessfully laid siege to the town in 1629 and trouble flared intermittently with Bantam, but in the mid-1640s peace treaties were concluded with both these neighbours.

Instructed to expel foreigners from places of Dutch trade, Coen closed Moluccan ports to the English and rivalry between the European competitors became progressively more ferocious until news of the Anglo-Dutch Treaty of 1619, with its proposals for co-operation, provided a brief respite; this ended with the execution of ten Englishmen at Amboyna (Ambon) in 1623. The English had found it increasingly difficult to obtain cargoes of spices in the Moluccas, and thus switched the locus of their activities to Macassar and Bantam, where shipments of both spices and pepper could be procured. Though not eliminated from the spice trade until the 1680s, Coen had driven the English from the Moluccas, and drastic measures, described by Geertz as 'a landmark in the history of mercantile brutality',[2] were now used to give the Dutch control of production. In 1621 Coen decided on a total conquest of the Banda Islands, source of nutmegs and mace. The population was ruthlessly exterminated and the spice gardens distributed to Company servants to work with imported slave labour. Cloves were more widely distributed in the Moluccas and output was rising; indeed, in 1622 the combined production of Amboyna and Seram was double world consumption. The Dutch secured their supplies from Amboyna, which itself produced sufficient to satisfy the demands of Europe and Asia, and therefore launched measures to eliminate clove-trees from other islands; in time, this policy proved so effective that cloves became scarce. Although the monopoly was never complete, the Dutch were now masters of the home of spices, and the English had ceased to be serious rivals. The Portuguese, however, still retained their hold on Malacca, once the chief entrepôt of the international spice trade but now of reduced commercial significance. But when this port fell to the Dutch in 1641, the Company was clearly the strongest power in the archipelago, and the inner seas of Indonesia 'for all practical purposes, had become a Dutch lake'.[3]

The Company greatly strengthened its monopolistic position in the Indies as all the major indigenous states disintegrated in the later seventeenth century. Moreover, by the 1680s the trading activities of rival Europeans had virtually ended, and by manipulating prices or by compulsory cultivation the Dutch were now able to regulate the output of the most profitable contemporary crops and thus turn the archipelago into what Furnivall somewhat grandiloquently terms 'one vast estate, literally, a plantation'.[4] In the Moluccas, the Spanish withdrawal in 1663 was followed by the recognition of Dutch suzerainty by Tidore in 1667 and by Ternate in 1683, leaving the Company as effective master of the home of spices, and enabling it by the use of methods that would receive universal condemnation at present, and had disastrous consequences for the inhabitants, to maintain close control of production. These methods included restrictions on food imports, the fostering of internal disputes, regular expeditions to destroy 'surplus' plantings, and forced cultivation; in Amboyna, for example, the cultivators were obliged to plant an additional 120,000 clove-trees in 1656 and a further 60,000 two years later, but in 1667 further planting was forbidden and in the 1690s trees were compulsorily destroyed.

Nevertheless, control of output in the Moluccas was not alone sufficient to give the Company the prized monopoly of the highly lucrative spice trade. Macassar (Makasar or Ujungpandang) in south-west Celebes, for long a primary focus of the commerce of the eastern isles and a major entrepôt for non-Dutch trade in spices, greatly extended its influence in the early seventeenth century to bring most of Celebes, the islands of Buton, Buru, and Sumbawa, and parts of coastal Borneo within its orbit. As it prevented the establishment of a complete Dutch monopoly of trade and shipping, the position of Macassar was intolerable, and the port was blockaded in 1636. The Company then began to gain allies among Macassar's dependencies, notably Bone, and with their aid a broken Macassar was compelled in 1667 after a fierce struggle to accept Dutch overlordship, to dismantle its defences, to expel all other Europeans, and to grant to the Dutch a monopoly of its trade. Southern Celebes was now placed under a Dutch governor with his headquarters in Macassar, and control of its former territories passed to the Company. This seizure of Macassar produced far-reaching shifts in patterns of trade and shipping in the eastern half of the archipelago, but by far its most important long-term effect was the stimulus it gave to the creation of colonies by Buginese traders throughout the archipelago, for beneath the tightening frame of Dutch monopolies the Buginese came to play an important political role in many of the surviving indigenous states, and to create their own commercial empire.

Control of the trade in cloves, nutmegs, and mace was the prime object of the Company in the seventeenth century. Drawn as they were from a restricted number of small islands in the Moluccas, a monopoly of these products was relatively easy to achieve by direct intervention in producing areas. With pepper, which also entered trade on a large scale, things were different however, for the vine was widely cultivated in Sumatra and in parts of Borneo. Failing to achieve anything like a complete monopoly, the Company had to be satisfied with such control as it could gain over the pepper trade through treaty contracts with the rulers of the chief producing and exporting states. To a large extent, this was achieved in Sumatra and, several years after the discovery of ore on the island in 1710, a similar arrangement was made to cover the trade in Bangka tin. Thus, in 1642 the Company was granted a monopoly of Palembang's pepper exports, and in 1659 obtained a privileged position in the ports of Acheh; thereafter, by undermining the power of the Sultanate of Acheh, the coastlands of Sumatra were brought increasingly under Dutch supervision. Less success attended moves to monopolise the pepper trade of the powerful south Borneo Sultanate of Banjarmasin. The Company was accorded exclusive rights there in 1635, but attempts to enforce these met resistance and Dutch residents were massacred. Renewed efforts were made two decades later and in 1664 the Company obtained a new monopoly of local pepper. Again, however, this proved illusory; English traders engrossed most of the produce and the Dutch withdrew, not to return until the 1730s when they established a settlement at Banjarmasin.

The Dutch were in the archipelago to make profits from commerce and to this end all the major islands save Borneo had been brought (by the late seventeenth century) within the framework of their monopoly system. The acquisition of territory, which necessarily brought administrative costs, was, however, totally unattractive and their early empire in the Indies, as with that of the Portuguese, comprised merely a string of strategically placed forts and trading posts. Yet, willy-nilly, as their commercial interests grew in the seventeenth century, it became increasingly necessary to protect them by an extension of territorial control. Generally, this was achieved by intervention in the internal affairs of indigenous states, a process clearly revealed and with the most profound repercussions in the case of Java.

There, in 1674, a prince from Madura, Trunojoyo (Trunajaya), led a successful rebellion against the current ruler of Mataram, overrunning much of his realm and sacking his *kraton*. Whilst in flight, the old ruler died; but a request for Dutch assistance was granted, the kingdom was reoccupied, and his successor was installed by the Dutch as Amangkurat II. The new ruler, who established his *kraton* at Kartasura in the Solo valley, was heavily indebted to the Company to which he made major commercial concessions; in addition, he ceded to the Dutch a tract of land south of Batavia together with the port and district of Semarang. Concurrently, internal dissension in Bantam permitted successful Dutch intervention in west Java, where, by a treaty of 1684, this state became a vassal of the Company which thereby obtained exclusive trade rights and enforced the withdrawal of the English to their newly established fort at Benkulen (Bengkulu) in west Sumatra. By the 1680s, therefore, the Dutch Company was already in direct control of considerable territory, and, with substantial influence in Bantam and Mataram, had become the dominant power in Java. With the opening of the new century, however, the Dutch were drawn even deeper into Javanese affairs and thereby greatly consolidated their position in the island. Thus, intervention in a succession dispute in Mataram in 1704 brought the Company a monopoly of the trade of this realm and control over additional territory, including eastern Madura. When military support was once more required by a ruler of this state some four decades later, virtually the entire northern seaboard of Java and the western half of Madura fell under Dutch control, and Mataram, based on a new *kraton* at Surakarta, became 'officially a vassal state of the Company'.[5] Largely because of further internal dispute, in 1755 the crumbling empire of Mataram was partitioned, the eastern half centred on Surakarta going to the Susuhunan Pakubuwono, and the western half to Sultan Hamengku Buwono I with his *kraton* at Jogjakarta. At the same time, a rebellion in Bantam required yet another costly military intervention to ensure the succession of a Dutch-supported Sultan, and this further strengthened Company authority in the west. By the middle of the eighteenth century most of Java's inhabitants were either governed directly by Batavia or were the subjects of various small Javanese states that had become effectively vassals of the Company with Dutch residents advising their rulers. This establishment of Company control in Java paved the way for a continuous intensification of Dutch influence on the island's people and economy, which in large measure is responsible for one of modern Indonesia's most outstanding dichotomies.

The Dutch Company reached the height of its power at the beginning of the eighteenth century; Batavia, the supreme symbol of its mercantilist and monopolistic policies, had become the political and commercial focus of an archipelago in which events were largely controlled by the Dutch. Yet despite this achievement, the Company was in a weakening financial position, chiefly because the profits accruing from its monopolies of archipelagic trade were declining. This trend continued throughout the century as spices became relatively less important and the activities of English and Buginese traders made it progressively more difficult to enforce the old monopolies. The serious implications of this change for the Dutch were partly offset by the introduction of new means of obtaining agricultural products for export; although efforts were made to enforce trade monopolies, a new system of 'Contingencies and Forced Deliveries' was introduced whereby either tribute in kind was levied on districts under direct Dutch control, or peasants were forced to grow particular crops for delivery to the Company at fixed prices. This produced a widening of the Company's interests to cover the actual production of export crops, of which coffee was the outstanding example.

Arabian coffee was introduced to Java by the Dutch in the 1690s. Plants were distributed to district chiefs around Batavia and Cheribon (Cirebon), and as the Company offered attractive contract prices for the produce, there was a rapid expansion of cultivation in the first quarter of the new century; output rose to 12 million lb. by 1723, and Java coffee soon found a place in the European market. This created a situation totally alien to the Company's experience; the mass production of coffee for sale at relatively low prices in an expanding European market foreshadowed the kind of development to come a century and a half later, but was greatly at variance with the current Dutch monopoly system of dealing in restricted supplies of low-bulk, high-value products. The price offered for coffee was thus drastically reduced; many bushes were removed, other holdings were neglected, and production fell so sharply that the Company was unable to secure sufficient for export purposes. It therefore applied a system of forced delivery to the production of coffee in the Preanger (Priangan) districts of west Java which it now controlled and, to ensure future supplies, made the annual planting of a stipulated number of bushes obligatory. The system instituted to organise this enforced peasant cultivation of coffee ultimately served as the foundation for the Netherlands Indies civil service; under the overall control of the Commissioner for Native Affairs, responsibility rested with the Regents assisted by supervisors or 'coffee sergeants'. These 'native' officials received a share of the output for their services; prices were fixed by the Company in accordance with European demand, so that whatever the state of the market, the peasant producers themselves made little from coffee cultivation. The application of the principle of 'Contingencies and Forced Deliveries' to coffee and other crops in the eighteenth century, rivetted Dutch interest on Java as the island quickly emerged as the principal source of the primary tropical produce which had come to furnish the bulk of the Company's profits.

A continuing theme of Indonesian history is the manner in which the differential impact of external forces has served to augment the cultural diversity of the archipelago, and this is as true of the era of the Dutch East India Company as it is of prehistoric times. Although authority rarely extended far from the coastal footholds, by the later eighteenth century few parts of the archipelago had escaped some Dutch interference. Yet, as Vlekke so clearly shows, significant regional differences in the nature of the European impact were already apparent.[6] As already seen, much of Java had passed under direct Company rule and the island's economy had been greatly modified to yield increasing quantities of selected export crops to the Dutch. The Western influence was stronger, and certainly more oppressive, in the Moluccas. The indigenous commerce of this area was destroyed by the erection of monopolies. By means of annual *hongi's,* or expeditions by fleets of armed *perahus* to extirpate trees elsewhere, the cultivation of cloves was restricted to Amboyna and that of nutmegs to the Banda Islands. Since the population of these islands was obliged to purchase its food from the Company at inflated prices, emigration became an attractive alternative to abject poverty. In Celebes, where the once-flourishing entrepôt of Macassar had suffered severe commercial decline as a result of Dutch intervention, the Minahasan territories of the north, to which the Company gained access a century earlier when it established a post at Menado, proved surprisingly receptive; many of its people accepted Christianity, so that it became in time 'one of the most westernized parts of the archipelago'.[7]

In Java, the Moluccas, and Celebes therefore, the activities of the Company contributed much to emerging economic, political, and social patterns; elsewhere, the Dutch had negligible effects on local cultures. Their presence in Sumatra was limited to a few small forts and trading posts, and although they held an exclusive right to handle the exports of pepper and tin from many states by treaty, their monopoly was regularly penetrated by Chinese, European, and indigenous traders, and they had little influence either on the planters of pepper or the miners of tin. Despite its exports of diamonds, gold, and pepper, Borneo experienced even less direct interference. The settlement at Banjarmasin permitted some control of the pepper trade, but in the west, a major source of gold and diamonds, posts opened at Sambas and Sukadana early in the seventeenth century were quickly evacuated, and the next venture, a factory at Pontianak in 1779, lasted only a few years. Nevertheless, the widespread political consequence of the Dutch presence in the Indies must not be overlooked. Even this abortive late eighteenth-century intrusion into west Borneo did disrupt existing politico-commercial relations, and was largely responsible for the rise to power of an adventurer, Abdul Rahman, as Sultan of Pontianak. By right of discovery, by conquest from the Portuguese, or as successor to the indefinite spheres of Ternate and Tidore, the Company had acquired claims to the Lesser Sunda Islands, the scattered islets of the south-east, and the coastlands of New Guinea in the course of the seventeenth century, but since these yielded little of value to the Dutch, they were of no real interest and, together with Bali and Lombok, they virtually escaped Western influence.

The monopolistic policies of the Dutch were most successful in the late seventeenth century; thereafter, conditions began to alter and, for a variety of reasons in the subsequent century, the decline in the Company's fortunes became progressively more obvious. This can be attributed partly to rampant corruption amongst its officials. Additionally, the Dutch presence disrupted but did not destroy indigenous politico-commercial structures, and the confused situation in the island world was marked by the predatory activities of fleets of traders-cum-marauders, and by the attempts of local rulers to use traditional political means to maintain their incomes and authority in the face of Dutch policies.

More important, however, as an era of expanding and diversifying trade, the eighteenth century witnessed a rapidly growing market for Asian products in Europe. Some of these, such as pepper, coffee, sugar, indigo, and tin, were produced in increasing quantities in the archipelago; others, such as tea from China, passed through *en route* to the West, and generated a rising demand for island produce to finance this burgeoning trade. The Company successfully retained its spice monopoly, but spices were of progressively diminishing significance as items of trade and, as Tarling has observed, the Dutch probably devoted so much attention to maintaining this monopoly 'that they neglected the new opportunities that opened up'.[8] Indeed, the growth of commerce and the broadening range of exports made it almost impossible to enforce the old monopoly system and offered strong attractions to other traders, notably the English, Buginese, and Chinese, to penetrate ever deeper into former Dutch preserves, thus contributing greatly to the fall in the Company's profits. The emergence of Bangka tin as a major export product provides an excellent case in point. Destined principally for the China market to pay for shipments of tea, there was a sharp rise in the island's exports between 1750 and 1780. The Company had possessed a formal monopoly of this trade in tin since 1722, but there is sound reason to believe that by the 1770s the Dutch actually received less than half the total output of the Bangka mines, most of which found its way to English and Chinese traders. Similar monopoly evasion occurred on the Malay peninsula, so that the Dutch soon came to regard the English as 'their masters in the tin trade of the Straits'.[9] Faced with this growing commercial competition, from about 1770 bankruptcy threatened the Company and in 1783 it stopped paying dividends.

The Company's problems also owed much to developments in Europe. When the Netherlands became involved in the Franco-British-American War in 1780, the British blockade of Dutch ports cut communications with the Indies. Although the Dutch were unable to ship exports to Europe, monopolies were not relaxed to admit foreign traders and the accumulation of unsold produce in Batavia's stores did little to help the Company's ailing exchequer. Moreover, in 1784 the Dutch monopoly of shipping in the archipelago was finally broken by the Treaty of Paris, and thenceforth British and other vessels were free to trade in the area. The French Revolutionary Wars delivered further blows to the Company's waning power. Holland was occupied by the French in 1795; its new government became allied with the invaders, and, to forestall a French takeover, the British occupied Dutch archipelagic possessions with the exception of Java. The accounts of the Company had shown a mounting deficit for many years and by 1791 this had reached 96 million guilders. After due consideration, it was decided to allow the Company's charter to expire at the end of 1799; the state, its chief creditor, then took over all its possessions and debts, the latter then totalling some 135 million guilders.

Partly under the influence of French revolutionary principles, in the last years of its life much criticism of the objects and methods of the Company was voiced in the Netherlands. When its surviving possessions passed to the state, a committee was appointed to consider the commerce and administration of the Indies; but its report, submitted in 1803, recommended few major changes. At the time, of course, communication between Java and the Netherlands was difficult; the authorities in Batavia used their relative freedom to capitalise on rising prices by opening Java's ports to foreigners and, in the early years of the new century, corruption was rife.

The situation changed radically with the arrival in 1808 of a zealous reformer, Herman Willem Daendels, as the new Governor-General. To increase efficiency and provide a greater degree of direct rule, he completely remodelled the administration, turning 'native' chiefs into salaried officials of the Dutch government. One of his most far-reaching reforms transformed the judicial system.

Recognising a distinction between indigenes and others, this was reorganised to provide Native Courts to deal with cases concerning only Javanese according to *adat,* whereas those involving foreigners were dealt with according to Dutch-Indian law by Councils of Justice. Charged on his appointment with strengthening the defences of Java, the armed forces were improved, fortresses erected, and an energetic programme of road-building was commenced. This produced one of his most spectacular achievements; using forced labour, a great trunk road was built through the entire length of Java, shortening the east-west overland journey from 40 to 6½ days. Moreover, Batavia had long been infamous as an unhealthy place and on his initiative its residential quarters were moved inland to Weltevreden. These reforms did much to remove the old Company structure, but Daendels retained, and indeed greatly extended, the compulsory cultivation of coffee. However, cut off from markets by the British fleet, the growing supplies of coffee proved difficult to sell, and burdened with the cost of his reforms, the financial situation deteriorated. In a vain attempt to replenish the exchequer, Daendels resorted to desperate expedients, including the sale of 'government domains' to private individuals. His dictatorial manner, the nature of his reforms, and his insensitive methods gained him enemies among the Dutch; in Java he aroused serious antagonisms by issuing 'new regulations for "ceremonial and etiquette" under which Dutch officials were forbidden to pay the traditional marks of honour to the ruling princes and must wear hats in their presence'.[10] After a brief period of intense activity, Daendels was removed from office in 1811.

The annexation of the Netherlands to the French Empire in 1810, Napoleon's designs on India, and the strengthening of the island's defences by Daendels, persuaded the British that it was strategically necessary to occupy Java. Arriving in August 1811, the British occupation forces met little resistance and Java and its surviving dependencies were soon surrendered. Much of the preparatory work for the invasion had been done by Thomas Stamford Raffles, who was now appointed Lieutenant-Governor in charge of the island. Having established British authority, Raffles launched an impressive programme of reform. He reorganised the government, dividing Java into sixteen Residencies, to provide for direct administration by paid officials. He sought to abolish slavery, and, although far from a complete success, his measures did produce a substantial drop in the number of slaves. His most significant innovation, however, was undoubtedly the renowned land-rent system, designed to replace the old, and in his view stultifying, contingencies, forced deliveries and compulsory services.

An investigation of land tenure led him to believe that all land was state property; occupiers were therefore tenants liable to pay rent for their land and were assessed according to the productivity of the land. Rents were to be levied on villages. Payable in rice or cash, rents were collected by village headmen, who were made salaried government servants, under the supervision of European officials. The first moves to introduce this revolutionary system began in late 1813 and, not surprisingly, met with serious problems. Its successful adoption presupposed far more detailed cadastral surveys than then existed, together with careful evaluation of land potential rather than the arbitrary estimates which had to be made; yet, in the long run, these were overcome and the system was retained by the Dutch after their return to Java.

Despite his hopes, Raffles found it necessary to maintain both the forced cultivation of coffee in the Preanger districts and compulsory services in the teak-producing areas. His reforms were concerned primarily with Java; elsewhere, his main achievement was the acquisition of the Bangka tin-mines from the Sultan of Palembang. Like Daendels before him, Raffles faced severe financial constraints on the implementation of his reforms, and, in his turn, was obliged to sell government lands to private individuals to bolster a declining revenue. He too failed to balance the budget. Moreover, his dream of making Batavia 'the centre of a new British empire of the islands',[11] revealed for instance in his attempts to extend British influence to west Borneo and in the tone of parts of his monumental *History of Java,* lacked official sanction, for the occupation of Java was seen as a temporary expedient caused by affairs in Europe. Faced with accusations of financial incompetence and dissatisfaction with his policies among his superiors, Raffles was recalled in 1815. Britain had already agreed to return Dutch possessions by the Convention of London in 1814, and, with the defeat of Napoleon, the transfer began.

Three Commissioners-General, including Baron van der Capellen, were appointed to restore Dutch government in the islands; arriving in Java in April 1816, they quickly resumed its administration, but full restoration of the remaining possessions was delayed by indigenous recalcitrance and disputes with the British. Faced with a dire need for revenue and apparently adhering to the principle that freedom of enterprise encourages production, the policies adopted by the returning Dutch were characterised by uncertainty as to methods and an absence of overall coherence. They decided to continue with Raffles's land-rent system, maintained the framework of his system of territorial administration, and confirmed his regulations relating to slavery.

They also reintroduced the dual system of justice and retained the forced cultivation of coffee in the Preanger districts. Van der Capellen took over as Governor-General in 1819 and, until his removal six years later, had to contend with a mounting and irreversible deficit. The new administrative machine was costly, falling crop prices in the early 1820s meant diminishing returns, especially from coffee, and the trade, now free, was mostly in foreign and chiefly British hands. Moreover, outbreaks of unrest in the Moluccas, Borneo, Celebes, Palembang, Bangka, and west Sumatra had proved a serious drain on resources. Fears over British intentions, compounded by the founding of Singapore in 1819, were not dispelled until the Treaty of London (1824) settled Anglo-Dutch political and commercial relations in the archipelago by arranging for a Dutch withdrawal from the Malay peninsula in return for the British posts in Sumatra and an undertaking that the British would make no further settlements south of Singapore.

The depressing financial situation was greatly aggravated by the outbreak of the so-called Java War in 1825. Discontent with Dutch policies was already widespread in the 'native' states when Van der Capellen succeeded in alienating the Jogjakarta aristocracy by interfering with their sources of income. Diponegoro (Dipanegara), eldest son of the deceased Hamengku Buwono III of Jogjakarta, was ignored for the succession and quickly gained sympathy as a liberator who would free the Javanese from the grip of the infidel Dutch. In the general unrest, Diponegoro led a revolt, took Jogjakarta, and conducted an effective guerrilla campaign in much of central Java until, in the later 1820s, the Dutch developed suitable retaliatory tactics. In 1830 Diponegoro offered to negotiate; when he visited Dutch headquarters, he was arrested and exiled to Menado in northern Celebes. Batavia annexed substantial additional territory from the two principalities and, although these preserved their identity as *Vorstenlanden,* Dutch sovereignty thus covered the entire island. The Java War was disastrous for all concerned. Rural life and economy were seriously disrupted. In battle, or through the ravages of disease and famine, nearly 15,000 Dutch troops and an estimated 200,000 Javanese died. Financed almost entirely by loans, the war had cost 20 million guilders and, with the opening of hostilities in Europe, the Dutch treasury, to quote Vlekke, was 'emptied to the bottom, in Holland as well as in Java'.[12] Rehabilitation was clearly imperative.

The arrival of Johannes van den Bosch as new Governor-General in January 1830 ended this period of uncertain and unprofitable policies. Adopting much of the old Company approach, he sought by state direction to raise the level of export-crop production in Java at the lowest possible cost. This he did by introducing the *Cultuurstelsel,* popularly known as the 'Culture System', but perhaps more accurately rendered as 'System of Forced Cultivation'. In essence, this meant that instead of paying taxes and rent in money the Javanese peasant was obliged to devote part of his land and labour to the cultivation of export crops prescribed by the government, to which he was forced to deliver the produce. The main crops involved were coffee, sugar, and indigo; of these, coffee, which furnished the bulk of the revenue derived from the system, was grown on previously 'waste' uplands, but in reality, the reserves of shifting cultivators. Villagers were also required to use one-fifth of their sawah land for the cultivation of sugar-cane. Supervision of cultivation was entrusted to Dutch and 'native' officials, who were rewarded with a proportion of the output of their districts. Initially, Van den Bosch had merely ordered the planting of 'adequate quantities' of coffee, sugar, and indigo, but various measures in the early 1830s greatly increased the element of compulsion and the system 'grew until it overshadowed and blighted the whole economic organization of the country, and nothing remained but the Government as a planter on a superhuman scale'.[13] Java came to resemble a large state-run plantation. Moreover, the sole right to ship the resulting 'government' produce to the Netherlands was granted to the Nederlandsche Handel-Maatschappij (NHM), founded in 1825 as an import-export agency for the Dutch government; this came to handle the majority of Java's exports and Amsterdam soon regained its position as a world market for tropical produce.

Financially, the new policy was immensely successful. Although the Preanger districts retained their importance, coffee-planting spread rapidly to formerly unoccupied hill-lands, or *Woestegronden,* and there was a sharp increase in sugar cultivation, particularly in physically favoured parts of east Java. Output of all export products rose dramatically and by 1840 the aggregate value of shipments of coffee, sugar, and indigo had risen to 58 million guilders. Unlike developments later in the century, this tremendous expansion owed little to an influx of capital or to improvements in methods of production; that it was due primarily to 'the organization of labour for State cultivation', as Furnivall suggests, can hardly be doubted, especially since the system permitted the government to discount labour charges, the largest item in production costs.[14] But it is often forgotten that world prices for coffee and sugar showed an upward trend in the 1830s. Whatever the causes, however, the deficit in Java's revenues was quickly cleared and from 1831 the colonial government regularly transferred its surplus—known as the *batig slot*—to the Dutch exchequer, the system proving, in Baud's words, 'the life-belt on which the Netherlands kept afloat'. Between 1831 and 1878, when the transfers ceased, the home treasury received 823 million guilders from Java and, among other things, this helped to finance the construction of the Dutch railways.

While it did much to promote development in the Netherlands, the *Cultuurstelsel* had more depressing effects in Java. It led to a deeper Western penetration of the rural economy than ever before, with direct repercussions on life and society at village level. The burden of work, and often of risk also, fell heavily on the peasants, and demands on their land and labour frequently interfered with food production; indeed, this was one of the principal causes of a succession of famines in central Java in the 1840s, and it also contributed to internal displacements of population. Clearly, the economic incentives for the villager were minimal; he was, as Van Niel observes, 'expected to give an inordinate amount of his energies and resources to the cultivation in comparison to the share of the profits he received'; harnessing his productive efforts by compulsion, the system 'did not allow or encourage him to break out of the confines of his traditional patterns'.[15] Yet, although it is usually condemned, far more objective and detailed research in the voluminous Dutch archives is needed before we can achieve a balanced assessment of the *Cultuurstelsel,* for its effects were not entirely detrimental, its impact was very uneven, and the failure of entrepreneurship and enterprise to emerge among the Javanese peasantry probably owes as much to inherent cultural impediments as it does to Dutch policy. To its credit, for instance, must be placed the introduction of new export crops, some of which later became important. And although its disruptive effects cannot be ignored, production of the prescribed crops never absorbed more than about one-twentieth of Java's cultivated land and directly involved less than a quarter of the population. Even where it did apply, there were significant regional variations in both the organisation and the effects of forced cultivation, depending in part on the enthusiasm and effectiveness of local Dutch officials. In the longer term, perhaps the outstanding feature of the period 1830 to 1860 was the intensity of Dutch interest in Java and their virtual neglect of the rest of the archipelago.

With constitutional change in the Netherlands in 1848 the colonies came under the control of the Dutch parliament, the States-General, in which there emerged several influential advocates of a more liberal approach. Seeking a far greater role for private enterprise and concerned for the interests of the Javanese. liberal opposition to existing policies gradually began to have effects, and measures to open Java to private capitalists in the 1850s produced some results. The immense success in the Netherlands of the novel *Max Havelaar,* published by Eduard Douwes Dekker under the *nom de plume* 'Multatuli' in 1860, gave the movement a tremendous boost; the appearance of this classic of Dutch literature 'helped to provide a popular background for those Liberals who wanted to make a serious effort to introduce their principles into the colonial administration'.[16] Their demands for the abolition of slavery were rewarded in 1860 and five years later compulsory labour in the government forest districts was ended. Indeed, during the 1860s much of the apparatus of the *Cultuurstelsel* was dismantled, the state progressively withdrew from direct involvement in cultivation, and a new commercial policy evolved based on free-trade principles. Forced cultivation of pepper was abolished in 1862, and was followed by that of cloves and nutmegs in 1863; indigo, tea, cinnamon, and cochineal in 1865; and that of tobacco in 1866. Significantly, however, these were the least profitable 'government' crops contributing little to revenue, whereas the compulsory cultivation of coffee and sugar, which together accounted for three-fifths of Java's total export earnings in 1865, was retained.

The shift from state direction to private enterprise was effectively consummated by two pieces of legislation in 1870, for these marked the beginning of a half-century of unfettered capitalist expansion, subject only to the vagaries of the world market. One of these provided for government withdrawal from sugar cultivation in twelve annual stages starting in 1878; only coffee then remained unfree, and forced cultivation of this crop continued in Java until 1917. Secondly, under the provisions of the Agrarian Law of 1870, individuals and companies were able to acquire heritable 75-year leases to government domain (i.e., uncultivated land to which no Indonesian had claims) and although indigenes were forbidden to sell their land to aliens, they were permitted to lease it to capitalists for periods of 5 to 20 years. By facilitating the acquisition of land, this law decidedly paved the way for a tremendous expansion of private plantation interests.

Since the arrival of Van den Bosch, who saw most of the Outer Islands as potentially 'unprofitable burdens' unsuited to the system of forced cultivation, the Dutch had concentrated heavily on Java. From the mid-nineteenth century, however, they became increasingly aware of the need to assert their position in the rest of the archipelago, if only to forestall the intervention of others; thus, it was largely from fear of British activities that efforts were made to consolidate Dutch authority in western Borneo. Billiton (Belitung), with its known deposits of tin ore, was occupied in 1851, and a conflict with the Sultan of Banjarmasin over the government exploitation of coal-mines at Martapura resulted in Dutch annexation of his territories in 1863. Meanwhile, moves were made to bring more of Sumatra under control and, after subjugation of the Lampungs, a treaty with the Sultan of Siak in 1858 extended Dutch sovereignty to Siak, Deli, Serdang, Langkat, and Asahan in the north-east. Relations with Acheh, which had claims to these states, were severely strained. In 1871 the British withdrew their objections to Dutch intervention in this northern sultanate. However, the capture of its capital Kotaraja, now Banda Aceh, two years later, signified the start of a lengthy and extremely costly campaign against active guerrilla resistance instigated by district chiefs and religious leaders, and although Dutch sovereignty was finally acknowledged in 1903, sporadic insurrections continued for several years thereafter. Closer attention was also paid to certain of the other islands and by the opening of the twentieth century control had been achieved over much of Sumatra, Borneo, Celebes, and the Moluccas, together with Lombok and northern Bali. By various means Dutch rule was then quickly extended over the remaining territories and by World War I the archipelago was effectively under a single authority. Nevertheless, save for a few enclaves of strong Dutch economic interest and occasional points of missionary activity, the Outer Islands remained for the most part the domain of scattered shifting cultivators largely undisturbed by Western influences.

The outstanding feature of the period after 1870 was, however, the efflorescence of private enterprise and the dramatic growth of export production. The adoption of more liberal colonial policies had created an environment conducive to increased investment in plantation and other ventures at a time when the opening of the Suez Canal, the rise of the steamship, and the growth of demand in the industrialising countries of Europe produced an expanding market for tropical produce. Much of the capital needed for the new developments was supplied by the NHM, which financed the erection of sugar factories and the opening of private estates; other ventures were backed by the newly established *Cultuurbanken,* or agricultural finance corporations, which specialised in financing plantations. Access to capital had immediate effects on the sugar industry. Improved machinery was imported, new factories were built, and more fertilizer was used; output more than doubled between 1870 and 1885 and sugar became Java's major export crop.

This period of affluence and expansion for the private planter in

Java came to an abrupt end in the early 1880s when disease hit both sugar and coffee, and prices fell catastrophically. Unable to withstand the losses, the interests of proprietary planters passed to large corporations, most with their headquarters in the Netherlands. In response to the depression improvements were effected in methods of production, in general efficiency, and in marketing, so that, for instance, the yield of sugar per hectare doubled in the last quarter of the century. New crops such as tea and cinchona were also introduced. Still using land rented from villagers, the sugar industry of Java grew to massive proportions in the first thirty years of the new century. Output doubled between 1900 and 1920 and, with the introduction of a new high-yielding variety of cane (POJ 2878) in 1924, doubled again by 1930. Sugar exports reached a peak of 2.9 million metric tons in 1929, when the area planted to cane totalled 200,000 hectares. During the same period Java became the major world producer of cinchona, and, after the adoption of Assam seed and greatly improved methods of preparation, many tea estates were opened, chiefly in the Preanger highlands, and exports of tea rose tenfold between 1915 and 1930. Moreover, soon after 1900 *Hevea* rubber was added to the list of Java's plantation crops and estates were developed both in the Preanger district and in the Besuki area of the extreme east.

With the extension of effective Dutch control, however, development was no longer restricted to Java and, as plantation organisation replaced the earlier cultivation by peasants under government supervision, the entire pattern of export production in the archipelago began to change. This found its most dramatic expression in the rise to prominence of north-east Sumatra as the plantation area *par excellence* in the Outer Islands. The success of Jacobus Nienhuys, who began to plant tobacco on the fertile volcanic soils of Deli in 1865, soon attracted others to the production of high-quality wrapper leaf for cigars; several companies were formed and 170 tobacco estates had been opened by 1889. Sited as they were 'in a primitive society on the fringes of European administration',[17] these pioneer companies had to provide for themselves the basic transport and other facilities, and, with their large concessions obtained on favourable terms from the local Sultan and through the use of imported Chinese labour, adopted a system whereby the land was planted with tobacco only once every six to nine years. When tobacco prices fell sharply in 1890, marginal estates either closed or turned to other crops; the surviving estates were consolidated into four large Companies and the N.V. Deli Maatschappij (Deli Company), established in 1869, achieved a dominant position in the industry. By 1928 Medan was encircled by 72 tobacco estates with a planted area of 50,000 acres. In the meantime, other plantation ventures had appeared. *Hevea brasiliensis* was introduced to north-east Sumatra in 1906 and vast areas of estate rubber were developed in Serdang and Asahan. Tea-planting began on elevated land around Permatangsiantar in 1911 and the first commercial planting of oil-palm that year in Asahan was followed by a tremendous expansion of this crop in the 1920s. The opening of sisal estates on the Simalungen hills after 1917 completed the patchwork pattern of large, corporate-owned plantations. With their indentured Javanese and Chinese labour, these plantations of Sumatra's *Cultuurgebied* were a unique product of this age of private enterprise.

Elsewhere in the Outer Islands the growth of export-crop production occurred primarily on indigenous smallholdings. The expansion of world demand for vegetable-oil products made coconut cultivation for the production of copra an increasingly attractive proposition and from about 1890 there was a steep rise in the acreage devoted to coconuts, notably in northern Celebes and western Borneo. An ideal smallholder crop, rubber was quickly adopted by indigenous farmers, particularly in southern and eastern Sumatra and coastal Borneo, and when the restrictions of the Stevenson Scheme were applied to Malaya in the 1920s, vast and unrecorded areas were planted by smallholders in Indonesia. Small-scale cultivation of other export crops was equally localised; pepper was largely confined to the Lampungs, Bangka, and the Riau Islands, and coffee to parts of Sumatra, northern Bali, and central Celebes. These 'growing points of peasant enterprise' in which smallholder production for external markets achieved immense importance were, as Geertz observes, 'islands in a broad sea of essentially unchanged swidden-making',[18] and, but for Schrieke's study of western Sumatra,[19] we would know little or nothing about the effects of this intrusion of cash-crop production into indigenous agriculture. Here is a field which merits a major research effort, for the way in which peasants respond to new commercial opportunities is fraught with significance for Indonesia's economic future.

Although the development of export-crop production was the more spectacular, there was a concurrent increase in mineral exploitation and a growth of private participation in the mining industry, which until 1860 had been entirely a government preserve. The rich alluvial tin deposits of Bangka had been worked under government direction since 1816, but the introduction of steam-driven machinery in 1890, and of dredges three decades later, brought a sharp rise in output. Tin-mining began on nearby

Billiton in 1852 and eight years later the mining rights passed to the Billiton Maatschappij; in 1923 this concession was transferred to a new company, with government the major shareholder, which in time also acquired the Singkep mines, where production began in 1889. The mining of coal to provide bunkerage for steamships began in south-east Borneo in 1849, and as with the fields developed later at Umbilin and Bukit Asem in Sumatra, this also was a government venture. The state thus possessed substantial interests in tin and coal, but the situation was otherwise with petroleum. The first successful attempts to exploit known deposits in the 1880s brought the formation of companies to provide suitable financial backing and led to the establishment in 1890 of the Royal Dutch Company to work fields in north-east Sumatra, and, later, to open those at Balikpapan and Tarakan in eastern Borneo. This company gradually absorbed the other oil concerns in the archipelago, and in 1907 amalgamated with the local subsidiary of the British-owned Shell Transport and Trading Company to form Royal Dutch Shell, whose concessions were developed by a new Company, the Bataafsche Petroleum Maatschappij (BPM). Royal Dutch Shell dominated the expanding petroleum industry, but in 1912 the Standard Oil Company of New Jersey formed a local subsidiary, the Nederlandsche Koloniale Petroleum Maatschappij, which subsequently gained entry to several fields. By 1930 Indonesia's oil production totalled 44 million barrels (6 million tons), the bulk coming from Borneo and Sumatra.

The total value of exports from the archipelago rose from 108 million guilders in 1870 to 1,801 million in 1925 and this enormous growth of production 'called into existence a new colonial world with a wholly new structure, political and economic'.[20] European capital flowed into the Indies, including substantial amounts from non-Dutch sources; indeed, although Dutch investment was dominant in the sugar industry, on the eve of World War I, half of the rubber companies in Java were British and nearly half the investment in north-east Sumatra was foreign European, principally British, Swiss, and German, and American. By 1930 Western investment in Indonesia had reached an estimated total of 2,000 million U.S. dollars.

The multiplication of plantations, mines, and commercial and financial institutions transformed the European population of the Indies. The number of Europeans (including Eurasians) rose from 59,000 in 1892 to 242,000 in 1930, whilst the relative numerical strength of government employees in the Dutch community was greatly reduced. At the same time, a distinction appeared between those who were locally born, regarded Indonesia as home, and had a close interest in local affairs (the *blijvers*), and those who came for a period of service with the intention of returning to the Netherlands (the *trekkers*); the former, who were in the majority, were predominant in government employment and in the sugar industry, the latter in mining, foreign trade, and in other estate ventures. Equally, there was a significant change in the distribution of Europeans, for whereas formerly they had concentrated heavily in Java, there were now substantial numbers in the emerging enclaves of Western enterprise in the Outer Islands, namely the *Cultuurgebied*, the 'tin islands', and the oilfields. Indeed, this phenomenal development of export production—which was of far greater significance to Indonesia than most historical studies suggest—served to accentuate further the differences between Java and the rest of the archipelago. As the old condiment and beverage crops gave way to industrial raw materials, Java's contribution to export earnings declined. While Java, with a rapidly growing population and little spare land, experienced increasingly severe and seemingly insoluble problems, unprecedented economic growth brought prosperity and change to the zones of Western investment and smallholder enterprise in the Outer Islands.

When Raffles placed the population of Java at 4½ million in 1815, he certainly underestimated total numbers. Nevertheless, for many reasons, notably the peace conferred by Dutch rule and improving health and transport facilities, the population of Java and Madura grew rapidly during the nineteenth century; numbers doubled between 1850 and 1880, rose to 28.4 million in 1900 and to 41.7 million in 1930 when over a quarter of the Districts of Java had densities exceeding 500 per square kilometre (or some 1,300 per square mile). Until about 1900 this growth of numbers was matched by an extension of the cultivated area and from the mid-nineteenth century much new land was converted into sawahs. By the early twentieth century, however, there was little scope for further extension, rural population was growing faster than the cultivated area, and there was a steady decline in the amount of cultivated land per head of population. By the 1930s peasant holdings averaged less than one hectare; many families possessed no land except their house-plots and associated mixed gardens, and perhaps a quarter of the population led a precarious existence, relying chiefly on casual employment.

Peasant agriculture in Java became progressively more intricate and elaborate as the burgeoning numbers were 'forced into a more and more labor-stuffed sawah pattern' and were absorbed on 'miniscule rice farms', a process Geertz has labelled *involution*.[21]

With worsening man-land ratios there was scant possibility of displaying initiative and enterprise in response to commercial opportunities, as was occurring in the Outer Islands; all efforts had to go into food production. Yet, the quality of peasant diet deteriorated, with an apparent decline in calorie intake. *Per capita* rice consumption in Java and Madura seems to have started its long decline shortly after 1850 and, if the figures are to be trusted, average annual consumption per head in the later 1930s was only four-fifths of that seven decades earlier and was substantially lower than the average for the Outer Islands. Falling rice consumption was counterbalanced by a sharp increase in the use of other foods, especially maize, tapioca, sweet potatoes, and soya beans, and adoption of these crops was officially promoted from the later nineteenth century either for off-season cropping on sawahs or for cultivation on dry fields (*tegalan*), so that by the 1910s they had been fully integrated into a diversified and increasingly intensive subsistence-oriented peasant agriculture. The structure of food-producing agriculture and its many problems are further analysed in Chapter 5.

After the ending of the *batig slot* in 1878 the Dutch showed a greater willingness to use Indies revenue for local purposes; the first railways were built, harbour facilities were improved, and, from about 1880 onwards, irrigation systems were modernised. By the end of the nineteenth century, however, it was becoming clear that the peoples of Java derived little benefit from the growth of export production and that indeed there was evidence that living standards on the island were declining. Rising criticisms of the liberal *laissez-faire* approach, conditioned largely by emerging moral and philanthropic ideals, produced a new attitude to colonial government. This was marked in 1901 by a declaration that in future government policy was to be based on the principle of the 'moral duty of the Netherlands toward the people of the Indies' and a year later a special committee was appointed to inquire into 'the causes of diminishing welfare in Java'. Known usually as the Ethical Policy, the new approach was essentially paternalistic, involving far greater government intervention than hitherto; as Furnivall so neatly puts it, this new approach was one of 'let me help you, let me show you how to do it, *let me do it for you*'.[22]

Using revenues in part derived from the expanding colonial economy and in part from grants-in-aid from the metropolitan government, strenuous efforts were made to improve 'native' welfare, particularly in Java. Very substantial sums were devoted to the improvement and extension of irrigation and flood control facilities, and, after the foundation of a Department of Agriculture in 1905, better methods of cultivation were introduced. Suggested initially years earlier as a partial answer to Java's population problem, the first attempts were made to promote Javanese settlement in the Outer Islands; but the movement of colonists to southern Sumatra in 1905 was not very successful and transmigration, primarily from east-central Java to southern Sumatra and central Celebes, did not become marked until the 1930s. In Java itself, the 'advancement' of peasant farmers seemed to require the adequate availability of rural credit; to displace Arab moneylenders and Chinese middlemen, state pawnshops were established, and in 1904 a start was made to provide a popular credit system. Much was also done to improve public health and transport facilities; more roads were constructed and a government subsidy was used to ensure the provision of regular inter-island shipping services on unprofitable routes. In spite of the cost, these projects met little objection from the non-official European community, for in general they were of greater benefit to them than to the peasant who, in large measure, merely experienced excessive interference by Dutch officials who often knew little of local conditions. Although a great deal was achieved, the government failed to solve the problems of Java. Despite the 'moral mission' of the Ethical Policy, employment opportunities did not expand and 'native' welfare continued to diminish. Nevertheless, it has to be remembered that no government of the time accepted overall responsibility for the welfare of the nation and that this was only enforced by the traumatic experiences of the Great Depression and World War II.

Education for Indonesians had been neglected in the nineteenth century and in 1903 only 190,000 pupils attended school in the Indies. From 1907 village schools were established with government support and the numbers attending rose to 700,000 in 1923 and to 2 million in 1940. But the spread of educational facilities failed to keep pace with population growth, and the literacy rate in the late 1930s stood at only 6 percent. Moreover, although technical, law, and medical colleges were established, training at post-secondary level was difficult to achieve and required prior attendance at Dutch-language school. In any case, within the colonial structure there were few opportunities for Western-educated Indonesians, and in 1940 out of a total of more than 3,000 higher civil servants only 221 were indigenes. In these circumstances, it is hardly surprising that the seeds of nationalism began to sprout early in the century.

The encouraging example of Japan's modernisation, coupled with a growing list of grievances which ranged from discrimination in government employment to the dominating role of Chinese middlemen, produced rising dissatisfaction with their inferior status under colonial rule among the small group of Western-educated Indonesians. This trend of ideas is clearly apparent in the now-famous letters of Raden Ajeng Kartini, daughter of the Regent of Jepara, which were first published posthumously in 1911.[23] It was also expressed in the appearance of the first national organisations in the Indies. *Budi Utomo* (High Endeavour) was founded in 1908 to promote culture and organise schools on a national basis, and soon gained supporters among the aristocracy, officials, and intellectuals. As a reaction against the Chinese hold on the *batik* or textile trade of Java, the *Sarekat Dagang Islam* (Society of Muslim Traders) was established in 1911. This was reorganised a year later as *Sarekat Islam* which, retaining its religious character, quickly became the first popular political movement, and, after its first nationwide congress in 1916, demanded self-government on the basis of union with the Netherlands. Dutch unwillingness to allow any meaningful Indonesian participation in government or administration was, indeed, a powerful stimulus to rising nationalist ideals. Some concessions were made, but they were exceedingly small. As a result of the Decentralisation Law of 1903 local councils were formed in Java with European, Indonesian, and Chinese members and in 1916 a *Volksraad* or People's Council was created. But it could only offer advice and, with a European majority, it was not a representative body.

During the second decade of this century socialist concepts gained converts among both Indonesians and Dutch Eurasians. Semarang became a focus of socialism and it was there that Hendrik Sneevliet, himself sympathetic to developments in Russia, founded the revolutionary Indian Social Democratic Club. This formed the basis for the creation of the *Perserikatan Komunist di India* (PKI) in 1920; communists quickly penetrated the new trade unions, fomented strikes in the early 1920s, and instigated revolts in west Java in 1926 and in west Sumatra in 1927. These were quashed by government, the PKI was banned, and many of its members were interned in New Guinea. The collapse of the communist movement left the stage of nationalist endeavour clear for *Sarekat Islam,* which had already called for independence and now started to show more concern for social and economic conditions. In 1925 a new constitution was drafted for the Indies which gave supreme executive and legislative power to the Governor-General. The powers of the *Volksraad,* however, remained insignificant and although it was given an elective majority, Indonesians held only thirty of its sixty-one seats.

Neither this, nor the policies of *Sarekat Islam,* could satisfy all the aspiring nationalists, especially those with more extreme views, and in 1927 Sukarno was instrumental in founding *Perserikatan Nasional Indonesia* (National Party of Indonesia). Imprisoned by the Dutch from 1929 to 1932 for his advocacy of a policy of non-co-operation, he was rearrested in 1933 and exiled. Faced with the severe economic problems caused by the Great Depression, government reactions to nationalist claims hardened in the 1930s; officialdom displayed a strong determination to preserve the colonial situation and only the more moderate were allowed free rein. Nevertheless, in 1936 the *Volksraad* did pass a motion requesting the metropolitan government to call a conference to discuss the question of self-government for the Indies. Nothing had been achieved when the Japanese successfully invaded the archipelago early in 1942.

NOTES

1 M.A.P. Meilink-Roelofsz., *Asian Trade and European Influence in the Indonesian Archipelago between 1500 and about 1630,* The Hague, Martinus Nijhoff, 1962, 177.

2 C. Geertz, *Agricultural Involution: The Process of Ecological Change in Indonesia,* Berkeley and Los Angeles, University of California Press, 1963, 50.

3 Fisher, *South-east Asia,* 136.

4 J.S. Furnivall, *Netherlands India: A Study of Plural Economy,* Cambridge, Cambridge University Press, 1944, 39.

5 Vlekke, op. cit., 216.

6 ibid., 200 ff.

7 ibid., 205.

8 N. Tarling, *A Concise History of Southeast Asia,* New York, Frederick A. Praeger, 1966, 60.

9 C.D. Cowan, 'Governor Bannerman and the Penang Tin Scheme, 1818-1819', *Journal of the Malayan Branch, Royal Asiatic Society,* vol. XXIII, pt 1, 1950, 54.

10 Hall, op. cit., 410.

11 ibid., 419.

12 Vlekke, op. cit., 287.

13 Furnivall, op. cit., 121.

14 ibid., 127.

15 Robert Van Niel, 'The Regulation of Sugar Production in Java, 1830-1840' in Robert Van Niel (ed.), *Economic Factors in Southeast Asian Social Change,* Asian Studies at Hawaii no.2, University of Hawaii, Honolulu, 1968, 106-7.

16 Vlekke, op. cit., 305.

17 G.C. Allen and A.G. Donnithorne, *Western Enterprise in Indonesia and Malaya,* London, Allen and Unwin, 1957, 99.

18 C. Geertz, op. cit., 116.

19 Schrieke, op. cit., 83-166.

20 Furnivall, op. cit., 212.

21 C. Geertz, op. cit., 80.

22 Furnivall, op. cit., 389.

[23] Raden Adjeng Kartini, *Letters of a Javanese Princess,* translated from the Dutch by Agnes Louise Symmers and edited and with an introduction by Hildred Geertz, New York, W.W. Norton and Co., 1964.

CHAPTER 4

To The Abyss, and Back

DESPITE THE TRAUMATIC IMPACT of the Great Depression, which was even more severely felt in the Netherlands Indies than in nearby Malaya which had a far more specialised economy, socio-political conditions in the Indies remained generally tranquil until the outbreak of World War II.[1] But in December 1941 the Japanese attacks on South-east Asia brought this stability to an abrupt end, and over the next quarter of a century Indonesia experienced a series of shocks which succeeded each other in breathless and bewildering fashion. It was not until after the establishment in 1966 of the 'New Order' of General Suharto, and after a ferocious blood-letting which had revealed to Indonesians and the world the magnitude of the differences among the peoples of the archipelago over the social and political organisation of their country, that Indonesia again achieved a period of stability and commenced seriously to grapple with its many pressing problems. The recent history of Indonesia can conveniently be divided into four periods: (a) the Japanese occupation and the revolutionary war, 1942-49; (b) Parliamentary government, 1950-59; (c) Guided Democracy, 1959-65; (d) the New Order, from 1966 onwards.

The Occupation and the Revolutionary War

The Japanese threat, of course, was long foreseen, but the Dutch proved as powerless as their allies elsewhere in South-east Asia to meet it. The financial stringency of the Depression prevented any large expenditure to increase military preparedness or economic strength, although a little had been accomplished; in the later 1930s an industrialisation programme was launched to reduce the degree of dependence on the outside world for manufactures, and this was later taken over by the government of independent Indonesia. But with virtually no heavy industries to support a large and sustained military effort, the Netherlands Indies could offer no effective resistance once Japanese air power had achieved command of the Eastern skies and seas for the Imperial forces. Within a few weeks of the first landings of Japanese troops (Sumatra, December 1941; Java, March 1942) effective resistance ceased. By mid-1942 South-east Asia for the first and only time in its history became on paper one political unit under Japanese control; but in practice the various Imperial forces did little to co-ordinate policy in the areas under their jurisdiction.

The Japanese military administration in the Indies was divided among three commands. One army command with headquarters in Singapore embraced Sumatra and Malaya, a second administered Java, and the remaining islands were placed under the control of the Imperial Navy. Although primarily designed to serve the convenience of the conquerors, this organisation nevertheless broadly corresponded to the traditional groupings of the Malay world. It restored the historic close connections of the lands on either side of the Malacca Strait, acknowledged the uniqueness of Java, and recognised the peripheral character of the remainder of the archipelago.

As elsewhere in South-east Asia, the swiftness and completeness of the Japanese victory stunned the indigenous people, and had the most far-reaching consequences. To many Indonesians the Japanese were liberators, and the Dutch colonial regime and the indigenous nobility, the *priyayi,* on which it had increasingly relied as a constraint to nationalism, were discredited; moreover, a large number of government jobs suddenly became available to Indonesians, although the Japanese rigidly held all the key posts. But to the Japanese themselves, occupation of the Indies was merely a means of maximising their war effort, and they improvised brilliantly with the limited industrial and infrastructural equipment acquired from the Dutch. Nevertheless, the harshness of their rule soon forfeited whatever goodwill they had gained as liberators, and in order to maintain an active popular support for their war effort, the Japanese army, as elsewhere in conquered South-east Asia, began to court the forces of nationalism.

That a policy of stimulating Indonesian nationalism would eventually have backfired against the Japanese themselves is clear from the experience of other parts of occupied South-east Asia, and in the eastern islands the conservative Japanese navy never permitted any expression of nationalist feelings. Of the three principal nationalist leaders exiled for some years in the mid-1930s, Hatta and Sjahrir to the Boven Digul camp in West New Guinea and Sukarno to Ende in Flores, Sjahrir maintained an active opposition to the Japanese, which restricted him and his followers to underground activities; both Sukarno and Hatta, however, were prepared to work with the victors. Sukarno, a graduate in engineering of the Bandung Technological Faculty, had already established himself as the most flamboyant nationalist by the early 1930s, and in 1927 had launched the Indonesian Nationalist Party (PNI) as a vehicle for consolidating all independence movements. This aim was unsuccessful, but his brilliant and inflammatory oratory enabled him to overshadow the more cautious Hatta, whose political experience had included service as a socialist member of the Hague Assembly in the 1920s. Faced with a Japanese ultimatum of collaborate or be eliminated, Sukarno capitulated and indeed made a virtue of necessity. Most studies of Sukarno by Western writers do not find this very reprehensible, but according to Alisjahbana, a leading Indonesian literary figure, this was entirely in keeping with character; Sukarno's basic beliefs, in his view, were always essentially Fascist, and showed many points of semblance to those of the Nazi myth-makers and their nineteenth-century precursors. Throughout his career, Alisjahbana claims, Sukarno was dominated by a craving for power, in which truth and principles were ruthlessly brushed aside whenever by doing so he could enlarge his personal authority.[2] Thus Sukarno's oratory sent many Indonesians to their deaths as *romusya* in Japanese labour camps, and his collaborationist activities were to prove a major impediment to Dutch recognition of the spontaneity and validity of the independence movement.

With new facilities for propagating their views, the nationalists began to forge bonds between the intelligentsia and the ordinary people, or *rakyat,* impossible in the Dutch period. Although the Japanese always intended to replace the Dutch language by Japanese and to compel its teaching in schools, there was insufficient time to carry out such a policy, and the administration was inevitably compelled to make greater use of the Indonesian language, or *Bahasa Indonesia,* which was given official status. Indonesian is very similar to the Malay spoken on either side of the Strait of Malacca, and although only a small proportion of the peoples of Indonesia speak this as their first language, through the rise of the emporium of Melaka (Malacca) and the growth of trade, Malay had become the *lingua franca* throughout the archipelago even before the arrival of the Europeans. Under Dutch rule the use of Malay extended greatly both in commerce and in administration, but the Dutch were opposed to granting the language formal status, and it was not until the occupation that *Bahasa Indonesia* passed into wide popular use and began to assume its present form.

The Japanese, nevertheless, soon found themselves obliged to impose sharp restraints on nationalist activities as it became clear that most leaders cared little for the Japanese war effort but a great deal for Indonesian independence. As the tide of fortune clearly began to flow against them, the Japanese were compelled to make concessions, but they never moved as far or as fast as nationalists demanded. Revolutions are always the product of a small group of determined men, who seize the right time to impose their will on the largely indifferent mass of the population, and the Indonesian revolution was no exception. But in creating conditions in which nationalists could generate mass support, the occupation was decisive, and in the *Peta,* a volunteer army of Indonesian officers and other ranks, and in other military and para-military organisations sponsored by the Japanese, it created the means by which the revolution was defended until the pressure of world opinion could be enlisted to ensure its triumph.

But as the revolution itself germinated during the occupation, so too did most of the pressing socio-political problems for which the Indonesian Republic has so far been unable to find a satisfactory answer. The many military organisations sponsored by the Japanese formed close ties with the new political parties that were launched soon after independence, and thus initiated the close connection of the armed forces and politics, a situation that has greatly hampered the maintenance of national cohesion and a high rate of economic growth. Closely linked with this question of the role of the armed forces in national life is that of the relationship of the outlying provinces (or regions) with the central authority and the national capital, an issue that has become more pointed through the growing disparity in the ratio of population to resources between Java on the one hand, and the Outer Islands, or *Tanah Seberang,* on the other. And not the least important legacy of the shortages, hardships, and social disruptions of the occupation was the liquidation of the benign and generally efficient and corruption-free bureaucracy of the Netherlands Indies, and its replacement by an enormously swollen, inefficient, and privileged kleptocracy, under which the institutionalisation of corruption and the black market was to proceed apace.[3]

In the face of continual Allied successes, the Japanese were compelled by the middle of 1944 to promise eventual Indonesian independence; but they remained reluctant to commit themselves to a definite date. In July 1945, when the Japanese cause was clearly lost, it was finally agreed that independence would be granted, and first to Java. A preparatory committee was set up under Sukarno to implement the decision, but nothing had been done before the Japanese surrender on 15 August 1945, under the terms of which the Imperial forces were to hand over their authority to reoccupying Allied forces. Unwilling to take any action that might prejudice their standing with the Allies, Sukarno and Hatta prevaricated, but their hands were forced. Impatient militant youth groups kidnapped the pair, and on 17 August persuaded Sukarno, according to some accounts at pistol point, to make a declaration of Indonesian independence. Sukarno was nominated President of the new republic, and Hatta Vice President, but the provisional constitution promulgated a week later left many issues undecided, a situation that encouraged much factionalism and intrigue.

Among the undetermined issues were the method of election not only of the President and the Vice President, but also of the supreme legislative body, the People's Congress (MPRS). As elections by universal suffrage were impossible at the time, it was decided that until they could be organised, the functions of the Congress were to be discharged by a Central Indonesian National Committee (KNIP) appointed by the President. This gave to the President great freedom of manoeuvre, and, in effect, an indefinite tenure. Yet despite the post-occupation vacuum, Presidential action to make the machinery effective in the face of the external threat to the new republic was far from vigorous, and whatever his other talents, Sukarno over the next two decades was repeatedly to appear as the man of words rather than of action.

To the government of the Netherlands, Sukarno, Hatta, and their followers, were flagrant Japanese collaborators; it failed to appreciate the magnitude of the changes wrought by the occupation and the strength of nationalist feeling, and despite the opposition of the socialists, who had long supported Indonesian independence, it was determined to re-establish its authority under one guise or another. It was, moreover, widely believed that the Netherlands could not withstand the economic consequences that would follow from loss of its tropical possessions, which, apart from their large export earnings, provided a great multiplicity of employment opportunities for a small European country with many signs of population pressure. This prognosis was to prove entirely false, but there were few indeed in the immediate post-war years who foresaw the remarkable subsequent growth of the world economy. In the Outer Islands, where nationalist activities had been suppressed and return by Allied troops was swift, the Dutch were able to return without difficulty, and to proceed with their plans for a federation of Indonesian states linked with the Netherlands through a common allegiance to the House of Orange. In Java, however, reoccupying British forces encountered increasing resistance from Indonesian units, and with the assault on Surabaya (October-November 1945), notable as the last occasion in which Indian troops fought under British command, the four-year war of independence was launched.

It was, in many ways, a war fought at half-cock, and apart from the two Dutch 'police actions', which were major military operations, the revolutionary war was largely a series of skirmishes and guerrilla actions which in themselves were far from decisive, and which resulted in remarkably little physical destruction. The real battle took place on the political front, in the court of public opinion, and in the newly formed United Nations. Indonesian resistance caught the imagination of a West embroiled in the Cold War, and with the passage of the Independence of India Act in Britain, which became effective in 1947, the fate of all colonial regimes was sealed.

Although a large but motley assemblage of nationalists, ranging from Muslim conservatives to extreme socialists and communists, followed a rigid policy of non-co-operation with the Dutch, the more influential Indonesian leaders, above all Hatta and Sjahrir, realised that a direct confrontation between the Netherlands forces and the unco-ordinated and ill-equipped Indonesian units could have but one result. Talks were therefore necessary to protect the republic's armed forces from destruction, and to win the battle for world opinion. It was vitally necessary to demonstrate that Indonesian nationalism was a genuine indigenous force and not *Nihon sei* (made in Japan); but this was impossible, argued Sjahrir and his supporters, while all political bodies remained within an originally Japanese-sponsored political front, and the government itself had a strong collaborationist complexion. Independent political parties, and a government that owed nothing to Japanese favour, were essential for the goodwill of the West; and in a crisis of survival, these pressures proved decisive. With the appointment of Sjahrir as Indonesia's first Prime Minister, Indonesia began a fitful ten-year experiment with parliamentary democracy.

Had Sjahrir's ministry received some genuine concessions from the Dutch the country's subsequent history might have been very different. Although successful in fending off an attempted *coup* of the extreme Left led by Tan Malaka, one of the founders of the original PKI (Indonesian Communist Party) in 1920 who later broke from the party and in 1948 established his own 'national communist' party (*Murba*), the government could not win acceptance for the Linggadjati agreement with the Dutch of March 1947, in which the republic conceded the principle of federal Indonesia; moreover, the charge of betraying the revolution made by the militants appeared all the more convincing when the Dutch, irritated at the delay in implementing what they considered were its terms, launched its first 'police action', reducing the republican territory in Java to the central portion of the island around Yogyakarta. The attack, however, precipitated the Indonesian question into the United Nations, where support for the fledgling republic proved strong. Through the United Nations a second agreement was arranged on board the USS *Renville* in December 1947, but this in turn could not be implemented by Amir Syarifuddin, who had succeeded Sjahrir as Prime Minister, because of the opposition of political groups hostile to a ministry of such marked leftist orientation.

Thus Indonesia's struggle for existence had become caught up in the conflict of power within the republic itself, a development that had indeed appeared almost inevitable since the declaration of independence, and both issues were to be resolved by force of arms. In a new political manoeuvre Hatta became Prime Minister in a cabinet responsible to the President and not to the Assembly (KNIP), and under the pressures of the Cold War and the severe economic and social constraints operating within the reduced republican territory, the lines between government and anti-government forces hardened rapidly. The communists quickly gained the ascendancy in an anti-government coalition organised by Syarifuddin, and, in effect, transformed it into an enlarged PKI. The communist leaders had apparently already decided on an attempt at a *coup* when their hand was forced by the rebellion of sympathetic army units in Madiun in September 1948. But by appealing for national unity at this stab in the back when all the republic's energies were needed to cope with the Dutch menace, Sukarno and Hatta were able to rally support to contain the rebellion; by December it had been crushed, with the death of Syarifuddin and most of the communist leaders. The PKI was destroyed as an effective force, and was to remain an underground movement until 1952.

This successful defence against a communist *coup* greatly enhanced Indonesia's standing in a West aghast at the communist takeover in Czechoslovakia earlier in the year, and when the Dutch launched a second 'police action' almost immediately afterwards to force on the republic acceptance of the federal system the Netherlands had been building up over the preceding three years, the attack encountered almost universal international opposition. Yogyakarta was speedily occupied and Sukarno, Hatta, and Sjahrir captured; but republican forces kept up guerrilla activities, thus preventing the Dutch from consolidating their control. The United Nations Good Offices Committee, which had assisted in the *Renville* agreement, was reorganised as a United Nations Commission for Indonesia, and a Security Council resolution calling for the release of the arrested leaders and for progress towards implementation of Indonesian independence, was passed. The decisive influence, however, was American economic pressure; by threatening to withhold Marshall Aid for the reconstruction of the Netherlands, the United States was in a position to force compliance with the Security Council resolution. Although it has been denied that any such threat was ever made, even a hint would have sufficed, for Indonesian leaders had long complained that economic aid to the Netherlands was being dissipated in heavy Dutch military expenditure against the republic.

Thus after a Round Table conference at The Hague late in 1949, a transfer of Dutch sovereignty over the archipelago to a federally constituted Indonesia was finally arranged. West New Guinea was excluded, however, and the future of this territory was left to be decided at a later date. As the area had always consumed more resources than it generated, it is difficult to see why the Dutch insisted on its retention, although it was hoped that the territory could come to provide a home for those Indies-born and bred Dutch and Eurasians who chose not to reside in the new republic. Although it was not realised at the time, New Guinea was to constitute an increasingly bitter field of dispute between the Netherlands and the new Indonesia, from which both parties suffered.

In the states created in the area under their control, the Dutch had relied heavily on conservative elements drawn largely from the aristocracy, and their governments possessed little real autonomy. With the withdrawal of the Dutch forces the federal structure crumbled rapidly, and within a few months most of the territorial units created by the Dutch had merged with the Indonesian Republic. Only the South Moluccas resisted the merger, for many Ambonese had served with the Royal Netherlands Indies armed forces, and were fearful of Javanese domination of the new state. An attempt to create an independent republic of the South Moluccas was suppressed by Indonesian Republic forces, but sporadic fighting continued for many years, and Ambonese *émigré* groups in the Netherlands still continued to agitate for an independent Moluccas in the 1970s.[4] With the promulgation of the Provisional Constitution of 1950, in which the President was reduced to little more than a figurehead, five years to the day after the original declaration of independence, the unitary Republic of Indonesia became a legal as well as a practical fact, and in the following month the country was admitted as the sixtieth member of the United Nations.

Parliamentary Government

Although Hatta had returned to the office of Vice President

following the success of the Round Table conference of 1949, the final achievement of independence did not appear to mark any great breach with the immediate past; for the next three years the country continued to be governed by the same broadly pragmatic and conservative groups drawn mainly from the Nationalist Party (PNI) and the *Masyumi* who had worked with Hatta to secure Western goodwill, but the rapid succession of ministries soon suggested that parliamentary democracy was a tender plant in the Indonesian socio-political environment. In harsh reality, a great divide had been crossed; the hardships and fears, but also the glamour and excitement, of the revolutionary struggle when differences between Indonesians could be set aside in the common cause, were behind, and the country no longer occupied the forefront of the world stage. Beset with the Korean War and a multiplicity of new and pressing problems, the United Nations hoped it had heard the last of the Indonesian question.

The problems of reconstruction that confronted the new country were daunting. The occupation and the revolutionary war had resulted in a great decline in agricultural and industrial production, and the country's infrastructure and productive equipment, above all, the transport system, were in a deplorable state. No immediate solution to these problems was at hand, and their resolution clearly demanded careful and rigorous planning, prolonged and dedicated application, and severe checks on any increase in personal consumption. But for the preparation and execution of such a policy, the administration and the bureaucracy were hopelessly inadequate. For those whose revolutionary fervour still burned strongly, moreover, such a Spartan regime lacked any appeal; for years, nationalist leaders had preached that the great natural resource endowment of their country would automatically ensure widespread prosperity once the imperial yoke was thrown off. And indeed, for a short period, the very high prices realised by Indonesian exports during the Korean War concealed the harsh reality of the country's parlous economic position, and suggested that the age of plenty had arrived.

The struggle for power which had been waged so ferociously throughout the life of the Yogyakarta republic was now subject to no restraint; it was no longer necessary to unite behind leaders acceptable to the West. Indonesia's political parties had within a few years come to number more than fifty, and although few of these were of any real importance, several had a substantial religious, ethnic, or regional appeal. Few had any coherent platform or policy, and many represented little more than the personal following of the founder, or leader. All in theory supported

Sukarno's famous *Panca Sila,* or five principles, but in practice their interpretation of these grand but nebulous concepts varied widely.[5] Most also professed an adherence to some kind of ill-defined socialism, although only the PKI was resolutely opposed to capitalism; the necessity for some private capital and enterprise in national development was generally conceded, although, wherever possible, co-operatives were to be favoured.

It has frequently been remarked that Indonesia's political parties all embraced various combinations of nationalism, religion, and Marxism, disparate and conflicting elements to the Westerner, but which Indonesians found little difficulty in reconciling. Many Indonesian leaders were devout Muslims, but had acquired some Marxist leanings through contact with Dutch socialists and through study abroad, and all were intensely nationalist in desiring an economy as well as a polity firmly under the control and ownership of indigenous Indonesians. But the pace and manner in which this was to be accomplished remained a source of deep division between the pragmatists and the extremists, an issue which was polarised by the terms of the transfer of sovereignty. These provided that Indonesia accepted financial obligations of some $550 million to the Netherlands in return for the assets of the Netherlands Indies government, and that private Dutch investment, valued at some $2,000 million, would be respected. But as Indonesia's own economic position became more parlous after the collapse of the Korean boom, these obligations became increasingly unacceptable to extremists, and the pressure for sharp limitations on the role of the alien in the national economy became linked with demands for a more flamboyant and aggressive foreign policy for completing the revolution, and liberating West New Guinea (or Irian).

Arranged in this line-up were, on the one hand, the *Masyumi* and the moderates of the PNI who had negotiated the transfer of sovereignty and who looked to Hatta for leadership, and, on the other, the PNI radicals and extremists identifying with Sukarno, together with the PKI, which despite the Madiun débâcle recovered spectacularly in the 1950s through a new policy of enthusiastic support of the President. Two other parties, the NU (Muslim Scholars) and PSI (Socialist Party), generally threw their support to the pragmatists, as did the small Christian parties. While all the major parties could trace their origins back before the war, they were essentially new organisations created after the Japanese surrender. The PNI appealed mainly to the bureaucracy and the *priyayi,* whereas *Masyumi,* a coalition of generally progressive Muslim groups, was supported by many indigenous traders and commercial houses. After a chequered history in and out of *Masyumi*, NU emerged in 1952 as an independent organisation representing the traditional and conservative Muslim viewpoint; unlike *Masyumi* which drew support from urban areas, NU was always a rural-based party. As the oldest party PKI had undergone several transformations since its foundation in 1920, but after 1953, under the leadership of Dipanegara Aidit, it grew rapidly into a powerful monolithic organisation, eventually becoming the world's largest communist party outside the Eastern bloc. The PKI controlled most of the labour unions, which, though virtually confined to the small modern economy sector, were strongly entrenched in estate, mining, and manufacturing industries, and in transport. Although appealing mainly to the nascent urban proletariat in Indonesia's rapidly growing cities, it nevertheless rapidly built up a strong grass-roots organisation in the countryside through its Peasants' Front (BTI), and became a powerful force in those parts of the country where agrarian problems were most acute, notably in Central and East Java. The distinguished Socialist Party (PSI), on the other hand, appealed mainly to the urban intelligentsia and its lack of a wide popular base was later to prove disastrous. Founded by Sjahrir to support the Hatta government after the extreme Left, which had signed the *Renville* agreement, had renounced it, PSI included some of the country's leading intellectuals and professional men such as Dr Sumitro, perhaps the country's most able economist and financial expert, and Finance Minister in the Wilopo cabinet of 1952-53. The PSI could also often rely on the support of another remarkable revolutionary figure, the Sultan of Yogyakarta, Hamengku Buwono IX, the only one of the more than 200 petty princelings and hereditary rulers of the Netherlands Indies to survive the revolution. By unequivocally backing the independence movement and making his city available as the capital of the republic, the Sultan became a national hero, and, while still retaining his title, became in effect the Governor of the *Daerah Istimewa* (Special District) of Yogyakarta, which possesses the status of a province.

Against this background of bitter party conflict, the moderate coalition ministries of Natsir, Sukiman, and Wilopo (1950-53) struggled to restore the shattered economy and to grapple with some of the country's more pressing problems. In West Java, North Sumatra, and in south-west Sulawesi, the militant *Darul Islam* ('abode of the Muslim faith') which stood for a theocratic Muslim state, was in open revolt against the Jakarta government. Rehabilitation of the run-down estate and plantation crop industries was being seriously affected not only by the depredations of *Darul*

Islam but also by the massive occupation of estate land in the Medan area of East Sumatra by successive waves of squatters from the Lake Toba highlands. The now grossly over-large Indonesian armed forces strenuously resisted any attempt to scale them down to the needs of a nation no longer fighting for survival, and worse, many senior officers had carved for themselves profitable little economic empires through controlling ports, harbours, and transport media, levying a toll on all traffic passing through their domain. Ministries, jealous of their powers of patronage, continued to act as if there were no limit to their expenditure, further augmenting the already swollen ranks of the underpaid and underworked government servants, or *pegawai,* making a mockery of central budgetary control, and sharply increasing inflationary pressures. All of these groups—*Darul Islam,* the squatters, and the armed forces—found support somewhere or other in the parties, and any prospect of strong government action always threatened the shaky coalitions. With the collapse of the Korean boom, euphoria at independence speedily gave way to deep disillusionment as Indonesia found itself faced with the difficult task of paying its way in a world that manifestly did not owe it a living, and militant nationalism became all too frequently a cloak for corruption and a merciless struggle for power.

A turning-point in the history of modern Indonesia came with the 17 October 1952 incident, in which the question of army reform became an issue that polarised moderate and extremist opinion to flash point, and clearly revealed to the country the depths of the divisions that had been papered over during the occupation and the revolutionary war. The 'incident' was precipitated by the desire of the Minister of Defence (the Sultan of Yogyakarta) and the Finance Minister (Dr Sumitro) to reorganise the expensive ill-disciplined and over-large army into a small but highly trained and well-equipped modern force. Many progressive officers, including the Army Chief of Staff, Colonel Nasution, supported the change, but it encountered strong opposition from those both within and without the army who saw the armed forces as revolutionary agents with a fundamental place in Indonesian society, many of whom would also have found their own positions and privileges threatened by the proposed changes. That Dutch military aid, the only then available, was to be used to carry out the reforms, enabled the opponents of the scheme to mobilise opposition in the country and in the provisional parliament, which on 16 October expressed no confidence in the Defence Minister. Next morning large crowds converged on the Presidential palace, urging the dismissal of Parliament but the retention of the Defence Minister and the cabinet;

these were followed by army units, including armoured forces, which ringed the palace, and a tense situation prevailed throughout the day. But Sukarno, increasingly chafing at the largely figurehead role assigned to him since adoption of the 1950 constitution and jealous of his position as Supreme Commander of the Armed Forces, was able to outmanoeuvre the Chief of Staff and his supporters. On this occasion, as subsequently, Nasution lacked the resolve to move against the President, and when later in the day Sukarno emerged to address the crowd, it was clear that he had triumphed. The Sultan retired to Yogyakarta, concentrating his energies on developing his own mini-state, and for the next decade took a limited role in national life. The Wilopo cabinet staggered on for a few more months, but it was clearly doomed, and with its demise also expired the hope of an effective parliamentary democracy in Indonesia.

Although the incident marked the triumph of the extremists over the moderates within the PNI, it represented also the first fruits of the newly adopted PKI policy of abandoning opposition to the Indonesian state and substituting an uncritical support of the President. Thereafter, Indonesia drifted steadily into the hands of those who rejected a modern mixed-economy state in which a high rate of economic growth was accorded a major priority in national goals, and while more and more began to be heard about 'completing the revolution', which with the passage of time was to become increasingly identified with the occupation by force if necessary of West New Guinea, in practice the 'continuing revolution' meant a consolidation of privilege and a hardening of the lines of social stratification. But a recrudescence of the trappings and attitudes of the traditional feudalism, with its preoccupation with symbols and monuments, might well be considered the antithesis of revolution. It is doubtful that any newly developing country, and certainly not one as large or as populous as Indonesia, can for long put aside any attempt to deal with its problems in a basically rational way; the communist alternative is omnipresent, and the rejection of pragmatism merely encourages its appeal and enlarges the basis of its support.

Thus the identification of interests between the President and the PKI conferred the mantle of respectability on the party, despite its proved history of treachery, and in the country at large PKI prestige and authority increased year by year; nevertheless, cabinet office and real power were denied it, for the opposition of the Muslim parties and of the army stood firmly in the way. The massive public support for the party was clearly revealed, however, in the two elections of September and December 1955, respectively for Parliament and for a Constituent Assembly which was to draw up a new constitution to replace the provisional one adopted in 1950. The elections, which it was hoped would restore credibility and respect to a Parliament whose perpetually feuding members possessed no popular mandate, were meticulously organised and were taken very seriously by the public, and in these first and perhaps the only really free elections ever to be held in the country, the very high electoral turnout suggests that belief in parliamentary institutions was more widespread and firmly rooted than either the President or his many admirers at home and abroad were later to suggest. Unfortunately, the September election was indecisive; four major parties, PNI, *Masyumi*, NU, and PKI, between them shared almost 80 percent of the total popular vote, but only some 6 percent separated the top and bottom parties of the foursome, respectively the PNI and PKI, with *Masyumi* and NU occupying intermediate positions. Its most important immediate consequence was the virtual elimination of the PSI, which thereafter ceased to exercise any real political influence. The election also revealed the strong regional and sectional appeals of the parties; the PNI, NU, and PKI all received their greatest support in Central and East Java, where social stratification was most rigid, whereas *Masyumi* was strongest in the areas outside 'inner Java', particularly the Sundanese lands of West Java, and Sumatra and South Sulawesi.

Yet the lengthy preparations for the poll itself, which had begun with the passage of the electoral law of March 1953, exhausted the country; bitter electioneering absorbed the energies of party leaders and members alike, and in the barrage of charge and counter-charge, promise and counter-pledge, the never very efficient machinery of government suffered further heavy abrasion. The economy performed dismally, with the important estate sector facing almost insuperable obstacles placed in its path in attempting to regain pre-war levels of productivity. Petroleum alone seemed free of the paralysis forced on export industries by a hostile government; but after a run of very good years, rice output after 1954 fell short of domestic demand, and year by year the level of rice imports grew. Corruption during the first Ali Sastroamijoyo ministry (July 1953-July 1955), a PNI-NU coalition balancing act supported by the communists but with *Masyumi* and PSI in opposition, became so flagrant that army intervention brought about its downfall.

After the brief caretaker ministry of Burhanuddin Harahap to implement the elections, only another patchwork coalition proved possible, also under the nominal leadership of Ali Sastroamijoyo, in which the two major Muslim parties combined with the PNI to exclude the communists. But by now intra-party divisions had become as pronounced as those separating the parties themselves; thus while the PNI extremists and the PKI attributed prime responsibility for the continued poor state of the economy to the machinations of aliens and imperialists, for many in the PNI the local Chinese were an even greater menace, a view that also had strong appeal to many in both Muslim parties. Yet the PKI never took an anti-Chinese stand, and with the final breach between Moscow and Peking, its traditional unwavering support of the Moscow line was replaced by a declaration of independence, which in practice meant a closer association with China. With this development came a substantial increase in the support, financial and otherwise, provided by the Chinese community to the party. Throughout South-east Asia communism is everywhere regarded, rightly or wrongly, as essentially a Chinese phenomenon, and in Indonesia the growing identification of the local Chinese with the PKI was to have serious consequences.

In its attitude to the Chinese, as in all things, the PKI supported the President, and it is to Sukarno's credit that he never attempted to capitalise on widespread anti-Chinese feeling. In view of his well-known distaste for economic matters, it was unlikely that the President was concerned with the deleterious effects that strong anti-Chinese legislation would have had on the faltering national economy, and while repressive measures might have provoked some reaction from Peking, experience elsewhere in South-east Asia showed that this was hardly an effective deterrent. But such a policy would have interfered with the President's increasing desire to cut a figure on the world stage, and to establish his claim as principal spokesman for the Third World, for which position there were other serious contenders. He had first enjoyed this luxury during the Afro-Asian conference at Bandung in May 1955, a genuine triumph of the first Sastroamijoyo administration, when under the President's auspices the two great leaders of the new Asia, Nehru and Chou En-lai, came together for the first and only time. One of the results of Bandung was an agreement with Peking by which the Indonesian Chinese were to be allowed to choose their future allegiance. The history of this agreement and its consequences for the Indonesian Chinese are discussed in Chapter 9.

To what extent the President was motivated by the agreement is uncertain, but he was quick to see that it was the dispute over West New Guinea that offered the best prospects of remaining in the world's limelight. His demand that the territory should be handed over to Indonesia received enthusiastic support from the PKI, but this was one issue on which most Indonesians thought alike, and there was no opposition from any of the parties. Nevertheless, the growing preoccupation with an adventurous foreign policy was far from the liking of many who believed that the government's first concern should be coping with existing internal problems rather than with adding new ones, and for its neglect of the economy the government came under strong criticism. The inflationary spiral was pricing what exports Indonesia could generate out of the market, and foreign exchange reserves continued to fall; but government response was merely to repudiate the financial obligations to the Netherlands assumed at the transfer of sovereignty, and to give further twists to the inflationary spiral through larger budget deficits. Corruption, as in the first Ali Sastroamijoyo ministry, had become a way of life to ministers and officials, and in a sensational incident the Foreign Minister himself, Ruslan Abdulgani, was arrested on a corruption charge by an army faction, without authority of the central government.

Yet the army was as corrupt as the parties. In Sumatra and Maluku (Moluccas) local army commanders themselves engaged in the profitable but illegal barter trade, occasionally using the proceeds to assist regional development, activities which usually had the full support of the local *Masyumi* or PSI organisations. To the peoples of the export-originating areas, a government policy of securing, as they saw it, maximum short-term advantage to the PNI extremists and Javanese interests, was especially infuriating. The deep-seated ethnic and cultural hostility between Java and the Outer Islands was heightened by a growing sense of economic subservience in the provinces to a Jakarta that was turning a deaf ear to their needs and aspirations, and to a Java that in making but a minor, and steadily declining, contribution to national export earnings while consuming a large and expanding share of total imports, was the principal cause of the country's mounting balance of payments problem. This subservience was detectable in the steady depreciation in the terms of trade between Java and the Outer Islands in favour of the former, as evidenced in the rate at which rubber could be exchanged for rice, and in irritants such as the transfer of outworn railway stock to the Sumatran systems with the introduction of new equipment in Java. Sumatrans and others correctly pointed out that such new stock was being paid for by the proceeds of their exports, and that their rubber and copra would bring far more rice on the world market, as was obvious from the flourishing barter trade.

Although economic issues had become a major cause of estrangement between Java and the Outer Islands, to the latter the progressively closer association of the President and the PKI was as much a matter of deep concern. Long frustrated by the constitutional limitations to his authority and throwing blame for the country's disunited and parlous state on to the internecine strife of the parties, Sukarno in October 1956 first hinted at his new concept (*konsepsi*) of 'Guided Democracy'; it coincided with increased unrest in the provinces, in which party differences had been reinforced by disaffection between local commanders and the central headquarters in Jakarta. Following an unsuccessful *coup* in Jakarta by the West Java garrison under Colonel Lubis, whose intervention had led to the fall of the first Sastroamijoyo cabinet and the arrest of the Foreign Minister in the second, local commanders in Sumatra hastened to declare their rejection of the authority of Jakarta. In North Sumatra, where the population was sharply divided by conflicting ethnic and economic interests and which contained a large Javanese estate labour force solidly controlled by communist-led unions, a *coup* against the central government was aborted by a counter-*coup* within the command. But in Central Sumatra, where the economically enterprising Minangkabau people formed a homogeneous group, local army commanders were successful in establishing a regional council with firm popular support. Dismayed at the perfidy of the President, Hatta resigned from the office of Vice President, and by early 1957 the regional revolts had spread to Sulawesi and Maluku.

The Sastroamijoyo administration was now on the point of collapse, and with the withdrawal of the support of the *Masyumi* members the way was open for the President to construct a government more to his liking. In amplification of his *konsepsi*, Sukarno argued for a new government in which all the major parties, including the PKI, would be represented, while Parliament would be supplemented by a new supreme advisory body, a National Council, in which various functional groups such as farmers, workers, businessmen, the defence forces, etc., would be represented, and which would conduct business in accordance with the traditional *mufakat* (consensus) principle instead of voting. Sukarno defended his desire to have communist representation in the government on the grounds that 'a house divided against itself cannot stand'. But only the PKI and other extremists expressed any enthusiasm for the proposal. For somewhat different reasons, both Muslim parties vigorously opposed the scheme, which merely confirmed the provinces in their defiance of the central government.

Some political scientists have viewed the history of Indonesia from the enunciation of the *konsepsi* to the institution of 'Guided

Democracy' some two years later, as essentially a successful attempt by the army to consolidate and legitimise the enormous gains it acquired through the imposition of martial law (technically a state of siege) in March 1957, which was pressed on Sukarno and the Ali Sastroamijoyo administration by Nasution as a counter to the declaration of a state of siege by the rebels in eastern Indonesia. The decree, which was in fact based on an old Dutch colonial law and was signed by Ali just before his resignation so that there was some question of its legality, not only catapulted army officers into positions of great political power, but provided all kinds of profitable openings in the economy. These fruits the army was determined to retain after the suppression of the revolts, and in this analysis, 'though it was not always evident, because of the dominant figure of Sukarno, the main driving force behind Guided Democracy was the army'.[6]

This view goes far to explain the strong intellectual commitment of several Western scholars, no Marxists themselves, to the PKI, whose virtue consisted in forming an effective force, which the other parties were not, standing squarely with the President in opposing a military takeover. But the view that Guided Democracy was master-minded by Nasution, as Lev suggests, is at odds with the conceded dominance of Sukarno. Sukarno was nobody's man, least of all Nasution's; on every occasion in which the two were in apparent confrontation, the army leader backed away, for he had no counter to the President's charisma. Believing that, as good nationalists, the PKI could be trusted, Sukarno genuinely wanted communist participation in the government, and it is not easy to see why the army should support a system which could only enlarge the status of its greatest enemy. And this is precisely what happened. Nothing that followed in the next few years suggested that the army was in control of events; its professional competence as revealed by the 'confrontations' was low; army unity was not preserved, for PKI infiltration of the officer corps augmented; and in 1965 Nasution narrowly escaped with his life and was effectively eliminated as a political figure.

Despite the resignation of the cabinet in March, the President could not have his way; it proved impossible to construct another cabinet with PKI representation, and the outcome was another unsatisfactory compromise. To break the deadlock, Sukarno used the device that had been employed to overcome opposition to the *Renville* agreement, namely, the appointment of an extra-parliamentary cabinet. His nominee as Prime Minister was Juanda Kartawijaya, a pragmatic and respected non-party man who had held office in many cabinets, and a professional engineer-economist who had formerly directed the National Planning Bureau. Although a few left-leaning extremists were given office, to win NU support no PKI members received appointments, and the new government, essentially a PNI-NU coalition with PKI support in Parliament, was saddled with the task of rehabilitating a country that appeared on the verge of disintegration. But neither in composition nor in inclination was it equipped for such a burden; it failed abjectly, and its failure spelt the doom of parliamentary democracy in Indonesia.

As a substantial proportion of its export earnings were being siphoned off by regional commanders, Indonesia's economic position continued to deteriorate, and mounting budget deficits increased the costs of export industries. But whatever Juanda's personal views, economic rationality found little place in policy, and under the combined pressure of the President and the PKI, the country swung sharply in the direction of xenophobic nationalism. In elevating the West New Guinea issue from a minor irritant into a major international dispute, Sukarno demonstrated his deep political acumen, for though the issue was totally irrelevant to the country's grievous socio-economic problems, which indeed would only be exacerbated with the incorporation of the territory into the republic, all Indonesians were aggrieved that the promised negotiations with the Dutch over the status of the territory that were to have taken place within a year of the transfer of sovereignty, had never been held. At a time of deep national division, any issue that could generate a façade of cohesion was doubly valuable; moreover, the dispute provided abundant opportunities for the exercise of the President's remarkable oratorical skills, and kept him in the forefront of the international arena.

Communist support for a National Council and for the return of Irian, was extravagant and absolute. The PKI, of course, had little interest in any programme for genuine economic rehabilitation; it sensed, correctly, that Indonesia was heading for total economic collapse, and the resulting chaos would probably provide just the conditions in which a bid for power could succeed. Moreover, vigorous prosecution of the struggle for Irian could hardly fail to produce a head-on confrontation with the Dutch, in which the latter's massive investments in the country would become hostage; moreover, in a prospective military conflict there could be a place for the creation of 'people's armed units', a standard communist technique for gaining power, and a much-needed insurance against hostile action on the part of the army. But deeply suspicious of communist intentions, the army central command feared the growing community of interests between the President and PKI; it had prevented the filling of the vacant position of Chief of Staff following Nasution's dismissal after the 17 October incident, and its united opposition to Sukarno's nomination of a leftist officer led in 1955 to Nasution's recall. But on the Irian question the army could not appear to be inferior to the PKI in patriotic ardour; moreover, it had always to justify the privileged position of its large establishment in a poverty-stricken country, and in a further trial of arms with the Dutch its powers and influence could only increase. The communists could thus not be permitted to make all the running. From their first beginnings Indonesia's armed forces had been involved in political activities, and Nasution now moved to consolidate and to expand the army's role in civil life through the Veterans' League and the establishment of army-sponsored youth, peasant, workers', women's, and religious organisations, thus creating a parallel range of bodies operating at all social levels to counter those established by the PKI. In behind-the-scenes manoeuvres with local commanders, Nasution also endeavoured to contain the spread of the regional revolts, and to prevent any formal declaration of disaffection.

An open conflict, however, was not to be avoided. Late in 1957 Indonesia's fourth application to the United Nations for the resumption of negotiations with the Dutch over the future of West New Guinea failed, despite the support of most Afro-Asian nations and the Soviet bloc. The debate had been preceded by much sabre-rattling from Sukarno, who threatened dire consequences for the world at large if Indonesia's just claim was refused. But the decisive action that followed on receipt of the decision in Jakarta did not originate with the President; it was the work of the PKI. Early in December workers of communist-dominated unions seized the vessels and other assets of the Dutch-owned KPM inter-island shipping line and of the NHM, a large Dutch trading company, and throughout the country the takeover of Dutch-owned estates, mines, and factories proceeded apace. While the cabinet dallied, it was clear that the takeovers had full Presidential approval, and although the army could not protest, it had been taught a lesson in tactics that it was to turn to account five years later. The fate of 'mixed enterprises', that is, those of joint Dutch and other foreign interests, of which the most important was the Shell subsidiary BPM, was unclear for some time, but eventually these were untouched. Many of the assets seized eventually passed into the control of government undertakings, but nearly a year was to elapse before Dutch assets were formally nationalised.

The seizures, which were patently illegal acts, further inflamed the *Masyumi* and other moderate leaders. Economically they were disastrous; the KPM services proved impossible to replace, for the sequestered vessels could not be operated, and the short-term consequences of the takeover were critical shortages of commodities of all kinds in the Outer Islands, some of which remained unvisited for weeks at a time. With the departure of the Dutch managers and technicians the productivity of estates and factories further declined, and with the Dutch also went most of the Eurasian, or 'Indo', population, that had elected to apply for Indonesian citizenship after 1949. But independence had undermined their economic and social position, and with the nationalisations most had no recourse but to leave the land in which they had been born and bred, for a distant one that few had ever seen. Fortunately, the Netherlands recognised its obligations to those whom it had always regarded as Dutch citizens, and since 1949 over 100,000 immigrants from Indonesia have been assisted to make new lives in the country.

In the Outer Islands the call for the restoration of the *Dwitunggal,* the 'duumvirate' of Sukarno and Hatta which had created the republic, was taken up with renewed vigour. Early in 1958 the moderates Natsir, Harahap, Sjafruddin Prawiranegara, and Sumitro, an array of *Masyumi* and PSI ex-ministerial talent, appeared in Padang after having secretly left Jakarta, and in February the local army commander, Colonel Hussein, presented Jakarta with an ultimatum. Failing the creation within five days of a new cabinet under either Hatta or the Sultan of Yogyakarta, the local council and its supporters would create their own government, and on 15 February, when no reply had been received, the Revolutionary Government of the Republic of Indonesia (PRRI) was proclaimed in Padang, with Sjafruddin and Sumitro as Prime Minister and Finance Minister respectively. The cabinet was agreed with the supporters of a parallel rebellion against the authority of Jakarta in Sulawesi, where Colonel Sumual, another hero of the revolutionary war, had issued a 'Charter of Continuing Common Struggle' (*Permesta*) in Makasar, but had consolidated his authority in the Minahasa peninsula in the north of the island, where the Christian Menadonese people, as with their neighbours in Maluku, had long mistrusted the Javanese. But it proved impossible to create any firm support for the regional cause in either North or South Sumatra, or in Kalimantan; the rebellion was effectively confined to Central Sumatra and North Sulawesi, and the 1,500-mile separation of the two centres of resistance posed problems of co-ordination that the rebel leaders were never able to overcome.

If the rebellion generated little support elsewhere in the

archipelago, apart from a few expressions of sympathy, it got none at all in the rest of the world. The Padang rebels could not even gain control of the rich oilfields of Central Sumatra, and Caltex, the country's largest individual earner of foreign exchange, continued to make payments to Jakarta under the instructions of the United States government. Shipments of American arms, paid for from the proceeds of the barter trade, did reach Padang, but it is doubtful if the regional leaders ever seriously contemplated sustained resistance. As essentially pragmatic men dedicated to rational economic and social policies in which some degree of regional autonomy and the use of local resources for regional development were basic, they made strange bedfellows with the flamboyant local army commanders, whose principal objective appears to have been to consolidate their privileges and influence. With the exception of the communists, Indonesian leaders have shown a commendable unwillingness to carry basic divisions to the point of a conflict of arms, whose ultimate consequences can never be foreseen, and it is probable that the regionalists felt that a forceful demonstration of protest would bring Jakarta to its senses. If this were so, they sadly miscalculated. After some inconclusive talks with Hatta the central government moved to suppress the rebellions, and as landings of troops in Central Sumatra and their advance inland met little organised resistance, it soon became clear that Jakarta had nothing to fear. With the occupation of Padang in April 1958 the Sumatra rebellion virtually came to an end; some rebel leaders took to the hills to continue guerrilla activities, but with the exception of Sumitro who went into exile for a decade, most of the important figures in the rebellion returned to Jakarta within a year or so. The suppression of the North Sulawesi revolt involved more serious fighting, which for a time appeared to be about to escalate sharply when the rebels unexpectedly obtained air support from Taiwan. But here also, resistance had degenerated into sporadic guerrilla activity by the end of the year.

The successful suppression of the revolts greatly enhanced the prestige of the army, although it was generally believed that the central command had never entirely lost contact with the rebel military commanders. To the wide ranging powers it had acquired through the declaration of a state of siege and the imposition of martial law, it now assumed direct authority over the reoccupied areas of Sumatra and Sulawesi, and added greatly to its material assets in the form of land and other property. The operations, nevertheless, had been inordinately expensive, one reason perhaps why the rebels felt that no serious campaign would be mounted against them, and coinciding with a pronounced fall in export prices, so accelerated the drain on Indonesia's foreign-exchange reserves that the statutory obligation of Bank Indonesia to maintain a formal reserve position was abolished. In accentuating the dislocations resulting from the precipitate exodus of the Dutch, it hastened the country further down the road to ruin, for in the fighting and the subsequent guerrilla operations many estate factories were destroyed and remained inoperative for many years afterwards. That final economic collapse was averted for a few more years owed much to the fact that in 1958 Indonesia, for the first time, began to receive substantial foreign economic aid. And as a result of Nasution's shopping expeditions abroad, it also began to acquire much military aid in the form of arms and equipment from Russia and other East European countries, a development that boded no good for the future.

With the elimination of the regional challenge, the way became open for the President to proceed with the implementation of his plan for a Guided Democracy, which the parties and the cabinet had frustrated. The authority of Parliament had been reduced by the establishment in mid-1957 of an appointed supreme council, the National Council, but the duties and responsibilities of the Council remained vague in the extreme, and national decisions continued to be taken, in so far as they were taken at all, by mutual compromises among the President, the cabinet, and the army commanders. But the regional revolts had greatly discredited the parties such as the *Masyumi* and the PSI which had most vigorously opposed the President, and in April 1959 Sukarno felt in a strong enough position to demand that the Constituent Assembly vote a return to the vague and provisional 1945 constitution, under which the powers of the President were potentially enormous. Three months later the Assembly was dissolved, and in an act of gross illegality the President reactivated the 1945 constitution by decree. Indonesia's tragic experiment with Guided Democracy was now well launched.

Guided Democracy 1959-65

Although acclaimed by the President as a formula for solving modern problems through a reorganisation of political and economic institutions in conformity with traditional Indonesian values, in practice Guided Democracy meant little of the sort. Nor did it effectively concentrate power in the hands of the President, if indeed that was ever its aim, for Sukarno continued to be constrained by the same influences that previously limited his freedom of action, most notably the army general staff, and the opposition of the Muslim devout to anything that smacked of godless communism. Nevertheless, if it did not give power to the President, it did deny it to anyone else.[7] In essence Guided Democracy was a palace or court government, in which the privileged participants endeavoured to extract for themselves the maximum power base from the national pool, and to acquire the financial resources to operate and consolidate it. It is, of course, impossible to credit that the President did not desire power, and his love of the trappings of power remained notorious to the very end. But it was essentially power without responsibility that Sukarno desired, 'the privilege of the harlot throughout the ages' as Britain's Prime Minister Stanley Baldwin once described it, and if this was not a very practical goal, it was one that he shared with many other prominent Indonesians, and especially with the Chief of Staff, General Nasution.

In spite of the fact that the National Council of 1957 had proved entirely ineffective, the President's machinery for negating the opposition of Parliament and the parties and for sloughing off responsibility for any action or lack of action was more of the same; in quick succession, a variety of large appointed non-voting councils of 'functional groups' was created, with ill-defined and overlapping duties. The 1945 constitution, it is true, had provided for a supreme sovereign body, the People's Congress (MPR) and a provisional Advisory Council (DPA), but the new bodies created by Sukarno lacked any real executive authority or control over the President, and merely debated issues that he chose to put before them. With the dissolution of Parliament in March 1960 elected bodies in Indonesia disappeared for more than a decade, and the President completed his new institutional structure with the creation of the 616-member People's Consultative Assembly, which included most of the appointees of the old National Council, and which, with appropriate irony, would eventually remove him from office. However, the day-to-day work of government continued, as before, to be in the hands of what was in reality the President's own cabinet, led by Juanda, who as First Minister virtually continued in his former office.

Ultimately, of course, the President could not escape responsibility for the state of the national polity and economy, which were to be conducted in accordance with the precepts of yet another of the bewildering profusion of acronyms spawned by the Indonesian Republic, Usdek. This was concocted from the five slogans of the President's political manifesto (Manipol), standing respectively for (1) *Undang-undang Dasar 45* (return to the 1945 constitution, or a strong presidential government); (2) *Socialisme à la Indonesia* (Indonesian socialism), illustrative of the President's large propensity for larding his oratorical outbursts with foreign words and phrases, and implying a major redistribution of wealth and income; (3) *Demokrasi Terpimpin* (Guided Democracy), essentially the orchestra of the complex conciliar structure under the baton of the maestro, Sukarno; (4) *Ekonomi Terpimpin* (Guided Economy), or the concentration of economic activity in the hands of state entities and co-operatives; and (5) *Kepribadian Indonesia* (Indonesian Identity), in practice braggadocio nationalism and a swashbuckling foreign policy. With the banning of the *Masyumi* and PSI in August 1960, Sukarno's triumph over his old rivals Hatta and Sjahrir was complete; and with the suppression of PKI activities by some regional army commanders as a kind of *quid pro quo,* all overt party operations were proscribed shortly afterwards.

Sukarno now appeared to be absolute master of Indonesia, and grandiose titles and eulogies such as Great Leader of the Revolution and President for Life were bestowed on him by the sycophant bodies under his control. The regime became more authoritarian, and forthright or outspoken criticism of the President became increasingly likely to result in arrest and imprisonment without trial. Nevertheless, Sukarno was no dictator, even if at times he behaved like, and indeed with the passage of time even came to look like, *Il Duce,* another collector of fancy titles and, according to some biographers, dictator against his will, who proved powerless to control the sweep of events that he had helped set in motion.[8]

But what in fact was there for the Indonesian revolution to oppose? For all his profound ardour and extravagant exhortations to Indonesians to 'throw themselves like logs on the fires of national revolution', and to pursue revolution 'to the abyss of annihilation', Sukarno had no programme for major social or economic change.[9] Of acronymic sloganeering there was a surfeit, but none of these semi-mystical incantations were ever translated into practical policies for action. Never did the Great Leader of the Revolution express any definitive views of the kind of Indonesian society he would like to see emerge, or, if he had any such opinions, the President for Life kept them to himself. His general social orientation, as befitted a good Javanese, was essentially conservative, and, although he continuously iterated a desire for modernity, in thinking that this could be grafted on to a traditional society without major trauma, he perpetrated a basic error common to many leaders of newly independent countries throughout the world. But there was never the slightest indication of how this union was to be effected. The most revolutionary social and economic changes that the President could have wrought clearly lay in rural life and in the traditional agricultural sector, and in the attitudes of mind that these engendered; but Sukarno could never give more than token support for land reform, for the obvious reason that the cultural values embodied in the Indonesian jingles *ramah-tamah* (good neighbourliness), *gotong-royong* (mutual aid), and *musyawarah-mufakat* (consultation and discussion and consensus) that he constantly paraded, were all deeply rooted in the Javanese agricultural tradition. And, as Indonesians commented more and more, if his innate conservatism and style of conducting public affairs recalled the behaviour of the Susuhunan of Mataram, the feudal princes of central Java, so too did his personal behaviour with its frequent and ruinously expensive foreign junketings, his love of ceremonial panoply and the splendid state occasion, and, not least, his excessive uxoriousness and sexual proclivity. Moreover, as always in the harems of the princely courts of South-east Asia, the wives of the Head of State wielded substantial political influence, especially his second wife Hartini, and the third, Ratna Dewi, a Tokyo bar-hostess whom Sukarno had met on his round-the-world tour of 1959, when pictures of Presidential cavortings with Italian film-star Gina Lollobrigida graced many European magazines.

It was on this lack of direction and preoccupation with the form of government, with its over-emphasis on slogans and symbols in place of the substance of concrete action, that the opponents of Guided Democracy focussed. Above all, the drift appeared to give far too much latitude to the PKI, the country's largest party, which, having been denied office, had escaped the odium of responsibility for Indonesia's deplorable socio-economic situation. As if in return for its total support of the President, the PKI always seemed to have Sukarno's ear; a Democratic League (LD), formed by prominent intellectuals and party leaders to perpetuate the ideals of liberal democracy, was ferociously attacked by the communists and speedily suppressed. But, unlike the President, the PKI wanted real revolution, not talk or trappings, and it knew precisely how to exploit the persistent shortcomings of independent Indonesia, which, despite the enormous advantages that it had conferred on the élite, had failed totally to improve the living standard of the average Indonesian.

Sukarno's basic ignorance of and antipathy towards economic issues was notorious, but although most of his many Western admirers have conceded that this was regrettable, they have held that it was but a minor detraction from his function as a nation-builder. But in reality it was disastrous, and, with poetic justice, proved to be the final goad to the forces that overwhelmed him. It is not enough, even in Third World countries, merely to pay lip-service to economic development. If governments anywhere are to survive, and recent events in eastern Europe are testimony to the truth of the matter, they must demonstrate not only a genuine commitment to the attainment of higher living standards, but be able to point to reasonable success in achieving them. Those braggard charismatic leaders of newly independent countries who in the late 1950s and 1960s plunged their national economies into ruin and kept the world in uproar, have mostly disappeared, and the demise of the remainder can confidently be predicted. In the chaos of economic collapse, the PKI could confidently expect to be able to mount a successful *coup,* and expediency reinforced ideology in generating violent PKI opposition to any manifestation of economic rationality that would promote the health and stability of Indonesia's mixed economy.

The creation of a 'national' economy, that is, one largely owned and controlled by indigenous Indonesians, had long been one of the most cherished of revolutionary goals, yet in practice virtually every act of 'Indonesianisation' appeared not merely to inhibit the capacity of the economy for further growth, but almost to prevent it from functioning at all. The traumatic effect of the Dutch take-overs was compounded by similar action against large-scale Chinese enterprise, and although any anti-Chinese measures could count on a large measure of public support, the move was justified on the grounds of promoting socialism, and as a reprisal for support of the *Permesta*-PRRI rebels by members of the Kuomintang party and the Taipei government. In 1959 all Chinese businesses in rural areas were ordered to be wound up or transferred to Indonesian co-operatives, and although the measure was enforced with varying degrees of severity in the regions, opposition to forcible removal by Chinese in West Java resulted in bloodshed and a sudden estrangement with Peking, which with the proved impotence of Taiwan had again reappeared as an unexpected protector of the Indonesian Chinese.

Thus having hamstrung the once efficient export-oriented industries, the government had now passed to throttling much of the country's distributive and procurement services, and the inflationary pressure of budget deficits was soon reinforced by growing physical shortages of consumer goods of all kinds. In August 1959 a precipitate devaluation by 90 percent of large-denomination notes, almost half the currency then in circulation, and of bank deposits exceeding 25,000 Rp., proved only the briefest of stop-gaps; allegedly aimed at hitting speculators, black marketeers, and other holders of hot money, the measures were also essentially anti-Chinese. But lacking a modern tax structure, or any means of fabricating an effective revenue-collecting machinery from the underworked, underpaid, and extravagantly overlarge bureaucracy, the state's only recourse was to the printing presses of Bank Indonesia, which over the next decade poured forth an increasing flood of new money. By 1967 the money supply had increased over 300-fold, and with successive devaluations of the rupiah and the periodic suspension of key imports through lack of foreign exchange, prices had risen over 1,500-fold.

Soaring inflation strains the fabric of any society, and, in an Indonesia with an already gross maldistribution of income, the effects on the poor and the economically weak were very severe. Uncontrolled inflation heightened social and economic inequalities, and in itself made for a more authoritarian and corrupt regime, although other powerful forces were also propelling the administration in the same direction. It was economic ineptitude that finally accomplished what had for long defied his opponents; the President's charisma vanished utterly in the confusion, rioting and demonstrations following the December 1965 introduction of a new rupiah to replace one thousand old ones, and enormous increases in the price of essential commodities and services. But by then the regime, or 'Old Order' (*Orla*) as it came to be called, had probably passed beyond redemption.

Thus, year by year, living conditions in Indonesia for the great mass of the population grew worse, for between 1958 and 1965 net national product grew slower than population increase, so that *per capita* product declined. But although the state was clearly heading for bankruptcy, it was military adventure that made collapse inevitable. Yet it is unlikely that the extremely aggressive anti-Western foreign policy pursued by Indonesia in the early 1960s was a deliberate attempt to divert popular attention from unpleasant reality at home. Compared with making revolution, domestic problems had never been regarded as compelling issues by the President, and although it was true that the future of Irian was perhaps the only topic on which there was a high degree of unanimity of Indonesian opinion, each component of the 'triangle of forces', the President, the army, and the PKI, had powerful reasons for desiring to force a decision. For the first time in its existence, the army had large supplies of modern weapons, provided under aid agreements with the USSR and other communist countries, which it was anxious to use in what looked like being a cheap and easy campaign which would ensure that the armed forces received the maximum credit for 'completing the revolution'. So rapidly did the new supplies arrive, and in such quantities, that on paper Indonesia had become a formidable military power, unmatched in Asia between India and China; in particular, the acquisition of powerful sea and air striking forces, in conjunction with the President's increasingly inflammatory anti-Western language, produced a minor panic in Australia. Yet the new equipment, which included such sophisticated hardware as Russian 'badger' and 'bison' bombers, submarines and a cruiser of the *Sverdlovsk* class (promptly renamed *Irian*), enhanced the importance of the other arms of the defence forces relative to the army, and, by appointing officers who were well-disposed towards him as senior commanders in the navy and the air force, Sukarno greatly augmented his own standing and authority. Never a homogeneous or single-minded force, the army was further divided against itself through the encouragement and promotion of leftist pro-Sukarno officers, and the President cultivated a major rival to Nasution in the person of General Yani, who in 1962 took over as Chief of Staff when Nasution was 'promoted' to the rank of Minister of Defence. In reality, of course, Nasution was effectively removed from direct control over operational troops. But although Yani removed several *panglimas* appointed by Nasution, he proved no puppet, and was to suffer death and mutilation at the hands of the communists in 1965.

Basking in the reflected glory of the magnificent new military equipment and of other massive Russian aid such as the Cilegon steelworks in West Java and the prestigious Senayan arena and sports complex in Jakarta, the PKI could apparently do no wrong. Its support for the Presidential sabre-rattling was almost hysterical, and it was the principal instigator of a series of mass demonstrations in favour of direct action for the return of Irian. Thus the army's attempt to keep direct control over the return of Irian movement proved unavailing, and in the face of a total commitment to confrontation of the Dutch by both President and PKI, it had no course but to fall into line.

From 1961 onwards, a series of minor hostile acts were mounted against the Dutch in West New Guinea, which included naval actions, landings on offshore islands, and an air-drop. These initial operations did the Indonesian services no credit, for they were badly bungled, and from each encounter the Dutch clearly emerged as the victors; survivors picked up by the Dutch from sunken Indonesian vessels were promptly repatriated, adding insult to injury. Nevertheless, it was clear that the small Dutch garrison could not offer serious and prolonged resistance to an all-out Indonesian attack, and the difficulty and expense of providing support from the home country were formidable. Moreover, the retention of West New Guinea, at best a face-saver from the 1949 agreement, had minimum appeal to the Dutch public, for the Netherlands was visibly much more prosperous without Indonesia than it had ever been when it controlled the Indies. As in 1949, it was the United States that provided the catalyst, and the United Nations the instrument. Under an agreement worked out with President Kennedy, the Dutch in 1962 agreed to withdraw and to hand over the territory to the United Nations. On 1 May 1963 Indonesia would assume responsibility for the administration under the aegis of the United Nations, and in 1969 a plebiscite would be held to determine whether the local population wished to remain a part of Indonesia.

The Dutch had, in fact, been rapidly preparing their half of the island for speedy self-government, as had the Australians in eastern New Guinea. The new agreement, as with that of 1949, was essentially face-saving, for once Indonesia had gained *de facto* possession of the territory, it was doubtful that a genuine plebiscite would, or indeed could, ever be held, given the sparse and scattered nature of the local population, its bewildering ethnic and linguistic diversity, and its immense social and economic backwardness with many villages living an existence essentially unchanged from that of the Stone Age. Having effectively occupied the territory, the Indonesians proceeded to strip it of everything valuable or removable, and there was soon evidence of some resistance to Indonesian rule from the local population, which proved embarrassing to Australia when refugees fled across the border. The ill-defined and for the most part undemarcated frontier with Papua-New Guinea appeared a potential source of future conflict, and Australian suspicions were intensified as senior Indonesian officials began to use the term Irian to refer to the whole island. Nevertheless, the world hoped it had heard the last of Indonesia and the Irian question; but Indonesia was not long to remain far from the centre of the world stage, and, with the acquisition of complete independence for the eastern half of the island, it is still too soon to be sure that the Irian question is finally settled.

However, progress in resolving the long-drawn-out dispute appeared to galvanise the administration into a greater measure of economic commonsense. The President's Economic Declaration (*Dekon*) of 1963 appeared to foreshadow more realistic and rigorous policies for promoting economic growth, and in the following year a United States Mission recommended massive economic aid for resuscitating the flagging economy, and for promoting export growth. It was not to be; almost immediately the country was plunged by the President, with full PKI support, into a new foreign adventure, which led to speedy and almost total ruin.

This new conflict arose from a proposal in 1961 by Tunku Abdul Rahman, Prime Minister of the nearby and prosperous Federation of Malaya, to link his country with Singapore and the British Borneo territories of Sarawak and North Borneo in a broader federation of Malaysia. The formation of this new state is analysed in a companion volume, but its immediate purpose was to thwart the possibility of an extreme leftist government appearing in Singapore, which had been virtually independent since 1959, and to cope with some of the more pressing difficulties that had arisen from the creation of two political units from what was essentially the unitary polity and economy of pre-war Malaya.[10] For centuries the Malay peninsula and the Borneo territories had been as much a part of Indonesian history as any of the islands that now constitute the republic, and the new state was clearly a matter of great interest to Indonesia; the proposal, moreover, was also of concern to the Philippines, which as successor to the Sultan of Sulu also had a claim to North Borneo, later renamed Sabah. The contending claims of the three parties to the British Borneo territories effectively wrecked the attempts of the late 1950s and early 1960s to create an embryonic regional association in South-east Asia (the Association of South-east Asia, or ASA, and *Maphilindo*), but Sukarno's initial reaction to the Malayan proposal was one of indifference. His hostility waxed greatly, however, after an unsuccessful *coup* by the communist-leaning Party Ra'ayat in December 1962 in Brunei. This small but oil-rich British-protected Malay Sultanate had declined to enter the Federation of Malaya in 1948, and was to stay aloof from the new federation of Malaysia. Party Ra'ayat's leader, Azahari, had violently opposed the formation of Malaysia from the beginning, and, with the routing of his forces by British troops, Azahari fled first to Manila and then to Jakarta, where he proclaimed the government-in-exile of the new independent state of North Kalimantan, thus in a sense reasserting Brunei's historic claims to the territories lost by it to Sarawak in the nineteenth century.

The PKI, with which Party Ra'ayat had maintained the closest of contacts, threw its whole weight in support of the rebels, and attacked the government for not immediately recognising the new state. Sukarno now denounced Malaysia as a neo-colonialist plot aimed at perpetuating the country as a Western puppet, and a violation of the wishes of the population of the Borneo territories. The Tunku was under great pressure to create the new state as soon as possible, and it is true that the arrangements worked out with Britain and the United Nations to avoid the delay of a full-scale plebiscite and to substitute a Commission of Inquiry under Lord Cobbold to investigate local feeling on the issue, did involve some restriction of the fullest freedom of expression. Given Britain's decision to withdraw, the Borneo territories would almost certainly have preferred full independence, a status that Britain had already granted to several smaller and less populous former possessions. But union with Malaya was infinitely preferable to incorporation within the Philippines or Indonesia, and there is not the slightest doubt that, for the majority of the territories' inhabitants, the latter possibility was anathema. Sukarno did not, it is true, directly claim the territories for himself, but he attacked the new state as violating the concept of *Maphilindo*, the vague community of the Malay peoples of Malaya, the Philippines, and Indonesia launched in Manila at a meeting of President Macapagal, Tunku Abdul Rahman, and Sukarno in 1963, and for perpetuating the existence of foreign military bases and Western capitalism in the region. 'Volunteers' from Indonesia were soon making forays across the border of Sarawak, and British and Commonwealth troops came to the support of the Malaysian forces in a rapidly expanding guerrilla war.

With more than a dozen years of experience of combating the communist terrorists in the forests of the Malay peninsula during the 'Emergency', the small Commonwealth and Malaysian units were more than a match for the Indonesians in this kind of jungle warfare. In the United Nations also, where for so long Indonesia had always commanded a sympathetic hearing, Indonesia found itself outmanoeuvred, and its only strong support came from the communist powers. Meanwhile, the arrival of substantial quantities of Chinese military equipment under aid agreements had once again raised Peking's standing in Jakarta, and this was further augmented when China announced that it might come to the assistance of Indonesia should the latter be attacked by British forces. With the official proclamation of Malaysia in October 1963, Sukarno ordered an all-out 'confrontation', but insisted that it was not the Indonesian forces that had taken up arms against the new state, but Malaysians in revolt against the Tunku.

These new developments provided further grist to the PKI mill, and after the death of Juanda the few remaining elements of rationality in Indonesian policy appeared rapidly to evaporate. After the elevation of Aidit to the rank of Minister without portfolio early in 1962, overt or covert communist representation in Indonesia's unwieldy cabinet steadily increased, as did PKI's influence in the small Praesidium or inner cabinet, in which Dr Subandrio, First Deputy Prime Minister and Foreign Minister, held Indonesia on a pronounced pro-communist-power course. Although forced to abandon its attacks on the army for initiating actions likely to encourage British reprisals, the PKI continued to exploit dissatisfaction among younger officers at conditions of service or with the corruption of many senior commanders, and built up strong support in the air force and Marine Corps. For despite their re-equipment and Sukarno's exhortation to all Indonesians to 'crush Malaysia', the Indonesian armed services seemed unwilling to engage the Royal Navy, the RAF, and other Commonwealth units defending Malaysia in serious combat with their new Russian and Chinese weapons. The Malaysians were not to be cowed, and invasion operations launched against the peninsula ended in ignominious surrender. Kuala Lumpur was also unmoved by Sukarno's announcement of a nationwide programme to recruit some 20 million volunteers to liquidate the Tunku's 'puppet state', and rejected all proposals for talks until the confrontation had been called off. Somewhat unexpectedly, the PKI suddenly found itself in trouble at home.

The army and the PKI had already brushed over the seizure of British and of other foreign assets in Indonesia as a reprisal for support of Malaysia; mindful of the events of 1958, the army moved swiftly to forestall occupation of the remaining foreign-owned mines, estates, and factories by PKI-dominated unions, and on this occasion all foreign assets, including those of countries such as Belgium and Italy which had no part in the Malaysian dispute, were sequestrated. But a more serious conflict threatened over the PKI's determination to use confrontation as a means of forcing the creation of a 'fifth force' through the arming of peasants and workers, an operation which the army was determined to prevent at all costs. In pursuit of this aim the PKI had taken up with vigour espousal of one of its dearest goals, and a potentially highly explosive national issue, the question of agrarian reform. From its reorganisation in the early 1950s by the triumvirate of Aidit, Lukman, and Nyoto, the PKI had pledged itself to land reform in Indonesia's crowded countryside, in conformity with communist policy throughout Asia of gaining power through promoting the cause of the land to the peasants who till it. It was largely through its highly organised Peasants' Front (BTI) that the communists had become a real power in the regional governments of Central and East Java, and the communists had strongly supported the legislation of 1960 for the reorganisation of Indonesian agriculture, and continuously pressed for action to implement the redistribution provisions of the new acts.[11] But resistance to change in traditional rural Java was enormous and, determined to force the issue, the PKI early in 1964 conducted an intensive field investigation into the agrarian situation throughout Java, under the personal supervision of Aidit himself. Objectivity, inevitably, was a secondary consideration; Aidit's report claimed to find massive evidence of landlord oppression and extortion, and in protest the PKI initiated a mass agitation which speedily culminated in a series of sporadic peasant revolts in Central and East Java, in which hungry and landless peasants were encouraged to occupy the property of those opposing reform. Several landowners were murdered, and the parties of the rural traditionalists, PNI and NU, strongly condemned the revolts and threatened forcible countermeasures. Only army intervention prevented the conflict from widening and threatening civil war in the countryside. But explosion had merely been deferred, and the sharp polarisation in rural life soon had bloody consequences.

At this sharp double-check to the PKI, at the hands of the army, the President felt obliged to come to the party's aid in an attempt to restore the balance of the 'triangle of forces', and to make another demonstration of his regard for the communists in conformity with his long-reiterated principle of *Nasakom* (an acronym compounded from the Indonesian for nationalism, religion, and communism). An opportunity existed in the efforts of the anti-PKI parties led by the *Murba* to form a united front, from which emerged the Body for the Promotion of Sukarnoism (BPS), which endeavoured to use the tenets of the President's pre-*Nasakom* period as a weapon against the PKI. But the device was too transparent, and in December 1964 the organisation was banned. One of its prominent figures, however, was Adam Malik, Minister of Trade and former ambassador to Moscow, from whom more was shortly to be heard. Soon afterwards all *Murba* activities were proscribed, and in September 1965 the party was dissolved.

On the political front the PKI now was without a rival, and although the President was probably sincere in his belief in the virtues of *Nasakom* and saw the communists as a genuine indigenous national force, to very many Indonesians, and to the world at large, he increasingly appeared in thralldom to the party. Piqued at Malaysian success in the United Nations, Sukarno in January 1965 withdrew Indonesia, child of the UN, from that body and commenced preparations for launching a rival organisation, a Conference of New Emerging Forces (*Conefo*), whose deliberations were to be held in 1966 in a grandiose new complex of buildings in Jakarta; very soon afterwards, work on the numerous Sukarno monuments in Jakarta pre-empted every railroad car and virtually all building supplies in Java. A few months later the

President proclaimed the formation of a Jakarta-Phnom Penh-Hanoi-Peking-Pyongyang axis, leaving no doubt to many observers that non-alignment was a thing of the past. With the triumphant celebration in May 1965 of the 45th anniversary of the foundation of the PKI, at which Sukarno embraced Aidit in Jakarta's Russian-built Senayan stadium, Indonesia seemed about to fall to the PKI like a ripe plum. Economic conditions, meanwhile, verged on the chaotic; the new waves of nationalisation had further disrupted production, inflation had got completely out of control, and, as a result, although it was not appreciated at the time, the government machinery had already broken down. Central budgetary control had disappeared, and the government simply lacked the financial resources to function as a unit; only those Ministries with special or secret funds of their own, or supplied from one or other of Sukarno's secret accounts, were able to remain fully operational.

Yet just when it appeared that nothing could prevent the PKI from coming to power for want of any alternative, everything was lost in a gambler's throw. Why the party should have decided to attempt to seize power in yet another *coup* when it seemed inevitable that within a year it would come by it legitimately is not entirely clear, but the most likely explanation is that it was moved by fears for Sukarno's health. The President had been in poor physical condition for some time; after earlier visits to the West, he had increasingly turned to Peking for treatment, and Chinese doctors were then attending him in Jakarta. In August the latter reported to the PKI that the President would not long survive, thus presenting the party with an agonising choice. Without the President to protect them from the army, Aidit and his lieutenants feared for their future and perhaps their lives; if they were ever to come to power, they apparently reasoned, it had to be with the full acquiescence and support of the President, who would thus bestow on them his own mantle of legitimacy as the founder of the country. If Sukarno had but a few more weeks of life, they had to act quickly; and in some such way the decision to mount the fourth *coup* of the extreme Left was taken.

Not that the party was unprepared for such an eventuality, for since early in the year it had been providing secret training for a striking force of its own in a remote corner of the Halim Air Force Base near Jakarta, using weapons smuggled in from China, probably through the help of the Foreign Minister, Subandrio. This necessitated approval of the chief of the Indonesian Air Force, Air Marshal Omar Dhani, who with Subandrio was later sentenced to death for complicity in the *Gestapu* (an acronym formed from

Gerakan September Tiga Puluh, or 30 September movement) plot. Whether Sukarno was apprised of the plot in advance is not entirely clear; but the balance of evidence strongly suggests that he knew that a pre-emptive strike against the 'Council of Generals' was being planned by the PKI, and did nothing to prevent it. This Council identified a group of senior officers of the Army High Command who had taken a consistently strong anti-PKI line, and who, the party alleged, having done their best to thwart the President, were now plotting to overthrow him; prominent members included Chief of Staff and Minister for the Army General Yani, and Minister for the Co-ordination of the Armed Forces, and nominally Minister of Defence, General Nasution. In August Sukarno was informed by Aidit of a group of revolutionary-minded officers who would help remove the obstructionists, thus ensuring the future of the Indonesian revolution. Sukarno's subsequent behaviour strongly suggests that he gave tacit approval to the removal of the generals, although he may have left some doubt as to his views on their fate.

The plotters had, in fact, overestimated the military units believed sympathetic to their cause, but the forces they were able to assemble, consisting of units of the Diponegoro and Brawijaya divisions, were formidable enough, and it was not a numerical inferiority that proved the communists' undoing, but Sukarno's hesitation once the *coup* failed to go according to plan. Key buildings in Jakarta were occupied in the early hours of 1 October, and in raids on the houses of the generals three were killed on the spot and three more were abducted to the Halim base, where the mutilated bodies of all six were thrown into a well, the notorious *Lubang Buaya* (crocodile hole). But in a highly dramatic incident which involved the fatal wounding of his daughter, Nasution was able to escape the communist executioners, and although too shaken to make much contribution to organising resistance to the *coup,* news of his escape convinced Sukarno, who had gone to Halim early in the morning, that the plotters could not carry the army with them. Effective opposition, however, was quickly mounted by the commander of the army's Strategic Reserve (*Kostrad*), Major-General Suharto, who was not deemed important enough to merit attention from the communist murder squads, and who would have escaped anyway, as he was not at home on the fatal night. Suharto was only one of the 300 army officers above the rank of brigadier, and had never previously commanded any attention from foreign scholars of Indonesia. He had, however, a distinguished record as a guerrilla leader in the revolutionary war, and had been in charge of planning a joint assault operation on West

New Guinea when the issue was settled by international negotiation. With a judicious blend of *musyawarah* and bluster, and by the threat of overwhelming force, Suharto was able to negotiate a surrender of the rebel commanders holding Medan Merdeka (Freedom Square) and to prepare for a move on the Halim base, where the revolutionary military plotters, the communist high command, and President Sukarno himself, were becoming highly alarmed at the turn of events.

The message of support that PKI leaders in the provinces were awaiting from Sukarno over the rebel-held Radio Jakarta never came; without Sukarno's approval PKI's mass demonstration machinery could not be made operative, for the party had risen to fortune as the consistent supporter of the President. With the arrival at Halim of the paratroops despatched by *Kostrad,* the rebellion collapsed; the plotters fled in various disguises, but all were soon apprehended. Aidit flew off to Yogyakarta, after vainly trying to persuade the President to accompany him, where he tried to build a power base in what had long been one of the party's principal strongholds, around the rebellious Diponegoro division. Aidit's strategy was to claim that the *coup* was nothing but an internal affair of the army, and to wait until the President had mollified the army by arguing that vigorous action threatened the country with civil war. It failed to work for Sukarno's admission that he had gone to Halim of his own free will, 'to be near an aircraft if that should be necessary', did the President irreparable damage.

With the discovery of the bodies of the murdered generals three days later, a wave of revulsion swept the country. In Jakarta angry mobs led by NU youth groups destroyed the headquarters of the PKI and the houses of the party's leaders, and in Central Java the communist high command prepared for a siege, ordering the elimination of local opponents in a wave of atrocities reminiscent of the events immediately preceding the Madiun rebellion of 1948. But this merely helped to trigger off the greater fury that was to come. As in 1948 also, communist resistance was brittle, and by the third week of October, the PKI's rebellious units had been eliminated by the crack paratroops earlier deployed at Halim. Aidit was caught in the Solo area, and summarily shot; only one of the party politburo eventually escaped. By mid-November virtually all organised communist resistance had ended, and Indonesia plunged into a bloodbath whose only parallel in recent times is the slaughter that accompanied partition of the Punjab and Bengal in 1947. The army did not initiate the killings, but it did nothing to prevent them, and once its disinterest was apparent, infuriated

Muslim organisations rounded up and slaughtered communists and their assumed supporters not only throughout Java, but also in Sulawesi and in parts of Sumatra. In Hindu Bali also, the nobility and upholders of the established order rounded on the communist troublemakers in murderous fury. Estimates of the dead range from a little less than 100,000 to more than half a million, but the exact figure will never be known. In Central Java and in Bali whole families of communists were slain, to prevent any possibility of revenge; in these areas one of the most remarkable facts of the fall of the PKI was the placidity of the victims and their calm acceptance of their fate; most merely asked for time to say a prayer, and then were taken away to be summarily shot or stabbed, and thrown into mass graves. Marxism clearly had made little impression on the minds of most PKI peasant supporters, and was merely another veneer on the traditional cultural base. Inevitably also, attacks were made on the Chinese and their property; in Kalimantan many were murdered by the local Dayak population, and in North Sumatra large numbers were incarcerated to await transportation back to China. Month after month the slaughter continued, although nowhere on the scale of the massacre in Central and East Java, where, in the eyes of the devout traditionalists, the communists had grossly violated the *adat* (customary law) regulating rural life. But it was impossible to liquidate all the PKI suspects, and when the orgy of killing died down from sheer exhaustion, the problem of what to do with the survivors and how to prevent any further resurrection of the party remained for government. Meanwhile, in Jakarta, Sukarno continued to act as if everything was as before; but after his equivocal behaviour at the discovery of the murdered generals the old panache was never recovered, and Sukarno's instinctive grasp of political reality seemed increasingly to elude him. The Indonesian polity and economy were in ruins, and new hands were necessary to rebuild them.

The New Order (Orba)

Sukarno's immediate objectives were to protect his own position and to protect the extreme Left from further attack; this he endeavoured to achieve through continued denunciations of the evils of *Nekolim* (neo-colonialism), which necessitated undiminished prosecution of the confrontation of Malaysia. But the sense of national outrage provoked by the murdered generals inevitably became directed towards the President himself as his close associations with the chief plotters gradually became known. By mid-October army pressure had forced him to appoint Suharto as Chief of Staff in place of his earlier nominee, General Pranoto, a known Sukarnophil, to whom the President had given the job on the death of Yani. Whether Sukarno could have continued to play off the country's many contending forces against each other is conjectural; on the face of it, his economic ineptitude alone stood firmly in the way of such an eventuality, for destitute and bankrupt Indonesia needed an immediate transfusion of massive Western aid if it were to survive at all, and that would certainly not have been forthcoming while a Sukarno with undiminished powers still occupied the Presidential palace. Suddenly, a new political force appeared, and, mobilising opposition to the currency changes and price increases announced in December, dealt the Presidential charisma a blow from which it never recovered. This was *Kami* (Indonesian University Students' Action Front), a body founded shortly before the *Gestapu* plot and with tacit army approval, which over ensuing years was to spearhead opposition first to Sukarno himself, and, with his fall, to that of the administration of the generals and technocrats which succeeded him.

Although unquestionably arranged in consultation with the army command, the student demonstrations showed great organising skill and attacked Sukarno at his weakest points, namely his unsatisfactory and equivocal explanations of his behaviour both during *Gestapu* and subsequently, and the gross mismanagement of the economy. Accustomed to the adulations of a semi-hysterical mass audience, Sukarno had no answer to these new demonstrations in Indonesia of 'student power' in which university and high-school students combined to fill the streets with hostile slogans and demonstrations, to invade parts of the Presidential palace, and even to occupy ministries. Assured of tacit army approval, *Kami* simply ignored the Presidential proscription on meetings of more than five students imposed in February 1966, and stepped up attacks on the new cabinet, which still included notorious PKI sympathisers such as Subandrio and Air Marshal Omar Dhani.

Indonesia's new strong man had already appeared. Yet it is not in the Javanese character and cultural tradition, with which as a village boy Suharto was deeply inculcated, to polarise issues into stark blacks and whites, nor to present questions in forms which require categoric affirmatives or negatives. For his part in suppressing *Gestapu* Suharto had earned widespread respect both in the country and in the armed forces; but he knew that the President still possessed supporters in the army itself, that Sukarno was still highly esteemed in Central and East Java, and continued to command favour with the PNI extremists, who had launched their own pro-Sukarno youth movement. A direct attempt to remove the

President from office, or injury to his person, could still precipitate civil war; thus the process of containing and neutralising the President had to be performed gradually and with the visible acceptance of the country as a whole, so that the important concept of legitimacy should be preserved. Thus it suited Suharto and his supporters, who included the important Indonesian national petroleum entities with their vital foreign exchange earnings, to allow the students to make the running, but to restrain *Kami* and other anti-Sukarno forces from pressuring for the outright dismissal of the President or for his trial for complicity in the *Gestapu* plot. But the President was told that the student clamour could only be stilled, and the Presidential position safeguarded, if the army were given special powers to ensure public safety and tranquillity. There was, of course, nothing to stop the army doing as it wanted already; the new measures were merely to publicise what would be, in effect, a major change in executive authority, and to give it the stamp of legitimacy. On 11 March 1966 Sukarno capitulated, and gave to Suharto all powers to restore order and to guarantee the President's safety.

Suharto had now become master of Indonesia, and his subsequent acquisition of the title of Acting President in March 1967, and of full President a year later, were merely titular confirmations of reality. Not absolute master, of course, for in multivariate Indonesia, with its many contending forces and interests, such a position is probably beyond reach, as Sukarno had found. Nor is it clear whether Suharto had actively sought this role or whether it was forced upon him by the pressure of events; but throughout his long duel with the President he continued to behave as a professional soldier owing allegiance to the lawful government, and to have legal authority for all his actions. But the President's tools began to be used against him, notably the MPRS, or People's Consultative Congress, the supreme sovereign body in the 1945 constitution, which was responsible for the election of the President and Vice President; purged of its former communist members and their sympathisers, it was now to call Sukarno to account for his conduct of the nation, and eventually to remove him from office.

Suharto's first exercise of his new authority in March had been to declare the PKI dissolved, an act which the President had refused to do; then began the lengthier process of the systematic elimination of leftist and 'Old Order' (*Orla*) influence in the cabinet, the bureaucracy, and in the armed forces themselves, and some of the more notorious leftists such as Subandrio were placed under arrest. But every attempt by Sukarno to assert his authority and to retain his creatures in the cabinet resulted in renewed waves of yet more massive student and activist demonstrations. Against a background of rising national agitation, and under pressure from the army and the MPRS, whose reconvening the President had done his best to delay, a major reconstruction of executive authority was finally forced on Sukarno. At its meeting in June, the MPRS had confirmed the special powers given to Suharto in March, stripped the President of his grandiloquent titles such as 'President for Life' and 'Great Leader of the Revolution', and, ominously, made provision for Suharto to take over as Acting President should the President become unable to act. With the formation of the 'Ampera' cabinet in July 1966, the President was reconsigned to the largely titular role he had held in the early 1950s; ironically, *Ampera,* from the Indonesian *Amanat Penderitaan Rakyat* (message of the people's suffering), was taken from one of Sukarno's own impassioned addresses. While Sukarno claimed that he was still the Prime Minister as before, he was tacitly ignored; real authority now rested in a triumvirate with General Suharto as Chief Minister, Adam Malik as Foreign Minister, and the Sultan of Yogyakarta as Minister of Economics and Finance.

The new streamlined cabinet had a great deal of urgent business to face. Malik had to convince a hopeful but still somewhat incredulous world that Indonesia had undergone a major and irreversible political change, and that the *Orla* madness had gone for ever. The Sultan had the difficult task of damping down the country's roaring inflation and reaching accommodation with its many creditors so that essential imports could again flow in; with exports amounting to scarcely $600 million in 1966, Indonesia owed more than $2,400 million, so there was no recourse but to ask for time and substantial aid funds to help restore the stricken economy. Indonesia's political orientation thus swung completely about; a World Bank mission was immediately invited to advise on the country's enormous economic problems while preparations were made for Indonesia to rejoin this organisation and other international bodies such as the IMF and the United Nations and its many special agencies, from all of which Indonesia had withdrawn a little more than a year previously. Relations with China were broken off, and had not been restored by 1975; the ruinous confrontation with Malaysia, which had never been palatable to Army High Command and which had been in a state of virtual abeyance since *Gestapu,* was called off, and, in concert with Malaysian forces, Indonesian units began to track down communist bands operating across the Sarawak-Kalimantan border.

Although Indonesia's indebtedness to the communist powers

for supplies of military equipment was a major obstacle, it was clear by the end of the year that the country would be able to reach agreement with its Western creditors, and to obtain sufficient aid funds to begin rehabilitation of the national economy and, in particular, of the important export industries. The Inter Governmental Group (IGGI), formed under the aegis of the World Bank, developed from the initial Indonesia aid and creditor group, still operated in 1975, despite Indonesia's almost explosive export growth after 1972.

To combat the heavy pressure against him, the President continued to rely on the strategies that had served him so well in the past; in his Independence Day address of 1966 Sukarno repeated the braggadocio appeals for continuation of the national revolution under his leadership, as in previous years. But the President seemed unable to appreciate that the old magic had disappeared, and his behaviour at the graves of the murdered generals on armed forces day in October appeared to many Indonesians as sheer hypocrisy. Moreover, the trials of prominent former figures in the cabinet and the armed forces such as Subandrio and Air Marshal Omar Dhani for complicity in *Gestapu* deeply implicated the President, and further eroded his popular basis of support. The demands from student groups, the press, certain army leaders, and of local councils that the President be put on trial for his involvement in *Gestapu* grew to a crescendo. In January 1967 the MPRS, chaired since its reactivation by General Nasution, began discussion of the President's fitness to remain in office, and behind the scenes strenuous efforts were made to persuade the President to resign. Sukarno's refusal to heed these entreaties produced a typically Indonesian compromise; although allowed to remain nominally in office, the MPRS decision of March 1967 obliged him to accept General Suharto as Acting President, so that the arrangement of a year earlier which provided for Suharto to act as President whenever the President himself was unable to perform this office, was reconfirmed. Suharto and the army had in fact forcibly restrained the students and other activists who wished to place Sukarno on trial; there was admittedly a danger of civil war being sparked off by any direct threat to Sukarno's person, but it is more likely that Suharto's sense of the fitness of things interposed on the President's behalf. From statements of Nasution and others, there is little doubt that the army had the evidence against Sukarno to obtain a conviction of complicity in the *Gestapu* plot, but there was no disputing the fact that only Hatta, in retirement since his resignation as Vice President in 1957, could contest Sukarno's position as father of the nation, and, as the country's first President,

Sukarno fulfilled the essential requirements of legitimacy for the traditional Indonesian ruler. There was also the uncomfortable fact that Suharto and his associates had all owed the President allegiance, and that in his name they had initiated actions for which the President was now being called to account—essentially the problem that Khrushchev faced in his attack on Stalin. It is generally believed that Suharto had given an undertaking to the President to protect him from bodily harm, and to preserve him from disgrace; the President's poor health, which had been a prime factor in *Gestapu,* probably also suggested that the problem of Sukarno would speedily resolve itself.

Thus the Sukarno era expired, and a year later, on 27 March 1968, General Suharto was sworn in as President of Indonesia in an unpretentious ceremony. Forbidden to engage in any political activity, the former President, who was never formally dismissed, retained the love of some of his wives and ex-wives but the affection of few other Indonesians; rejected and discredited, he lived a virtual prisoner in the palace at Bogor. Sukarno had once declaimed that on his tombstone he did not want written 'Here rests His Most Exalted Excellency the first President of the Republic of Indonesia', but 'Here rests Bung Karno, the Tongue of the Indonesian People'.[12] Even this request was to be denied him, as was also that for a last resting place in Jakarta. But Sukarno had generated too many inflammatory passions and aspirations to be allowed a potential cult centre in the national capital after his death, and when this occurred on 21 June 1970, Sukarno was buried in an unmarked grave at Blitar in East Java, next to that of his mother, the town in which his turbulent life began some 69 years previously. With the death of the former President, all geographic references to the name of Sukarno were eliminated.

Meanwhile, the round-up of communists and suspected sympathisers continued, against a background of reports of renewed PKI resistance and plots. How far these reflected genuine PKI movements of resurrection is not clear; they were certainly convenient excuses for the retention of special powers and privileges by the army, and several were undoubtedly manufactured for that purpose. The large numbers of those detained without trial in prisons and concentration camps in Java began to generate international criticism, and not until October 1970, after much uncertainty and hesitation, did the government make up its mind as to the fate of the 100,000 or so detainees. These were to be divided into three categories: those in Class A and directly involved in the *Gestapu coup* were to be put on trial; hard-core and unrepentant leftists suspected of complicity were to be confined as settlers on agricultural camps on Buru island in the Banda Sea; and those in Class C, nominal members of communist organisations, were to be freed or resettled in official transmigration schemes in Sumatra or Kalimantan. Those banished to the rugged infertile island of Buru faced a lifetime of hard labour, although, with the passage of time, the spartan quality of prison-camp life has been a little relaxed; the settlement of the 'colonies' inevitably also brought about conflicts with the local population.

Indonesia had been readmitted to the world community and its multinational organisations, but one manifestation of Sukarno's intransigence still remained, namely the discharge of Indonesia's obligations to the United Nations in respect of Irian. Sukarno had repudiated the provision in the 1962 agreement for Irianese, or Papuan, self-determination in 1969 on the future status of the territory, but for any Indonesian government the possible loss of the acquisition was not to be considered. Suharto could not afford the risk of being outflanked by the Left; nevertheless, it was highly necessary for the country to make some gesture of compliance with the United Nations agreement, and, after playing for time, Suharto announced that Indonesia would honour its obligations. But how to obtain the appearance of popular support for continuation of the merger with Indonesia from an illiterate and backward population, which, had it been capable of understanding the issues at all,would probably have indicated strong opposition, was not so difficult a problem; South Africa and Rhodesia, faced with a similar necessity of demonstrating to a sceptical world a facsimile of indigenous approval of their respective policies, had perfected an appropriate technique, which Indonesia borrowed. In a so-called 'Act of Free Choice', a selection of well-drilled chiefs and headmen voted overwhelmingly on behalf of their tribes for continuation of incorporation within Indonesia. The deliberations were observed by a United Nations mission, but in practice no really free expression of Papuan opinion was permitted, or was possible. Leaders of a Free Papua movement, which had generated several minor revolts and demonstrations against Indonesian rule, endeavoured to generate support in Australia, black Africa, and in the United Nations, but all efforts to gain a hearing were fruitless; whatever the merits of the case, the world simply did not want to hear any more about an issue that it hoped had long been settled. There was, it is true, some adverse comment from the United Nations mission, and some pungent criticisms in the Australian press; but greatly relieved at the fall of Sukarno, Canberra had no desire to create any difficulties for his successor.

Irian Jaya, as it was renamed, soon proved a lucrative acquisition. Though long a minor producer of petroleum in Dutch days, new discoveries had eluded prolonged exploratory drilling; suddenly they were found, and on the southern flanks of the island's mountainous backbone large ore bodies of copper and of other minerals, on which preparatory work had been slowly proceeding during the Dutch administration, were finally confirmed. But harnessing these resources, which became possible through Indonesia's changed attitude towards foreign investment, may yet prove fraught with danger; the eastern half of the island has, in all probability, an even greater endowment of physical resources, and the state of 'Niu Gini' will certainly ensure that it receives an adequate share of the proceeds of their development. Irian Jaya's resources, on the other hand, will have to be shared with over 125 million Indonesians. Indonesia, it is true, has itself allocated funds for Irian's development to supplement those supplied from foreign donors as part of the United Nations agreement. But despite the island's overall backwardness, the eastern portion of New Guinea is substantially the more developed, and as this economic disparity enlarges, as seems highly likely, it could have major political repercussions. Meanwhile the sporadic outbreaks of active opposition to Indonesian rule have continued, and groups of refugees from time to time seek sanctuary by fleeing across the now well-demarcated border into Papua-New Guinea.

Posting to service in Irian, in fact, proved a very satisfactory means of disposing of those senior officers who, though sympathetic to *Orba*, created some misgiving in government as commanders of fighting troops in Java, so close to the centre of power. The problem of the many Sukarno sympathisers in the armed forces and senior commanders too closely associated with *Orla* created greater difficulties, being essentially part of the general problem of a chronic superabundance of general officers. Gradually, elderly senior officers have been retired, or removed from the active list where they could be found other jobs; nevertheless, there were still more than a hundred generals in 1973, and the imposts levied by regional commanders on the local economy continued to generate much criticism, particularly from student organisations.

While thus consolidating his support among the armed forces, Suharto took steps to remove the massive disincentives to production of *Orla*, and to resuscitate the economy as speedily as possible; these goals had been publicised to the world in the country's requests for substantial aid resources and for a rescheduling of its foreign debt. The most immediate problem facing the *Ampera* cabinet was to slow down the rate of inflation; but Indonesia's creditors also insisted on rigorous suppression of the smuggling, or barter trade, and compensation for, or restoration of, the sequestrated properties. These, the government announced, would be returned to their original owners subject to certain conditions, and in 1967 a new Foreign Capital Investment Law was passed, guaranteeing freedom from nationalisation. New investment was slow in materialising, but by 1970 American, European, Japanese, and Australian companies were scrambling for places in an investment bonanza. The pattern of this investment creates some serious misgivings, as it has been overwhelmingly directed towards mineral production, above all petroleum, and other extractive industries such as timber, which offer the prospect of rapid high rates of return and speculative profits, but which generate relatively little employment opportunities in relation to the size of their investment.

In mid-1968, on being confirmed by the MPRS as full President for a further five years, Suharto also obtained approval for changes in the cabinet; the Assembly's powers of independent action have remained as limited and as ill-defined as when Sukarno created it, but, as with all of Suharto's decisions, the move was thus clothed in a mantle of legality. The new Development cabinet, as it came to be called, was substantially smaller than its predecessor and contained significantly fewer ministers from the armed forces. Its most notable feature, however, was the appointment of Dr Sumitro Djojohadikusumo, who had returned from exile abroad in 1967, as Minister of Trade. The new economic pragmatism was also visible in the appointment to cabinet rank or to high positions in the administration of a number of highly competent professional economists, former students of Sumitro who had received further training abroad, most at the University of California at Berkeley; prominent among these new recruits to high-level government service from the intelligentsia were Dr Ali Wardhana, Minister of Finance, and Dr Widjojo Nitisastro, Chairman of the National Planning Council (*Bappenas*) and economic adviser to General Suharto. Under the overall direction of the Sultan of Yogyakarta, who as 'overlord' Minister of State for Economic, Financial, and Industrial Affairs was charged with ensuring the wellbeing of the whole economy, this team of technocrats was largely responsible for the rapid turn-around of the economic situation in Indonesia over the following period of the First Five-Year Plan (*Repelita* I), and for the achievement of a rate of economic growth in the 1970s that could stand comparison with that of some of the world's economic front-runners, and notably with the country's near neighbours, Singapore and Malaysia. The Plan, and the degree of success achieved in reaching its objectives, is discussed in succeeding chapters.

Ironically, Suharto thus demonstrated that Sukarno's move back to the 1945 constitution, under a strong and determined President, which Sukarno never was, could produce both political stability and rapid economic growth. Yet despite the odium that they had incurred for their pathetic and self-interested performance before 1965, the parties nevertheless represented a part of the political process that had been vital in achieving independence, and obstinately remained the chief vehicles for the expression of sectional and regional opinions that were still too powerful to be ignored. Indonesia, in short, despite the accepted importance of the armed forces in political life, was not prepared to accept an overt military regime of the typical Third World model, as the army well knew. Thus although the Suharto government had little love for the parties, it had to accept them in part, and to ensure that they remained amenable to control.

In its mid-1968 session, the MPRS had decided that the long-postponed elections for a new Parliament (DPR) should be held not later than July 1971, and in the long run-up to the elections, government and military pressure on the parties steadily mounted. The necessity for a reduction in the number of the country's splinter parties had been voted by the MPRS in 1966, and party leaders were now bluntly told to resolve their differences and to fuse their organisations. Some parties, of course, such as the proscribed PKI and certain of those suppressed by Sukarno, were no longer in the field. But the very large and very divided Muslim community posed a major problem; since the suppression of the *Masyumi* by Sukarno in 1960, Muslim liberal and progressive elements had felt denied a legitimate voice. Ironically, *Masyumi* itself was a shifting coalition of very diverse elements, 'an elephant with beri-beri' as one of its leading figures, Sjafruddin Prawiranegara, had described its ponderous and often enfeebled behaviour; but the resurrection of *Masyumi,* many of whose leading figures were still *persona non grata* to the army for their part in the *Permesta*-PRRI revolts, would present a potential danger to the continued dominance of army interests, which the government could not tolerate. Yet it was impossible to accommodate the more liberal Muslim elements, either within the traditional NU, or in the small regional Muslim parties, the PSII (Islamic Association Party) of West Java and the *Perti* (Islamic Education Movement) of Sumatra, both of which had survived largely because of their unimportance. Thus despite its resolve to reduce the number of parties, the government nevertheless found itself involved in the creation of yet another;

but in the new Indonesian Muslim Party (PMI), or *Parmusi* as it came to be called after its foundation in 1967, the old leaders of *Masyumi* were forbidden to hold office. In addition to its close surveillance of the legally permitted parties, the government also proposed to keep the parliamentary Assembly on a tight rein through a political party of its own. Sukarno had toyed with the idea of a national front under his leadership, but had rejected it, probably for fear that control would be wrested from him by the army.[13] The government's sponsorship of a Joint Secretariat of Functional Groups (*Sekber Golkar* or, more simply, *Golkar*), comprising members of the armed forces in non-military functions, police, government servants, teachers, workers, etc., to contest the election, suggested that Sukarno's fears were well-founded. Moreover, to make doubly sure that the House of Representatives remained docile, the government would appoint another hundred nominees, mostly from the armed forces, to the new body, in addition to the 360 elected members.

It was clear that the administration was determined that *Golkar* would win the election and by a large majority; but even candidates from other parties were subjected to a close scrutiny to ensure that all potentially hostile elements were excluded. *Golkar*, although tracing its origin to 1964, was made an effective force by Major-General Ali Murtopo, long a close associate in arms of Suharto, a member of the powerful Council of Special Assistants to the President (*Aspri*), and anathema to most student organisations and to many intellectuals. Thus direction of *Golkar*'s election campaign was entrusted to the personally very popular Adam Malik, who exploited his great standing in the Outer Islands to the full. But there were many charges of official heavy-handedness and intimidation during the campaign, and, as further rein on the parties, all discussion of the 'New Order' and all political activity at the village level were forbidden. The election was thus far from free in the Western sense, or indeed in comparison with those of 1955, and, inevitably, it produced the desired result. *Golkar* won comfortably with 236 seats against the combined nine other parties' 124, and gained control of all 26 provincial and of most district assemblies.

Dismayed by their heavy defeat at the hands of what they regarded as an army-dominated organisation, the parties immediately came under further pressure to sink their differences and to form themselves into two major groupings, so as to constitute with *Golkar* a three-party Assembly. As even the Islamic parties had never been able to agree on a common policy, this was to ask a great deal, but the government was adamant on carrying out this 'reform' in time for the next session of the MPR. Under the 1945 constitution the MPR was theoretically the country's supreme policy-making body, and was responsible for the selection of the President and Vice President; in its new session the organisation would be for the first time a properly constituted body, dropping the 'provisional' (from the Indonesian *sementera*) from its old title of MPRS. It was to consist of the members of the DPR together with representatives drawn from the regional assemblies, to which would be added other nominated members drawn from functional groups, and on 12 March 1973, the anniversary of the granting of special powers to General Suharto by President Sukarno in 1966, the new President intended to deliver an account of his stewardship of the nation as required by the constitution, and would be confirmed in office. To meet this date the parties were virtually presented with an ultimatum, and early in January the four Muslim parties regrouped as the United Development Party (PBP) and the five remaining independents as the Indonesian Democratic Party (PDI). Thus at last the desired reduction in the number of parties was achieved, but at the cost of all vitality, which was precisely the army's intention. The Muslim parties promptly announced that their merger related specifically to political activities, and that in other matters they would retain their identity. But the prospects that the two organisations might work together to form an effective opposition to *Golkar* remained faint in the extreme.

To the background of an impressive deployment of armed strength in the capital, President Suharto presented his report on the appointed date, and was duly confirmed in office for a further term of five years; the office of Vice President, vacant since the resignation of Hatta, was conferred on the Sultan of Yogyakarta. The MPR also approved a cabinet reshuffle, the representation of the armed forces being somewhat diminished, and, to the surprise of foreign observers, Dr Sumitro was effectively demoted to what appeared to be the unimportant position of Minister of Research. The serious, almost colourless, ceremony formed a striking contrast with the carnival-like state occasions in the days of Sukarno.

Thus for the first time in the history of the republic, the provisions of the hastily compiled 1945 constitution had been complied with. Since that date Indonesia had indeed travelled to 'the abyss of annihilation', to use Sukarno's words, but it had drawn back. Indonesia's foreign-exchange reserves stood at a record level, the economy was healthier than it had ever been, and Indonesia's standing in the world community and with its neighbours was high. Yet it was obvious that the Indonesian revolution was not, as Sukarno had boasted, more important than either the American or the Russian revolutions; what the world saw was merely another poor and apparently overpopulated country struggling, and with modest success, against a multiplicity of pressing problems. To many Indonesians this pragmatic but lacklustre government left something to be desired, and the perilous but exciting years of Sukarno in retrospect appeared even attractive. And to others, among whom were certainly to be counted the student organisations, even pragmatism had lost its appeal; economic development, as it always does initially, had increased inequality and public awareness of it. Corruption was as rampant as ever, and the privileges of the commanders of the armed forces as entrenched; both appeared at their apogee, as the students saw it, in *Pertamina*, Indonesia's national oil company, ironically the most dynamic national organisation in the economy, but virtually a state within a state and subject to no ministerial control, more than half of its board made up of high army officers, and presided over by an organising genius who nevertheless lived in a style commensurate with that of the oil-sheiks of the Middle East, and who encouraged similar flamboyant and extravagant living standards among his subordinates. Parliament was reduced to a cipher, and the members of the Presidential Council of Assistants, all senior officers, behaved exactly as Vice Presidents in their own right. Religious intolerance and open conflict, never a serious problem at any time previously, began to assume major proportions, and the appointment of General Panggabean, a Christian, as Commander of the Armed Forces, perhaps as a precautionary move to counter the influence of the Muslim General Nasution, Chairman of the MPR and long Indonesia's senior soldier, who with a little more resolution might perhaps have become President himself, created much Muslim concern.

The Chinese problem, moreover, still remained. The administration accepted that, for the time being at least, Indonesia could not dispense with the skill and capital of its Chinese population, and had tried to damp down expressions of anti-Chinese feeling. But rising prices, the result of the worldwide inflationary problem, and of an unexpected drought in 1972 which forced up rice prices, again caused an upsurge of resentment of the Chinese dealer and middleman, and in October sporadic anti-Chinese rioting broke out. The situation had scarcely been restored when on 15 January 1974 a far more serious outbreak of rioting mounted by the student organisations took place in Jakarta, in protest against the state visit of Prime Minister Tanaka of Japan. Although primarily an attack on 'ugly Japanese' economic domination, the demonstrations were also directed against the government itself, which was charged with selling out Indonesian resources to the Japanese and to other foreigners at bargain prices. This new demonstration of student power drew much of its inspiration from Bangkok, where Tanaka had already received a similar treatment from the university and high-school students who a few weeks previously had staggered the world by ejecting what had appeared to be a solidly entrenched military regime. The student protest was not, in fact, very rational, for Japanese behaviour in Indonesia was far from venal, and if their businessmen endeavoured to drive a hard bargain, this was no more than normal business ethics accepts. The demonstrations also appeared to owe something to the encouragement of the students by outsiders, political figures from the old *Masyumi* and PSI according to the Presidential assistants, but perhaps also a section of the army itself. The rioting was also an expression of dissatisfaction with the government of technocrats, who, as the students saw it, had produced few discernible gains for the ordinary Indonesian. Perhaps the students, or those behind them, thought that they could emulate the heroes of Bangkok, who in a few days of bloody street fighting had overthrown the government, and certainly since October the Presidential Council of Special Assistants had come under heavy attack.

Indonesia was clearly not as stable as it had appeared to the outside world, but Suharto moved with his customary speed and efficiency to restore the situation. The Council of Assistants was disbanded, and the President himself took over from General Sumitro, Deputy Army Commander, command of *Kopkamtib,* the army organisation for the restoration of security and order which Suharto himself had set up in 1966, following his receipt of special powers from Sukarno. But what had erupted was also a question as old as the nation itself, the role of the armed forces in national life; Indonesia's fractious generals were quarrelling again, perhaps over the succession. Suharto himself was merely *primus inter pares;* an unknown before 1965, he had worked closely with Murtopo and Sumitro, the two principal disputants, for many years. With his aides Suharto had been slowly endeavouring to impress a more civilian stamp on the administration, partly to promote greater national cohesion, and partly to prepare for the expanded international role that Indonesia would have to play in implementing its proposed Second Five-Year Plan (*Repelita* II). Although Commander-in-Chief under the constitution, Suharto had tried to reduce his personal military involvement, stepping down from the position of Army Commander in favour of General

Panggabean (a Sumatran), and attending the session of the MPR in civilian dress. Perhaps this was no more than window-dressing, and the President had now been obliged to resume a more obvious military role. But with the office that brought him to power again under his control, Suharto felt able to allow the contending generals to retain their other positions, and, in effect, reconstituted his council of aides under another guise.

But the basic issue born of the occupation remains, and Indonesia still clearly shows the marks of its violent recent past. The weakness of its political institutions and the lifelessness of *Golkar* and the parties are as much a danger as the vicious infighting of the 1950s. Throughout the Third World the politicians have shown repeatedly that they cannot provide efficient and progressive government, and the generals who have regularly displaced them have often shown a similar ineptitude. How the conflict will be resolved in Indonesia is still obscure.

NOTES

[1] Throughout this work the term Malaya is used in its geographical sense, that is, the Malay peninsula and its offshore islands.

[2] S. Takdir Alisjahbana, *Indonesia: Social and Cultural Revolution*, Kuala Lumpur, Oxford University Press, 1966, 169-70. Alisjahbana's savage indictment is in marked contrast to the tributes paid to Sukarno by most foreign writers, although Willard A. Hanna's *Bung Karno's Indonesia*, New York, American Universities Field Staff, 1961, is a notable exception. J.D. Legge, *Sukarno*, New York and London, 1972, provides many sympathetic insights into Sukarno, but strains credulity by giving the former President the benefit of every doubt.

[3] The Netherlands Indies administration was not quite so free from corruption as writers such as Furnivall and Myrdal claim. In the indirectly administered territories in particular, the planters had devised effective means for ensuring that poorly paid government officers did not make life too difficult for them. See pp. 158-9.

[4] When Dutch-Indonesian relations began to improve after 1965, the activities of the Moluccans became a considerable embarrassment to the Netherlands government. In 1970 extreme security precautions were taken to protect General Suharto from attack on his first visit to the Netherlands.

[5] The *Panca Sila* were first iterated in an address given shortly before the end of the Japanese occupation; they came to be regarded as the epitome of nationalist aspirations, and were embodied in the preamble to the constitution. They are usually translated as belief in God, humanism, Indonesian independence, democracy, and social justice.

[6] Daniel S. Lev, *The Transition to Guided Democracy*, Ithaca, Cornell University Press, 1966, 59.

[7] Hanna, op. cit., x.

[8] The similarities between Sukarno and Mussolini have received inadequate recognition. Sukarno admired the Italian leader sufficiently to use Mussolini's own words in his Independence Day address of 1964 during the confrontation of Malaysia, urging his countrymen to spend the year living in danger *(Vivere Pericoloso)*. In acronymic-prone Indonesia, 1964 thus inevitably became *Tavip*, from the Indonesian *Tahun* (year) and the Italian words.

[9] From the Independence Day address of 1960, perhaps the apogee of Sukarno's many flamboyant and auto-hypnotic oratorical outpourings.

[10] J.M. Gullick, *Malaysia,* London, Ernest Benn, 1969.

[11] See below, p. 137.

[12] Hanna, op. cit., 3.

[13] H. Feith, 'The Dynamics of Guided Democracy', in Ruth T. McVey (ed.), *Indonesia,* rev. ed. New Haven, 1967, 364.

CHAPTER 5

Poverty, Food Production and Population

INDONESIA'S POVERTY IS OBVIOUS even to the casual visitor. It is also reflected in the general lack of reliable statistics, and any account of national product and its sectoral composition involves much uncertainty. In the early 1970s, however, agriculture probably generated about half of Gross Domestic Product, and absorbed about three-fifths of the labour force. This large disparity, which is found in all Third World countries, suggests that agriculture is much less efficient than are non-agricultural activities. Nevertheless, it is not so inefficient as the figures would appear to indicate, for national accounting techniques undervalue the contribution of farmers to their own subsistence.[1]

Food Production

Yet there is no question that the large agricultural sector, and its generally low productivity, are the principal architects of national poverty, for the Indonesian farmer's productivity is low even in comparison with that of his counterpart elsewhere in South-east Asia. Only in the successor states of Indochina, whose agriculture has been disrupted by prolonged warfare, is the value of output per farmworker lower than in Indonesia, and in nearby Malaysia output per agricultural worker is nearly four times as high.[2] True, the net value of output per cultivated hectare is comparatively high by South-east Asian standards (although still substantially below that of Malaysia), but to achieve this requires a very large labour input. Malaysia deploys less than one-third as many workers per hundred cultivated hectares as does Indonesia, and elsewhere in South-east Asia only in Vietnam does the intensity of labour use in agriculture exceed the Indonesian level. Farmers of such low productivity cannot receive large incomes, and many have pointed out that the traditional *gotong-royong* is a euphemism for shared poverty.

Throughout the Sukarno era agricultural output grew at a rate that barely kept pace with population increase. Since 1966 there has been a much larger government commitment to raising agricultural productivity, and important gains have been achieved in both food and cash-crop production. Yet in relation to the resources committed success had been but modest, and by 1973 it was clear that Indonesia would not attain all the agricultural goals of *Repelita* I, the First Five-Year Plan. Between 1967 and 1972 more than $100 million, much in foreign-aid funds, was invested in an attempt to achieve self-sufficiency in rice by 1974, the end of *Repelita* I. But despite the new irrigation works and the extended employment of the technical innovations of the so-called 'Green Revolution', the magic goal, as in so many other Asian countries, always receded just as it appeared within reach. In the early 1970s rice output was increasing at about 6 percent per year, and success seemed assured. But in the latter half of 1972 a drought in Java again forced Indonesia to embark on an international shopping expedition for scarce and costly supplies, and rice prices, which had remained fairly stable for some years, again pursued the upward gyrations of the days of Sukarno. But flood or drought, and in Indonesia many kinds of crustal instability, are certain to occur from time to time. Realistic planning must allow for such contingencies.

Given Indonesia's great physical diversity, wide differences in agricultural practices and in the productivity of both land and worker are only to be expected. One distinction, however, is paramount: productivity is substantially higher in the Outer Islands, the *Tanah Seberang,* than in Java, and there is evidence to suggest that this disparity has widened in both colonial and independent eras alike. In view of the reputed fertility of Java's volcanically derived soils, this may appear anomalous, but it results from two contrasting systems of agriculture, the *sawah,* or inundated ricefield, and the swidden, or 'fire-field', a slash-burn shifting or bush-fallow agriculture widely practised throughout the humid tropics, and formerly common also in Europe, for the term swidden is an Anglo-Saxon one. In large part also, this division corresponds with a preoccupation with food-crop production for subsistence on the one hand, and with export-oriented, largely tree-crop production, on the other.

These dichotomies, of course, are not complete, for about one-third of Indonesia's rice area of some 8.5 million hectares is located in the Outer Islands. In Bali and Lombok, agriculturally as well as geologically extensions of Java, in the highland basins of the *Bukit Barisan* (range) of Sumatra, in newly established 'transmigration' colonies of Javanese settlers in South Sumatra, and in parts of the southern peninsula of Sulawesi, the flooded ricefield is a very conspicuous element in the landscape. But elsewhere in the *Tanah Seberang,* the rice harvest is largely dry or hill rice (*padibukit*) grown on impermanent fields and dependent on natural rainfall alone. In Java such dry rice (*padigogo*) is relatively unimportant. Dry fields in Java are permanent and are largely devoted to the production of rice substitutes and supplements. Wherever possible, they are converted into sawahs through the provision of supplementary water. Nor is Java without areas of export-crop production, for West Java and Besuki in the island's eastern extremity both possess extensive plantings of rubber, and at higher elevations in Priangan in the west, and to a lesser extent on several of the great circular volcanic massifs of Central and East Java, there are coffee and tea estates, and smallholder plantings. Physically and economically, in fact, it is legitimate to regard West Java (*Jawa Barat*) as more akin to the *Tanah Seberang* than to the 'inner Java' of the two provinces of Central Java (*Jawa Tengah*) and East Java (*Jawa Timur*), which constitute the cultural hearth of the Javanese people. Nevertheless, the distinction between the two parts of Indonesia is fundamental. The sawah system of Java is largely a subsistence one, and is inward-looking in the sense that commercialisation is limited and a traditional value system is perpetuated. Geertz has described this situation as one of 'agricultural involution', and his analysis receives comment later in this chapter. Swidden agriculture, in contrast, has been more easily penetrated by, and absorbed into, a monetised commercial economy, and, in its greater responsiveness to the price mechanism of the world market, could be termed 'outward-looking'.

Yet both are essentially alternative ways of solving the basic problem confronting the farmer in the humid tropics, namely, how to combat the rapid decline in fertility consequent on cultivation, and how to make available in the soil an adequate supply of the soluble nutrients necessary for successful crop production. Tropical soils are thin and, unlike temperate soils, do not contain large humus accumulations; thus the traditional temperate world techniques of maintaining fertility on continuously cultivated land such as crop rotations involving nitrogen-fixing legumes, periodic fallows, and the use of organic, particularly animal, manures, are either inappropriate or present very great difficulties. The sawah system solves the problem by inundating the field; the swidden farmer does so by abandoning his fields for many years before resuming a cycle of cultivation.

THE SWIDDEN

It is clear that the swidden system is much the older, and that, in some still imperfectly understood way, sawah agriculture has evolved from it. But as shifting agriculture has long been regarded as primitive and of low productivity, the differing orientations of the two systems may appear paradoxical. In a sense, the only true swidden cultivators in Indonesia at the present are, as elsewhere in South-east Asia, the few scattered groups of pagan aborigines in remote or inaccessible mountain fastnesses; these are people whose way of life is so closely bound up with the swidden system that they cannot be divorced from it without destruction of their cultures. True swidden cultivators always resist the enforced adoption of the sedentary life of the sawah system, but most swidden groups could not avoid some contact with the Hindu-Islamic 'great tradition' of Indonesia, from which they acquired some knowledge of sawah agriculture, and even for groups for whom such contact was limited such as the Toraja of Central Sulawesi, the Dutch colonial regime brought many changes in both agriculture and social organisation. On the other hand, peoples such as the Batak of the Lake Toba area of Sumatra, or the Minangkabau of Central Sumatra, originally both wet-rice cultivators, took increasingly to swidden-like cash-crop production as the Netherlands Indies became more integrated in the world economy, and as indigenous farmers were allowed to respond to the price stimuli of the world market. Primitive or not, the swidden system seemed to be far more adaptable to socio-economic change than was the sawah, with its rigid cultivation cycle season after season.

The flexibility of the swidden arises directly from its apparently inchoate and confused pattern of cultivation. The swidden farmer solves the problem of diminishing soil fertility through the use of long-term fallows, which may range from as little as seven to twenty or more years. While the swidden is under cultivation, the growing crops are supported from the stock of nutrients present in the body of the original forest, part of which are released by burning the material felled in making the swidden clearing, or *ladang*. Sites for new swiddens are chosen in the forest towards the end of the rainy, or rainier, season; they are of varying shapes and sizes, and are selected entirely on the basis of the cultivator's profound ecological knowledge of whether or when an area is fit for cultivation. Wherever possible, the labour of having to fell very large trees is avoided by choosing sites in secondary forest, but some large trees may be left standing in the swidden, and valuable wild fruit-trees such as the durian are always preserved. The felled material is allowed the longest possible time to dry out, as a good burn is essential for success; then, towards the end of the dry season, the swidden is fired. Apart from the burn no preparation of the soil of any kind is undertaken, and with the onset of the rains seeds are sown, often in association, in holes made with a dibbling stick.

After the initial clearing the work of cultivation is very slight, a great contrast with the heavy labour inputs demanded by sawah cultivation, especially as it is practised in Java. Apart from protecting the growing crops from wild animals and some limited weeding, the swidden needs little attention, and time is left the cultivator for other activities such as the chase, or a wide variety of religious observances. When weeding becomes difficult or onerous, it is usually the signal for the swidden to be abandoned. Moreover, whereas the sawah produces a seasonal harvest, that of the swidden is protracted, and one of the main objectives of the cultivator is to make it as continuous as possible. This is accomplished by growing a very wide variety of crops, and of different maturation periods, which are each planted in the parts of the swidden that experience has proved best. Thus cereals such as dry rice and maize, starchy roots and tubers such as yams, sweet potatoes, taroes and tapioca, a wide variety of pulses and leafy green vegetables, many kinds of fruits including annuals, herbaceous perennials such as bananas and pineapple, or even perennials such as papaya, jackfruit, and durian, can all find a place in a swidden. This multiplicity of crops not only provides a balanced diet, but is also an insurance against natural hazard; some or other of the swidden crops will succeed, whatever befalls. But with the passage of time yields progressively decline, pests of many kinds invade the clearing, and eventually it is abandoned to regenerating secondary forest. After an interval of many years, depending on the one hand on such physical factors as the aspect and elevation of the land, the nature of the subsoil and the parent rock, the precipitation regime, and the previous vegetational community, and on the other, on the numbers of the swidden group and the land available to them, the swidden may be reoccupied. But boundaries of new swiddens are seldom the same as those of the past, and no records are ever kept.

The close-knit many-storeyed structure of growing plants in the swidden, from tall fruit-trees or even the natural trees left standing, to trailing vines and ground creepers, has been likened to an attempt to reproduce the multi-layered structure of the original forest, and where population densities are light enough to permit the recovery of the forest and the replacement of the elements lost through cultivation, most scientists at present believe that the swidden system is essentially conservative of resources, and is an acceptable form of land use. What constitutes a maximum safe level of population density is, however, far from clear; 50 persons per square kilometre which may be permissible in some areas may be far too high a density in others. But if insufficient time is allowed for the natural rehabilitation of swiddens before their re-occupation, great and perhaps even irreversible damage to the soil can result.

It is possible that as much as 2 million hectares of forest land are cleared in Indonesia each year by swidden cultivators, but much of this is in isolated or upland areas unsuitable for commercial forestry, and the *permanent* loss of forest land through the extension of the continuously cultivated area, and through the depredations of modern mechanised forestry which in Indonesia borders on timber-mining, present ecological problems of at least equal concern. Moreover, the greater part of the loss arises through the practices of groups such as the Lampung people of South Sumatra, whose swiddens are not of the multiple-cropping type described above, but produce either cash crops such as rubber and coffee, or dry rice.

The incorporation into the swidden system of perennials capable of producing a cash income was easily accomplished; pepper was already a ladang crop when Europeans first penetrated into South-east Asia, and, with rising demand, its cultivation was taken up so widely that on occasions there were problems of over-supply. Coffee also proved well-suited to the swidden system, and European planters used a modified version of the swidden to produce the famous Deli wrapper tobacco, an industry which is discussed in the following chapter. But an even greater impact resulted from the introduction of *Hevea* rubber. As a natural forest tree, rubber is ideally suited to swidden cultivation; it removes nothing from the soil, for its latex is merely a hydrocarbon synthesised by the plant from the carbon dioxide of the air and from soil water. It seeds freely, and new seedlings can compete successfully in regenerating secondary forest, or *belukar*. By planting a few rubber seeds during the swidden cycle, the cultivator is thus able at very little cost in time and labour to create a capital asset capable of producing an income stream for many years. Simple both to grow and to process, natural rubber is an ideal crop for the small farmer in the humid tropics, and it is scarcely surprising that production by indigenous farmers grew rapidly in this century. Many former swidden cultivators have become essentially smallholders, primarily dependent on their cash incomes, but growing dry rice for their own subsistence. The extent to which they engage in the latter activity depends largely on their assessment at the beginning of each season of the relative prices of rice and rubber.

In terms of the productivity of the land, swidden agriculture is far from inefficient. In addition to the produce of the many interplanted supplementary crops, dry-rice yields of a thousand to 1,500 kilograms per hectare are commonly achieved, as against a national average of a little more than 2,000 kilograms per hectare in the period 1965-70.[3] This latter figure, moreover, includes the contribution of a second harvest, taken on almost one-third of the sawah area of Java, and also that from the new high-yielding rices, which accounted for about 12 percent of the total rice area of Indonesia in 1971. But in terms of output per man-hour, the swidden is very much more rewarding, for its modest yields are gained with very little labour, and much of that not really arduous. Swidden cultivators are thus always reluctant to adopt other forms of agriculture, and such behaviour represents sound economic judgement, not indolence, as colonial administrators throughout the intertropical world once commonly believed. Swidden cultivators knew that the change would involve them in a great additional labour for an inadequate return.

This suggests, of course, that colonial agricultural policy operated under serious misconceptions, and it is only since the end of the colonial era that the surprisingly high labour productivity of the swidden has become widely recognised. In a remarkable heterodox study, which draws heavily on the experience of Indonesia and of certain African countries, the Danish economist Boserup has argued that initially the shift from swidden to sedentary rice agriculture represents retrogression, and that it is only the pressure of population numbers on limited land resources, and which makes a higher output per unit area mandatory, that compels the change.[4] This is, essentially, the Malthusian Principle of Population stood on its head. The Malthusian analysis is an equilibrium of misery, in which the level of subsistence can never be more than that which just enables the labouring population to replace itself; its numbers are rigorously fixed by available food supplies, which reflect the scarcity of land and the diminishing return to every additional unit of labour applied to it.[5] To Malthus, population was what the modern social scientist calls a 'dependent variable', whose size was automatically determined by other factors. But the experience of much of the Third World, where rapid population growth has been, and still is, an undoubted fact, does not support this, according to Boserup; population growth is given (that is, population becomes an independent variable) and food supplies are made to match through changes in the farming system and the reduction and eventual elimination of the fallow. The resulting fall in the productivity of labour is a great psychological shock, which is met through a reduction in the valuation placed on leisure, and an increase in that placed on the virtues of hard work. Once this is accomplished, Boserup argues, the way is open for further technological advances, and a dense population can ultimately produce large long-term gains in economic development.

This analysis has generated much controversy, but in Java over the past 150 years a Boserup-like mechanism may have operated. Once widespread, the swidden (termed *humah* in West Java) is now limited to a few relic survivals among the Sundanese peoples of southern Banten and Priangan. In the physically and ethnically similar Lampung region of South Sumatra, the swidden is also steadily losing ground. But the replacement in many parts of South Sumatra of a forested landscape with its swidden cultivators of rubber and dry rice, by a sawah landscape of Javanese immigrants through the mechanism of the transmigration programme is not an autonomous agricultural change. It is an act of policy involving a high degree of government subsidy. Although rationalised as primarily serving economic ends, the transmigration programme has never been subjected to rigorous appraisal in cost: benefit analysis, and in fact serves a multiplicity of ends, many of an ill-defined or even nebulous character, which, it is claimed, will promote national strength and cohesion. Thus although the programme has never been required to provide a predetermined level of income, or living standard, it is expected to assist cultural and spiritual development, which have the advantage of not being susceptible to measurement.

Swidden cultivators in Java were important producers of coffee and other tree crops until access to forest land became denied them, partly through the retreat of the forest itself through rapid population growth and partly through the operation of the Dutch *Woestegronden* policy, under which all land unencumbered by native rights, as the regenerating forest reserve of the swidden system apparently was, was claimed as state property. Thus Java failed to gain a rubber smallholder industry at the turn of the century; its exports became more and more confined to products of estate agriculture, particularly sugar, and with the collapse of the industry after the Great Depression, Java has been largely reduced to the position of a pensioner, living off the export earnings of the Outer Islands, and unable to feed itself. The even more rapid population growth in the *Tanah Seberang* in this century, although on a much smaller base, also converted Sumatra and Kalimantan into food-deficit areas, but from the proceeds of their rubber sales, swidden smallholders could usually purchase imported rice at lower real cost than that of raising dry rice on their own ladangs.

But how long such imports will be available is problematic, and the problem of the rice deficit in the Outer Islands is further examined below.

Ultimately the superior responsiveness to economic change of peoples whose material culture is largely swidden based, reflects the basic psychological differences between sawah and swidden farmers, and, particularly, their differing attitudes towards land. It is a commonplace that when a commodity is plentiful and freely available, any unit is not valued particularly highly, and land is no exception. The traditional swidden group had virtually limitless land, and no conception of landownership in the Western sense. All members possessed some right of usufruct as members of the group, within the territory which through custom and tradition was recognised as the group's domain. The cultivator established his claim by simply clearing and planting his ladang, and the Sumatran coffee or rubber smallholding was largely created in the same way. Thus in contrast to the Javanese *petani,* who, if he is a good Javanese, placidly accepts his ordained place in the sawah system, swidden-smallholders possess a much more commercially oriented attitude towards land, which is valued not so much for its own sake and for the status which landownership confers, but for its capacity to produce an income stream. To maximise this, cultivators themselves decide on the optimum product mix, according to their assessment of present and future differential prices.

This finds a parallel in the different attitudes towards land among the Chinese. For the Chinese in the Nanyang, land is valued in hard practical terms, and there is little of the traditional peasant 'good earth' viewpoint of their ancestral homeland. It is not surprising, therefore, that many of the indigenous peoples of the Outer Islands have developed great skill in trading, and not infrequently can compete with the Chinese on almost equal terms.

THE SAWAH

The soil of the flooded ricefield is protected by its water cover from the rapid physical and chemical deterioration which inevitably results from continuous cultivation in a humid tropical climate. The water cover maintained during the growing season may be entirely derived from rainfall, and even in the early 1970s nearly one-third of Indonesia's sawahs were of this type. Run-off during the rainy season is prevented by the retaining bunds, and an impervious subsoil prevents the impounded water from percolating downwards. Many kinds of soils are suitable for the construction of sawahs, for with cultivation they speedily acquire their own properties, and after some centuries of monoculture the original soil characteristics are often impossible to determine. But because of their permeability, limestones are unsuitable, and in Java such areas contrast markedly with the sawah-covered plains, both because of their accidented landforms and their distinctive patterns of land use. Thus except for a narrow coastal fringe, the island of Madura is devoid of sawahs and, in common with other limestone areas of Java, possesses living standards which are among the lowest in the country.

But even in generally pluviose Indonesia, rainfall in any one season can depart substantially from average conditions, and rain-fed sawahs involve a significant element of hazard. Supplementary water is sometimes available naturally through the seasonal extension of swamps or through the flooding of rivers, whose regimes are a function of the seasonal precipitation and of the lithology, vegetation, and land use within the catchment basin, all of which affect run-off. Indonesia has many regional varieties of wet-rice cultivation adapted to such conditions. Yet all of these are also at risk from time to time, and for the maximum security irrigation is highly desirable. Irrigation also confers an additional benefit, in that as yield is closely related to the amount of water available during the growing season, which may vary from 12 weeks for quickly maturing varieties such as the modern 'miracle rices' to as much as 7 or 8 months for some traditional long-term varieties, it results in a larger crop. Improved water control is thus often a cheaper and more convenient means of increasing output than is expanding the sawah area; moreover, when it permits the taking of more than one rice crop per year, the cultivated area itself is effectively increased.

Irrigation in Indonesia is of two main types, indigenous or semi-technical, using traditional methods and materials, and locally organised and controlled, often on some co-operative basis such as the Balinese *subak* which has in addition other social and religious functions, and serving discrete small areas, typically minor river valleys. Such irrigation may occasionally show a high degree of technical sophistication; stream levels are raised by earth and brushwood dams, water is carried long distances in bamboo conduits, and the Balinese have developed great skill in cutting tunnels through the volcanic tuff. Indigenous irrigation, however, is largely confined to intermontane valleys and highland margins. It could not expand on to the broad coastal plains, for its techniques were inadequate to cope with the great yet very fluctuating discharge of the major rivers, nor could it provide storage, highly desirable for multiple cropping and virtually essential for the successful dry-season cultivation of high yielding varieties. Thus the extension of irrigation over the coastal plains came in the colonial period, with the use of European technologies and modern materials. Technical irrigation involves major regulatory works and lengthy concrete distribution canals, and although such works in Java began as private undertakings, their size and public importance soon led to their operation as official undertakings. Typically, however, and as with indigenous works, such irrigation is of the gravity-deviation type relying on the run of the river, and primarily intended to safeguard the main crop, that is, the crop taken at the end of the rainy season, which in Java is April in most districts. During the dry season river levels and storage capacities permit the serving of only a very limited area with sufficient water for a *padigadu* (off-season) crop.

The earliest technical irrigation systems date back to the time of the Culture System, but following the creation of the Netherlands Indies Irrigation Service, whose origins date from 1886, Irrigation Divisions were demarcated, and works on major rivers were gradually constructed. The largest were those on the Citarum and Cimanuk serving the north-coast plain of West Java, but many smaller districts were created in Central and East Java, where a major stimulus was provided by the growth of a largely European-owned sugar industry. A peculiarity of irrigation in the Netherlands Indies, and which has been continued in independent Indonesia, is that water is provided free. Such a system does not encourage optimal use of the water supplied, and means that those without irrigation facilities subsidise those possessing them.

Present policy, however, is to upgrade modern irrigation systems through the provision of regulatory storage facilities, which can equalise discharge from year to year. This involves expensive high dams, and is usually part of multipurpose water storage and utilisation projects incorporating power production, industrial development, flood control, and the extension of multiple cropping. One such development is the Jatiluhur scheme on the Citarum river near Purwakarta which possesses some 150,000 kw. of electric power and provides 250,000 hectares of wet-season rice with full water control and 80,000 hectares with water for a *padigadu* crop. The Brantas, which has been an important irrigation area since the 1890s, is also to be equipped with major additional works; this highly erratic river is peculiarly susceptible to flooding, partly because of variations in rainfall from year to year, and partly because its course often becomes choked by the debris from volcanic activity. Though attractive to foreign-aid donors, multipurpose projects are very time-consuming to construct; Jatiluhur was inordinately long in gestation, being virtually 20 years behind schedule.

Because it permitted only limited *padigadu* cropping, the growth of modern irrigation since the 1890s paradoxically coincided with a remarkable extension of the cultivation of rice substitutes as the population curve trended sharply upwards. Crops such as maize, tapioca, sweet potatoes, chick-peas, ground-nuts, soya beans, and other pulses, collectively known as *polowijo* (Javanese, *palawija*), were increasingly planted on sawahs during the dry season (April-October, sometimes called east monsoon) in Java, and throughout the year on permanent dry fields, or *tegalan*, which to maintain fertility required treatment with buffalo or ox manure, crop rotations, and fallows. Where constructed on sloping land, *tegalan* are usually elaborated terraced. Thus despite the extension of irrigation, there was a steady decrease in this century in the share of sawahs in the total harvested area. By the outbreak of World War II this proportion had fallen to some 45 percent, strong evidence to many of severe population pressure, for side by side with this diminution there had occurred a reduction in the contribution of rice to daily food intake, and an increase in that from rice substitutes, particularly that from tapioca. Gruel (*sega ojek*) made from the roots of the hardy and quickly maturing tapioca has become the principal food of the poorest classes in rural Indonesia, and in limestone areas is virtually the staff of life. Though its virtues were extolled by President Sukarno in his famous 'Go to Hell!' speech on foreign aid in 1964, in fact a tapioca diet is a very deficient one, as it consists of almost pure starch with little fat or protein.

Such changes permitted the sawah system to support a greatly enhanced population in the face of the mounting difficulty and expense of extending the sawah area. In *kabupaten* (the former regencies, or districts) with half or more of the total area under *tanah darat* (cultivated land less house lots, or sawahs plus *tegalan*) rural population densities range between 500 and 750 persons per square kilometre, and in those where double-cropped sawahs constitute half or more of the total area, as in parts of the north-coast plain of West Java, the plains of Central Java on both north and south coasts, in the Yogyakarta-Surakarta area and in the Solo-Brantas delta, densities can reach 1,500 persons per square kilometre. How far these patterns are reflected in the distribution of size of holdings is uncertain. There are no reliable statistics of landownership, and land offices have more than their share of the common shortcomings of the generally over-large, underworked, and underpaid Indonesian bureaucracy. This difficulty is compounded by the remarkably relaxed and casual attitude of most Indonesians towards the recording of ownership or of transfers of ownership. The legal owner registered in the Land Office is often not the *de facto* owner recognised by the population, and although the legislation of 1960 limiting the area that could be owned by any individual precipitated a rush on the part of the larger landowners to register plots in the names of children and relatives, everybody accepts that nothing has really changed. In every village, the real owners of each plot are known and accepted by the population, and that the authorities may not know is of no concern.

Probably most families in Java own some land, although in what may well be a large majority of *desas,* the number of those who own no sawah is larger than that of those that do; but what they own often cannot provide a minimum of subsistence throughout the year. Pelzer, quoting a 'survey' of 1957, a time when the country appeared to be falling apart and was far too stressed to devote anything like adequate resources to such a formidable task, reported that some 90 percent of all sawah farmers owned less than one hectare, and that 70 percent had less than 0.5 hectares; he concluded that many apparently independent farmers were in reality sharecroppers of moneylender landlords.[6] Some more recent sample surveys indicate that in *kecamatan* (subdistricts) with overall population densities of more than 500 persons per square kilometre, holdings of arable land per family head of less than one hectare comprise 70 percent or more of all holdings, and that those of less than half a hectare per family head range from 20 to 50 percent of the total. Unless it is double-cropped sawah, half a hectare is insufficient to support the average family throughout the year. The smaller the total holding, the more intensively worked is the house lot (*pekarangan*), whose fruits, vegetables, and other rice supplements under extreme conditions can provide up to two-fifths of a family's total calorific intake. In the most densely populated areas, many *desas* have an incidence of landlessness of more than 25 percent of all households, and extremes of more than 40 percent have been recorded. The very poorest do not even own a house lot or residence of their own, and are entirely dependent on wage labour.

Some authorities have concluded that the small size of Java's farms has arisen through the pressure of population increase and the absence of a law of primogeniture. Geertz, however, denies this, and suggests that the average size of holding remained largely constant at about one hectare over the nineteenth century; any reduction that has occurred is a comparatively recent development, arising from European modifications of *adat,* or customary law.[7] This would not really be surprising; the *preferred* size of holding is that which will keep the average family in modest comfort throughout the year, and is large enough to meet all the social obligations that a Javanese of such standing incurs in his *desa*. These, Geertz argues, have increased with time. One hectare of sawah, a hectare of *tegalan*, and one-fifth of a hectare as *pekarangan* are together large enough to meet all these requirements. Hence two hectares was adopted as the minimum holding in the Basic Agrarian Law of 1960, and transmigration schemes in the *Tanah Seberang* endeavour to provide holdings of around this size. It is significant that Javanese settlers in Sumatra show little inclination to acquire holdings of substantially larger size, even when it would be possible for them to do so. But the physical fragmentation of holdings is generally avoided, especially when a division is made among siblings. However, the number of claims or shares in the produce of a piece of land can increase enormously with the passage of time. Javanese agrarian organisation is one of extreme complexity; farmers may work their own land, they may be tenants on the land of another, or they may let part of their own land, either for cash or for shares, and they may combine all or any of these activities. The farming family, however, seldom relies on its own unaided labour; social pressures compel the use of a great deal of hired labour, and, in many Javanese *desas,* all who wish to labour in the harvest of any owner for a share of the crop have traditionally been allowed to do so.

Yet Indonesia's problem is not small farm size, but low farm productivity, for the examples of Japan and Taiwan demonstrate that these are not necessarily linked. Geertz attributes this situation, and the 'involution' in Javanese farming, to Dutch colonial policy, and, above all, to the growth of the sugar industry, which rented village rice-land under the terms of the Land Rents Ordinance of 1870 for sugar production. His analysis is plausible and is politically convenient; most Third World countries and their apologists find it necessary to attribute national shortcomings or deficiencies to the iniquities of colonial policy. Nevertheless, it leaves many issues unexplained and in a sense begs the question. Dutch colonial and agricultural policy could not have developed in the way that it did had it run completely counter to indigenous social beliefs and institutions, and though based in part on major misconceptions, the laws of 1870, which were the cornerstone of that policy, attempted to safeguard native rights as they were perceived at the time. The sugar industry receives further comment in the following chapter, but its extraordinary organisation in the Netherlands Indies, utterly unlike that of the sugar industry anywhere in the world, can hardly be taken for granted. Sugar could easily have been grown as a herbaceous perennial on unirrigated land in Java, just as in the West Indies or in the nearby Philippines, and as indeed it is on innumerable *pekarangan*. As almost always in colonial history, European enterprise initially operated hand in hand with local institutions. The Dutch perfected a system which in outline already existed, and to suit their own ends; significantly, independent Indonesia has shown no desire to discard its inheritance.

The most distinctive feature of the industry was its unique linking of estate cane production with peasant rice cultivation through an elaborate machinery in which the European enterprises rented village sawah land over a long period of years. Though given formal status in the Land Rents Ordinance of 1870, which made possible continued access to indigenously owned land by large-scale capitalist enterprise, the system had established itself much earlier. In essence, the legal owner became part tenant, working on his own rice-land in wet seasons when it was not occupied by cane and on his *polowijo* crops in dry seasons when the land was not so pre-empted, and as part coolie labourer for the estate. Not more than one-third of the village rice-land could be under cane in any wet season, and the land so used had to be released for a rice crop in the following wet season. But whereas the rice cycle was completed in less than six months, cane occupied the land for some 14-16 months; planted early in one dry season, it was harvested in that of the following year, moving over the land in a manner reminiscent of the 'Three Field' system of medieval Europe, and completing seven cycles in 21 ½ years, the maximum lease permissible.

In Geertz's view the system was not only extortion, but while making population increase inevitable, denied it any chance of participating in a genuine agricultural revolution and condemned it to a stagnating productivity. The first charge is certainly true; the payments for the use of his land together with his wages never compensated the *petani* for the loss of his food crops.[8] But the second fails to carry conviction. Even at its height, the sugar industry never affected more than some 10 percent of the total sawah area of Java, and in fact remained largely confined within the same irrigation districts, whose development it had done much to stimulate. True, it occupied the best sawahs in the country, but they were the best because the sugar industry had made them so, with the best water control, the most meticulous soil preparation (land prepared for sugar planting was thrown into a series of deep square ridges and furrows), and, a fact that Geertz fails to mention, very heavy application of fertilisers. Traditional *indica* varieties in Indonesia show little response to fertilisers, particularly the nitrogenous types used by the sugar industry; yet it is difficult to reach any other conclusion but that, in some way, the superior cultivation practices for cane were largely responsible for the undoubted higher rice yields in sugar districts. But how these higher yields were swallowed up in denser populations is not explained, nor can Geertz or anybody else provide convincing reasons for the rapid overall increase in Java's population during the nineteenth century, although he believes that the key factor was the elimination of famine through improvements in transport. But there remains the possibility that in sugar districts larger families were economically advantageous. As the industry grew, it became the largest employer of labour in rural Java and the largest source of cash earnings; at its apogee before the Great Depression, it generated over half a million jobs, from whose loss the island in a sense has never recovered.

Indeed, throughout the inter-tropical world, the major problem facing the European planter was seldom access to land, but the labour to work it for the production of the often exotic commodities needed for an export market. In Java, the feudal organisation of traditional society, in which the ruler was strictly the custodian of the communal lands, enabled the planter to obtain both. The traditional rulers of Mataram remunerated their senior officials (*patih*) through the grant of a *lungguh,* an area from which the grantee was legally entitled to receive the taxes and other obligations due to the ruler; today, many *pamong desa* (village officials) hold a *lungguh* in lieu of pay. The collection was usually entrusted to the official's steward (*bekel*), but even before the fall of Mataram, the rights derived from the ruler were sometimes transferred to non-indigenes in return for a capital sum and the payment of taxes; essentially, the planters, or *landhuurders,* took the place of the *patih* or *bekel.* With the passsage of time, and increasing contact with Europeans, these officials usurped more and more rights, abrogating to themselves many of the privileges of ownership.

In the indirectly ruled principalities of Yogyakarta and Surakarta, the agrarian organisation inherited from Mataram endured largely unchanged right up to 1918. In the directly administered areas, the mantle of custodian of the land passed to the *lurah,* or village headman, who is now an elected official. In conformity with general European colonial policy, the Dutch administration pressed for the replacement of the traditional *adat* system of land use by the Western concept of individual ownership. But the planters were often able to resist this by dealing directly with the *lurah* in leasing village land, and often illegally acquiring *de facto* ownership by buying land in the name of indigenes.

But what the planters had really purchased were the traditional feudal rights due to the ruler, namely the *pajeg* (tax) of one-half of the rice crop and the cultivators' obligations for service for the *corvée,* military duties, and for other state and ceremonial occasions. The planters had no right to the land itself. That they were able to acquire the land for their own purposes and to mobilise the labour force of its cultivators, was possible only because indigenous officials had already distorted the system through their own impositions and usurpations. This, of course, was greatly to the advantage of the European planters. Nevertheless, they merely accepted the system as they found it, and were not responsible for its creation.

If, moreover, 'involution' is intended to indicate a high and increasing degree of labour utilisation, the sawah system of Java is far less involuted than is rice production in Japan, south China, or even in the Tonkin delta of North Vietnam. In all of these, many labour-intensive operations still unknown in Java are regularly performed. Yet productivity is very much higher in Japan, and is probably higher also in south China; moreover, it is rising, almost explosively so in Japan, where a large domestic rice surplus has been created. The sugar districts are clearly not the most depressed parts of the island; on the contrary, both at present and in the past their living standards appear high by local standards. The direst poverty is found in the limestone areas where the sawah has never been able to penetrate.

THE RICE SITUATION

Indonesia's rice shortage is of long standing. At the turn of the century *per capita* consumption of rice was some 110 kilograms per year, but by the early 1970s this had declined to some 100 kilograms, of which only 90 were supplied from domestic production. Additionally to its rice imports, Indonesia also imported large quantities of wheat, flour, and other foodstuffs, and although some of these were made available on concessional or aid terms, the food deficit constituted a large claim on foreign exchange. As the continued availability of rice from traditional exporters is uncertain, the desirability of national self-sufficiency is obvious. But Indonesia has found this goal elusive, and although in the early 1950s and again in the later 1960s success appeared within sight, ensuing unfavourable weather showed how delicately poised the rice situation really was. Significantly, after each setback the deficit has tended to grow. Rice imports in the early 1960s averaged over a million tons a year, substantially higher than those of a decade earlier, and their subsequent decline was largely the result of the country's exhaustion of its cash and credit to acquire more.

In 1971 self-sufficiency was confidently predicted by the end of the 1973-74 season, but in 1973 over 1.3 million tons were imported, and in 1974 almost 1.8 million tons. During the 1974-75 season rice output increased by nearly 6 percent, and once again it was claimed that the rice problem had been virtually solved. But forecasts based on the results of one or two good seasons are highly suspect. The rice situation seems unlikely to yield to the heroic measures of 'crash programmes', particularly when they commit the country to continued heavy reliance on expensive imported inputs.

Over the two decades following independence, rice production doubled, partly through increases in the cultivated area, and partly through higher yields; both of these were assisted through improvements in irrigation. But for much of the 1950s output grew at scarcely 1.5 percent per year, much lower than the rate of population increase, and the greatest gains came in the 1960s with the introduction of high-yielding varieties from the Philippines, the so-called miracle rices IR5 and IR8 (known in Indonesia as PB5 and PB8, after *Peta Baru,* or 'new Peta', Peta being one of the parents of the new varieties in the breeding programmes of the International Rice Research Institute near Manila), and with the development at the new Central Agricultural Research Station at Bogor of domestically bred high-yielding varieties such as Pelita, Bengawan, and Dewi Syntha. After 1965 the political situation became much more favourable for the deployment of foreign aid in promoting the wider adoption of these superior rices, which because they needed substantially larger inputs in the form of fertilisers, pesticides, and water control, were very much more expensive to cultivate than the traditional varieties. By 1971 almost 12 percent of Indonesia's sawahs, or some 20 percent of those of Java, were planted with high-yielding varieties, and with rice output expanding in the early 1970s at about 6 percent per annum just when Thailand and certain other Asian producers were finding rice in over-supply, fears were expressed that the target *per capita* consumption of 120 kilograms from home sources by the end of *Repelita* I would precipitate Indonesia also into an unfamiliar surplus situation.

As earlier noted, these gains were not realised cheaply. But after the dry season of 1972 it was clear that they were in large part the product of fortuitous circumstances, such as favourable weather, the speedy occupation of the best-irrigated areas by the new rices, the high return on the repair and renovation of neglected irrigation systems, and relatively low-cost fertiliser imports. New irrigation works will be more costly and will take time to complete, fertiliser prices have soared with the energy crisis, and although

Indonesia has started to harness potential for developing a large fertiliser industry from its natural-gas resources, this also will take time to bring to fruition. Future gains in rice output will thus be both more difficult and expensive. Yet merely to maintain the situation, rice output must grow by at least 3 percent per annum to cope with population increase and losses in storage.

Thus by the end of the First Five-Year Plan Indonesia was about one million tons short of its rice target, and it was evident that imports would be needed for some time to come. As elsewhere in Asia, the 'Green Revolution' had failed to live up to the optimistic forecasts of five years or so earlier. The difficulties of promoting the widespread adoption of an imported technology by a traditional industry had been grossly underrated, and, as elsewhere in Asia also, the first concern of Indonesian farmers was not yield but taste; they much preferred the lower-yielding but more palatable varieties bred in the country to the tasteless imports, PB5 and PB8. At both the local and national levels, the organisation of the Department of Public Agriculture (*Japerta*) was totally inadequate for carrying through an agricultural revolution of the kind needed. While in Jakarta policies were amended, discarded, and new ones adopted with bewildering rapidity, at the sub-district (*kecamatan*) level senior officials were regularly rotated every four years or so in conformity with government policy, thus making continuity in the prosecution of any programme virtually impossible. Agricultural extension officers were too few in numbers and had far too many responsibilities, among which were the making of estimates of area and production for more than 50 crops within their sub-districts, a task which in itself would have taxed the resources of a sizeable survey team. Typically, these unfortunate officials had to deal with several thousand individual and widely scattered farmers, many of whom were almost impossible to reach by wheeled vehicle at times in the wet season, and with minimal transport facilities.

Contact with individual farmers was thus both fleeting and sporadic, and it was largely to overcome this problem that the unique experiment was devised from which developed the programme known as *Bimas* (*Bimbingan Massal,* or mass guidance). This was essentially an attempt to popularise the new technologies which had been among the objectives of earlier programmes such as the Rural Education Centres set up shortly after independence, the Three-Year Emergency Programme of 1959-61, and the Padi Centres of 1961-64, but it differed in a radically new approach to accomplishing these ends. Farmers were to be instructed in the new techniques by senior students of agricultural colleges, who would live in the *desa* with the farmers for whom they were responsible for the entire crop season. The first pilot project in Krawang, a historically famous rice area of West Java, with students from the Agricultural College of Bogor, was able to establish very favourable student-farmer ratios, and, being closely supervised in an accessible area only 60 kilometres from Jakarta, was a resounding success. This was achieved not so much from the students' technological knowledge, but from their enthusiasm and interest, by which they were able to gain the confidence and co-operation of the farmers. Extended in the 1964-65 programme on some 11,000 hectares located in 15 provinces, student-farmer ratios suffered some dilution, but the approach was again successful. The programme was now expanded into a major national movement, and, with the new name of *Bimas*, was taken away from the Directorate of Public Agriculture and placed under independent high-level administrative authority. For 1965-66 the target was some 150,000 hectares, and for 1966-67, 480,000 hectares; these in fact were achieved, but the resources which had made possible earlier success had become grossly overextended, and there was a great falling-off in effectiveness. Even with an increase in the farmer to student ratio there were insufficient students to go round, so that students of other faculties of the universities and a substantial number of high-school students, all of whom had little to offer the farmers, became involved. But even the better-qualified students were able to give effective supervision to only one-fifth of the farmers they had been assigned, nor were they able to live with their charges throughout the crop season. Inevitably also, the aftermath of the *Gestapu* revolt compounded the programme's difficulties.

In the earlier projects, farmers had been provided with the necessary inputs, for which they eventually made payment in the form of a share of the incremental output. Other variants and subschemes made their appearance after 1968, by which time overextension of the original approach was obvious in the form of large arrears and defaults in payment for inputs. Private foreign interests such as the Swiss CIBA organisation and Sumitomo of Japan made agreements with government for the provision of fertilisers and pesticides against payment after the harvest; this was *Bimas Gotong Royong*, which, after 1970 when direct credits were made available for the purchase of inputs, became known as *Bimas Intensifikasi Massal* (mass intensification *Bimas*), or, simply, *Inmas*, which continued in operation side by side with the original *Bimas* approach. Military formations were also occasionally involved in these projects, such as the scheme organised for the

Krawang area by the Siliwangi division. These new variants produced many complaints from padi-growers; fertilisers were often of less desirable types and highly priced in real terms, as the incremental yield was often, so farmers charged, deliberately overassessed. Nevertheless, *Bimas* and *Inmas* had the backing both of the World Bank and IGGI, the international aid consortium, and by the end of *Repelita* I new programmes were to operate over some 4 million hectares.

The new technologies, however, are not open to the landless and the poor, and their impact on total employment in the village is uncertain; cultivation of the new rices was substantially more labour-demanding than that of the traditional varieties, but, because of the need for alternative methods of harvesting, it is not clear that total employment has increased. With tall-standing indigenous varieties, each panicle is harvested individually by means of the *ani-ani,* or harvest knife, which is concealed in the palm of the hand as the head together with a portion of the stalk is severed; in this way, the 'rice-spirit' is not offended. Modern high-yielding varieties are short in stature and have a sharp flag-leaf below the fruiting head, which necessitates harvesting with the *arit,* or sickle; as they are foreign, it is reasoned that the rice-spirit is not offended by this treatment. But because the ripe ears drop readily from the panicles, modern varieties have to be threshed in the field by the harvesters, who remove the grain in baskets; with indigenous varieties, on the other hand, the fruiting heads are tied into bundles and carried from the field on shoulder-yokes. Thus the traditional harvest is an extremely labour-intensive operation, employing up to 500 workers per hectare, and to harvest just one *petak* (an individual sawah) may temporarily occupy all the available labour of the *desa*. Traditionally, all who wished to participate in the labour of the harvest for a share of the crop have been allowed to do so. But growing landlessness, which has increased the numbers of would-be harvesters, who are usually women, and the social pressures which have tended to push up the share awarded to them, are operating in conjunction with the differing harvesting requirements of the new varieties sharply to restrict this old custom. The practice of selling the standing crop in the field to a middleman for cash, who then arranges for the harvest by a small team of his own, appears to be spreading fast, and, if continued, could have serious social consequences.

Social pressures in Java act to compel the employment of labour beyond the value of its marginal product, and it is remarkable that, despite the very small size of holdings, a relatively small part of the total farm labour requirements are performed by the owner and his family. With the spread of high-yielding varieties this proportion seems to have declined still further. The cultivation of the new rices, however, is seldom possible to tenant sharecroppers, for the inputs are too expensive, and as irrigation improvements lead to the replacement of off-season *polowijo* by high-yielding rice, the tenant is gradually reduced to the status of a labourer.

Under such conditions, the question arises of the potential contribution to enhanced productivity of agrarian reorganisation and land reform, long a highly contentious issue in Indonesia. Since *Gestapu,* however, discussion of this issue has been discouraged, and it has received little priority. Yet it was an important and much-debated question in the first decade of independence, and although its principal protagonist was the PKI, there were many in other parties who viewed the increasing incidence of landlessness with deep concern. In 1960 the Basic Agrarian Law and the Sharecropping Law were promulgated, which were to provide a new framework for the ownership and use of land in place of the old Dutch legislation. The former restricted the right of ownership to Indonesian citizens, and fixed a maximum size of holding according to a scale based on population density. In *kabupaten* where population density exceeded 400 persons per square kilometre, as in Java and Madura, the maximum permissible was 5 hectares of sawah or 6 of *tanah kering*. But where population densities fell below 50 persons per square kilometre, as in large areas of the *Tanah Seberang,* owners were allowed up to 15 hectares of sawah or 20 of dry land. Land owned in excess of these limits was to be acquired by the state against compensation in government bonds, and redistributed to the landless and to those whose holdings were too small to provide a minimum of subsistence. The act also fixed a legal minimum of two hectares: this was largely a political gesture, as it could only be provided through a shift of population from Java to the other islands on a scale far exceeding anything ever conceived in transmigration programmes. Just to provide the legal minimum to all of Java's sawah-owners would have required some 18 million hectares, or twice the cultivated area of the island. The Sharecropping Law required all tenancy agreements to be registered and to be effective for not less than 3 years for sawahs and five for *tegalan;* the tenant's obligations, moreover, could not leave him with less than half the crop in the case of sawahs, and two-thirds for dry fields. Implementation of the measures was entrusted to local committees, which with excessive optimism was scheduled to be completed within three years in Java and in five in the Outer Islands. But, as noted, large landowners circumvented the law through multiple registration, and the intricate network of tenancy and sub-tenancy in the *desa* was ill-suited to precise definition in a legal document. Ironically, while it is true that in general Indonesia possesses no highly privileged class of really large landowners such as exists in the Philippines, and whose holdings could constitute a basis for land reform, it has created one since 1957 in the form of the armed forces. Most of the armed forces' properties consist of ex-foreign-owned estates planted to tree crops, but the armed forces are frequently in the position of landlords growing food crops. But its close association with the PKI gave the cause of land reform a bad name, and the work of acquisition and redistribution proceeded very slowly. Nevertheless, by 1972 about a million hectares had been redistributed under the legislation.

This, of course, had minimal impact in a situation in which over 90 percent of all sawah-owners possess less than one hectare. Nor has the government at any time been prepared to give market forces a free rein in stimulating peasant initiative to increase output. In Java, where there is a rice harvest of some magnitude in every month of the year, an enormous multiplicity of individual producers, and an inadequate transport system, it is doubtful if there is any better allocative mechanism than the market. Government, however, has long endeavoured to secure certain political objectives through fixing rice prices and those of key inputs such as fertilisers. Some of these goals, such as increasing the participation of indigenous Indonesians in milling and marketing, occupations which, as elsewhere in South-east Asia, have long been dominated by Chinese, appear desirable. More open to question is the practice of providing a subsidised rice ration to a privileged élite, notably the bureaucracy and the armed forces.[9] But the political necessity of keeping the cost of living from spiralling in the rapidly growing urban areas conflicts with the need for high enough farm prices to encourage farmers to make the additional investment to raise output, and Indonesia has been no more successful in reconciling these two goals than have other Asian countries. The main aim of the Logistics Bureau (*Bulog*), the government rice-procurement agency which purchases rice from co-operative mills at the sub-district level, is in fact to secure the rice that government needs to meet its commitments to its privileged employees, and, hopefully, to exert some influence on prices in the Jakarta and other major urban markets. But differential pricing inevitably encourages hoarding by peasants, and with the drought of 1972 *Bulog*'s purchases fell far short of its target. It remains true, however, that in comparison with certain other Asian countries the longer-term food prospects of Indonesia are far from unfavourable. An enormous area of potentially cultivatable land awaits development in the Outer Islands, and mounting oil and gas revenues should finance the construction of the plants required for the production of the other inputs necessary for the harnessing of these land resources. Yet the fact that the country can now easily finance the import of rice and other foodstuffs in any amount has inevitably tended to reduce the sense of urgency; but in another quarter-century Indonesian oil and gas will be largely exhausted, and population will be at least twice that at present. Since 1970 large additional resources generated by the commodity boom have been committed to expanding and accelerating the transmigration programme, but all efforts so far have not even succeeded in the more limited and immediate aim of making Sumatra self-sufficient in rice. To expedite attainment of this goal, in 1974 contracts were signed with the Hawaiian estate company C. Brewer and with Mitsui of Japan, for the lease of large areas of land in the Palembang district for double-cropped rice production with semi-mechanised methods. In this resurrection of the 'rice plantation', a form of enterprise that had disappeared from Java during the Great Depression, old and discredited methods of production had, as in the case of the sugar industry, again demonstrated surprising resilience in modern Indonesia.

Population

In food production, as in so many other respects, the nation's future depends largely on a fuller utilisation of its rapidly growing labour force. In population, as in geographic area, Indonesia is the giant of South-east Asia, its total of 126 million people in 1973 encompassing over two-fifths of the region's inhabitants. Even more than that of its neighbours, the economy is characterised by an extremely low participation rate (the share of the total population gainfully employed) and by a low number of workdays per year per worker, both in agricultural and non-agricultural activities. These untapped human reserves appear as great a potential asset as the archipelago's promise of a growing stock of physical resources. But in relation to the rate at which the latter are becoming available the structure, size, and rate of growth of the population are among the biggest obstacles to the elimination of poverty and a rapid improvement of living standards. With birth-rates remaining high and mortality falling, the annual rate of population growth has accelerated from about 2.1 percent during the 1960s to over 2.3 percent in 1974; while this is lower than the rates in most South-east Asian countries, Indonesia's population is already so large that a growth-rate of this magnitude yields an absolute increase of 2 ½ to 3 million people a year, or an annual increment the size of the population of Singapore. Moreover, there is still scope for substantial reductions in death-rates, particularly infant mortality, and all the signs indicate a further rise in annual growth-rates which could exceed 3 percent by the later 1980s, and which would give Indonesia a total population of over 200 million by 1991.

Many of the nation's most acute problems arise because, unlike nineteenth-century Europe, this population growth has not been accompanied by a corresponding expansion of employment opportunities or a rise in *per capita* productivity through industrial growth and the modernisation of agriculture. Although it has certainly generated economic growth when measured by the yardstick of total physical output, the Suharto government's encouragement of foreign investment in such capital-intensive extractive industries as mining and forestry and the failure of the 'Green Revolution' to fulfil its earlier promise have done little to upgrade productivity. Indonesia's population remains overwhelmingly rural; over three-fifths of the workforce is engaged in agriculture, the greater part of which consists of peasant farmers, sharecroppers, or landless labourers only marginally touched, if at all, by official development planning; moreover, while the larger cities are growing fast, principally through rural-urban migration, productive urban employment expands far more slowly. Poverty thus pervades both rural and urban areas enmeshing most Indonesians, and particularly the people of Java, in a seemingly inescapable low-income trap. The extreme youthfulness of the population, in which the proportion under 15 years old rose from 42.1 percent in 1961 to 44.1 percent in 1971, imposes a heavy dependency burden on existing workers, but it also means that problems of employment and food supply will become more, not less, acute in the last quarter of this century and the real test of the New Order's economic policies must be the extent to which they mitigate the intricate interrelated problems of rural and urban poverty, for if these persist, greater social and political unrest is inevitable. Yet, while the need fully to harness a rapidly growing labour force in ways which suitably augment national production and personal incomes is as urgent as anywhere in Asia, it has long been compounded by the political and economic repercussions of the severe maldistribution of the nation's inhabitants between the nuclear island of Java, 'full to overflowing with people and cropped to capacity',[10] and *Tanah Seberang*, or 'the land beyond', with its immense relatively empty spaces. Despite more than three-quarters of a century of concern and attempted solutions, this extreme imbalance remains one of Indonesia's most intractable problems.

Geertz's portrayal of this contrast in terms of 'plenum' and 'vacuum' is oversimplified.[11] With over nine-tenths of the national territory, little more than a third of its population, and an average density of only 23 per square kilometre in 1971, the Outer Islands—and particularly Kalimantan and Irian which together comprise half of Indonesia's land area but account for only 5 percent of its population—do contain immense sparsely-peopled areas in which shifting cultivation is the most widespread agricultural system. But to tar the whole of *Tanah Seberang* with the same brush is to mask significant variations with important developmental implications; North Sumatra, South Sulawesi, and South Kalimantan, for instance, are much more densely settled than are other parts of the Outer Islands. Additionally, the admittedly massive problems of Java have diverted attention from certain significant long-term trends. For some considerable time Java's population has been growing more slowly than that of the Outer Islands, several of which, notably Sumatra, record rates markedly higher than that of the nation as a whole. Indeed, with a quarter of Indonesia's land area, Sumatra's share of its population has grown from 13.6 percent in 1930 to 17.5 percent in 1971 and this single island, which includes all the major migrant-receiving provinces except DKI Jakarta, now contains almost half of all the people in the Outer Islands, and occasional pockets of population pressure, as in Tapanuli, are beginning to emerge. Clearly, in the long run it is as necessary to promote development to absorb this more rapid increase in the Outer Islands, where marked increments in productivity seem possible, as it is to face Java's existing problems.

With only 6.9 percent of Indonesia's land area, Java accounted for 63.8 percent of the total population in 1971 and had an average density of 565 per square kilometre. Despite its mountainous character, over two-thirds of this excessively crowded island is under cultivation, most conspicuously in the form of elaborately intensive wet-rice farming; where soils permit widespread adoption of this form of agriculture, as they do on the north-coast plains and lowlands adjacent to volcanoes in Yogyakarta and Surakarta, rural densities often exceed one thousand per square kilometre, but less crowded areas frequently occur nearby, particularly on unirrigable limestone terrain. One of the most densely peopled agricultural regions in the world, Java is nonetheless a curious anomaly in South-east Asia. Fertile soils, a high percentage of cultivated land, elaborate agricultural techniques, a dense population, a larger proportion of the workforce in non-agricultural employment than the national average, well-developed road and rail networks, numerous towns and large cities, and the majority of the nation's industrial activities, these are attributes which elsewhere in the region signify the most developed or dynamic sectors of the economy. Yet although Java has long received the bulk of government development expenditure, in Indonesia these very attributes combine to yield a sombre picture of an island at the nation's heart beset by concentrated and deepening poverty for which no adequate solutions have yet been found.

It is often suggested that the current size of Java's population is not the result of a sudden upsurge in numbers in the twentieth century, as is the case generally in the tropics, but that it has been caused by the unusual combination of persistent relatively high rates of growth operating over a long period of time. Commonly this apparently exceptional situation is attributed to the increasing penetration and influence of the Dutch in the life of the island from the early nineteenth century, with particular weight being given to the reduction in mortality associated with the establishment of peace and order and to the introduction of medical and health facilities, especially smallpox vaccination. Recently, however, closer scrutiny of these oft-quoted views has revealed that there is no sound evidence that Java did experience high rates of population growth in the nineteenth century.[12]

No censuses were conducted in Indonesia during the nineteenth century. In the most complete colonial enumeration, that of 1930, only rough estimates were made for some parts of the country and even the 1961 census excluded Irian, which was not then under Indonesian jurisdiction, merely including an estimate for its population. In consequence, calculations of past rates of growth have relied heavily and injudiciously on inadequate and incomplete data and especially on Raffles's total of 4.5 million for the population of Java in 1815 and Bleeker's figure of 9.4 million for 1845. Uncritical use of these figures, both undoubtedly far below the actual totals, has seriously exaggerated subsequent rates of growth. Taken at face value, for instance, they indicate an average annual increase in the island's population in the first half of the nineteenth century of 2.48 percent, a rate unbelievably higher than that at present; equally, unqualified acceptance of the official figures for Java of 29.98 million in 1905 and 34.43 million in 1920 implies an annual growth-rate of a mere 0.93 percent in the first two decades of this century. Java has always been Indonesia's most populous island and Peper has concluded that its population was substantially larger in 1800 than has been suggested hitherto, probably totalling between 8 and 10 million.[13] In his opinion,

Java's population grew at less than 1 percent a year in the first half of the nineteenth century and at between 1 and 1.5 percent in the latter part of the century; in the first four decades of this century the annual rate of growth was about 1.5 percent. In other words, starting from a much higher base than has been accepted before, the population of Java under Dutch colonial rule expanded because of a progressive increase in the rate of growth. If this is so, then although the numbers involved are large, the demographic history of the island is not unusual.

Peper also takes a fresh look at the reasons cited to explain the supposed trends in the growth of Java's population. As he points out, against the inferred effects of Dutch pacification (which, incidentally, can hardly be invoked to explain the growth of Bali's almost equally dense population) must be set the ravages of the Java War (1825-30), in which an estimated 200,000 Javanese died, and a quarter of the inhabited and cultivated area sustained damage. But recent work casts even more serious doubts on the ability of Dutch measures in the fields of public health and medicine to have had the influences on death-rates with which they are usually accredited. Smallpox vaccination, the only public health measure in the nineteenth century, was very limited in scale and was largely restricted to areas with concentrations of Europeans, particularly military personnel; indeed, there were smallpox epidemics in the earlier part of the century, the vaccination system was not made more effective until after 1850, and total eradication was not a real possibility until about 1930. Moreover, in view of the minimal medical facilities available—there were, for instance, only 53 doctors in Java in 1870, half of them employed by the army, and the existing hospitals were almost exclusively military establishments—treatment for diseases such as cholera, malaria, plague, and typhus was generally denied to the vast majority of Java's inhabitants in the nineteenth century, and spread only slowly in the early decades of this century. The history of public health in Java is, indeed, more in accord with Peper's interpretation of the history of population growth as a successive rise in rates of annual increment than with earlier views of a long-sustained increase; and this newer interpretation seemingly affords a more satisfactory explanation of the acknowledged mounting pressure on the land, the key to Java's most serious problems.

Nonetheless, staggering though these are, Indonesia's population problems are not simply a matter of overall size and regional imbalance in distribution. Of at least equal importance, if less well known, are the direct effects on age structure, developmental needs, and future growth prospects of the country's peculiar demographic history in the last thirty to forty years. The 1940s produced for Indonesia a 'hollow generation' which is most clearly evident in Java. The Japanese occupation and the subsequent revolutionary struggle caused many casualties, disrupted the economy, and produced a deterioration in living conditions with serious food shortages which were especially acute in 1944 and early 1945. Concurrently with the rise in mortality, as a result of the break-up of families and the postponement of marriages, birth-rates fell dramatically and remarkably small numbers of children were born between 1942 and 1946. In sharp contrast, Indonesia experienced 'a tremendous population upsurge' during the 1950s with an apparently continuous rise in the rate of annual growth.[14] The reunion of families and the marked improvement in *per capita* incomes and living standards brought a return of the crude birth-rate to the pre-war level of over 40 per thousand, thus engendering a 'baby boom'; concurrently, the start of a belated health revolution through vigorous campaigns to extend public facilities and to reduce the incidence of disease, particularly the eradication of malaria, caused a pronounced decline in death-rates more sudden than occurred in the industrialising countries of the West in the nineteenth century.

Although the entire country was affected to some extent, the results of these abrupt changes were most apparent in Java; at the 1961 census 15.6 percent of the island's population had been born between 1952 and 1956, whereas only 7.7 percent had been born between 1942 and 1946. The existence of these two adjacent cohorts of vastly different sizes has necessarily raised serious implications as they proceed through their life cycles. The very smallness of the numbers born in the 1940s greatly facilitated the expansion of educational facilities and the reduction of illiteracy in the subsequent decade, without making unbearable demands on available finance. By the later 1950s and early 1960s this 'hollow generation' meant that there were relatively small numbers of new entrants into the job market, and, even though teenagers recorded the highest rates of unemployment in 1961, the need to expand employment opportunities was less than it might have been; and as this generation moved into the reproductive ages, it caused a temporary lessening of the birth-rate. But the 'hollow generation' is being followed through this cycle by a cohort which is twice as large. Initially, this greatly increased pressure on the educational system, but as those born in the 1950s enter their late teens and twenties, two inevitable developments are occurring. Firstly, there has been a huge increase in the size and a radical rejuvenation of the total labour force, which is likely to grow twice as fast between

1971 and 1976 as it did between 1961 and 1966. Secondly, a rapid upsurge in births in the present decade is unavoidable simply because of the sudden massive increase in the number of women of child-bearing age. Coupled with the distinct probability of a speedy reduction in death-rates, nearly three times as high as in neighbouring West Malaysia, and particularly in infant mortality, which accounts for about half of all deaths in Indonesia, this will bring a quickening in the rate of population growth, which promises greatly renewed pressure on employment possibilities in the near future. Indeed, with the country's population likely to double within the next thirty years, Indonesia's as yet unfulfilled need adequately to utilise its tremendous supply of manpower and to ensure a more equitable distribution of rising incomes, is becoming ever more desperate.

In their efforts to grapple with these manifold problems of population, employment, and food supply the governments of independent Indonesia have relied largely, and with equally little success, on policies introduced in the Dutch colonial era. Attempts to increase agricultural production in Java through the rehabilitation, improvement, and extension of irrigation facilities, the introduction of new high-yielding varieties of rice, and the provision of appropriate inputs, credit, and guidance have not produced a noticeable rise in rural living standards primarily because most holdings are already so small that even with these improvements farmers are unable to meet the rice needs of their own families. Moreover, with only an estimated 100,000 hectares of unused potential rice-land now available in the island, and which because of technical difficulties would require very large investments of time and money to convert into sawahs, there is little prospect of extending the cultivated area to absorb additional surplus labour or to augment the output of food. Equally, as was the case with the Dutch in the 1930s, the promotion of manufacturing industry in Java since independence has failed to match the growth of the island's labour force (see below, Chapter 7). As yet, therefore, neither modernisation of agriculture nor an expansion of manufacturing has been sufficient to absorb more than a tiny fraction of Java's annual increment and the basic elements of the country's present population strategy are the speedy dissemination of family planning and the transfer of large numbers of people to the more empty *Tanah Seberang*. Whether these can be any more successful in alleviating the problems is highly questionable.

Fears about the apparent overpopulation of Java and the 'diminishing welfare' of its inhabitants spread among the Dutch at the close of the nineteenth century, and to relieve the growing pressure a programme of colonisation (*kolonisatie*) was started to arrange the movement of people from densely settled parts of Java to the largely empty Outer Islands.[15] The first resettlement scheme was established in 1905 in Lampung, south Sumatra, with colonists from the overcrowded residency of Kedu near Jogjakarta, and other schemes followed in south Sumatra, Celebes, and south-eastern Borneo. None of these was very successful, however, and by 1922 only 23,000 settlers had been moved from Java; official interest waned, and during the rest of the 1920s the number leaving Java averaged less than 500 a year. With the severe unemployment caused by the depression of the early 1930s the idea of *kolonisatie* was re-examined, and under the charge of a newly created special commission the programme accelerated suddenly; by 1939 76 settlements had been started, mostly in Lampung and Bengkulu. But the rate of movement fell substantially below expectations; the Dutch never managed to transfer more than 60,000 in a year, the total number moved between the start of the programme and the Japanese occupation was under 200,000, and there was a huge gap between the number leaving Java each year and the annual increase in the island's population.

Now seen as desirable both as a means of easing the plight of Java's landless peasants and as a method of furnishing labour to the Outer Islands, colonisation—which became known as transmigration (*transmigrasi*)—was begun again under a special department of the newly independent government in 1950. Although Javanese peasants were as reluctant as ever to leave and the Department of Transmigration faced financial problems and administrative difficulties, not the least because of unsatisfactory co-ordination with other agencies involved in establishing new schemes, more colonists were moved between 1951 and 1960 than the Dutch had resettled in forty years; the numbers involved, however, were still totally insufficient to have any impact on Java's worsening problems. In consequence, the Eight-Year Development Plan (1961-68) included an immensely ambitious proposal to move 390,000 families (representing 1.5 to 2 million people) by 1968; but the numbers actually moving in the early 1960s fell far below the targets. In 1964 therefore Sukarno proclaimed that transmigration had become 'a matter of life or death for the Indonesian people' and launched a grandiose, and utterly unsuccessful, new plan to resettle 100,000 families in 1966.

Despite its failure to bring the promised rewards either in relieving pressure in Central and East Java, which have supplied the bulk of the migrants, or in stimulating development in the principal recipient areas of Sumatra and Kalimantan which, on the contrary, show distinct signs of becoming 'little Javas' reproducing all the social and economic inadequacies of the homeland, the Suharto government has persisted with transmigration. It has had no more success than its predecessors, however, and only 54,200 colonists were settled between 1967 and 1970. Undismayed by this long history of ineffectiveness, undoubtedly caused partly by poor organisation and administration, by insufficient finance, and by a frequent failure to select suitable sites for settlements, some of which have been in areas where irrigation facilities were absent or would be impossible to provide, the Directorate-General for Transmigration Affairs now proposes to move over 450,000 families from Java and Bali during the Second Five-Year Development Plan (1974-79).

Whatever its curiously tenacious attractions for the official mind or its possible propaganda value for governments seeking to create the impression of dealing with crucial problems, on any reasoned assessment transmigration can do little more than inflict an insignificant dent, and that at great expense, in Java's problems. It is highly probable that over the last two decades voluntary migration from the other islands to Java, and especially to Jakarta, has exceeded the outflow of transmigrants, a situation which suggests that it might be more appropriate to channel greater investment to the Outer Islands to persuade potential Java-bound migrants not to leave, and a process which might, incidentally, in the long run also create destinations economically more attractive to the Javanese than the typical resettlement scheme. But, in any case, at current rates of growth the annual absolute increase in Java's population is over 1.5 million, so that for transmigration to have any noticeable effects it would need to be on an enormous scale, possibly involving coercion, and far beyond the capacity of existing shipping facilities, financial resources, and administrative machinery to provide. Significantly, having projected Java's future population so that he could compare the effects of out-migration and a decline in fertility, Widjojo Nitisastro concluded that 'a "normal" decline in fertility will have a comparable, if not a stronger, impact on the future growth of Java's population than an out-migration of 200,000 young persons annually'.[16] That the island's population problems can be solved even partially by transferring large numbers of its inhabitants to other parts of the country is an impossible dream which is slow to fade. Even though the effects cannot be immediate, the only realistic course is to focus on generating more employment opportunities within Java, and on reducing the number of future births.

Convinced that Indonesia could support, and indeed required, many more people, Sukarno continuously stressed the desirability of increasing the population. There was some interest in modern methods of birth control in the early 1960s, mostly among the better educated and the women's organisations, and clinics were established in larger cities, but this incipient family-planning movement was denied official support. In the first years of the New Order voluntary organisations received more encouragement and a spate of surveys and reports, including the proceedings of the first congress of the Indonesian Planned Parenthood Association held in Jakarta in February 1967, drew attention to the need for urgent and vigorous action.[17] In 1969 the government sought the assistance of the United Nations Development Program and of the World Bank to permit the introduction of a comprehensive family-planning programme, and this objective was incorporated into both the First and Second Five-Year Development Plans. Initially the programme has been restricted to Java, Madura, and Bali, where it was hoped to achieve a target of 3 million acceptors by the end of the First Plan. Numerous clinics were opened providing the pill and other devices at a small charge; an evocative poster campaign supported the call for a maximum of three children per family, which on some estimates could reduce the rate of growth to 2 percent a year, instead of the traditional five or more, and, in an effort to reach rural peasants, familiarisation courses were run for *dalang,* the storytellers at the *wayang,* or shadow puppet, performances so popular in Java.

According to recent official statements, the family-planning programme now seeks to reduce the annual rate of population growth to 1.2 percent by the end of the century. No matter what measures are introduced or how aggressive the campaign, this is almost certainly an unattainable target. There does seem to be a genuinely widespread desire for smaller families and Indonesia's many ethnic groups have a variety of customary methods of contraception which should facilitate adoption of modern practices. As with other much-heralded developments, however, the government's administrative machinery, which appears to treat the distribution of contraceptives much like the distribution of fertilisers or pesticides, may prove too weak and cumbersome to allow the establishment of a fully effective programme, and certainly the results achieved so far have not lived up to earlier expectations. In any case, of course, the effects of a family-planning programme are long in coming and a successful campaign in wholly propitious circumstances could not significantly influence growth-rates for several decades. In the 1960s Indonesia's crude birth-rate was still over 40 per thousand; even the most vigorous programme is unlikely to reduce this rate by as much as one per thousand per year, which would bring it down to 25 per thousand in 1990, a rate already achieved by Singapore.[18] While they make the need for birth control more urgent, there are two other reasons for doubting whether such a programme can have as great an impact on growth-rates as some believe. As noted earlier, because of the 'baby boom' of the 1950s, very large numbers of future mothers are now entering the childbearing ages and in consequence even a decline in the birth-rate will not mean that fewer children are born than at present. Moreover, as general health facilities improve, there is every likelihood of a significant drop in mortality, and if family planning succeeds only in offsetting this decline, current rates of population growth will persist. It is not unreasonable to suppose, therefore, that Indonesia will have a population of about 240 million by the end of this century.

The inevitable conclusion is that the only prospect of improving the lot of the large and rapidly growing number of Indonesians is suitably to increase the tempo of economic activity. What has been and is being done in this respect is the subject of the following chapters, throughout which several questions recur. Are the measures which have been introduced sufficient to cope with the problems? Are they initiating the necessary structural changes in the nation's economy so that activities associated with higher productivity and higher incomes embrace increasing numbers of people? Should the government of Indonesia perhaps aim first at maximising employment of its huge supplies of manpower rather than seek the highest possible rates of conventionally measured economic growth? To what extent is there justification for recent criticisms, particularly by more youthful Indonesians, that developments fostered by the Suharto government have merely emphasised the dualism between expanding modern-sector industries such as mining, forestry, and large-scale manufacturing, all of which create relatively few new jobs in proportion to their investment, and the largely unchanged sectors of agriculture and petty urban employment which, with their low productivity, afford pitifully poor living standards for a growing mass of the population? Finally, does the 'modernisation' now in process in Indonesia resemble the thin veneer of earlier cultural intrusions in that it is causing a widening gap between the small numbers who benefit from the resultant social and economic transformation and who become increasingly oriented to the acquisition of material possessions, and the majority, whose numbers increase yearly, who continue to eke a meagre livelihood on tiny farms and city streets, and who must devote the bulk of their expenditure to food?

NOTES

[1] For a discussion of this point in the context of South and South-east Asia, see Gunnar Myrdal, *Asian Drama,* New York, 1968, 492-9.

[2] The FAO *State of Food and Agriculture 1972* estimated the output per Indonesian agricultural worker in 1970 as some US $126, as against $492 for the Malaysian farmworker. As Malaysia's large immature plantings of oil-palm and high-yielding rubber have come into bearing, and with the boom in commodity prices in 1973-74, the disparity has widened with time.

[3] Unmilled rice; the variety of terms in Indonesia for rice in different stages of preparation necessitates caution in examining statistics. *Padi* is strictly rice cut from the field in the traditional manner, with part of the stalk attached to the ears; after being allowed to dry, this becomes dry *padi* (*padi kering*), and when threshed is called *gabah.* Milled rice is *beras,* and its production involves a substantial weight loss, depending on the extraction ratio. In FAO publications, paddy means unmilled rice; by using an appropriate extraction ratio in milling (typically 65-70 per-cent), a figure for the milled rice equivalent may be obtained.

[4] Ester Boserup, *The Conditions of Agricultural Growth,* London, Allen and Unwin, 1965.

[5] Malthus originally produced no satisfactory theoretical basis for his argument, nor was it supported by any empirical evidence, although he was driven to attempt both by criticism. It was, in fact, nothing but a principle—explicitly, a conservatively useful belief, made to justify a repressive social policy in early nineteenth-century Britain.

[6] Karl J. Pelzer, in Ruth T. McVey (ed.), *Indonesia,* New Haven, 1963, 126.

[7] Clifford Geertz, *Agricultural Involution,* 97.

[8] Competition for irrigation water enforced the cultivation of *polowijo* in the dry season; cane had priority, in fact, in the use of water at all times.

[9] Apart from its other economic distortions, this unquestionably encourages government officials to have large families. A very senior official confided to one of the authors that with six children he was able to obtain a rice ration large enough to avoid buying rice on the open market, and that many *pegawai* set themselves this goal.

[10] Fisher, *South-east Asia,* 287.

[11] Geertz, *Agricultural Involution,* 12-15.

[12] Widjojo Nitisastro, *Population Trends in Indonesia,* Ithaca, Cornell University Press, 1970.

[13] Bram Peper, 'Population Growth in Java in the 19th Century: a New Interpretation', *Population Studies,* vol. 24, 1970, 71-84.

[14] Widjojo Nitisastro, op.cit., 124.

[15] The classic study of the Dutch colonisation programme is K.J. Pelzer, *Pioneer Settlement in the Asiatic Tropics,* New York, American Geographical Society, 1948.

[16] Widjojo Nitisastro, op.cit., 234.

[17] Masri Singarimbun, 'Family planning in Indonesia', *Bulletin of Indonesian Economic Studies,* no. 10, 1968, 48-55.

[18] Nathan Keyfitz, 'The Long-term Prospect for Indonesian Population', *Bulletin of Indonesian Economic Studies,* vol. 9, no. 1, 1973, 107-9.

CHAPTER 6

Production for Export

THE VITAL IMPORTANCE of enlarging export earnings in Third World countries is heavily stressed by all development economists, and in most realistic national development plans the export sector is given special encouragement. National development inevitably necessitates a large increase in imports, which in the last analysis can only be paid for by enhanced exports; loans and most other forms of international aid in effect amount to a mortgaging of future exports. Indonesia has long been an important supplier of several key commodities to the world market, but because of its very large population, *per capita* foreign trade is very low, and is likely to remain so for the foreseeable future. No conceivable expansion of Indonesia's booming petroleum industry can greatly modify this situation, nor can it do very much in itself to raise the country's present very low *per capita* product. Over the present century, moreover, far-reaching changes have occurred in the structure and geographic origin of Indonesia's export trade, changes which have greatly complicated the problem of maintaining national cohesion.

It was seen from Chapter 3 that right until the end of the nineteenth century, Java, the most populous island, had long been the principal source of exports, and that export production was closely linked with indigenous agriculture. But with the coming of capitalist forms of enterprise, export production, for reasons which are analysed below, shifted progressively to the Outer Islands, above all to Sumatra. The potential consequences of this development were inadequately appreciated by the Dutch administration, largely because it took place so slowly; even by the 1920s, some 30 percent or so of export earnings still originated in Java, and although this share fell heavily in the 1930s, it was always hoped that this was a purely temporary phenomenon. But the range of Java's exports steadily diminished, becoming more and more dominated by sugar, and in fact the Great Depression gave the sugar industry a blow from which it never recovered, largely because it was primarily responsible for the growth behind tariff barriers of a modern sugar industry in what had long been Java's principal sugar market, British India. As a result of the occupation and the revolutionary war, the sugar industry was almost totally destroyed, but apart from a few years in the mid-1950s when a half-hearted attempt was made to restore an export component to the slowly rehabilitating industry, all of Java's sugar has been earmarked for domestic consumption.

This change, however, meant that Java's mounting food deficit and import bill were increasingly financed by the exports of the Outer Islands. But the structural changes described below, arising from the rapidly increasing importance of the mineral industries, have almost reduced Java's export contribution to vanishing-point; Jakarta, nevertheless, now disposes of foreign exchange resources inconceivable in the mid-1960s, whose allocation is fraught with consequence for Indonesia's economic well-being, and perhaps even its survival as a unitary state.

Agricultural Exports

Production for sale in more distant markets has long been a distinctive feature of Indonesian agriculture. The pepper from Sumatra and Borneo, and the cloves, nutmeg, and mace of Amboyna and Banda, constituted a highly organised trade well before the arrival of the Europeans, and during the colonial period the range of agricultural exports grew steadily. Some of these new exports consisted of crops long grown in the country for local consumption, but many were importations, brought by the Portuguese and the Dutch from the New World or from Africa. From the Americas came tobacco, cacao, tapioca, cinchona (source of the drug quinine), and, most important of all, Para rubber (*Hevea brasiliensis*). From Africa came coffee and the oil-palm. More than 40 crops featured in the export trade of the Netherlands Indies by the outbreak of World War II, although those of major importance never amounted to more than ten or so. Many of the crops introduced by Europeans, however, never developed a significant export trade, although they established an important place for themselves in indigenous subsistence agriculture.

During the eighteenth century Java supplanted the 'spice islands' as the principal source of export crops, and its dominance lasted until the end of the nineteenth century. Rice and indigo were initially of greatest importance, but during the nineteenth century coffee and sugar became the chief export items. Direct European interest in export-crop production was for long fitful and dilettante. But with the so-called Liberal period from 1870 onwards, and the new policy of assigning to private capital a major role in colonial economic development, direct European participation grew rapidly; the volume and range of agricultural exports augmented greatly, and by the turn of the century the European joint-stock company had firmly established itself as the dominant unit in export-oriented agriculture. These developments involved major changes in the geographic distribution of both public and private investment, and the preoccupation of the Dutch with Java, which had endured for almost three centuries, was gradually displaced in favour of one with Sumatra, where the physical and socio-economic environment proved especially favourable for export-crop production on a large scale. Java, it is true, retained its grip on its old export staples, coffee and sugar; but for a variety of reasons it proved unable to attract more than a very modest share of the investment in new lines of export-oriented agricultural production, many of which showed a high propensity for growth. Outside Java and Sumatra, Borneo and the Minahasa peninsula of Celebes with the islands to the north alone appeared capable of providing congenial environments for the development of the new agricultural activities made possible by the expanding world market for agricultural raw materials and foodstuffs. While Dutch capital inevitably spearheaded the development of corporate agriculture, the very liberal investment laws of the Netherlands Indies and the ease with which land could be acquired attracted much British, American, Franco-Belgian, Australian, and other foreign capital; indeed, among major industrial nations, only Japanese interests were unrepresented. The consequences of this massive investment in export-oriented agriculture, both by indigenous Indonesians reacting to the stimuli of the market and by aliens, were to be far-reaching.

By the outbreak of World War II the Netherlands Indies could well claim to represent the apogee of tropical export agriculture. The colony was on the threshold of becoming the world's largest exporter of natural rubber, and it was by far the largest exporter of copra, palm-oil, pepper, cassia, quinine (a vitally important drug in the days before synthetic anti-malarials), kapok, and tapioca. It was the second largest exporter of sisal, and but for the intervention of the war would quickly have attained the premier position. Before the onset of the Great Depression, it had been the second largest exporter of cane sugar. It was the third largest exporter of coffee and tea, and, with probably the world's lowest costs of production at the time, was steadily improving its competitive position in the production of the latter as against that of India and Ceylon. It was also the source of what was, and indeed still remains, the world's most highly priced agricultural product, the incomparable Deli cigar-wrapper tobacco. Its enormous estates attained levels of efficiency unmatched elsewhere in the world, and in rubber, tobacco, palm-oil, tea, quinine, and sisal, accounted for the greater part of total output, and for an even higher proportion of the best grades. But despite their undoubted efficiency, in many lines of production the estate industries were under increasing pressure from the competition of indigenous smallholders.

Smallholders and estates together generated some 60 percent of the Netherlands Indies export earnings in the 1930s, and although the volume of agricultural exports fell heavily during the Great Depression, with the notable exception of sugar most items had made a great recovery by the outbreak of World War II. But the trend was unmistakable; the traditional structure of export-originating agriculture appeared to be strongly reasserting itself, and the war and its aftermath merely accelerated this change. For until approximately the mid-nineteenth century, indigenous farmers had always constituted the principal source of exportable agricultural products; but as a result of the economic policies of the Liberal period, by the turn of the century some 90 percent of agricultural exports originated in the estate sector. Estate output continued to rise until the eve of World War II, but in the present century there has been a progressive increase in the contribution of indigenous growers to total export earnings. By 1914 their share of agricultural export earnings reached almost one-quarter, and by 1938 some 40 percent. With independence, the decline in the relative importance of the estate sector proceeded even more rapidly. By the mid-1950s estates contributed scarcely 40 percent of such earnings, and by 1970 less than 30 percent, despite the fact that throughout the lifetime of the republic a significant proportion of estate industry and for some years the whole of it, had been absorbed within the public sector.

To some extent at least, this decline was more apparent than real; moreover, it needs to be assessed against a background of stagnating or declining export-crop production, for it is impossible to draw any other conclusion but that independent Indonesia has so conducted its affairs that it has operated strongly to discourage both estate and smallholder enterprise alike. The proof of this contention is the remarkable upsurge of rubber and palm-oil production in nearby Malaysia, where a highly nationalist yet economically rational government has not only provided conditions under which estates have been able to attain rising levels of efficiency, but has also greatly stimulated smallholder production and, indeed, has devised machinery by which smallholders have been able to enjoy the fruits of technical progress in both field and factory, and to participate in capital-intensive enterprises previously closed to them. But in Indonesia, only in natural rubber has the pre-war level of output been exceeded, a largely fortuitous occurrence for which the Indonesian government can claim little credit. Output levels of most of the impressive array of agricultural exports of the Netherlands Indies had still not been regained by 1970; and in some lines there appeared virtually no possibility that the pre-war export volume could ever be regained, either because production had virtually ceased, as with sisal and cinchona, or because rising domestic demand appeared likely further to constrain any exportable surplus, as was the situation with coconut products. Much of the responsibility for this plight of the export-crop industries can be attributed to the excesses of the Sukarno regime, but it is surprising that the New Order has shown so little inclination to follow the example of Malaysia. Significant steps, it is true, have been made by the Suharto regime to improve the productive efficiency of the estate sector, including the government's own rundown estates; moreover, the glittering prospects of Indonesia's oil, gas, and other mineral and extractive industries, have operated to reduce the necessity for facing the difficult task of raising agricultural export earnings. As it was doing extremely well from the commodity boom of the early 1970s, and export earnings rose from some $600 million in 1965 to almost ten times this amount in 1974, it was unlikely that the administration was much moved by the realisation that it might have done substantially better still. More importantly, however, through its failure to take more positive steps to revitalise smallholder enterprise, the government was neglecting an obvious and effective way of ensuring a greater degree of much-needed social justice in an Indonesia in which every advance in economic fortune appeared to be accompanied by a progressively more inequitable distribution of wealth. Throughout the Third World the desire for economic growth is being steadily tempered by a rising clamour for a greater measure of social justice, and this development the Indonesian government will neglect at its peril.

The diminishing role of agricultural exports in the national economy is striking. With the destruction of much of the physical equipment of the important Netherlands Indies mining industries during World War II, agricultural products accounted for over 80 percent of total export proceeds in the early post-independence years, but with the gradual rehabilitation of mining activities and the failure of export-crop industries as a whole to grow, this proportion had fallen back to the more normal figure of some 60 percent by the mid-1960s. But thereafter decline was rapid; with the new Foreign Investment Law of 1967 and the opportunities open to the great multinational corporations for large profits in extractive industries, petroleum, timber, and metalliferous mineral production boomed, and by 1970 agricultural products contributed less than 40 percent of total export income. The rapidly rising income from oil exports had pushed this share to below 20 percent by 1972, and by 1974 it appeared that possibly no more than 10 percent of Indonesia's foreign-exchange earnings would be derived from its traditional agricultural staples, a situation scarcely conceivable a decade earlier.

A progressive shift away from a preoccupation with agriculture is of course regarded by most economists as evidence of substantial economic development in inter-tropical countries. In Indonesia these developments, however, did little to reduce the share of the workforce engaged in agriculture, or to increase incomes outside the great urban foci. In the early 1950s a distinguished development economist and one-time United Nations adviser to the Indonesian National Planning Board confided to one of the authors that he could not recommend the planting of a single additional rubber-tree in view of the menace of synthetic rubber. But as Little has argued, the opportunities for stimulating development and for raising rural incomes in Third World countries through the expansion of agricultural exports have been consistently and grossly underrated.[1] Smallholder rubber production in Sumatra, in fact, has been a profitable activity in Indonesia whenever the producer has been able to acquire the necessary inputs, but all too often he has encountered major difficulties in marketing his output, for over large parts of southern Sumatra many pre-war roads have disappeared. Moreover, he has been compelled to dispose of his output through official channels which have paid him substantially less than the market price, and in a soft and, until the later 1960s, a steadily depreciating currency, with which it was often impossible to buy the things that he considered necessary to persuade him to increase production. This situation inevitably encouraged the growth of a flourishing illegal barter trade across the Malacca Strait with Singapore and Malaysia, while in eastern Indonesia coconut smallholders similarly endeavoured to dispose of their output through illegal trading with the Philippines. The barter trade was estimated by IGGI, the international aid consortium of Indonesia's principal Western creditors, as costing the nation some $200 million annually in the mid-1960s; a decade later the government had still not succeeded in suppressing it completely. Indeed, it would not be too much to claim that both the rise of an important smallholder export-crop sector in the Netherlands Indies and its fitful survival in independent Indonesia occurred in spite of, rather than because of, government policy; the smallholder has never received much but lip-service. The relative decline of the estates since 1950 owes less to any encouragement or incentives to smallholder production than to the fact that, as alien-owned and managed enterprises, they were particularly vulnerable to an often irrational and xenophobic nationalism.

Thus crops whose production was largely an estate prerogative show heavy declines in output and export levels of the immediate pre-war years; these are products that for technical reasons need complex, lengthy, and expensive processing at the site of production or in close proximity to it, and include *kina* (cinchona), sisal, oil-palm, tea, and sugar. Before World War II some tea-leaf and a little sugar were also produced by smallholders under contract to estate factories, but the poorer quality and lower yields of smallholder output made integration with the handling of the estate's own output through the factory difficult, and most sugar-mills refused to handle such material even after official restrictions were lifted. On the other hand, crops whose cultivation required only inexpensive inputs, and whose processing was quickly and easily accomplished, were admirably suited to smallholder production, and in coconuts, pepper and other spices, kapok and tapioca, estates were never of any importance. In some crops of major export significance, such as coffee, tobacco, and, above all, natural rubber, smallholders and estates competed vigorously. In all of these, however, the simple methods of the past are being rapidly replaced by more sophisticated field and factory techniques in other major producing countries, a development that augurs ill for the Indonesian smallholder.

Nearly all of these export items are derived from either tree crops or herbaceous perennials, and, as noted earlier, smallholders have found production particularly attractive wherever it has been possible to incorporate it within the swidden system. The usual heavy clearing and planting costs of tree crops, and the long wait for these plantings to come into bearing, involve neither monetary nor opportunity costs (under swidden conditions), and, with improved transport both within the Netherlands Indies and outside, native growers reacted promptly to the price stimuli of the world market. The sawah system, in contrast, offered fewer and less rewarding opportunities for such cash-crop production. Production of perennials on ricefields themselves was out of the question, and although the *pekarangan* (house lots) supported dense stands of coconuts with a sprinkling of other exportable crops such as kapok, there was seldom any surplus for sale outside the village itself. Thus export-crop production was possible only through complex arrangements which periodically released land from rice production, and whose organisation required both capital and political power; it was also necessarily limited to the production of annuals, or of perennials which could be treated as annuals, a requirement which both sugar and tobacco satisfied. Hence, although Java did acquire a substantial estate sector, in large part through historical accidents in certain parts of the island which greatly facilitated planters' access to land, it never developed an important smallholder industry, and the link between the village and export production established under the Culture System was broken. Outside the sawah system, at elevations in west Java and on certain of the great volcanic massifs of the central and eastern portions of the island, a few indigenous farmers produced tea or coffee, usually in association with nearby estates. But from the most important of all smallholder activities, natural-rubber production, Java was almost totally excluded.

Political pull, of course, often reinforced technology in tipping the balance of advantage in favour of the estates, and although the Netherlands Indies government long declined to become a party to international restriction out of concern for 'native rights', the planters, as with their counterparts in contemporary Malaya, never lacked opportunities for impressing on government that rubber cultivation was a serious business best left to European enterprise. Moreover, there were many ways in which the planter could exert pressure on poorly paid government officers to take a charitable view of estate shortcomings or of infringements of regulations in order to cut costs. One such method was the practice of holding a public auction for the personal effects of retiring or transferred officials; those who had served the planters well could be sure of a good attendance, and bids far in excess of the real worth of each item. In the indirectly administered territories, the principalities of Jogjakarta and Surakarta in Java (the *Vorstenlanden*), and in the sultanates of east Sumatra, the planters were able to acquire land on extremely favourable terms which in practice involved the suppression of indigenous rights in the use of land. How the planters were able to acquire their extraordinary privileges in the *Vorstenlanden* has already been related; here, they not only possessed the right to use half the village rice-land each wet season, instead of one-third as in the directly administered parts of the island, but they also enjoyed the use of compulsory unpaid labour. Even after this feudal anachronism was finally removed as a result of the conversion introduced in 1918, the planters were still able to use as much land as before, and were compensated for the loss of unpaid labour by a reduction in their rent payments; not until 1935 were they obliged to pay the full rent.[2]

In the East Sumatra sultanates also, the planters' privileges were entrenched through historical accident. Nienhuys and the early planters preceded the effective imposition of Dutch rule, and the great estate companies such as the *Deli Maatschappij* and the *Senembah Maatschappij* which succeeded them always insisted on the integrity of the contracts negotiated with the rulers by the pioneers, in all dealings with the Batavia government. In return for a cash payment and a rental, which even with upward revisions with the passage of time was always low in relation to the real value of the land, the planters obtained access to vast areas of land over which it is doubtful that the local ruler exercised any real authority or enjoyed any rights at the time. The pre-colonial Malay sultanate on either side of the Malacca Strait was essentially a closely confined downstream, or *kuala*-based, entity, and the densely forested *ulu,* or headwaters, was avoided by all Malay peoples wherever possible; the transformation of the Malay princely state into a political unit embracing the whole of a catchment area was a deliberate act of European colonial policy. Under these 'agricultural concessions', the rights of the indigenous population in the land were ill-defined; in practise they were heavily restricted or suppressed as the planters sought to preserve the quality of the superb Deli tobacco. This, it was discovered, was best accomplished through a modified form of swidden agriculture, in which the land was allowed to revert to *belukar,* or secondary forest, for some 7 to 9 years after the taking of a tobacco crop. At such times it appeared that the indigenous population could use the land for food crops, but as virtually all of these were soil-depleting, more and more were proscribed, or cultivation forbidden entirely.

From tobacco the companies moved into the production of rubber, oil-palm, tea, and sisal, which was the last estate crop to appear in the Netherlands Indies. Although several non-Dutch organisations, such as the American Goodyear and U.S. Rubber Company; the British agency house Harrisons & Crosfield; and the Franco-Belgian Socfin also carved out agricultural empires from the forest, the Deli company so dominated the old east coast that the term 'Deli region' came to be attached to the collective sultanates of the area, and not merely that of Deli itself. The company owned and operated the Deli Spoorweg, the only private railway to survive into the independence period and still a profitable concern when finally taken over in 1958, and the city of Medan, the principal metropolitan focus of northern Sumatra with a population in the mid-1970s of virtually one million, was entirely its creation. Medan, in fact, was a company town, built as the administrative and service centre of the company's numerous enterprises. The company also provided the electricity and water-supply systems, built both the Sultan's *istana,* or palace, and the *masjid* (mosque), and constructed and operated the famous Hotel de Boer, a primary focus of planter social life.[3]

Access to large areas of land on virtually give-away terms was by no means the only advantage enjoyed by the Sumatran planters. The great estates were hacked out of the jungle at stupendous speed by virtually private armies of indentured Javanese labourers, whose conditions of life and work were all too often ruled by a Draconian discipline. Although the planters' preference was to continue to rely on the Chinese labour which had been employed by the pioneers, and whose organisation and supply could be conveniently left to the Chinese themselves, the use of Javanese immigrants resulted from the intervention of the Netherlands Indies government, which even before the turn of the century was concerned with the growing problem of landlessness. Immigrants were engaged under 'Coolie Ordinances', which made it a criminal offence for an indentured worker to leave his employment before the expiry of his articles and the full discharge of his debt. Although the proportion of 'free labour' in the east-coast estates grew steadily with the passage of time, penal-sanction clauses still governed indentured workers until the Great Depression, and even during the 1930s a central fingerprint registry was still maintained in Batavia to keep check on estate labourers who might attempt to return home. Not until 1941, almost on the eve of the Japanese attack, were the last relics of penal sanctions and the indenture system finally swept away.

This sad history, so strikingly different from that of the estates in the Malay peninsula, superimposed on a long tradition of debt bondage and the use of compulsory unpaid labour for government purposes in the Outer Islands, goes far to explain the uprisings against the *Oostkust* sultanates in 1946, and the post-independence difficulties of the foreign estates.[4] The picture was not entirely dark, of course. Planters' organisations such as *Avros,* the famous Rubber Planters' Union of east Sumatra, accepted that good labour relations were as important as scientific research in maintaining a high level of efficiency, organised an improved labour recruitment service, and urged improved dietary and living conditions for estate workers. The Netherlands Indies government continually sought to ensure that the legal obligations of the estates to all workers were scrupulously observed, and to uphold native rights in land. But there is no question that abuses of the Coolie Ordinances were common, and the fall-back position of the planters on the sanctity of their contracts with the rulers created endless delays. Hence in 1919 the government decided that no further agricultural concessions could be granted, and that as existing ones expired, they would be replaced by *erfpacht* leases, granted by the Batavia government under the provisions of the Agrarian Law of 1870. This enabled government to lease land unencumbered by native rights to aliens for up to 75 years, and was a major instrument in the policy of encouraging private capital investment in export-crop production. *Erfpacht* leases were first made in West and East Java, and were issued largely in respect of hilly or upland areas suitable for perennials, although the lessee could cultivate whatever crop he liked. But they never had time to become really important in Sumatra; as the concessions themselves ran for 75 years, conversion was slow, and even in 1938 almost 950,000 hectares was held under such tenure out of a total estate area of some 2.5 million hectares. Virtually all of this enormous area, much of which was unused because of the special requirements of the tobacco industry, lay in northern Sumatra.

Its resolve to preserve indigenous rights in land also caused the government to move against the privately owned estates possessing freeholds. These *particuliere landerijen* traced their origin to the land sales in west Java made by the Daendels and Raffles administrations of the early nineteenth century. By the end of the century many of these had been acquired by Chinese and were used for the cultivation of coffee and other cash crops. European companies also acquired title to some of these lands, and in 1910 Anglo-Dutch Plantations (later Anglo-Indonesian Plantations Ltd) acquired the largest and most famous of these estates, the P & T Lands (*Pamanoekan en Tjiasemlanden*). One of the pioneers of rubber cultivation in the Netherlands Indies, the company proceeded to create the largest rubber estates in Java. But abuse of their workers and tenants by the Chinese estate-owners, and a desire to make some show of reducing the economic privileges and position of the Chinese, had long caused government to consider acquiring privately owned estates, and developing the land for the public welfare.

This policy was finally launched in 1910, but financial stringency made acquisition a slow and fitful process; by the outbreak of World War I about a dozen estates had passed into government hands, and these, together with those properties developed by government for experimental research with new crops such as cinchona and oil-palm, constituted the government estates division of the Department of Agriculture. This well-managed unit, with a long record of scientific research and commercial profitability, passed as part of the assets of the Netherlands Indies government to independent Indonesia, when it was reconstituted as the *Pusat Perkebunan Negara* (National Plantation Centre), which with reorganisation eventually expanded to absorb the whole estate industry of the country with the takeover of all foreign estates in 1964. Proximity to the capital, for some of the P & T Lands lay within the Batavia Residency, made the few European-owned estates extremely tractable; Anglo-Indonesian Plantations continued to maintain excellent relations with the Indonesian government after the transfer of sovereignty, and in all probability was Java's largest single source of foreign-exchange earnings in the Sukarno period. The European estates in West Java avoided the squatter problems that plagued the East Sumatran estates in the post-war period, and their close association with the army in the guerrilla warfare with *Darul Islam,* for estates were prime targets for attack, made their position with the authorities somewhat more favourable than that of their Sumatran counterparts. But even when all forms of estate-land tenure were declared void in 1958-61, private freeholds accounted for less than 9 percent of the total estate area, and a substantial part of this had long been utilised for subsistence cropping by Sundanese or Javanese tenants.

Throughout the 1950s, the question of estate access to land remained a major issue in national policy. Without the assurance of a continuation of their leases for a reasonable period, the companies were not prepared to make the new investment necessary for improved efficiency and for a continued high level of export earnings, which, as noted, amounted to some 30 percent of the national total in the early 1950s. But this the weak and unstable coalitions could concede only at their peril. The question was pressing, for many of the early concessions and leases had fallen in, and the remainder would do by 1965. Much turned on what constituted a reasonable period. Suggestions for a 30-year extension were unattractive to the companies, as this would allow only one cycle of cultivation; after 30 years the productivity of the rubber-tree falls off, and oil-palms become too tall for economic harvesting. To justify the heavy investment in replanting, in new processing plants, and generally rehabilitating properties heavily damaged or neglected during the occupation and the revolutionary war, would, so the companies argued, need three cycles, a demand that no Indonesian government could concede.

Both in Parliament and in the country hostility generated by the past history of the estate industry was strong. It was further fed by the squatter problem, an issue that not only polarised the question of indigenous versus alien rights in land, but challenged the government's role in development policy and administered the final blow to the Wilopo cabinet. To stimulate local food production during the occupation, the Japanese invited inhabitants of the Batak highlands to settle on unused land in East Sumatra, much of which consisted of the 'reserves' of the tobacco estates, in accordance with their practice of cropping only every eight years or so. Long experience had shown the planters that any attempt to crop at more frequent intervals produced a great decline in quality, and as Deli tobacco was a speciality product, competing with other luxury items not on the basis of price but on its consistently superb quality, any diminution in the latter threatened the whole future of the industry. By occupying reserve land, squatters rendered the normal cycle of cultivation impossible, and a decline in both quantity and quality of output was inevitable. To have removed squatters established over many years would have required a major operation, but the problem was heightened by the continued influx of new waves of settlers, some of whom also squatted on land prepared for planting.[5] Although tobacco estates were most affected, some tea and sisal estates also suffered invasion, and the latter industry, the most capital intensive of all the estate industries of the Netherlands Indies, never recovered. Some estates in northern Tapanuli, a minor area of estate production, were also affected.

The squatters, it is true, were not local inhabitants, and their moral case was not perhaps as strong as it might otherwise have been. But they were well organised, and received enthusiastic support from left-leaning party wings and from the resurgent PKI. Squatters, whether urban or rural, constitute a most intractable problem for government in underdeveloped countries, for they have a strong moral case and usually develop substantial political strength. But they are a direct challenge to the authority of government itself. If not speedily removed, they invariably provoke further rounds of squatting, the expense and difficulty of removing them increases, and land earmarked for other purposes is sterilised and major development projects imperilled. They pay no taxes, for to require them to do so is an admission of legitimacy. For government to move against them is difficult and dangerous, but delay is worse still and is an encouragement to further defiance of government authority.

So it was in Indonesia. The *Masyumi* coalitions were conscious of the need to increase export earnings of the estates, and knew well that uncontrolled squatting in a country with Indonesia's agrarian structure could have potentially explosive consequences; that such fears were well grounded has already been seen. But all that was politically possible was a series of 'stand-still' agreements, in which the rights of existing squatters were conceded to their parliamentary supporters in return for a ban on new incursions. This demonstration of weakness produced its inevitable results, and after the fall of the Wilopo government no further serious effort was made to grapple with the squatter problem. The Deli company after many warnings finally withdrew from production, and gave notice that it would bring action in the courts of whatever country in which Indonesia or Indonesians attempted to market tobacco produced from its properties. A confused legal battle resulted, in which the marketing of Deli tobacco was transferred from Amsterdam to Hamburg and other centres, and sales were slow and laborious. Changing tastes in the market for tobacco, moreover, boded ill for Indonesia; a substitute for the perfect Deli leaf could be found in homogenised tobaccos and the plastic mouthpiece threatened all cigar-wrapper tobaccos. The increasing preference for the light Virginia tobaccos, even in Indonesia itself, prejudiced also the dark filler tobaccos of the old *Vorstenlanden* and Besuki. But, as with sugar, the revolution had virtually destroyed the old basis of the industry in Java, in which the companies rented village rice-land under the provisions of the Land Rents Ordinance of 1871. Thus, whereas the inter-war Netherlands Indies usually derived between 5 and 10 percent of its export earnings from tobacco, post-war Indonesia found itself a net importer.

There were other difficulties, however, confronting all estates. Labour was now well organised, and the Plantation Workers' Union of Indonesia (*Sarbupri*), one of the largest in the country, was solidly controlled by the communists and their supporters. On many estates a recalcitrant and hostile labour force did not work long enough to keep even patched-up processing machinery operating near optimum levels of output. Under Indonesia's rampant inflation, moreover, labour and other locally derived inputs became increasingly expensive, reducing Indonesia's competitive position in world markets; furthermore, the companies' ability to finance replanting and the re-equipping of estate factories was further jeopardised by discriminatory exchange rates for the rupiah which had the effect of reducing income from sales overseas, and by high taxes on profits. The acquisition of import licences for essential inputs, machinery, and spare parts involved inordinate labour and usually much bribery of officials. The issue of visas for key personnel from abroad encountered the same difficulties, invariably compounded whenever Dutch nationals were involved. Estates also suffered losses from pilfering, and from the tolls levied by the *panglimas* (local army commanders), which took a variety of forms.

Under such conditions, the estates operated much as they did during the Great Depression. Investment and maintenance were reduced to the barest minimum, and managers and their staffs not infrequently demonstrated great skill in keeping old equipment in operation with salvaged material.[6] However, by the mid-1950s, several companies had decided to run down their operations in Indonesia; properties were rapidly written off, and those whose operation presented special difficulties, or which were unlikely ever to repay the costs of rehabilitation, were sold off to Indonesian buyers at a fraction of their replacement cost. Companies by this time were very willing to comply with the government request for the employment of Indonesians in managerial capacities, for these could more easily reach accommodation with local officials and the *panglimas*, sometimes through the use of 'sweeteners' which some Europeans at least had scruples against using. By underdeclaring output and under-invoicing exports, an estate could create a margin for itself; sharing this with the appropriate officials could enable it to keep in operation even when the position on paper appeared hopeless. In conjunction with the large losses from pilfering, particularly serious in the case of rubber estates, such practices suggest that estate output may not have declined as much as appeared. But the regional revolts of 1957-58 were a further disruption to the East Sumatran estate industry; rebel forces not only impeded regular operations, but by attacking estate factories at times brought production to a complete standstill. Even after the collapse of the revolts, guerrilla bands continued to menace estates, and in one attack the factory of one of the largest oil-palm estates was completely destroyed. A decade later, this estate was still inoperative.

The years of Guided Democracy were traumatic in the extreme for the estate industries. In 1958 the freeholds of all privately owned estates were abolished, and all Dutch-owned estates were taken over, as described in Chapter 4. Administration of the newly acquired properties was entrusted to a new body, the *PPN Baru*. But inevitably, Indonesia's slender resources of technological and managerial estate expertise were still further extended. The concern of the army at this extension of the influence of its leftist rivals soon found expression in the attachment of army officers to several estates, although these took little part in the individual estate operations. Two years later, all foreign-owned estates were made subject to the new Basic Agrarian Law, which was directly derived from Article 33 of the 1945 constitution; this laid down that the land and water, and the natural resources therein, were to be controlled by the state and were to be utilised for the Indonesian people. Only Indonesian citizens could own land in fee simple, but corporations legally registered in Indonesia could apply for conversion of existing land rights to a new right of enterprise-use *(guna-usaha)*, although this could not exceed 20 years' duration. The Basic Agrarian Law also provided for the issue of new rights for up to 25 years, with the possibility of further extension. This provision was, of course, of minimal interest to the companies. Even in Malaysia they were by this time well launched on a policy of reducing their landholdings and concentrating effort on the best properties, and the acquisition of new land for their Indonesian affiliates in the face of Indonesia's increasingly hostile sociopolitical climate for foreign investment was out of the question. But if the new legislation did not go very far to meet the requirements of the companies, it did end the uncertainties of the past, although it was clear that conversion would involve an undertaking to step up replanting and research, and even a cession of part of the planted area. Yet scarcely had the companies begun to comply with the new requirements and the PPN undergone further transmogrification through a merger of the old and new organisations, than Indonesia again showed that economic considerations were to be entirely subservient to foreign policy. In 1961 all Socfin (a Franco-Belgian pioneer of the oil-palm industry in South-east Asia) properties in Sumatra were taken over as a reprisal for the murder of Patrice Lumumba in the Congo, and in 1964 nearly 150 British, American, Swiss, French, and Italian estates were also seized, as reprisals for overt or covert support of the new state of Malaysia.

It may just be true that in 1960 the PPN was performing about as well as could reasonably be expected given the enormous difficulties it confronted in the form of political pressure and rampant inflation, and the 1957 ban on strikes did ease some problems.[7] But its greatly enlarged responsibilities and Indonesia's steady drift into economic anarchy heavily eroded both morale and effort, and the hopes of the early 1960s of averting further deterioration of the capital stock of the estate industries were not realised. Nevertheless, the American estates, though placed under 'surveillance', experienced little or no interference, and were able to retain their own managements. If this appeared odd in the light of Sukarno's extravagant anti-American outbursts, there were nevertheless good reasons for adopting a more benign attitude towards the American properties, for United States espousal of the cause of Indonesian independence had several historical antecedents. Aceh vainly sought American military assistance in combating the encroachments of the Dutch, even offering the cession of part of its territory; but many Americans strongly supported the cause of Acehnese independence.[8] Americans had long endeavoured to eliminate the ugly face of Dutch capitalism in the Indies; the American estates had never employed indentured labour, and, through the adoption of discriminatory duties on commodities produced by penal-sanction labour, the United States put heavy pressure on the Dutch to abandon the practice. The American estates, moreover, had pioneered with improved housing, medical attention, and diet for their workers, and were much more generous than were their British and Dutch counterparts in making the fruits of their large research programmes available to others. They had refused to resume operations after the Japanese surrender so long as Dutch rule continued, and their Sumatran properties were first worked by *Avros*. Moreover, American enterprises, under instructions from the State Department, resisted all rebel blandishments during the regional revolts of 1957-58, and continued to pay taxes and duties to the central government.

Governments, of course, are not noted for their gratitude, and, despite this impressive record, technical reasons were probably more telling, just as in the case of the petroleum industry, which also remained largely free from interference. There were some small and isolated American properties, but even most of these were attached to units of enormous size, employing many tens of thousands of workers; with all the resources of Indonesian trained manpower in estate operations strained to the utmost, it was easier to turn a blind eye to the continued autonomy of the American giants. The American rubber estates in east Sumatra included the largest of their kind ever created, very large even in relation to other giant rubber estates elsewhere in South-east Asia. Through amalgamation of several units, HAPM (Hollandsch-Amerikaansche Plantage Maatschappij), a subsidiary of the United States Rubber Company (Uniroyal), by 1912 had created a few miles north of Kisaran a solid block of some 30,750 hectares (76,000 acres), and in 1925 this was raised to nearly 32,000 hectares (79,000 acres). Goodyear's Wingfoot estate of some 16,200 hectares (40,000 acres) east of Rantauperapat, created between the wars, was the world's second largest rubber estate, and its Dolok Merangir property north of Permatangsiantar reached nearly 6,900 hectares

(17,000 acres). The largest rubber estates elsewhere in South-east Asia are the 12,000-hectare (nearly 29,000 acres) Chuup estate of Socfin in Cambodia, but largely inoperative since the extension of the Vietnam War, and the Tanah Merah estate of Guthrie or the Ladang Geddes of Dunlop, both in peninsular Malaysia and nearly 7,300 hectares (18,000 acres) apiece. Keeping the enormous processing plants of these American giants in operation was a formidable problem, and the fact that they were 'captive' further complicated the economics of operation.[9] Thus, although the smaller and isolated American estates could not escape the problems faced by the entire industry, the larger units were left to their own devices. They had, however, also suffered severely. HAPM, renamed PTUS (US Co. Ltd.) after independence, found that some 7,000 hectares of trees had been removed to make way for food production during the occupation, and it was compelled to cede 30 percent of its total planted area in return for a 12-year extension of its exploitation rights under the provisions of the Basic Agrarian Law. In contrast to the British-and Dutch-owned estates, however, the American giants had launched vigorous replanting programmes in the early 1950s. Nevertheless, despite the more favourable age distribution of their material, even the American estates were operating at only about half their potential capacity by the end of the Sukarno period.

As part of its agreements with Indonesia's creditors, the *Ampera* cabinet in 1966 undertook to return all sequestered properties to their previous owners, and at long last it appeared that some of the more serious obstacles to a rehabilitation of the estate industries might be removed. Yet few of the British companies viewed the prospects of a return to Indonesia with any enthusiasm; to extend to Indonesia the far-reaching technological improvements in both field and factory of their Malaysian operations would require very heavy new investment whose future profitability was obscure in the extreme, and even to provide housing and accommodation for staff would pose serious problems, as this the government declined to return.[10] London Sumatra Plantations Ltd (a Harrisons & Crosfield subsidiary), the largest of the British groups in North Sumatra, however, joined Goodyear, Uniroyal, and some of the largest other foreign estate companies in pledging very large sums for the rehabilitation of their properties during the Second Five-Year Plan.

With the possibility of a revitalised and profitable private-sector estate industry after two decades of decay and neglect, there remained the problem of the estates within the public sector. That the reports of the early 1960s of mismanagement and deterioration of the government's own estates were broadly true, is suggested by the decision of the World Bank a decade later to make three loans totalling some $42 million for the rehabilitation of government rubber and oil-palm estates, a sum almost equal to that pledged by the large foreign estate companies; commenting on the condition of the government estates in the Lampung area of South Sumatra, the bank noted that only about one-quarter of the total estate area of nearly 35,000 hectares remained under cultivation.[11] But smallholders, it was clear, would have to wait for the Second Five-Year Plan for any substantial government assistance.

SMALLHOLDER RUBBER

Until its displacement by petroleum in the later 1960s, rubber was Indonesia's largest net earner of foreign exchange, and it is the only export crop whose production is substantially above that of the pre-war years. But the brilliant future that was predicted for the industry after World War II based on its large and buoyant smallholder sector and its very favourable age composition of producing material *vis-à-vis* contemporary Malaya has not been realised.[12] Malaysia's output of over 1.3 million tons in 1971 was probably half as much again as that of Indonesia, and will be more than twice as large long before 1980; moreover, it comprised a far higher proportion of sophisticated and technically classified material. That rubber is extraordinarily simple both to grow and to process, yields a regular year-round income with very little labour, is tolerant of a wide variety of soils, and can withstand substantial abuse and neglect, makes it highly attractive to estates and smallholders alike. About 700 of the 1,100 or so estates in Indonesia are planted to rubber, with a total planted area of a little more than 500,000 hectares. But the area and output of the far larger smallholder sector are very imperfectly known; the official figure of 1.3 million hectares is that derived by the Dutch in discharging the Netherlands Indies' obligations under the International Rubber Agreement (1934-41) and was a gross underassessment even at the time.[13]

The rubber industry came to the Netherlands Indies from Malaya, and was likewise exclusively an estate interest in the early years. As in Malaya also, the planting interests exerted heavy pressure on government to discourage direct smallholder competition with estate lines of production. But although the growth of socialist representation in the Hague Parliament led to a greater concern for native rights, the final abolition of restrictions on smallholder production and trade coincident with the great rubber boom of 1908-12 merely bowed to the inevitable. Improvements in transport both within the Indies and outside had brought many indigenous farmers within the compass of the world market, and, as earlier noted, favourable prices for coffee, copra, and rubber led to a marked expansion of smallholder output; the government could not have prevented such a development, even if it had wanted to do so.

Smallholders provided further striking evidence of their responsiveness to price stimuli during the Stevenson Restriction Scheme (1922-28), when the British territories of Malaya and Ceylon, which then controlled more than two-thirds of world output, endeavoured to force up prices by restricting output and prohibiting new planting. The result of this 'price umbrella' was a great expansion of smallholder planting in the Netherlands Indies, which refused to become a party to restriction out of concern for 'native welfare.' By 1934 smallholder output virtually matched that of estates. When the Dutch finally acceded to restriction under the International Rubber Agreement (1934-41), only gradually did the enormous area of smallholder plantings and the smallholder's very low costs of production become apparent. All estimates of smallholder output proved in fact to be far too low. In densely forested and thinly populated southern Sumatra and southern and eastern Borneo, to differentiate between ladang rubber and *belukar,* or secondary forest, was enormously difficult, and the figures of smallholder area based on a 'tree count' of the mid-1930s were spurious. Because of the virtual impossibility of determining smallholder output and regulating it at its source, Dutch control was largely exercised through special export taxes, but it is clear that much new planting continued even after prohibition. Some of this was the result of self-sown seedlings, but in view of the enormous area potentially suitable for rubber and the limited resources for policing it, large-scale evasion was all too easy, although the authorities at the time considered the danger slight.

Indonesia thus inherited a major industry that the colonial power knew little of, and certainly had done nothing to promote; moreover, because of the large extent of new planting in the interwar period, it had a much more favourable age composition of trees than had its Malayan smallholder counterpart, which, except for a few years in the depths of the Great Depression, had never been free of restriction since the early 1920s. This large new mature area could generate a great increase in output once market conditions became favourable, and in 1950, with the high prices of the Korean War, Indonesia swiftly became the world's largest producer and exporter, displacing Malaya from the premier position. But in 1947 planting restrictions in Malaya were finally abandoned, and, beset with the pressing problem of the 'Emergency', the British firmly set the country on the path to full independence, with a strong commitment to the maintenance of a high rate of economic growth.

But as has been shown, the latter never had any high priority in newly independent Indonesia, which, having lost the advantage of what had been, in effect, unilateral restriction by Malaya, continued to act in a manner that was a positive disincentive to the exercise of peasant initiative. Over large parts of Sumatra and Kalimantan, pre-war roads had disappeared, pushing up smallholder costs enormously. Imported inputs became difficult and expensive to obtain, and smallholders had no opportunity to upgrade their production from the traditional slab and lump rubber, which required remilling for acceptance in foreign markets, an operation still largely performed in the ports of the Malayan peninsula. Unrealistic prices set by government agencies encouraged producers to do what they had always done when times were hard and prices were low—resort to the barter trade. Such trade had been quite common during the Great Depression.[14] Given the extraordinarily favourable conditions for the smuggler, with an intricate physical interlocking of land and sea, it is doubtful that it can ever be completely stamped out.

Most important for the future, nearly all of the smallholder rubber consists of unselected material of low productivity, as indeed does most smallholder new planting as well. Modern high-yielding clonal material can yield more than two metric tons of rubber per hectare annually, but all such material is in very short supply in Indonesia, for to produce it is both time-consuming and expensive. Malaysia's large block-planting and replanting schemes have been closely linked with the development of special facilities for propagating such material, and indeed, on government-financed schemes the use of unselected material is forbidden. The estates, moreover, have long been engaged in developing improved clones in the research and development estate units of the respective agency houses, and this private research effort is buttressed by a first-class national research institution, the Rubber Research Institute in Kuala Lumpur, which touches all sections of the industry. Few of these things exist in Indonesia; as noted, private research by the estate sector was moribund throughout the greater part of the Sukarno era, and the government estates, many of which were initially research units of the Netherlands Indies Department of Agriculture, were in even poorer shape. With large areas still capable of being brought under cultivation, new planting is certainly easier for the Indonesian smallholder than his

Malaysian counterpart, who, lacking access to new land, must suffer the temporary income loss inevitable with replanting. But there is an elaborate official machinery to finance a large part of this cost, and although Indonesia has tried to emulate the Malaysian organisation, its replanting schemes are largely on paper, and nothing comparable with the Malaysian State Rubber Replanting Boards yet exists. Hence, by 1970 the Malaysian average smallholder output of nearly 785 kilograms per tapped hectare (700 pounds per acre) annually was probably more than twice that of the Indonesian smallholder industry, and the disparity was steadily widening; indeed, this figure was probably far in excess of that of the Indonesian estate sector.

Far-reaching changes in factory techniques have accompanied those in the field in Malaysia's ebullient rubber industry, and the traditional unsophisticated ribbed smoked sheet (RSS) is rapidly giving way to crumb rubbers, latices, and technically classified rubbers of guaranteed chemical and physical characteristics. Such plants offer substantial economies in both capital and operating costs, and can use all kinds of *hevea* material, including cup-lump and scrap. Indonesia's first crumb-rubber plant did not commence operations until 1968, but development thereafter was rapid; by 1971 output had reached 100,000 tons, and production of 250,000 tons was forecast for 1973, out of a total rubber output of 850,000 tons. Yet despite the government's desire to cut out the middleman and processing services performed for Indonesian smallholders by Singapore and Penang, and to encourage direct exports of locally processed material, few smallholders have access to the new facilities for producing more sophisticated rubbers.

OTHER CROPS

The prospects of a few other export crops merit brief examination. For most of these the immediate goal is to regain pre-war levels of output and exports, but, as mentioned, for some, such as *kina* (cinchona) and sisal, the prospects seem dismal. Nor does it seem at all likely that Indonesia can ever export more than 2 million tons of sugar annually, as it did in the 1920s, and the most pressing task of the sugar industry is to expand so as to satisfy the domestic market. For oil-palm products and tea, however, such a target is perhaps attainable.

The Netherlands Indies oil-palm industry, the most efficient in the world in the 1930s, has suffered greatly. Unlike rubber, which can withstand much abuse and which will even repay lengthy neglect with an additional 'flush' output when tapping is resumed, the oil-palm needs constant and meticulous attention; if this is not given, rapid deterioration is inevitable. Unharvested fruits left on the tree or fallen on the ground encourage rats and other pests which are difficult to eradicate. Fruits must be harvested when exactly ripe, and the bunches carried immediately to the processing factory, if a high-quality product with a low 'free fatty acid' content is to be maintained. There are substantial economies of scale in palm-oil production, the principal product of the South-east Asian estate industry (the kernels, which yield an oil similar to that of coconut oil, are a by-product); transport systems are elaborate and factories large and expensive structures, with pressurised 'digesters' for cooking the fruit bunches and hydraulic presses for expressing the oil.

An oil-palm estate thus requires a diligent and efficient labour force, capable of maintaining a continuous supply of perfectly ripe fruit to the factory, which in turn must be kept in operation at or near full capacity for as long as possible. Independent Indonesia has never been able to meet these conditions, and in consequence has been bypassed by a modern agricultural bonanza at least as spectacular as that of the great rubber boom early in this century. Rising world demand for fats and oils in the post-war period has sparked an almost explosive growth in oil-palm cultivation, for the tree has by far the highest yields per unit area of any oilseed crop. Its principal beneficiary has been Malaysia. The oil-palm industry came to Malaya from east Sumatra during World War I, but development was very slow, and by 1939 the industry was less than half the size of that of the Netherlands Indies. Really rapid growth, however, came after the end of the 'Emergency' (1948-60), when the country's full potential for the crop was slowly recognised; one after the other, estate companies which had never previously participated in production replanted old rubber or coconuts to oil-palm wherever soils and terrain were suitable, and a large programme of new planting was launched by the government itself, with much technical assistance from the estate sector, for its block-planting smallholder schemes. In a little more than a decade over 350,000 hectares were replanted or new planted to oil-palm, and Malaysia zoomed to the position of world's largest producer and exporter while the Indonesian industry stagnated. Perhaps fortunately for Indonesia, its traditional competitors, Zaire (ex-Belgian Congo) and Nigeria, were themselves stricken with acute political and economic disorganisation, but all of these producers' losses were Malaysia's gain, and the country is now indisputably the leader of the world industry.

Restoring competitive efficiency in the Indonesian oil-palm industry is thus a much more demanding problem than that confronting its natural rubber. The PPN was never capable of operating efficiently even the estates it acquired from the Netherlands Indies, and coping with those acquired by takeovers of the Sukarno period was an impossible task. Damaged and worn-out factory equipment has not been replaced and the lack of replanting (oil-palms are replaced when they become too tall for safe and economic harvesting) means that estates have a large stock of over-tall trees which cannot be properly harvested, thus ensuring a continuation of the pest problem. In 1971 it was announced that one of the three World Bank loans for the resuscitation of government estate agriculture would be allocated to oil-palm, and that some 8,000 hectares of new plantings would be made in Sumatra during the Second Five-Year Plan. This, however, is hardly enough to ensure Indonesia's customary place in the industry, and there are still no plans for smallholder participation. As the oil-palm has traditionally been a speciality of but a few Agency Houses, Indonesia does not have the range of expertise now available to the Malaysians; its own estate companies are, in any case, preoccupied with the rehabilitation of their own neglected properties. The gap between the two producers seems certain to widen further before it begins to narrow.

Tea is also an estate industry, but has a minor smallholder component. Unlike rubber and oil-palm, it is a crop of the highlands, and the most important producing area is the Priangan highlands south of Bandung around Malabar and Sentosa, where the industry is entirely an estate operation. The largest estates, however, are located in the Permatangsiantar (usually, Siantar) highlands of East Sumatra, which also contains some smallholder production of green leaf for processing at estate factories. Tea production is extremely labour-intensive, and the rising cost and militancy of labour have greatly reduced the industry's competitive standing. Many gardens (as estates are usually called in the tea industry) were overdue for replanting even by the mid-1950s, but most European estates, through careful pruning and control of blister blight, had managed to keep their material reasonably healthy and productive. As with all Indonesian agriculture, however, the ban on the import of pesticides with the foreign-exchange difficulties of the 1960s and the rising price of fertilisers made operations increasingly more difficult. The industry's main need, however, is still for a more productive labour force, which has become all the more necessary with the entry of East African producers, especially Kenya and Malawi, into large-scale production. These have the world's lowest costs in the industry, and have the advantage of substantial help from the Commonwealth

Development Corporation in setting up a smallholder industry linked with central processing. Labour problems in fact compelled the larger Siantar estates to contract for part of their leaf supply to smallholder tenants, but the productivity of the smallholders is still far too low. Java and Sumatra tea have always been quality products in the industry, unlike the 'fillers' of Assam, and for the maintenance of quality there again appears no substitute for the experience of the estates.

The government's tea estates in Priangan have also been the subject of a World Bank loan. In the early 1950s much of the *kina* of this area was replanted to tea in view of the pre-eminence of the new synthetic anti-malarials developed during World War II, but continued production of quinine has nevertheless been found desirable, and World Bank assistance has been extended to rehabilitating what was once considered the greatest achievement of the Dutch plantation industry in the Indies.

A final mention may be made of the sugar industry, which has already received comment in connection with indigenous agriculture. The industry is now entirely state-owned, the substantial Chinese interest having been taken over in the 1950s even before the appropriation of the Dutch interests. Several of the mills destroyed during the revolutionary war were rebuilt with loans from *Bank Industri Negara,* but output and sugar yields have greatly declined. Villages in sugar areas of East and Central Java are still compelled to release rice-land for sugar cultivation in return for rents fixed by the central government, but these have always been low in real terms. Sugar areas nevertheless appear among the most prosperous districts in Java, and have a high proportion of their sawahs under high-yielding rices. But output is insufficient even for domestic needs, and since the 1960s much has been heard of the need for a new industrial structure, in which sugar would be grown as a dry crop in the *Tanah Seberang* much as it is in the greater part of the inter-tropical world. After vainly trying to establish a viable industry in Sumatra, the government has finally sought assistance and a United Nations Development Program study has contracted with the two well-known British sugar groups, Tate and Lyle and Bookers, to advise on the prospects of a new industry.

This survey of the agricultural export industries underlines that although there is a definite and perhaps necessary place for state participation in large-scale export-crop production, partly to provide much-needed competition for private-capital estate activities which tend towards oligopoly, and partly to ensure a place for smallholder participation in the interests of social justice, the experience and technical skill of the private estate sector is a valuable national asset, and that whatever the record of the past, the destruction of the estates is a major national disaster. Moreover, as the experience of Malaysia testifies, the foreign-owned estate companies are quite prepared to assist the state to establish its own enterprises, either direct, in joint venture, or on a smallholder contract basis with factory central processing. True, these services come at a monetary and political price. But the experience of Malaysia, with a natural-rubber industry nearly twice as large and an oil-palm industry four times as large as its respective Indonesian counterparts, is eloquent testimony that it is one well worth paying.

Mining Industries

Unlike the production of export crops, mining is highly localised and employs only a tiny fraction of the nation's labour force. Nonetheless, it has become progressively more important in Indonesia's economy, and whereas less than 15 percent of total export earnings were derived from mining in 1928, in 1972 this proportion stood at about three-quarters. Since the later 1960s petroleum has been the premier export, and with the expectation of continuously high petroleum prices, indifferent prospects for the nation's rubber industry, and the likelihood of increased production of other minerals, the mining sector will long remain a principal source of revenue. Yet, in view of popular myths about Indonesia's wealth of resources, three remarkable features of this development require emphasis.

Firstly, the great economic importance of mining is based on the exploitation of a narrow range of minerals and fossil fuels; indeed, apart from the outstanding role of petroleum and tin, only coal, bauxite, nickel, and manganese have been worked to any extent in the recent past. Although maps of so-called 'mineral resources', littered as they are with pictorial symbols, leave a different impression, many known deposits are too small and isolated to warrant commercial exploitation. Secondly, there is a surprising poverty of knowledge about Indonesia's geology and mineral deposits. Geological work of high quality was carried out under Dutch rule, but it was largely academic, concerned with problems such as orogenesis and vulcanism, and, notwithstanding its involvement in production, the Netherlands Indies government was more desirous of promoting commercial agriculture than of stimulating the development of mining. When Van Bemmelen published his two-volume *The Geology of Indonesia* in 1949, broad patterns were known, but there had been little detailed geological mapping, and other than unpublished results of work by private companies, only a limited assessment of mineral potentialities. Although foreign geologists were hired for investigatory work under Sukarno, even in 1970 only 5 percent of Indonesia's land area had been surveyed in detail; general reconnaissance had been done in three-quarters of the country, but one-fifth of its area remained geologically unknown. To remedy this deficiency, in recent years foreign contractors have been encouraged to undertake mineral exploration. Frequently granted prospecting rights to huge areas in less well-known parts of the country, these contractors are obliged to report their findings to government after a fixed period, and then have first option for further exploration or for the working of any suitable deposits. The first contract of this type signed under the Foreign Investment Law of 1967 gave Freeport Sulphur Indonesia, a subsidiary of the American Freeport Sulphur Company, the right to search for copper in the Ertsberg of Irian. In addition to the massive search for offshore oil and gas, later contracts have covered exploration for nickel in Sulawesi, Halmahera, and Irian, and bauxite and uranium in Kalimantan, while the American Kennecott Copper Corporation has acquired rights of general mineral exploration in large parts of Central Java, West Sumatra, and Irian. Though much of this work is incomplete, several important finds have been made, including, for instance, confirmation by Freeport Sulphur Indonesia of significant copper-ore reserves in Irian, from which exports began in 1972, and the discovery of bauxite by the Aluminium Company of America (ALCOA) in West Kalimantan.

Despite its current importance, however, the development of the mining sector was retarded in the first fifteen years of independence by a combination of government inactivity and outdated regulations inherited from the colonial era, and in general production fell. For much of the nineteenth century the right to exploit minerals was held exclusively by the Netherlands Indies government, and although in areas outside effective Dutch jurisdiction production was in non-government hands as in the west Borneo gold-fields,[15] within the territories controlled by the Dutch the government itself operated the mines, as with tin in Bangka and coal in south-east Borneo. Private foreign investment in mining began with the working of the Billiton tin deposits after 1860 and rose to prominence with the growth of the petroleum industry. The Mining Law of 1899 established the principle that mineral resources were the property of the state, in which was vested the right to mine. Under this law and its subsequent amendments in 1910 and 1918 which were designed mainly to reserve an increased proportion of profits for government, provincial administrations were responsible for issuing prospecting licences. Concessions for exploitation were granted by the Governor-General for a maximum of 75 years to the holder of a prospecting licence who could 'prove the presence of the mineral or minerals he wants to mine in the area concerned and the technical possibility of their exploitation'.[16] Certain regions were reserved for prospecting and exploitation by or on behalf of government which in 1918 also acquired the prospecting and mining rights to all fossil fuels. These rights, however, could be transferred to private enterprise under special contracts. After independence the government expressed its intention of introducing new legislation to govern mining; but this was delayed and a law of 1951 stated that no new concessions would be granted for mining until fresh regulations were enacted. By preventing exploration, this seriously hampered development of the industry and it is only since the introduction of a new Mining Law in 1960 and, more particularly, the Foreign Investment Law of 1967, that there has been a sustained growth of output. Although the most striking increases in output have occurred in the petroleum industry, production of tin, nickel, bauxite, copper, and manganese is also rising.

OIL AND GAS

Production of petroleum began in the 1880s and by the Japanese occupation the Netherlands Indies was the world's fifth largest oil producer. As an easily recognisable separate foreign component in the economy, the industry had a chequered history in the strongly nationalist early years of independence. Output grew slowly, but the industry was hampered by being confined to production from pre-war concessions. After 1963, however, petroleum products displaced rubber as the country's principal export earner and since the late 1960s the petroleum industry has been the most dynamic sector of the economy. Output in the early 1970s rose rapidly and the future prospects of large oil and gas strikes both on land and offshore are bright. Apart from its vast continental shelf and an insularity affording relatively easy seaborne transport, the Indonesian petroleum industry is favoured in other respects. In a world increasingly concerned with pollution, Indonesia's oil is of low sulphur content, and commands a premium price. As the only major producer between the Middle East and the American Pacific coast, it is well located to serve the growing demands of Japan for both oil and gas; in 1973 Japan took some 71 percent of Indonesia's total exports of crude oil and nearly 91 percent of its exports of refined products, together meeting some 15 percent of Japan's total oil imports. Indonesian oil is increasingly in demand in the

United States and in South-east Asia, and its availability is independent of the Israeli-Arab conflict which bedevils the Middle East industry; domestic consumption is slight, so that nearly 80 percent of total production is available for export, and, despite an anticipated 14 percent per annum increase in domestic consumption over the period of *Repelita* II, this proportion will remain unchanged. Finally, Indonesia's unique production-sharing system ensures that companies know exactly what their future costs will be, and avoids the endless haggles over 'posted' and realised prices in countries where the old concession system prevails. In fact, Indonesia in the early 1970s offered the foreign oil-producers the most profitable deal available in any major oil-producing country, and, with the Middle East countries moving rapidly to complete nationalisation, it is scarcely surprising that the country elicited a great many applicants for new production contracts.

Until the late 1960s, the only foreign oil companies in Indonesia were those with concessions from the Netherlands Indies government. The oldest, and the largest producer in colonial times, was the Bataafsche Petroleum Maatschappij (BPM), formed by a merger in 1907 of the Royal Dutch and Shell companies; such was the origin of the world's second largest oil company. BPM possessed concessions in Acheh, north Sumatra, south Sumatra, east Java, and in eastern Borneo, and operated a refinery at Plaju near Palembang. Renamed PT Shell Indonesia after independence, when its concessions in northern Sumatra and Java were not restored, this company suffered most from nationalist pressures, although as a 'mixed enterprise' it escaped the nationalisations of 1957. Also dating from before World War I was the local subsidiary of Jersey Standard (Esso, later Exxon), the Nederlandsche Koloniale Petroleum Maatschappij, with concessions in south Sumatra and a refinery at Sungai Gerong, also on the Musi river near Palembang. This company, in which Mobil also possessed an interest, became PT Stanvac Indonesia after independence, although Mobil's interest disappeared in 1960 with the break-up under American anti-trust legislation of the Standard Vacuum Oil Company. Another pair of the seven great 'major' oil companies began operations between the wars, through the creation of the Nederlandsche Pacific Petroleum Maatschappij, a subsidiary of Standard Oil of California (Socal, or Chevron) and the Texas Corporation (now Texaco); NPPM began operations in the mid-1930s inland of Dumai in north-central Sumatra, and is now known as PT Caltex Pacific Indonesia. During the occupation and revolutionary war, oil installations suffered heavy damage, but after some delay these were restored and the refineries at Plaju and Sungai Gerong were rebuilt and extended. To facilitate this the Netherlands Indies government had instituted 'let-alone' agreements, which were taken over and continued by the Indonesian government. These permitted the companies to retain the balance of their foreign earnings and to remit profits, in return for a fixed payment into the Indonesian Foreign Exchange Fund.

Both Shell and Stanvac had explored most of their existing concessions prior to the occupation; denied new areas to work, both found it difficult to expand production after independence. In contrast, Caltex had only commenced to work its central Sumatran concessions when the Japanese attacked; with the development of its rich Minas fields in the 1950s, Caltex soon emerged as by far the largest producer. Caltex did not have a refinery in the country, so that while production of crude oil rose substantially between 1949 and 1964, the output of refined products was comparatively stagnant. Most of this production originated from oil produced from 40-year concessions granted under the 1918 amendment of the 1899 Mining Law, and these were rapidly approaching expiry date. By the later 1950s each of the foreign companies urgently needed new concessions to replace those already worked out, or due to expire. But a decision on new exploration was held up pending a new mining law to replace the old colonial legislation, for all nationalists wanted an industry under Indonesian control. The future of the petroleum industry inevitably involved the whole question of the place of foreign capital in Indonesia and the financing of its grandiose yet unrealistic Eight-Year Development Plan of 1961-68, drafted by a judge better known as a poet and mystic, and full of revolutionary symbols; and on this issue Indonesians had long been deeply divided. With the transition to Guided Democracy, all of the three components of the 'triangle of forces' had acquired a piece of the oil industry, which they were determined to enlarge.

The state had in fact an interest in the industry since its birth through its heritage from the Netherlands Indies government, which entered into a joint venture with Shell in the Nederlandsch-Indische Aardolie Maatschappij (NIAM) in the early 1920s. The company operated concessions in north Palembang and Jambi in Sumatra, and on the island of Bunju off the east coast of Borneo, near Tarakan. The organisation was integrated with Shell's other operations, and the transfer of sovereignty produced little change. In the political stress of 1958 the company was taken over by the state and renamed PT *Permindo* (*Perusahaan Minyak Indonesia*), but Shell continued to provide technical assistance and training for the new organisation, perhaps in expectation of reconsideration when the concessions were due to expire in 1961. In that year, however, and in consequence of Indonesia's new Mining Law, the company was reorganised as PN *Pertamin (Pertambangan Minyak Indonesia).* It was by far the largest of the three state entities, and with an efficient, but conservative, management was expected eventually to take over the whole state interest in the industry; politically it was less clearly aligned than the other entities, and having long worked with foreign capital was moderate in orientation.

The second in both size and seniority, and the organisation that eventually triumphed, scarcely surprisingly as it was the army's company, arose from the pre-war Shell operations in Acheh and north Sumatra, which had yielded over a million tons of crude in 1938. After the occupation the area was held by republican forces and the Dutch never returned; but for years the whole of northern Sumatra was in turmoil, first over the *Darul Islam* rebellion, and, in the later 1950s, the regional revolts. Under these circumstances, the army wielded considerable political power. In the late 1940s local worker interests, which initially had received the fields directly from the Japanese at the time of the surrender, attempted to resuscitate the damaged Pangkalan Brandan and Rantau fields which had suffered heavily from Allied bombing, and for many years there was a confused struggle for control. The operation of these fields was the subject of several major scandals, and in 1954 working was entrusted to a single enterprise, *Tambang Minyak Sumatera Utara* (TMSU). This, however, failed to solve the conflict over political control, and in 1957, a time of great national crisis, the army itself decided to intervene, and reorganised the working of the former BPM North Sumatra concessions as PT *Permina (Perusahaan Minyak Nasional).* To direct this operation, General Nasution chose one of his principal staff officers in the PRRI campaign, Colonel Ibnu Sutowo, a Javanese physician with a distinguished record in the Army Medical Service and as a field commander, and *panglima* of South Sumatra at the commencement of the rebellion. This appointment proved decisive; under the brisk new management output rose rapidly, the first exports of crude were begun, and in 1961 the entity was reconstituted under the new Mining Law as a state company (PN *Permina*).

The third and smallest of the state oil undertakings also originated in an old Shell concession that was not returned after the occupation. This was the Cepu area of Java, where the fields were approaching exhaustion, so that its retention by the fledgling republic caused the company no great concern. Cepu had always been a stonghold of left-oriented labour unions, and its PKI defenders were driven out by the army at the time of the Madiun revolt. Still under leftist leadership, operation of the fields passed to *Perusahaan Tambang Minyak Indonesia* in 1949, which unsuccessfully tried to take over also in northern Sumatra. In 1961 this became PN *Permigan (Pertambangan Minyak dan Gas Bumi Nasional),* and was in effect created as a counter to the army's *Permina.* It remained PKI-dominated until its dissolution after *Gestapu.*

The three state enterprises created under Indonesia's new Mining Law, promulgated in 1961, thus broadly corresponded to the country's three major political forces, the President or government, the army, and the PKI, and coincided with great changes in the organisation of the international industry. Based on the principle of the 1945 constitution that all minerals are the property of the state and shall be worked for the benefit of the people, the new law declared that all existing concessions were at an end, and that the state alone had the right to mine. However, foreign companies could be appointed as contractors for those operations which state entities could not, or could not yet, undertake for themselves, and relations between state bodies and contractors would be governed by 'contracts of work'. Existing concessionaires would, however, receive favourable consideration in the allocation of contracts in the areas within which they were operating. The contracts would involve a division of the profits, but based on realised and not 'posted' prices, and under certain conditions the state could take part of its share in the form of crude.

This did not give the country complete control of the management of the industry as Sutowo had desired, but senior personnel of his organisation had been prominent in drafting the new legislation, and played a major part in the new Bureau of Oil and Gas (*Migas*) set up by Chairul Saleh, Third Deputy Prime Minister, who appeared increasingly to assume the mantle of Sukarno's heir apparent. But it was a step forward in Indonesia's search for a new structure for the industry. The companies, not surprisingly, strongly resisted; what made them change their minds was the swiftly transforming world oil industry under the pressure of the 'independents', mainly domestic American producers who had long looked enviously at the majors' practice of producing oil cheaply in the Middle East and elsewhere and selling it dear in North America and in other Western markets, together with a host of new national oil companies such as Italy's energetic ENI. The year 1960 also witnessed the creation of the Organisation of Petroleum Exporting Countries (OPEC), which was to prove the most successful cartel ever created. If the majors would not accept the new conditions, it was clear that there were others who would, and it was the agreement in 1962 with Pan American Oil, a subsidiary of Standard Oil of Indiana, that convinced the majors that they had to yield. Under this agreement Pan Am became a contractor to *Pertamin*, and received a large block in Central Sumatra to the west of Caltex. The agreement involved a stipulated investment in exploration in the first eight years of the contract's 30-year term, the relinquishing of 25 percent of the contract area after five years and of an additional 25 percent after 10 years, the payment of cash bonuses, and a division of profits in the ratio of 60 to 40 between the state and the company. *Pertamin*, however, subsequently obtained the right to take a 20 percent portion of crude production, which it could sell itself.

These provisions were in general adopted in the so-called Tokyo agreements of 1963, which were a by-product of Sukarno's unsuccessful meeting with Tunku Abdul Rahman over the proposed formation of Malaysia. Actually, the new arrangements were not quite so unique to Indonesia as Sutowo has claimed, for in 1958 Argentina had adopted the same system of employing private capital on a contractual basis under state jurisdiction, to find and produce oil in return for a share in the output. But the Illia administration repudiated the agreements in 1963, and it was left to Indonesia to put the system to the test. The three majors were each assigned to one of the state concerns as contractors, and were allowed to choose new concessions, Shell making selections in South Sumatra and East Kalimantan, and both Stanvac and Caltex selecting new areas in Central Sumatra. Sutowo, however, had used a modified form of production-sharing in 1959, in arranging a loan from Japanese interests for the supply of equipment and for technical assistance for TMSU, which would be repaid in crude oil on the scale of 40 percent of the increased production made possible by the loan, above a threshold output level.[17] To provide these services the Japanese interests established the Japanese North Sumatran Oil Development Corporation *(Nosodeco)*, which later became a marketing agent in Japan for Indonesian state oil in a joint venture with *Permina*. The inordinate demands for new energy for Japan's booming economy were also a major factor in accelerating change in the world oil industry, and, in Indonesia as in other leading producers, greatly assisted national oil companies in breaking the monopoly of the majors.

By 1963, however, PKI had emerged as a major political force, and the hopes of a speedy resolution of the companies' difficulties were soon dashed. With the confrontation of Malaysia the demand for outright nationalisation augmented, and in 1965 the three majors, in common with all other foreign enterprises, were placed under government supervision and threatened with the renegotiation of their contracts. With the rising political tension in the country, oil exports fell by almost a third between 1961 and 1964, compounding the country's financial problems. Once again, the heaviest weight of nationalist, and communist, pressure fell on Shell. In 1964, following the United Nations agreement on West New Guinea, *Permina* purchased the assets of Sorong Petroleum, the successor to the Netherlands New Guinea Petroleum Maatschappij, which had found oil in the Klamono area of the Vogelkop (Bird's Head) peninsula before the occupation. Although operated by Shell, all three foreign companies had an interest in the NNGPM, but prolonged and expensive exploration had produced little new success, and the organisation had been on the point of withdrawing from operation before the UN handover; *Permina* again raised the purchase money by a loan against future production. In 1965, Shell decided that the obstacles to continued operation in the country were too great, and that it would be best for the company to withdraw, and to dispose of its assets, perhaps to return when political and economic conditions were more propitious. A purchase price of $110 million was eventually agreed, to be paid for over a five-year period from the proceeds of production. As the effective head of *Migas,* Sutowo played an important part in the negotiations, as a result of which *Permina* took over all Shell's operations including its two large refineries at Plaju and Balik Papan. The organisation had grown immensely in stature. After the sale, relations with Shell, which provided technical assistance to ease the transfer, proved amicable, and Shell returned to the country in 1971 through a share in an offshore consortium. The TMSU had made the first shipments abroad of state-produced crude in 1958, and in 1966 its successor *Permina* made the first exports of refined products.

In the critical year 1966 General Sutowo played a key role in the development of the Indonesian industry, being effectively in control of *Migas.* Chairul Saleh, who was absent in Peking during *Gestapu,* remained as Minister of Mines until early 1967, but his close identification with Sukarno deprived him of authority. Early in 1966 Sutowo moved to consolidate all state exploratory and production activities under *Permina,* and with the collapse of the *Gestapu* plot placed the directors of *Permigan* under arrest, and handed operation of its interests to *Permina.* The first production-sharing contract, which was to set the pattern for the whole future development of the Indonesian oil industry, was concluded between *Permina* and Independent Indonesian American Petroleum Company (IIAPCO), a consortium of private American interests, shortly after the formation of the *Ampera* cabinet, and covered a large area of the Java Sea. The new government assured both Stanvac, which had also been on the point of selling out, and Caltex that their 'contracts of work' would continue to be respected until their expiry in 1983. With this assurance, and aided by the 1967 Foreign Investment Law, Caltex intensified its operations, and in 1974 accounted for about 70 percent of the national crude-oil output of about 1.4 million barrels per day (70 million metric tons per year). Most of this still originates in the old contract-of-work areas, but both Caltex and Stanvac also have newer concessions on a production-sharing basis. In the late 1960s Caltex discovered new fields at Petapahan, Sintong, and Suram in Central Sumatra, and in 1971 agreed together with Stanvac to convert all the old concession areas to production sharing on expiry of the work contracts.

In 1969 integration of the state oil industry was finally achieved after nearly three years of preparatory work; *Permina* swallowed its rival to become PN *Pertamina (Perusahaan Negara Pertambangan Minyak dan Gas Bumi Nasional,* or State mining company for oil and natural gas). By this date the production-sharing contracts between *Permina* and its foreign contractors had proved eminently practical arrangements, and their numbers thereafter grew rapidly. The contracts of work under the 1960 Mining Law had been approved by Parliament and thus had the force of law. But Sutowo argued that the state should receive a more equitable share of the proceeds than the 20 percent of crude output it could claim under the contracts of work, and that it still lacked complete managerial control. Both of these objectives were achieved in the agreement with IIAPCO, which at the same time provided the foreign concessionaire with safeguards for the proper use of its money, and assured it of a reasonable profit if oil were discovered within its area. The agreement was virtually identical with one which *Permina* had been on the point of completing with Union Oil in 1963, but from which the company withdrew at the last moment, and provided that (1) full management control would rest with the state enterprise, (2) the contract would be based on a division of production and not of profits, (3) the concessionaire would bear all costs of finding and producing oil, but that these could be recovered from subsequent production up to a maximum of 40 percent of output, (4) the remaining production would be divided between the state entity and the company in the ratio of 65 percent to 35 percent, and (5) all equipment imported by the company would become the property of the state entity, and that the company would use other services provided by the entity.

The advantages of this arrangement to the foreign investor were very substantial, for he knew precisely what his obligations to the state would be in real terms, whatever the level of output and irrespective of the price of oil. Moreover, the right to expense up to 40 percent of total output was exceedingly generous. In practice the maximum has tended to become the minimum, and in the first half of 1974 this meant that the companies were realising nearly half of the going price of oil, then over $12 per barrel, on every barrel they raised, when costs of production were less than one-quarter of this amount. Under the circumstances, and with its income rising less rapidly than production, it is scarcely surprising that *Pertamina* decided to increase its share of the divisible portion of production to up to 85 percent when the price of oil exceeded $5 per barrel.

In 1967 Sutowo became Minister of Mines, and obtained government approval of the principle that with the exception of the existing concessions, and in especially difficult terrain, the state entities would explore for and work all on-shore deposits. New foreign entrants were to be encouraged to explore for and produce oil under production-sharing agreements in areas where the state entities lacked the experience or technical ability, and, in particular, offshore. By the late 1960s it was clear that the continental shelf of South-east Asia was potentially rich in oil and gas; moreover, the technology for discovering them existed, and was rapidly improving. Against a background of increasingly militant nationalism in 'host' countries in the world oil industry, and a string of OPEC victories over the companies, it was inevitable that the generous Indonesian terms would precipitate an oil rush as new applicants scrambled for concessions. Offshore working is expensive, and occasionally dangerous, but it did mean that the companies did not have to operate in the often isolated and swampy or forested areas in which many of the Indonesian land deposits occur. Moreover, they did not need to provide the same range of amenities and services for their employees, they were less reliant on local labour and on the frequently inadequate transport and other facilities, and, working at sea, there was no danger from political unrest or hostility.

But the rise of foreign offshore operations certainly had international political repercussions; Malaysia, Thailand, Cambodia, South Vietnam, the Philippines, and even Burma which since 1962 has tried to seal itself off from the outside world, were all involved in claims to the seabed on the continental shelf, and jurisdiction over the shallow seas of South-east Asia took on new significance. To the east of Kalimantan there was no problem, but the precise delimitation of the maritime boundary with Malaysia did present difficulties, particularly in the Strait of Malacca and in the South China Sea, where Indonesian possession of the Anambas and Natuna Islands produced a large northward projection of Indonesian rights between peninsular and eastern Malaysia, in a zone of major interest to potential foreign exploration. The situation was clarified in 1969 when Indonesia and Malaysia reached agreement on their common boundaries in the Malacca Strait, to the east of peninsular Malaysia, and to the north-west of Sarawak; subsequently Agip, Continental, and Gulf were granted large blocks in the Indonesian portion of the South China Sea and Mobil obtained a concession in the Malacca Strait adjoining its blocks in Malaysian waters. Later Indonesia also reached agreement with Australia on the delimitation of their international boundary in the Arafura and Timur Seas.

The early participants in offshore exploration, once Indonesian waters had been opened to them in 1967, were Japanese companies and the subsidiaries of North American independents. Among the Japanese entrants, for instance, the Kyushu Company obtained a block of 52,000 square miles off South Kalimantan and JAPEX (Japanese Petroleum Exploration Corporation) received an area eastward of Tarakan and Balikpapan off East Kalimantan, while early North American interests included Canadian Refining Associates with a block off south-east Kalimantan and IIAPCO with a huge area north-west of Java extending to the coasts of south-east Sumatra, Bangka, and Belitung. While the major international oil companies shunned Indonesia in this initial phase and chose to concentrate their activities in parts of the world they deemed more settled politically, to these smaller operators Indonesia offered a field in which competition for leases was relatively easy. Up to 1969 over $US 100 million had been invested by foreign oil companies, yet, except for TOTAL (Compagnie Française des Petroles), which had concessions on land and offshore in south-east Sumatra, the majors were scarcely represented. However, by 1970 the major companies began to compete for the few remaining unallocated offshore blocks and were clearly prepared to pay dearly for an interest in blocks already held by others. In that year British Petroleum acquired a block off north-east Kalimantan and also bought an interest in the Kyushu Oil/Union Carbide concession off south-east Kalimantan, while in 1971 Shell International signed a contract with IIAPCO to join forces to explore and develop the latter's massive allocation in the west Java Sea. By

1971, when total foreign investment in the industry had risen to almost $US 300 million and over 40 contractors were operating, all the major international companies had entered the field.

This offshore exploration took several years to fulfil its promise, but there was a rapidly increasing number of commercially exploitable strikes of oil and gas off Sumatra, Java, and Kalimantan, and, between 1968 and 1972, 43 new oil- and gas-fields, both on land and offshore, were discovered. By the early 1970s several of the offshore fields had come into production, notably IIAPCO's Cinta Field off north-west Java, the Arco-IIAPCO Arjuna Field north-east of Jakarta, and the Attaka Field of the Union Oil-JAPEX combine close to the Santan terminal in East Kalimantan, which was reportedly yielding 100,000 barrels of crude daily by the end of 1973. Though much of this exploratory work awaits further proving and development, it has already contributed to the remarkable increase in Indonesia's crude-oil production since 1966; the national target of producing one million barrels a day was achieved in 1972 and by early 1975 this had risen to 1.5 million barrels daily. As more offshore fields enter production and recent discoveries on land are exploited, annual crude production is expected to increase from its level of 476 million barrels (about 65 million metric tons) in 1973 to 720 million barrels (nearly 100 million metric tons) in 1978-79, the last year of the Second Development Plan. Exploration has also proved substantial reserves of natural gas and in this same period Indonesia is likely to emerge as an important producer for both the domestic and export markets. There are already American plans for offshore facilities to liquefy natural gas from the Arjuna Field near Jakarta and an agreement has been signed with the Pacific Lighting Corporation of Los Angeles to export this to the United States. *Pertamina* is itself proceeding with the construction of two liquefied natural gas plants, one in Aceh and another near Balikpapan. Proposals have also been announced to supply the Philippine market and to sell 7.5 million metric tons of liquefied natural gas annually to Japan in the 20-year period starting in 1977, production to come from the Badek Field in East Kalimantan and the Arun Field in Aceh.

This recent boom in the petroleum industry has certainly done much for the country's financial position, but its multiplier effects on the economy as a whole have been relatively slight. This is partly because when offshore operations began, the companies concerned used Singapore as the regional base for their supply, maintenance, and other activities and foreign workers on their rigs took their recreational leave in the island republic. By the early 1970s, however, the Indonesian government was endeavouring to alter this situation. Appropriate office space and housing were made available in Jakarta and the government has stipulated that companies operating in Indonesia must either get their supplies within the country or through its ports; they have also been instructed to employ Indonesian rather than Singapore nationals on their rigs. Efforts are now being made to provide suitable support facilities and allied services; a new logistic centre for offshore working has been opened at Tanjung Cikoneng in north-west Java and there are ambitious proposals to turn Batam Island, 20 kilometres south-east of Singapore, into the principal focus of the industry with a refinery and petrochemical plants. Coupled with intensification of exploration and the start of offshore production, these measures have made it more desirable for foreign operators and various allied support industries to transfer to Indonesia, and this has brought greatly increased use of Jakarta. Nonetheless, apart from occasional examples such as the recently completed project to pipe natural gas from *Pertamina*'s Prabumulih Bapat Field to supply new industries in Palembang, the burgeoning oil and gas industry remains essentially a distinct, separate segment within the economy which has not yet stimulated further manufacturing growth. Moreover, the total labour force employed in the industry in only about 54,000, of whom some 36,000 work for *Pertamina,* so that directly and indirectly it has done little to solve the nation's problem of surplus labour. Significantly, when rubber production was the major export industry in late colonial times, it was capable of involving large numbers of Indonesians and, through its smallholding sector, ensured wide diffusion of any rewards; the highly sophisticated, capital-intensive petroleum industry which now dominates exports does not afford similar possibilities for labour absorption or easy dissemination of development.

This rapid growth carried *Pertamina* in 1974 to the status of being numbered among the world's 200 largest industrial organisations outside the United States, and in many countries around the world its sea-horse trade mark was becoming increasingly familiar. Not only was it Indonesia's largest industrial enterprise, but it was its only large indigenous corporation; increasingly, and perhaps inevitably, it found itself more and more involved in activities often far removed from the petroleum industry. Apart from its many subsidiary activities and supply services for the industry, it operated hotels and hospitals, its own airline; it had become involved in the iron and steel industry, and in the development of rice estates. In 1971 PN *Pertamina* was reorganised as *Perusahaan Tambangan Minyak dan Gas Bumi Negara,* retaining its acronym

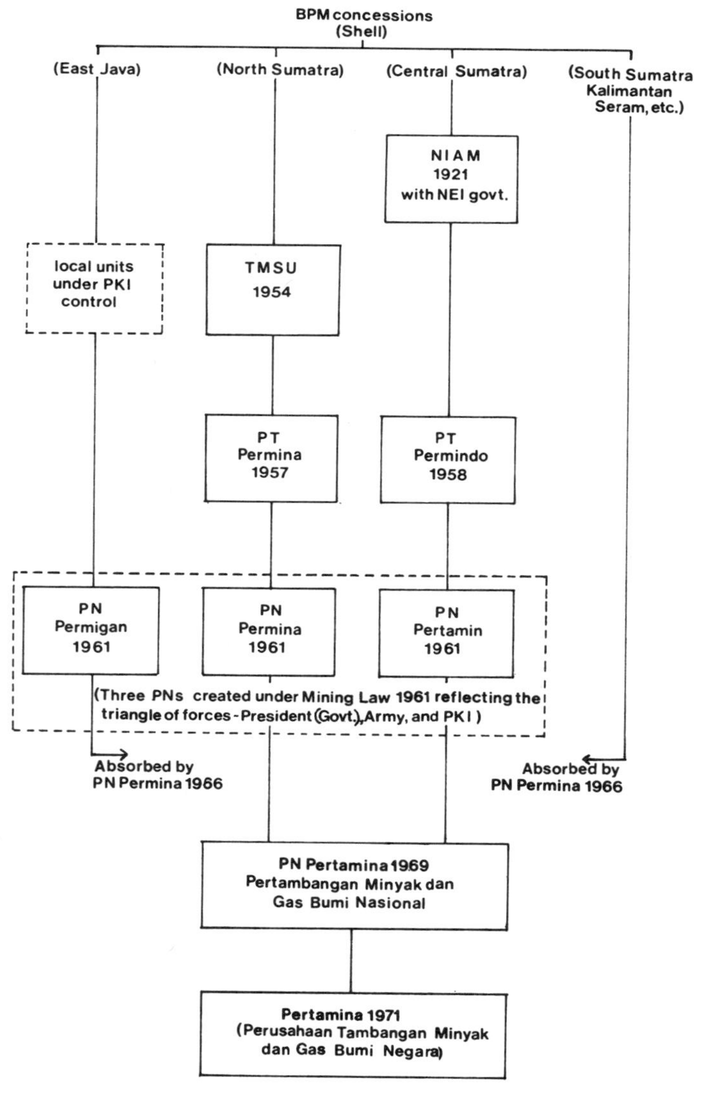
THE EVOLUTION OF PERTAMINA 1971
(Perusahaan Tambangan Minyak dan Gas Bumi Negara)
BPM concessions
(Shell)
(East Java)
(North Sumatra)
(Central Sumatra)
(South Sumatra
Kalimantan
Seram, etc.)
NIAM
1921
with NEI govt.
local units
under PKI
control
TMSU
1954
PT
Permina
1957
PT
Permindo
1958
PN
Permigan
1961
PN
Permina
1961
PN
Pertamin
1961
(Three PNs created under Mining Law 1961 reflecting the
triangle of forces - President (Govt.), Army, and PKI)
Absorbed by
PN Permina 1966
Absorbed by
PN Permina 1966
PN Pertamina 1969
Pertambangan Minyak dan
Gas Bumi Nasional
Pertamina 1971
(Perusahaan Tambangan Minyak
dan Gas Bumi Negara)

Pertamina, and its relations with government were specifically defined. The law obliged *Pertamina* to obtain government approval for any activity outside the oil and gas industry, but if it ever did so until 1975 at least, permission was never refused. On paper the entity appeared clearly under the direction of its Commissioners (who included Mohammed Sadli, the Minister of Mines, and Widjojo Nitisastro, the head of *Bappenas*), and the cabinet; but this was scarcely borne out in practice, for the organisation 's freewheeling financial operations scarcely seemed to have the stamp of prior cabinet approval. Some of its subsidiary activities such as the Krakatau steel complex at Cilegon and the Sumatran rice estates were undertaken at the specific request of President Suharto himself, but Sutowo's own ambitions for *Pertamina* seemed boundless—and so were the entity's demands for capital. In speedy succession *Pertamina* took on a list of projects that even a corporation many times its size would have considered a formidable programme—a floating fertiliser plant at Attaka off the east coast of Kalimantan; a large oil refinery and LNG plant at Cilacap in South Java with a pipeline to the Cilegon steel complex; a large terminal and refinery at the entrance of the Sunda Strait at Semangko in South Sumatra; another large refinery on the Malacca Strait in North Sumatra; an extension of the petrochemical plant at Plaju near Palembang; and, most grandiose of all, the Batam scheme. This is almost a mini-national development plan by itself, and aims at converting the scantily populated grassland waste of the small island of Batam into the principal administrative, supply, and trans-shipment centre for the entire South-east Asia oil industry, and into a major industrial and commercial centre. The ambitious long-term development plan calls for refineries, power stations, and supporting infrastructure, 7 miles of wharfage, shipyards, and oil-rig plants, a free-trade industrial zone, agricultural development, and tourist amenities. Thus by the mid-1980s the island should have a population of some 100,000, and constitute a formidable rival to Singapore, a development the island republic, mindful of its former rivalry with the now decayed port of Tanjungpinang in Batam's neighbour island, Bintan, initially viewed with deep concern. Later reflection, however, made it clear that if the scheme ever develops as envisaged at all, a matter of considerable doubt in mid-1975, the pickings for Singapore will be very substantial, and that the two islands would develop in symbiosis.

Keeping these many balls in the air presented Sutowo with growing difficulties, particularly as in the 1970s the organisation for the first time had severe financial constraints imposed on it.

During Vice President Agnew's visit to Indonesia in 1971 it was discovered that *Pertamina* had exceeded the borrowing ceiling for the whole country agreed by the government with the IMF and IGGI, the international aid consortium for Indonesia. Assurances of future good behaviour helped smooth over the affair, but henceforth *Pertamina* had to undertake to seek government approval and the consent of these international bodies for any loan of over $100 million, and running for less than 15 years. Such long-term loans were not easily come by, being largely available to governments only, so that Sutowo had to find alternative ways of raising capital to avoid the necessity of obtaining official approval, always a lengthy and cumbersome procedure. Sutowo tried several methods of raising funds that would circumvent his restrictions, but was finally driven to large-scale use of short-term bank credit, which he calculated could be successively rolled over through *Pertamina's* burgeoning revenues arising from the quadrupling of the price of oil after the Yom Kippur War.[18] But with the downturn in the world economy, the reappearance of a large oil surplus, and, most damaging of all, growing cut-price Chinese competition in Indonesia's biggest market, Japan, *Pertamina* by early 1975 faced a financial crisis of truly gigantic proportions, and although it did not technically default, it had to fall behind on payments both to its foreign creditors and in its transfers to the government. There is little doubt that many foreign bankers, dazzled by the high living and spending style of Sutowo and his associates, had lent, even pressed, funds on *Pertamina* without any real knowledge of the organisation's true cash-flow position (for it had never published any accounts), merely on the understanding that *Pertamina* was indeed 'Indonesian national oil'. One of the biggest lenders, First National City Bank of New York, may have offended Federal regulations which prohibit any United States bank from committing more than 10 percent of its total loans to any one borrower. Be that as it may, the banking community's concern for a rescue operation, perhaps the biggest in corporate history, is understandable. In mid-1975 *Pertamina* owed an estimated $2,700 million (about as large as the entire debt bequeathed to the nation by Sukarno), of which $1,650 was owed to foreign creditors and the balance to the government, against assets of perhaps $3,100 million.

In the crisis, which had produced a large and very unwelcome shortfall in Indonesia's foreign-exchange reserves, Suharto, as usual, acted quickly. Bank Indonesia announced that it would accept responsibility for *Pertamina's* foreign indebtedness, and the company was temporarily relieved of making transfer payments.

1 Associated with high population densities, wet-rice fields (*sawah*) occur on flat river or coastal plains or, as in Bali, on carefully constructed flights of terraces on hillsides

2 Despite the small size of their holdings, farm families in Java seldom rely on their own unaided labour for planting and harvesting

3 The traditional method of harvesting each rice pannicle individually with a small hand knife (*ani-ani*) is not suited to the new high-yielding varieties

4 Fish is a major source of animal protein in most Indonesian diets and large supplies of fresh fish are available daily

5 Introduced from South America in the 1850s, cinchona became an important plantation crop in West Java

6 Developed in the late nineteenth century, the Deli tobacco plantations became famous for their high-quality cigar wrapper leaf

7 Pertamina has constructed several new refineries since it acquired that at Plaju (above) in 1966

8 The world's largest off-shore tin dredge, *Bangka 1*, was built at Clydeside and afterwards towed to Bangka where it began operating in 1966

9 In its buildings and canals early Batavia was reminiscent of contemporary Dutch towns. Once neat and picturesque, most canals are now choked with rubbish

10 The restored residence of Governor-General de Klerk (1777-80), built outside Batavia's walls

11 Increased use of the motor car in the early twentieth century was accompanied by an extension of typically European suburbs on what were then the southern fringes of Batavia

12 Characteristic of all large Indonesian towns in colonial times was the distinctive Chinese quarter consisting, as in Semarang, of rows of multifunctional shophouses

13 Jalan Thamrin in Jakarta symbolizes the injection of a 'modern' high-rise profile into the traditional Indonesian townscape

14 Traditional *kampung* housing shows distinct regional variations. Javanese dwellings, like this in Yogyakarta, are built at ground level

15 Like these timber dwellings on the south bank of the Air Musi in Palembang, *kampung* houses in the Outer Islands are usually raised on stilts

16 Much of Indonesia's urban population is employed in tertiary activities. Many engage in hawking and petty vending, like these sidewalk vendors outside Yogyakarta's market

17 Production of fine-quality *batik* by labour-intensive methods remains important, particularly in Yogyakarta and Surakarta

18 *Becaks* vie with motor vehicles in central Jakarta. To discourage further in-migration, since 1972 *becaks* have been excluded from the city centre and from some residential districts

19 The large-scale manufacturing plants set up by Western concerns in the major cities during the 1930s included Unilever's soap factory in Batavia opened in 1934

20 Mohammed Hatta (b. 1902) with his daughter. Vice President from 1945 to 1956, he resigned because of disagreement with Sukarno

21 Sukarno (1901-70), the 'Tongue of the Indonesian people', displays hi charisma and oratorical skills at the opening of the Japanese Trade Fair i Jakarta late in 1965

22 Indonesia's first parliamentary election in September 1955 was taken ver seriously by voters and the turn-out was high. The result was indecisive

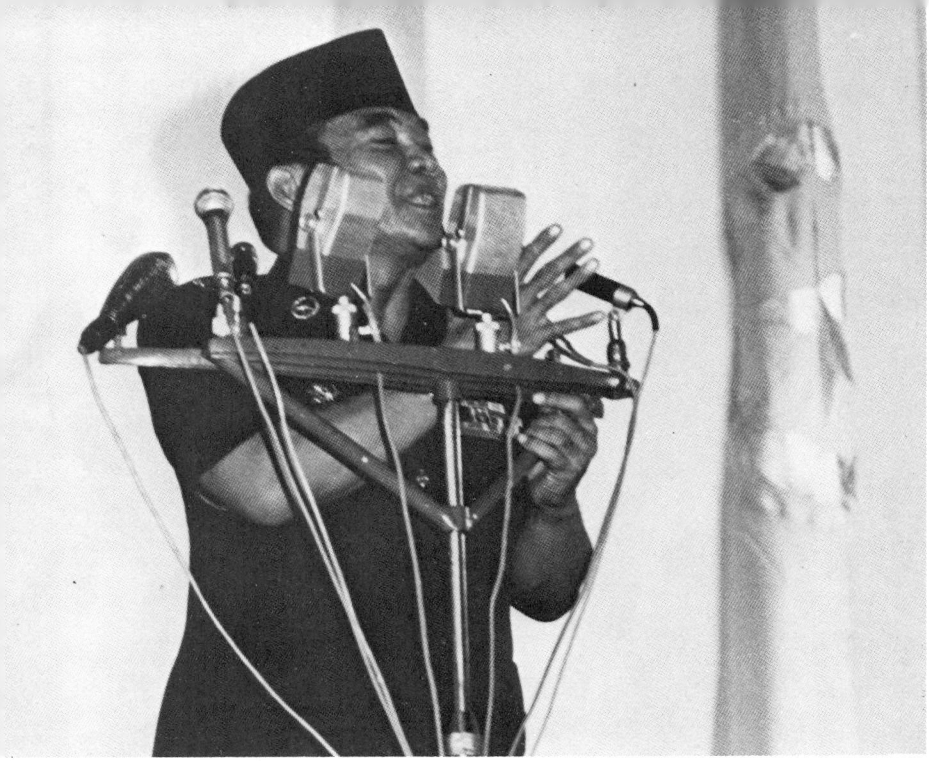

TANDA GAMBAR DALAM
PEMILIHAN UMUM
FRONT MARHAENIS
PARTAI NAHDLATUL 'ULAMA'
N. U.
TANDA GAMBAR N.U.
DALAM PEMILIHAN UMUM
PARINDRA

23 Led by Dipanegara Aidit (1921-65), Secretary-General since 1951, a PKI delegation visited Peking in August 1965 where they were met by Chou En-lai and Teng Hsiao-ping

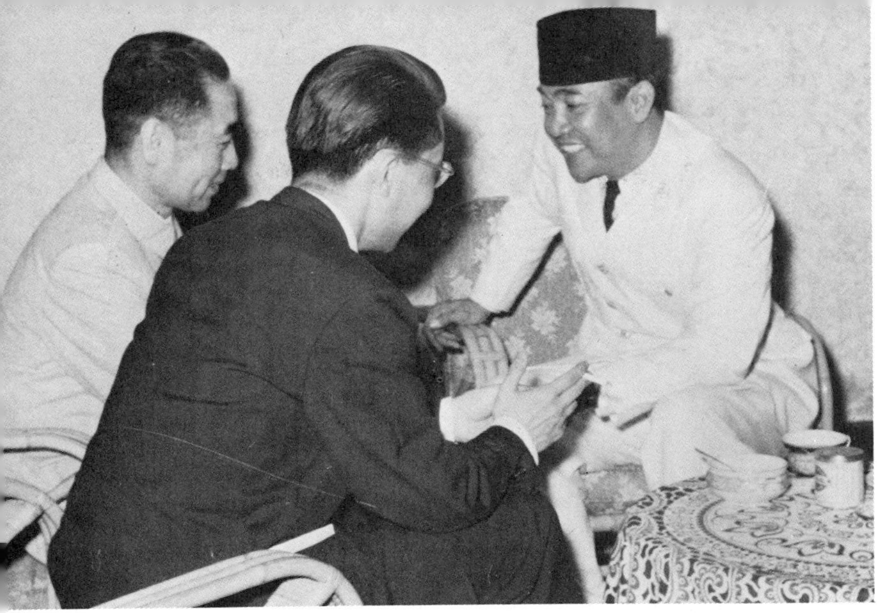

24 The Bandung conference in May 1955, attended by Chou En-lai, enhanced Sukarno's desire to be spokesman for the entire Third World

25 Sultan Hamengku Buwono IX (*right*), Minister of State for Economic, Financial, and Industrial Affairs and, since 1973, Vice President; and Dr Sumitro Joyohadikusumo, currently Minister of Research

26 Although Suharto effectively gained power after the abortive 1965 *coup,* he was not sworn in as President until March 1968. He is seen here addressing Parliament in 1972

But while the technocrats were made responsible for investigating *Pertamina*'s ancillary operations such as the steel complex and fertiliser plants, General Panggabean, the Defence Minister, was charged with scrutinising *Pertamina* itself—thus keeping control effectively within the army. Understandably, there was little reluctance on the part of international bodies or of financial institutions to continue to lend directly to Indonesia itself, although the view in some quarters of Jakarta that *Pertamina* had been the victim of a vast capitalist plot to tie the country indissolubly to the West seems far-fetched in view of the manner in which *Pertamina* lent itself to the operation. There is little doubt that this, in fact, is one of the most important results of the *Pertamina* crisis, and, with the final collapse of South Vietnam, Indonesia is confirmed as the principal barrier to any further spread of communist influence in South-east Asia. It has also underlined Indonesia's continued dependence on foreign aid; to extricate *Pertamina* will require funding larger than that deployed in *Repelita* I, and the price of moving too far and too fast has been dramatically demonstrated. But for many Indonesians, *Pertamina* and its adversary in government, the technocrats, are both tarred with the same brush; they have helped to perpetuate and enrich the already overprivileged élite, and their furious activity has left the *petani* entirely untouched.

TIN

Although petroleum has long occupied the premier position as a source of foreign-exchange earnings in the mining sector, in 1973 Indonesia regained its former position as the world's third largest producer of tin after Malaysia and Bolivia. To the east of Sumatra, the Indonesian tin islands of Bangka, Belitung, and Singkep are southerly outliers of the world's greatest stanniferous province extending from Yunnan through Burma, Thailand, and the Malay peninsula and the old river valleys of these islands, with their seaward projections, contain easily worked alluvial deposits of high-quality ore. Largely through Chinese enterprise, exploitation of the Bangka deposits began in the 1710s and by the later eighteenth century, when annual exports probably exceeded 3,500 tons, this island was the leading producer in South-east Asia.[19] The Sultan of Palembang ceded his mineral rights on Bangka to the British in 1812, during their brief occupation of the archipelago, and four years later the Bangka mines became the property of the Netherlands Indies government which continued to operate them through its Bureau of Mines until the Japanese invasion. Meanwhile, in 1860 the Billiton Maatschappij obtained mining rights to the recently discovered Billiton deposits and in 1923 exploitation of these passed to a joint venture between the company and government, the Gemeenschappelijke Mijnbouw Maatschappij Billiton, which, through a subsidiary, also controlled production in Singkep. In 1940 Bangka yielded 53 percent of total output, Billiton 41 percent, and Singkep a mere 5 percent. Throughout the 1930s production was restricted by quota under the International Tin Agreement, but it exceeded 50,000 tons in 1941, the last full year of operation before the invasion.

As in the Malay peninsula, Chinese labour has always been dominant in the industry, but both before and after independence tin-mining in Indonesia has differed significantly from that in its neighbour. Strung out along the western foot of the main ranges, exploitation of Malaya's tin deposits was the prime stimulus for the growth and location of the peninsula's zone of most rapid development, bringing in its train roads, railways, estates, and towns. In contrast, Indonesia's tin islands are physically divorced from the mainstream of national economic life, presenting localities which, save tin, 'have practically no other possibilities for economic development except for a few Malay or Chinese owned rubber and pepper plantations'.[20] Moreover, whereas tin-mining in Malaya is conducted by a multiplicity of European companies and smaller Chinese operators, the Indonesian industry is largely a government enterprise now controlled by the State Tin Corporation (PN *Timah*). At independence, the Indonesian authorities inherited total control of the Bangka mines and a 62.5 percent share in the joint venture working those on Belitung; this latter arrangement, which was renewed in 1953, ended five years later with the disruption of diplomatic ties with the Netherlands. Finally, the Indonesian industry has relied to a much greater extent on the use of dredges, both on land and offshore, and it has a far smaller proportion of gravel-pump mines which, with their lower capitalisation and greater flexibility, can respond more readily to price fluctuations.

Despite wartime damage to equipment, the tin industry was speedily rehabilitated after the occupation. Pre-war production levels were regained in 1948 and, with new dredges at work, output in 1954 equalled peak level attained before World War II. Thereafter, however, production fell almost continuously until the change of government in 1966, principally because of shortages of suitable managerial and technical staff and failure adequately to maintain or replace equipment resulting in the closure of some mines. Output declined from 32,100 tons in 1950 to 22,600 tons in 1960; by 1966 it had dropped to a mere 12,500 tons, the lowest figure for eighty years.

With the additional incentive of higher prices, the industry since 1966 has been revitalised through an accelerated investment programme designed to augment output and to safeguard its future by a search for new deposits. The state corporation has improved the industry's productive capacity by the repair and replacement of rundown equipment and new dredges have been introduced, including the largest in the world, *Bangka I,* capable of working offshore, which was built on Clydeside, towed to Bangka, and began operating in late 1966. Before the occupation part of Bangka's output was treated in the island's two working smelters at Muntok and Pangkal Balem, the rest going to Arnhem in the Netherlands. After 1949 the obsolescent Muntok smelter was partly restored, but the bulk of Indonesia's concentrates were shipped to the Netherlands for treatment until 1959; they were then diverted to Malaysia until confrontation broke this link in 1963, when they reverted to the Netherlands and, to a lesser extent, the United States; when political relations with Malaysia were resumed, so were shipments to that country's smelters. To avoid this heavy dependence on foreign treatment, the Muntok smelter has now been expanded to an annual capacity of 24,900 tons and can deal with virtually the entire output.

After a quarter-century without exploration, there was an urgent need to locate new reserves. Apart from its own investigations, since the passing of the Foreign Investment Law of 1967, PN *Timah* has signed exploratory contracts with several overseas companies. The first was with the Dutch concern, N.V. Billiton Maatschappij, which agreed to undertake offshore drilling in the drowned valleys around Bangka and in the vicinity of the Karimata Islands off south-west Kalimantan; in 1972 this company reported the discovery of new deposits in the waters close to Bangka. Additionally, the Broken Hill Proprietary Company Limited (BHP) has contracted with PN *Timah* to explore and develop the primary deposits of Belitung. Although still substantially lower than that of four decades earlier, output of tin reached 22,490 tons in 1973 and it is currently expected to rise to 25,500 tons by 1978-79. Through rehabilitation and renewed exploration the industry is now more able to respond to attractive price levels than was the case a decade ago and it will remain an important source of export earnings.

OTHER MINERALS

In addition to petroleum and tin, in late colonial times Indonesia also produced coal and small amounts of many other minerals including bauxite, manganese, nickel, phosphate, limestone, gold, and silver. Although the economic significance of some of these has waned, a few offer distinct prospects of future growth, and the recent intensification of exploration may reveal hitherto unknown resources.

At various times coal has been mined in several parts of the archipelago, but deposits are generally poor, and while they can be used for electricity generation, none is suitable for making metallurgical coke. To supply the fuel demands of steamships, the Netherlands Indies government started mining coal in south-east Borneo in the mid-nineteenth century; later, it opened two important fields in Sumatra, one at Umbilin near Sawahlunto in 1892, the other at Bukit Asem near Muaraenim in 1919, and a number of private collieries were developed in eastern Borneo. By 1941 total production of coal had risen to almost 2 million tons, nearly three-quarters of which came from the Sumatran fields. The mines were severely damaged during the occupation and full restoration was long delayed. The industry became entirely state-owned with the nationalisation in 1958 of the sole remaining private mine, that of the Koninklijke Paketvaart Maatschappij (KPM), the Dutch inter-island shipping company, at Parapatan in East Kalimantan, and since the closure of that mine production by the State Corporation PN *Tambang Batubara* has been confined to Sumatra. Substantial amounts of coal were still exported in the early 1950s, but during the 1960s output fell continuously and production in 1972 totalled only 179,000 tons, less than one-tenth of pre-war levels. Coal-mining has never been particularly profitable in Indonesia and this decline partly reflects the diversion of attention to the more attractive petroleum industry; but it is also the result of greatly reduced productivity on the part of the industry's largely Javanese labour force, the failure to maintain or replace equipment, and the inadequacy of transport facilities. The main consumers of present output are electricity generating stations, the Indarung Cement Factory at Padang, and the national railways, although the latter are increasingly turning to diesel haulage. After years of neglect, the current world energy crisis has rekindled official interest in coal, and, in order to augment fuel supplies, government incorporated proposals for the rehabilitation of the Bukit Asem mines in its Second Five-Year Development Plan and this is now in hand.

While experience thus far with coal has been disappointing, output of bauxite and nickel has grown enormously. Production of bauxite from the aluminous laterites of Bintan Island, south-east of Singapore, was begun in 1935 by the Nederlandsch Indische Bauxiet Exploitatie Maatschappij, a subsidiary of the Billiton

Company. Before the occupation the island's reserves were estimated at 17.5 million tons, and since the deposits were easily worked in opencast with excavating equipment, output rose quickly to 275,000 tons in 1940. Operations were resumed immediately after the war and production, destined for the booming Japanese market, increased from 400,000 tons in 1948 to 701,000 tons in 1966; thereafter, output accelerated and stood at 1.28 million tons in 1972. Shelved because of the invasion, Dutch colonial proposals to establish a domestic aluminium industry based on the hydroelectric potential of the Asahan river flowing from Lake Toba to the Strait of Malacca in North Sumatra have figured regularly in government planning since independence. Despite further setbacks in 1974, with Japanese assistance, these seem likely to go ahead sooner or later, and an aluminium smelter complex is planned at Kuala Tanjung on the coast east of Permatangsiantar. Exploration by the Aluminium Company of America has recently revealed good prospects for bauxite-mining in West Kalimantan and through its subsidiary, PT Alcoa Minerals of Indonesia, the company plans to begin exploitation and to establish an aluminium-processing plant at Tayam.

Deposits of nickel were discovered in several parts of Celebes in the last decades of colonial rule. Mining began in south-east Celebes in 1938 for shipment to Japan and exports reached 55,574 tons in 1941. Although earlier plans for the local treatment of the ore did not materialise, nickel production was continued by the Japanese during the occupation. With independence, however, the industry sank into oblivion, until the renewed growth of world demand, and particularly of Japanese requirements, brought a revival in the late 1950s. From a mere 13,700 tons in 1961 output had grown to 117,400 tons in 1966; it then shot up dramatically to 935,000 tons in 1972. Recent exploration has revealed deposits of nickel in Kalimantan, Maluku, and Irian, some of which may soon be worked. Production thus far has come entirely from the Pomala area of south-west Sulawesi, but a new nickel-smelting plant is under construction at Soroako in Central Sulawesi.

Apart from small amounts of gold and silver, which have been mined for centuries, the range of mineral exploitation has been widened lately by the production of copper in Irian and of manganese at Karangnunggal in West Java, and there are confident predictions of increased output of both; kaolin is also now exported to Japan from the Minahasa regency in North Sulawesi. That Indonesia possesses reserves of several hundred million tons of iron-ore has been known for over half a century. For the most part, however, these comprise low-grade lateritic deposits in Sulawesi and Kalimantan which are unsuitable for treatment in conventional blast furnaces and, since they afford little basis for the creation of an iron and steel industry, they remain unworked. Indeed, although production of some of these minor minerals will certainly grow, in the foreseeable future petroleum and to a lesser extent tin will continue to dominate the mining sector and to serve as the nation's major earners of foreign exchange. Nevertheless, the rapidly increasing population in both the towns and the countryside will have to be absorbed in more labour-demanding forms of activity.

NOTES

[1] I.M.D. Little, Tibor Scitovsky, and Maurice Scott, *Industry and Trade in Some Developing Countries*, London, Oxford University Press, 1970, ch. 7.

[2] The land situation in Yogya is described in D.W. Fryer, 'Jogjakarta: Economic Development in an Indonesian City State', *Economic Development and Cultural Change*, vol. 7, 1957, 452-64.

[3] A graphic if somewhat fictional account of planter life in the east coast during the early years of this century is to be found in Ladislao Székely, *Tropic Fever*, New York, Harper, 1937.

[4] Malaya achieved a modern system of labour relations, in which a breach of contract between employer and employee was merely a civil offence, more than a quarter of a century before the Netherlands Indies. The British planters, moreover, were never above the law.

[5] The squatter problem is discussed by Karl J. Pelzer, 'The Agrarian Conflict in East Sumatra', *Pacific Affairs*, vol. 30, 1957, 151-9.

[6] As managers' pensions were generally related in some inverse way to the capital expenditure they had incurred during their service, the incentive to improvise was strong. A West Java tea estate visited by one of the authors in 1956 had just renovated its boilerhouse and added a complete new withering room entirely with the aid of materials produced on the estate itself or collected from dumps and scrapheaps in Bandung and Jakarta.

[7] J.A.C. Mackie, 'The Government Estates', in T.K. Tan (ed.), *Sukarno's Guided Indonesia*, Jacaranda Press, Brisbane, 1967, 66.

[8] This fascinating story, and the long and little-known history of American involvement in Sumatra, is described in J.W. Gould, *Americans in Sumatra*, Martinus Nijhoff, The Hague, 1961.

[9] The analogy is taken from the 'captive' coalmines owned by the United States iron and steel, and chemical, companies, and, before World War II, the railroads. The rubber estates of the great tyre manufacturers were established to provide their parents with an assured supply, free from the bewildering and unpredictable oscillation of natural-rubber prices. Their output was thus delivered to a single market, and their operations were merely part of the total costs of producing motor-vehicle tyres. Within broad limits (in practice, to keep total liability to taxation to a minimum), the companies' internal pricing policy could be what they liked.

[10] The shortage of housing is a major impediment to the growth of the national economy, and finding accommodation for key personnel is a perpetual problem for foreign companies. Rents for such housing have typically to be paid in hard currencies and for three years in advance. In Jakarta such housing could easily cost more

than $1,000 a month in 1970, and with the rapid expansion of the oil industry demand greatly exceeded supply.

[11] Reported in the *Straits Times* (Kuala Lumpur), 5 January 1973.

[12] P.T. Bauer, *The Rubber Industry: A Study in Competition and Monopoly*, Longman, London, 1948, ch. 19. Seldom can the predictions of a professional economist have been wider of the mark.

[13] ibid., 100-3.

[14] ibid., 30.

[15] James C. Jackson, *Chinese in the West Borneo Goldfields*, University of Hull Occasional Papers in Geography no. 15, Hull, 1970.

[16] A.L. Ter Braake, *Mining in the Netherlands East Indies*, New York, 1944, 22-3.

[17] A.G. Bartlett *et al.*, *Pertamina: Indonesian National Oil*, Djakarta, Singapore, and Tulsa, 1972, 157.

[18] A sympathetic view of Sutowo's operations and of *Pertamina*'s financial problems is given in the *Far Eastern Economic Review*, 'Batam: An Island Dream Turns Sour', vol. 88, 2 May 1975, 72-4, and 'Sutowo: Down but Not Out', vol.88, 30 May, 51-8.

[19] James C. Jackson, 'Mining in 18th Century Bangka: The Pre-European Exploitation of a "Tin Island"', *Pacific Viewpoint*, vol. 10, no. 2, 1969, 28-54.

[20] Ter Braake, op.cit., 43.

CHAPTER 7

Urbanisation and Manufacturing Industry

Urbanisation

WITH ABOUT 18 PERCENT OF ITS POPULATION classed as urban in the census of 1971, Indonesia's level of urbanization is lower than that of many developing nations. But, as one of the world's most populous countries, its total of 21 million urban dwellers is greater than many national populations, including those of several of its neighbours. Jakarta, the capital, is the most populous city in South-east Asia, and Indonesia contains more large urban centres, including two others with over a million, than any other nation in the region. In recent decades these larger cities have grown rapidly, and on some projections Indonesia could possess ten 'million' cities by the year 2000 and Jakarta's inhabitants could exceed 12 million. The nation thus faces the prospect of urban agglomerations as large as any in the present-day West with scant hope of most city-dwellers ever reaching present Western levels of living. Rural Indonesia certainly has its problems, but the low-income and slowly industrialising urbanisation now in progress and the long neglect of urban facilities also demand urgent attention. The towns and cities of Indonesia, however, are far from homogeneous, and, recently as in the past, they have been affected differently by various processes of change.

Remarkably little is known about urban origins in Indonesia, but cities were in existence by the early centuries of the Christian era, both in commercially favoured localities in the Outer Islands and in the central more densely peopled parts of Java. It is common to divide these cities into two broad types and to suggest that, because of their varying functions, these exhibited differences in internal arrangement and in social and economic characteristics. Indeed, although some changes occurred with the passage of time, for over a millennium there was a clear distinction between early inland Javanese capitals such as Kediri or Majapahit on the one hand, and such emporia of archipelagic commerce as the north Java ports of Bantam or Tuban and Outer Island trade centres such as Srivijaya or Acheh, on the other. Little now remains of these early cities, primarily because of the flimsy building materials used, but archaeological traces of ancient inland royal capitals have survived in Central and eastern Java as has a contemporary description of fourteenth-century Majapahit in Prapanca's *Nagarakertagama*. Together with suggestive features in present-day Yogyakarta and Surakarta (Solo), these afford evidence of a distinctive longstanding tradition of urban design associated with the kingdoms so important in the island's earlier history.

These inland Javanese capitals were the seats of government for dynasties ruling land-based agrarian domains. The city served as custodian of a sophisticated courtly culture, deriving its wealth chiefly from the exaction of taxes and tribute from the surrounding rural populace. Characteristically, the major elements in the city's structure displayed a north-south alignment and were so arranged as 'to symbolize the cosmological universe and to emphasize the king's palace from which all power radiated'. Such a capital 'was not merely the largest city, chief consumer of agricultural surpluses, cultural hub and political centre of the kingdom; it was also the magical catalyst that guaranteed coalescence of the realm'[1] and the fall of a kingdom, dynastic conflict, or the death or defeat of a ruler, frequently heralded the demise, and often almost total abandonment, of an earlier court centre as the seat of government was transferred to a new site. The dominating feature of these cities was the *kraton*, the walled palace precinct enclosing the ruler's private residence and accommodation for his relatives, religious and secular officials, and numerous servants and artisans. Close by lay a large public square, or *alun-alun*, used for ceremonial and other occasions, around which were arranged the other major public buildings. Surrounding these, on a more or less rectangular street pattern, were the bamboo and timber dwellings of the poorer Javanese urban residents, many of whom retained close links with farming.

As trade expanded both within the archipelago and beyond, representatives of another type of city emerged on the north coast of Java, and along the shores of Sumatra and Borneo. In the case of the former, ports such as Tuban and Gresik were coastal foci of 'Javanese political and maritime power',[2] serving as points of export for the produce of interior kingdoms, particularly rice, and as entrepôts for the flourishing trade in spices from the eastern isles. Flanking the sea route between China and the West and with sparsely peopled undeveloped hinterlands, the early ports of Sumatra and Borneo were stapling points for international and regional trade. Although usually they contained a royal quarter and they were often also centres of religious learning, whether of

Buddhism or later of Islam, these various harbour principalities differed significantly from the inland capitals; their commercial functions were dominant, they had large foreign populations, and they served as points of entry for new ideas and influences. Unlike their counterparts in the cities of interior Java, the rulers of these coastal principalities derived most of their incomes directly or indirectly from the flow of commerce through their harbours.

Bantam in north-west Java is frequently cited as an example of this type of city. In the late sixteenth and seventeenth centuries Bantam became 'one of the principal points of the international Asian trade',[3] attracting a substantial traffic in Chinese junks; the Sultan's palace, the *alun-alun,* and the mosque occupied prominent places within the town walls, but the outstanding features of the city were its markets and its large contingents of foreign, particularly Chinese, merchants and traders. A broadly similar picture can be sketched for every noteworthy early Indonesian port for which records exist. By the later seventeenth century, for example, the north Sumatran port of Acheh (now Banda Aceh) was a major entrepôt for the exchange of Indian textiles, archipelagic produce, and Chinese silks and ceramics; it was also the point of departure for South-east Asian Muslims making the pilgrimage to Mecca and an important regional focus of Islamic scholarship. Contemporary descriptions reveal that Acheh contained a large stone royal palace, 'with excellent dwellings provided with gardens', similar to the *kratons* of Java, but because of its stapling function the localities devoted to the peddling trade which characterised contemporary commerce were equally important. 'There are two large market places in the town', Nicolaus de Graaff wrote in 1641, 'one in the centre and the other at the upper end thereof, where Indian merchants, both Moorish and heathen, sit with all sorts of wares for sale'.[4] As with all such port cities, Acheh had a substantial, partly transitory, foreign population, mostly Gujeratis and Chinese, who occupied ethnically segregated quarters; for the most part, the indigenous inhabitants lived in pile dwellings of bamboo and thatch, and were employed partly in fishing and in food production. Despite the advent of Europeans at the close of the sixteenth century, these earlier patterns associated with the traditional inland Javanese capitals and the harbour principalities survived widely in the Indies until the later nineteenth century and provided part of the basis from which the towns and cities of modern Indonesia have developed.

It is sometimes suggested that the larger cities of Indonesia became more alike under Dutch rule to the extent that a 'model' of the late colonial city can be formulated. This approach masks the operation of a variety of influences which, in reality, had created a diversity of urban forms by the eve of independence. For long, the Dutch had little direct effect on the archipelago's cities. Except in Jakarta (then Batavia), headquarters of their mercantilist aspirations and where Jan Pieterszoon Coen had sought to build 'a faithful copy of the old Dutch towns' replete with canals and 'stuffy tightly-packed, many storied houses',[5] the presence of the Dutch before the nineteenth century—and of the English in West Sumatra—was apparent in the forts and factories they attached to existing settlements and, indirectly, in the effects of their activities on earlier patterns of trade. The length of Dutch control and its degree of political and economic impact differed substantially in the various parts of the archipelago. West Java and Semarang may have been under Dutch rule from the seventeenth century, but the 'native states' of Jogjakarta, Surakarta, and Banyumas were not brought under full subjection until the third decade of the nineteenth century and, for the most part, the Outer Islands were affected even later. The final extension of Dutch rule over all the islands did bring the erection in the present century of a full-scale colonial governmental structure with various urban centres serving as administrative foci, and the coincidence of propitious economic circumstances and more liberal colonial policies fostered an efflorescence of private European enterprise chiefly in mines and plantations, which led to a dramatic expansion of export production. Both developments resulted in a marked increase in the European population of the Indies; nevertheless, only selected localities, principally in Java and north-east Sumatra felt the full effects of these changes. Elsewhere, the influences of colonial rule were less pervasive and cities retained many indigenous features reflecting local cultural variations. Since the urban centres of modern Indonesia have grown out of the legacy of this differential impact of colonialism, the contrast between the essentially 'colonial' cities strongly influenced by the Dutch and the cities which remained largely indigenous in character is of lasting importance.

The majority of the archipelago's towns and cities fall into the latter category. Even where they served as seats of colonial government, Europeans formed a tiny proportion of total population, in most cases less than 2 percent in 1930, and the colonial presence was an intrusive element symbolised in the fort, the governor's residence, and in the nearby small European quarter. In all cities of this type Indonesians formed over four-fifths of the population in 1930. Such were Jogjakarta and Surakarta, traditional capitals of the *Vorstenlanden,* as well as a multitude of smaller coastal and inland centres in Java, and most urban centres in the Outer Islands were similar. The hub of the layout of Jogjakarta and Surakarta, for example, was still the *alun-alun* and the large walled *kraton* encompassing the palace and the dwellings of the court officials, guards, and specialist artisans, a royal enclosure which in Jogjakarta housed 15,000 people in the later 1920s. Almost all the rest of the city comprised purely Javanese *kampungs* of tiled houses built at ground level. In both cities the impact of the Dutch was small; it took the form of a fort immediately north of the *alun-alun,* a tiny European quarter nearby, and a few hotels, clubs, banks, and administrative offices. In essence, Jogjakarta and Surakarta were traditional indigenous capitals retaining their roles as custodians of Javanese culture; indeed, Surakarta was described at the time as 'the heart of native Java, the Java of the Javanese, the stronghold of native life and tradition'.[6]

This continuance of earlier forms is also discernible in the Outer Islands as, for instance, in Palembang, supposed heir to the Srivijayan thalassocracy and commercial centre of much of southern Sumatra.[7] A representative of the Dutch East India Company was established there early in the seventeenth century, but the city did not come under direct Dutch rule until the 1820s. Before that time the focus of the urban area was the Sultan's walled palace and the large stone mosque nearby on the left bank of the Musi river, an area encircled to north and west by the timber dwellings of the lesser princes and principal chiefs. Immediately to the east, fronting the river, lay the Chinese quarter, scene of much of Palembang's commerce. With the imposition of direct colonial rule the palace area was converted into a fort occupied by Dutch military and civilian personnel; their numbers were always small, however, and they totalled less than 2,000 in 1930. Cities such as Palembang did not witness any marked growth of new governmental or residential zones, or of associated recreational facilities, and, since there was little European involvement in production or trade, there was only a slight infusion of Western-style businesses. When these did emerge, as with petroleum refining at Palembang, they tended to be physically separate, self-contained exclaves. The overwhelmingly dominant form of residence in these cities was the *kampung,* and the economy remained largely traditional, with trade in Asian hands and industry small-scale and often domestic. As in much of Java, Dutch colonial rule did not bring radical changes in the character of the city.

In complete contrast were those urban centres owing much more to direct colonial influences: the principal ports of north Java, Batavia, Surabaya, and Semarang; selected administrative centres in interior Java such as Bogor and Bandung; commercial and administrative centres in areas of plantation development in the Outer Islands, of which the outstanding example is Medan; and, for different reasons, fashionable hill resorts such as Puncak in Java and Berastagi in the Lake Toba area in northern Sumatra, which represented small escapist urban inliers born of a belief that it was desirable, if not essential, for Westerners in the tropics to retreat periodically to the cooler hills to protect their health. In addition to their more rapid growth in late colonial times, the first three of these groups shared many similarities. In particular, apart from a substantial Chinese element, they all had a large resident European population which, in the cases of Batavia, Surabaya, and Bandung, exceeded 20,000 in the 1930s. In company with their roles as seats of high-level administrative and commercial functions, this brought significant influences on patterns of residence, and a marked concentration of institutions and facilities, including clubs, restaurants, shops, and public services such as water supplies, sewerage, and hospitals, all designed primarily, if not entirely, for the European residents. Indeed, it was in these cities that both the monopoly of wealth and power enjoyed by the ruling European élite and the sharp cultural, residential, and occupational segregation typical of a colonial plural society found their most marked expressions. Occupying the lowest rungs of colonial society, indigenous Indonesians formed the majority of the population, yet, although in total their *kampungs* occupied much of the urban area, these tended to occur around the city's periphery, on river-bank land avoided by the Europeans, or squeezed into gaps elsewhere. Here, it was not the Indonesians but the small discrete European community which was most prominent and which occupied a disproportionately large amount of space. Thus, in Bandung, admittedly one of the more extreme examples, Europeans comprised only 12 percent of the population in 1930, yet they occupied 52 percent of total urban space, principally in the northern half of the city; although 78 percent of Bandung's inhabitants were Indonesians, these occupied only four-tenths of the urban area.[8] In consequence, although a minority in the city's population, this small European component exerted the greatest impact on the urban format, an influence clearly apparent in the changing location and character of its residential areas.

Batavia, Surabaya, and Semarang, for example, were all characterised by an elongated north-south development with relatively slight lateral growth and during the colonial era each experienced a progressive movement of better-quality residential areas southwards to higher ground away from the swamps near the river mouths, while concurrently the docks were moved seawards. In

Batavia, for instance, the original seventeenth-century walled Dutch town, with its fortress housing the governor-general, the senior officials, and a garrison, lay near the mouth of the Ciliwung river. From the later seventeenth century wealthy officials began to leave the cramped residences of the notoriously unhealthy old town, building spacious mansions for themselves outside the walls; this process accelerated after serious epidemics in the 1730s and a string of 'country houses' emerged south of the city. The first major shift of European residential areas in Batavia came, however, in the early nineteenth century. For reasons of health and defence, Governor-General Daendels (1808-11) developed a new government-residential area on slightly higher ground at Weltevreden 5 to 6 kilometres to the south. Now vacated by the Dutch, the partly demolished old town became a commercial centre occupied by Chinese and Indonesians and the 'garden town' of Weltevreden arose as the new European residential focus, acquiring in time its own European shopping centre. Subsequently, with the extension of properly surfaced roads and an increased use of motor vehicles, new European suburbs developed even further south at Gondangdia, Menteng, and Meester Cornelis (now Jatinegara) and Weltevreden lost much of its residential character as the number of shops, offices, and hotels in the area increased. Though the major shifts came later, both Surabaya and Semarang experienced broadly similar developments culminating in the emergence of elegant European villa quarters in hilly areas to the south.

During the long Dutch residence in these Javanese cities the typical Dutch dwelling also underwent modifications in style and form. The early cramped and stuffy houses lining the canals of the old town soon gave way to more spacious mansions and an era of ostentatious living with multitudes of servants. Linked with a growing interest in tropical gardening and the emergence of a mixed European-Indonesian 'mestizo' culture among the Dutch inhabitants, a new phase of European suburban development began in the early nineteenth century. This was marked by the so-called 'Indian' style of dwelling which adapted certain features of local housing to the needs of a wealthy European élite; elegant, capacious villas in extensive well-groomed grounds were set out around open squares or along wide tree-lined streets, frequently at densities of no more than one or two dwellings per acre. The rapid growth of the European population of these cities in the late nineteenth and early twentieth centuries and a marked extension of European residential areas, not infrequently at the expense of existing *kampung* quarters, then brought a reversal to progressively more Western forms which created an increasingly artificial

European environment in several of the larger cities. In terms of residence, this became apparent in a turn towards less pretentious more Western-style dwellings set in small neat gardens on carefully planned street systems. But it also brought a proliferation of specifically European-oriented social, cultural, and sporting facilities, which took up a substantial part of total urban space but were mostly closed to all but a tiny section of the population. Additionally, in the first third of this century cities of this type acquired a Western-type Central Business District, with a sudden rash of newly-built offices, banks, hotels, retail stores, and other service establishments catering principally for a European demand. By the late 1930s the most prominent features of these cities were the abundant and imposing buildings of colonial government departments, the often magnificent premises of the banks, agency houses, and commercial companies, and the extensive well-kept suburbs of villas and bungalows; all three were predominantly European. As 'urban islands of Europe-in-Asia'[9], these cities furnished a framework for the future very different from that afforded by those with a stronger retention of indigenous characteristics.

In the light of this historical survey, it is not surprising that the towns and cities of modern Indonesia exhibit considerable variety. Marked differences in the ways they were affected by colonial rule and the differential impact of the social, political, and economic forces operating since independence have produced a situation in which patterns of growth and change are complex, with widely differing combinations of inertia and transformation, and of the modern and the traditional. Many of the recent changes have had some effect on all the larger urban centres. This is especially true, for instance, of the broadening of their administrative and educational roles. Indeed, one of the more important causes of urban growth and change after 1949 was the expansion and Indonesianisation of national, regional, and local administration in forms designed to serve the purposes of social and economic development, and the generation of a greater national consciousness. The growth of health, educational, and other services, particularly the universities and other training institutions, the enlargement of the police and military establishments, and increasing state involvement in the economy brought a substantial extension of government responsibility and a proliferation of national and provincial government departments and agencies. In consequence, there was a sharp rise in the number of civil servants and other public employees in the larger cities, in which the use of land for government and public purposes became increasingly prominent.

In varying degrees, all urban centres also show the imprint of the political and economic vicissitudes of the last quarter-century. Under Sukarno, preoccupation with other matters and diversion of funds into monumental status symbols resulted in serious neglect of the urban infrastructure in a period of rapid city growth; public facilities such as roads, water and power supplies, schools, and medical services deteriorated and were totally inadequate to cater for the greatly enlarged populations. By the late 1960s, for example, the water-supply systems of Jakarta and Bandung were capable of serving only two-fifths of actual demand and school facilities in the capital could cope with only about half of its children. 'Since inadequate resources were committed to solving urban problems', one Indonesian has observed, the nation 'now finds itself faced with one of the most serious situations in Southeast Asia as far as urban affairs are concerned'.[10] The extent of the problem was revealed by surveys conducted in the late 1960s by the *Direktorat Landuse* of the Ministry of Home Affairs which showed that substantial parts of every city lacked what were deemed to be 'adequate urban facilities', meaning a combination of piped water and electricity supplies, a proper sewage system, and surfaced motorable approaches. Since the advent of the New Order in 1966 increasing attention has been devoted to improving the situation and to devising more effective means of urban planning and control. City transport facilities are being upgraded and extended through road and bridge construction and rehabilitation and the introduction of new buses and taxis; new power stations are permitting an extension, and greater reliability, of electricity supplies; and, with foreign assistance, urban water-supply systems are being renewed. That much remains to be done is indicated by a 1972 estimate that Jakarta then required at least three times its current road mileage to meet the increasing volume and congestion of traffic. After a long period of progressive rundown in their physical infrastructure, however, the cities of Indonesia are at last beginning to move towards the standards already present in nearby Malaysia and Singapore.

Proper assessment of the varying effects of recent changes, however, requires some form of classification of the nation's urban centres. In the early 1960s, Hildred Geertz proposed a division into two categories.[11] The first of these she termed 'metropoles'. These are the large cosmopolitan cities such as Jakarta, Surabaya, or Bandung which serve to link Indonesia with the outside world and which also act as integrating centres for the political, economic, and intellectual life of the nation, and which contain, for instance, the principal government offices, the major industrial and commercial establishments, the universities, and the foreign diplomatic and business communities. Her second category, the smaller centres with a primarily local orientation, she termed 'provincial towns'. Although they vary in form, function, and size, these centres are typified by their outlying location, by their relative lack of sophistication, and by their much closer integration with their immediate hinterlands; generally, life in these 'provincial towns' centres on trade and local regional administration.

Consideration of the changes in the last decade, and the much greater information now available, suggests a somewhat different twofold division. Firstly, there are those centres most affected by recent processes of growth and transformation. In general, these have shown the highest rates of population increase and the most marked growth of functional diversity with the establishment of new larger manufacturing establishments and the upswing in commercial and financial activity. It is, indeed, these cities which have been the principal beneficiaries of the recent increase in domestic and foreign investment in commerce and manufacturing and in the nation's new growth industry, tourism, which brought a total investment of US $185 million in luxurious new hotels between 1969 and 1972, mostly in Jakarta. These are the cities which display, at least in parts, an increasingly modern or 'internationalised' outward appearance through the products of the associated building boom, the new office blocks, banks, hotels, and shopping centres which, as symbolised by Jalan Thamrin, the capital's main thoroughfare, are injecting a new high-rise profile into a traditionally one- and two-storey townscape. In addition, they have seen the speediest adoption of the trappings of world youth culture as indicated in styles of music, hair, and clothing and the rise of student power. Apart from the sprawling capital Jakarta, which has recorded the largest absolute increase in numbers and has experienced the greatest changes, this category also includes the provincial capitals of Java and the major administrative and commercial centres of the Outer Islands. Somewhat similar, though smaller, are those towns located in areas now affected by renewed or novel exploitation of natural resources, usually arising from foreign participation; such, for instance, are those centres linked to the very rapid growth of petroleum output.

These centres of change differ greatly from the majority of *kabupaten* (regency) capitals, from the foci of traditional cultures such as Yogyakarta or Bukittinggi, and from the multitude of smaller market and administrative towns, particularly those in less accessible parts of the country or in areas which have either been bypassed by recent economic developments or which have declining resources. Characteristically, these have shown lower rates of growth, they have received only a slight infusion of modern elements, sometimes merely a new hotel, and they have retained many traditional features; to a large extent they possess an essentially unchanged physical form. These urban centres have experienced what Evers terms 'static expansion'. Their population has grown, albeit often slowly, but this has been accompanied by

> more of the same type of institutions, more people in the same type of occupations, some elaboration of existing social patterns rather than evolution of new structures. We should expect in these towns no drastic changes except population growth and with it the expansion of residential areas but without new patterns of residential segregation. In short, population growth without development.[12]

Taking as his example Padang, the predominantly Minangkabau provincial capital of West Sumatra, Evers points out that the fourfold increase in the city's population between 1930 and 1971 has not generated the kind of changes to be seen in the nation's largest cities. Despite the recent expansion of the Indarung Cement Factory, originally established there in 1910, Padang, as with many similar places, has remained 'a town of small traders and government officials'. Typically, those who advance in social and economic status in centres of this kind move to the larger cities and contribute to the changes occurring in them. This distinction between centres of transformation and centres of static expansion should not be pushed too far, for there are many elements in the former largely unaffected by change and all the nation's cities have multitudes of squatters; but unless current trends alter significantly, the contrast will produce an increasing diversification of Indonesia's urban scene.

One of the most obvious changes in the cities of Indonesia in the last quarter-century has been the multiplication of their populations. Jakarta, with 1.34 million inhabitants in 1949, housed 2.97 million in 1961, and 4.58 million in 1971; in the same period Surabaya and Bandung attained the status of 'million' cities and others, such as Medan, Semarang, and Palembang, passed the half-million mark. This explosion in numbers caused a marked expansion of the urbanised area, which has often trebled since the 1930s, frequently spreading far beyond the city's legal boundaries typically as peripheral low-income residential zones, a process of spatial growth which, like the less centralised location of many new government offices, partly reflects the modern role of motorised transport for intra-urban travel. Although the contribution of the natural increase of the existing city population is often underrated, the rapid growth of these larger cities is mainly the result of the inward movement of rural peoples. Rural-urban migration is not new in Indonesia, for it was certainly occurring on a significant scale in later colonial times, but the stream of city-bound migrants has reached unprecedented proportions since independence. Net in-migration to the capital, for example, has probably exceeded an average of 100,000 a year since 1948.

In terms of urbanisation, this has two important consequences. Firstly, the migrants are usually in the younger age-groups, mostly between 15 and 35 years old. This has immediate effects on the urban demographic structure, exaggerating its predominantly youthful composition with the alarming implications for future growth indicated by one estimate that the annual *natural* rate of increase of Jakarta's population is currently 2.5 percent. Secondly, a high proportion of the city's inhabitants are first-generation in-migrants and their young offspring. In 1961, for example, only 51 percent of the capital's population had been born there and, since half of these were under 10 years old, many must have been the progeny of parents recently arrived in the city. Conventional interpretations derived from Western experience would indicate that these cities have large numbers of recent arrivals still adjusting to the urban environment; but their very numbers suggest that equally they may be helping to forge future patterns of urban life.

Characteristically, new arrivals seek the assistance of relatives, friends, or fellow villagers already in the city and these links often determine where they settle and, less frequently, the type of occupation they enter. Migrants from particular rural districts therefore tend to cluster in specific areas where they partly re-create 'the same structure as in the rural villages'[13] and all larger cities have 'the characteristics more of an agglomeration of villages than of a very large metropolis'.[14] Frequently migrants live and work within a community comprising members of their own cultural group. They retain close contacts with their home villages, remitting cash and returning regularly for ceremonial and other occasions and often, as with the Batak migrants in Medan, they may have 'more meaningful links' with their rural relatives than with their alien urban neighbours.[15] According to Critchfield, it is rare to meet anyone in Jakarta 'who does not name a village as his real home or view his stay in the city as anything but transitory until he can save up enough money to return to his village'.[16] Certainly, this fosters retention of regional rural cultures in the urban setting, but it is debatable whether this means that the cities are simply being infected with rural values. Alternatively, it seems more likely that, although superficially similar, the ethnicity of migrants is manifested differently in accordance with the specific socio-cultural context of each large city and that diverse processes of interaction and change are at work; the tendencies outlined above are therefore more marked in some cities than in others and this is contributing to the increased differentiation of urban centres.[17]

It is difficult to identify the causes of this massive cityward drift of country folk, but one thing is abundantly clear: the migration has occurred primarily because the depressed rural economy, especially in Java, has offered only the spectre of declining man-land ratios, rising underemployment, increasing indebtedness, and an ever wider application of 'shared poverty'. For the majority, severe economic hardship, coupled with the hope of a better life in the city, rank as the principal reasons for deciding to move. In addition, other factors have played some part in the process. The recurrence of disorder and insecurity in the countryside, for instance, particularly the regional disturbances of the later 1950s in West Java, Sumatra, and Sulawesi, apparently drove many to seek refuge in cities, as did similar conditions in the mid-1960s. For some, migration has probably been partly a response to the social and psychological attractions of the large urban centre; to the villager, the city often carries the glitter of prestige and glamour, it exudes an aura of modernism, progress, and opportunity enhanced by the patina of apparent wealth and sophistication of those migrants who return home, either temporarily or permanently. Moreover, since secondary educational facilities are rarely within easy reach of villages and institutions of higher education are located in larger urban centres, there is little alternative for those seeking educational opportunities but to move, and, having moved, they do not usually return permanently to their villages. Finally, it must be remembered, particularly since some parts of the nation provide more migrants than others, that in certain Indonesian cultures temporary migration is traditional, as with the Minangkabau custom of *merantau* which takes many young western Sumatran males away from home. All the available data suggest, however, that for most rural-urban migrants economic considerations are paramount.[18]

The scale of this rural-urban migration has had direct repercussions on the physical and economic structure of the larger cities. In colonial times, Indonesian urban dwellers occupied their own distinctive *kampung* quarters, many of which had become increasingly congested by the 1930s. Urban house construction was curtailed during the Japanese occupation (1942-45) and in the succeeding Revolutionary Period (1945-49) destruction occurred in several cities; since then city authorities have been chronically short of funds and, especially in the Sukarno era, where public money was spent, it rarely went into housing. Meanwhile, to cater for the continuing influx of poor migrants squatter shacks proliferated on suitable vacant land, sometimes towards the city centre or alongside railway tracks, but most frequently around the periphery. As a result, the *kampung*-style squatter area, with its wooden huts and an almost total absence of normal urban amenities, is now the principal form of land use in the nation's cities, even in those characterised earlier as centres of transformation. The authorities are faced with 'the seemingly insurmountable task of providing water, sanitation, housing, education, transportation, law and order, and above all, jobs'[19] for the squatters, who probably now form between a quarter and a third of the inhabitants of each large city. Whatever the success of rehousing programmes in Hong Kong and Singapore, these squatter *kampungs* are unlikely to prove a short-lived feature of the Indonesian urban scene. In view of the numbers involved, the problem is not one of how to eradicate them, but of how to improve them, a fact the Dutch recognised half a century ago and an idea gaining increasing support at present. Since 1968 the Jakarta city authorities have improved several *kampungs,* including those near the airport at Kemayoran, and this kind of improvement, with subsidies from local administrations, has been incorporated into the nation's Second Five-Year Plan (1974-79). Fortunately, experience in the capital shows that squatter communities do respond to a modest amount of assistance. 'House fronts are painted, bamboo walls plastered with old newspapers and painted white, flower boxes appear, rubbish heaps vanish and a general air of hope and confidence seems to displace the old apathy'.[20] For the foreseeable future, this *kampung* housing, whether improved or not, will remain a major feature of Indonesia's cities.

Recently Soekanto claimed that

> Indonesia has no general social structure which can serve as a framework for the entire society. The country is composed of a large number of fluid groups, which tend to be parochial. Ethnic, religious and ideological groupings are more important than class differences in Indonesia.[21]

Nonetheless, the population of each city does show a distinction between a small, relatively affluent élite and the rest of the inhabitants who are overwhelmingly poor. Whereas racial differences enshrined in the legal subdivision of the plural society were largely responsible for patterns of residence in colonial times, since independence these have become increasingly determined by socio-economic status. The great majority of the urban population, many of whom are recent arrivals, are in low-income unskilled or semi-skilled jobs, often casual or irregular, and they tend to be conservative and traditional in their interests, activities, and behaviour, and relatively unsophisticated in modern ways. Though some are vagrants with no fixed places of abode, most—and this includes junior government employees and students—live in the extensive *kampung* and squatter areas, particularly in the outer parts of the city, within which, as has been seen, they have often formed homogeneous neighbourhoods through the residential concentration of those from similar rural homelands.

At the same time, however, the exodus of Europeans and Eurasians after independence, which was accelerated by the subsequent nationalisation of foreign enterprises, together with the enlargement of the bureaucracy and the armed services, resulted in the emergence of a new segmented Indonesian urban élite comprising senior government officials and military personnel, wealthy businessmen, and professionals. Many of these were trained overseas and they are more progressive and more knowledgeable of Western values and practises; through their greater wealth, they have a wider spectrum of interests and desires and access to the greatest range of urban amenities and facilities, and they are more oriented towards a modern 'internationalised' life-style, marked by material possessions and spending patterns. For the most part, this new élite moved into the older areas of high-quality dwellings, the villas and bungalows, formerly occupied by Europeans, so that patterns originating in the colonial era have strongly influenced the distribution of high-status groups in the modern city. In Bandung, for instance, the housing erected in the early twentieth century to the north of the city centre for Dutch colonial officers is now occupied by wealthier Indonesians, and, as in most cities, these remain the 'most expensive and beautiful residential sections'.[22] Additionally, where new housing has been built with public funds, it has been predominantly for this group, for the main objective of government has been to provide accommodation for its employees and for military personnel. In Jakarta two thousand new dwellings were constructed in 1951 alone specifically for senior officials and their families, and although Kebayoran Baru, the satellite town south-west of the capital, was conceived originally as a balanced community intended to contain a high proportion of low-cost housing, in practice it has developed into a modern upper- and middle-class area. Moreover, the state-owned oil corporation has recently constructed for foreign contractors operating in Indonesia, air-conditioned dwellings, with associated recreational facilities, at Tomang on the outskirts of the capital. Patterns of residence in the modern city, and particularly in those centres which have grown most rapidly and contain the greatest numbers of high-income earners, thus display a sharp dichotomy between a partially Westernised affluence, one measure of which at present is the number of people with direct access to supplies of pure water and electricity (which in Jakarta amounts to only one-eighth of the total population), and the mass of the urban poor. Whether expressed in terms of wealth and poverty, modernism and traditionalism, transformation and continuity, this same dichotomy permeates all aspects of urban life in Indonesia. It reflects the essential dualism characteristic of all Third World cities, the sharp distinction between the small proportion of the population engaged in the capital-intensive modern sector of the economy, in which incomes are high and regular, and the majority who are associated with the labour-surplus traditional sector in which self-employment in tiny business units and open and disguised unemployment, and the low and irregular incomes these bring, are typical.

Manufacturing Industries

Whatever happens in the rural areas, modernisation of Indonesia's economy to bring higher levels of productivity, income, and living standards will inevitably require a sharp rise in non-agricultural employment and, in particular, an expansion of urban-based manufacturing industries. As throughout South-east Asia, however, the present occupational structure of Indonesia's cities shows a heavy dominance of largely non-productive tertiary activities and over half the total employed urban population is in services, retailing, and similar occupations. With an enormous bureaucracy several times larger than in colonial times, government is a major employer although its innumerable departments and agencies are patently overpopulated with underemployed officials, clerks, office boys, and the like. Overt and concealed unemployment is indeed widespread and the rapidly growing city population, swollen by unskilled, inexperienced migrants, is engaged principally in such marginal low-paid occupations as hawking and petty trading, shining shoes, begging, or *becak* (trishaw) driving, 'the kind of employment which keeps a man from absolute starvation but contributes practically nothing either to the economy's development or to his own acquisition of skills and confidence'.[23]

In view of the size of the cities and their very large share of the nation's manufacturing activity, a remarkably small proportion of their inhabitants, probably less than a sixth, is in industrial employment. When cities in the West reached comparable sizes, their tertiary sectors were of a far higher level and they had substantially more industrial employment. In Indonesia, the growth of city population has been much more rapid than the increase in industrial employment and production, and, to a large extent, the nation remains heavily dependent on imports for manufactured goods. Despite some recent development, Indonesia has experienced urbanisation almost without industrialisation. Yet, as Wertheim observed nearly two decades ago, there is only one conceivable solution to the continued explosion of city population and increasing demands for adequate urban employment: 'speedy and energetic industrialization'. 'Only by rapidly increasing the urban population's production', he continued, 'can work and food be found for everyone'.[24] Rooted as it is in the nation's dualistic economic structure, with its combination of peasant agriculture and production of raw materials for export, the problem is not new; but in its current form it reflects the relative failure of changing official policies on industrialisation and urban employment during the last half-century.

Although the question of encouraging industrial development to redress the diminishing welfare of Java's population was raised in the early 1900s, and, in response to difficulties during World War I, a Commission for Factory Industry was appointed in 1916, effective colonial policies to promote manufacturing did not emerge until the 1930s. What industry there was in Indonesia until that time was either traditional in nature or owed its presence to the development of an externally oriented colonial economy, the latter including the plants processing raw materials for export and the metalworking and repair shops associated with the plantations, mines, railways, and shipyards. Most important in terms of numbers of units and employees were the innumerable, largely traditional, cottage and small-scale industries dispersed through the villages and towns. Most numerous were those producing cheap serviceable articles such as bamboo products, pottery, roofing tiles, or agricultural implements to meet the everyday needs of villagers. There were also many long-established handicraft industries producing, for instance, *batik*, or silver, gold, brass, and copper ware for a wider market. Particular towns were noted for special products—Tasikmalaya and Juwiring for umbrellas, Bareng for cutlery, Jogjakarta, Surakarta, and Pekalongan for *batik*. These industries were overwhelmingly Indonesian, and frequently involved a putting-out system whereby materials were supplied by a middleman or *bakul* who received the finished product in return for a small payment. Many had suffered severe competition since the mid-nineteenth century from imported Western goods, but they remained virtually the only form of consumer-goods production.

The Great Depression had serious repercussions in Indonesia, causing widespread suffering and unemployment particularly in the sugar districts of Java. At the same time, the Dutch became perturbed by the rising popularity of cheap imported Japanese manufactures. Although it was not the intention of the colonial government to transform the essentially rural-agrarian economy by industrialisation, the promotion of manufacturing was now seen as a matter of greater urgency. Efforts were made to devise a programme which would encourage small-scale enterprise and also lead to the establishment or expansion of labour-demanding industries producing essential consumer items currently imported in large quantities. A protectionist trade policy was introduced, restrictions were placed on the import of certain manufactured goods, and import duties on essential machinery and raw materials, including cotton and rayon yarn, were reduced or eliminated. As supporting measures, various government services were created to improve techniques of production and marketing and a Credit Fund for Small Industries was set up to provide capital on easy terms for small-scale industrialists. By 1941, there was a special budget allocation to provide subsidies for large undertakings deemed beneficial to the community and country. Additionally, industrial concerns in the Netherlands were invited to establish manufacturing or assembly plants in the Indies and the agency and import houses already operating there were persuaded to invest in manufacturing. These moves represent the beginnings of what subsequently became increasing government participation in the process of industrial development, but they should be kept in perspective; the capital spent by government on industry in 1940 was a mere 1.6 percent of its total expenditure and the credit extended to manufacturing that year was less than one percent of all credit funded by government. Nonetheless, the results were not unimpressive and on one estimate manufacturing industry's share of national income rose from 7.4 percent in 1930 to 9.8 percent in 1939.

The growth of cottage and small-scale industry during the 1930s, and especially in the later years of the decade, was seen by Wertheim as 'a symptom of an important dynamic evolution in Javanese society'.[25] A clear illustration of the trend was the enormous rise in the production of the locally preferred clove-based cigarettes known as *kretek*. By 1940, 69 *kretek* factories employing about 24,000 regular workers were in operation, principally in Central and East Java, in addition to a multitude of domestic producers whose numbers rose substantially in the period of peak demand after harvest; in consequence, imports of cigarettes dropped by about four-fifths during the decade. One of the most outstanding changes of this period occurred, however, in the textile industry, particularly in its weaving sector. Largely confined to Java, weaving is an ancient indigenous industry traditionally relying on simple handlooms to produce the coloured woven *sarongs* so widely used in the past by both men and women. The last decade of colonial rule witnessed a tremendous expansion of this industry with more than a sevenfold rise in the number of large weaving-mills and the creation of several thousand small, modern weaving establishments owned and operated by Indonesians, a process symbolised by the remarkable development of the handweaving industry in the Majalaya district of Bandung Regency.[26] But this period also brought significant shifts in technology. The improved wooden handloom with automatic shuttle developed by the Government Textile Service in Bandung for use in the home or in small weaving sheds gained speedy acceptance and the number in operation rose from 500 in 1930 to 49,000 in 1941. The introduction of a new simple mechanical loom suitable for medium and large mills had equally dramatic effects, with the number in use increasing from 40 in 1930 to 9,800 in 1941.

The 1930s also brought the emergence of a small, totally new, modern industrial sector in the larger, more Westernised, cities of Java. Despite the high cost of electricity, high freight charges, a shortage of skilled labour, and other deterrents, Western concerns began to invest in the country's first large-scale manufacturing plants: Goodyear opened a tyre factory in Bogor, Unilever and Van den Burgh established soap, margarine, and cooking-oil plants, Bata a shoe factory, General Motors a vehicle-assembly plant in Batavia, and a Dutch syndicate built a large textile-mill at Tegal. These various developments established patterns which have yet to show any notable change. Seven-tenths of the industrial establishments and over four-fifths of the industrial workers recorded in 1940 were in Java, with the heaviest concentrations in the vicinity of Batavia and Surabaya. In terms of employment, the country's principal manufacturing industries were those concerned with foodstuffs, textiles, and metal goods and repairing. Although manufacturing then accounted for possibly an eighth of the total employed population, 2.5 million of these worked in cottage and small-scale units; only 300,000 were employed in mechanised factories and these varied greatly in size. When the Japanese occupation intervened, a few seeds of future development had been sown, but the occupational structure still called for drastic refashioning.

The immediate concern of the rulers of newly independent Indonesia in the late 1940s was rehabilitation after the occupation. Largely because of the temporary effects of the Korean War, however, signs soon appeared of an economic recovery which seemingly justified the high hopes born in the revolutionary struggle. So far as manufacturing is concerned, broad post-war trends are clear. Although little new development of manufacturing occurred in the first five years of independence, output rose in the early 1950s and the share of manufacturing industry in net domestic product apparently grew from 9.5 percent in 1951 to 12 percent in 1957; some allowance, however, has to be made for Indonesia's shaky economic statistics in the Sukarno era. Already by mid-decade, however, inflation and political shifts foreshadowed what was to come. Sukarno and the PNI rose to political dominance, corruption and administrative inefficiency became normal, and policies became increasingly nationalistic and less economically rational as attention was focussed on achieving national solidarity, on 'continuing the revolution', on sloganeering, and on the creation of prestige symbols, all of which absorbed scarce resources sorely needed to promote industrial growth. Concurrently, progressively more ambitious industrial development programmes were devised and there was increasing direct state involvement in manufacturing, largely in an attempt to correct what was seen as one of the gravest defects of colonial rule, namely, the social and economic distortion caused by its emphasis on raw-material production for export and transference of the profits to the Netherlands. Meanwhile, foreign companies withheld new capital investment because of fears for the future which were duly confirmed by nationalisation. The ten years up to 1966 saw an overall decline in manufacturing output; in the early 1960s the proportion of the workforce employed in industry was lower than it had been thirty years earlier and by 1965 manufacturing industry's share of net domestic product had dropped to 11.8 percent. Industrial growth in Indonesia has yet to recover fully from the setbacks and false starts it experienced during the disastrous years of Sukarno.

The Emergency Industrialisation Programme of 1951 had two broad objectives and was fully successful with neither. Firstly, it sought to use substantial amounts of foreign aid to establish a series of large-scale government manufacturing projects principally to produce items required in the drive for national development. Among the top-priority projects scheduled for completion in 1953 were a large cement factory at Gresik and a large spinning-mill at Cilacap, both in Java. Largely because of shortage of funds and poor organisation, all these projects were seriously delayed and the Gresik cement plant did not open until 1957. Secondly, the strong element of mutual co-operation among Javanese villagers was to be harnessed by establishing co-operatives, or *perusahaan induk,* in order to expand and improve cottage and small-scale industries to yield more consumer goods for the domestic market. On behalf of local manufacturers of a particular product, these co-operatives would purchase materials, if necessary they would do preliminary processing, they would advise on techniques and undertake marketing. Most of the co-operatives planned in this so-called 'Induk Programme' were operating by the later 1950s, but, chiefly because of administrative defects and the poor quality of the products, they were far less successful than was hoped.

Lack of success with these earlier plans and the rise of Sukarno's concepts of Guided Democracy and Guided Economy brought an extension of direct government participation and an increased preoccupation with heavy industry which are apparent in Indonesia's First Five-Year Plan (1956-60). In addition to proposals for a future steel plant, this involved several large basic industrial units, mostly to be financed by overseas loans, including caustic soda and glass plants at Surabaya and a fertiliser (urea) factory at Palembang, which were intended to serve as catalysts for further industrial growth. It was also hoped to encourage medium and small-scale industries and, to relieve acute employment problems, priority was given to the development of manufacturing in East and Central Java. With about 18 percent of proposed public development expenditure earmarked for manufacturing, mainly as foreign exchange for the import of capital goods, this plan incorporated very ambitious targets; by 1960 domestic production of fertilisers was to rise to 100,000 tons, cement output was to reach 900,000 tons, and an additional 130,000 kw. of generating capacity was to be provided. Significantly, however, although few of the major projects fell far behind schedule and the number of industrial establishments increased, this was not accompanied by a marked growth in total manufacturing output or employment; indeed, in many spheres production fell, sometimes dramatically. One of the most startling examples is the case of the bicycle-assembly industry; whereas the number of plants in existence rose from 8 in 1955 to 46 in 1961, production of bicycles fell from 25,600 to

24,400 in the same period. The causes of this paradoxical situation are many and complex, but they certainly include the opportunistic way many new plants were established with easy government credit, rising inflation and the deflationary measures of 1959, and difficulties of acquiring imported raw materials and spare parts because of shortage of foreign exchange. Additionally, product design and production programmes were not always geared to 'reasonable and stable economic prospects' and many of the new plants had so wide a range of varieties of a single type of product that 'economic production is hardly conceivable'.[27] Moreover, the later 1950s witnessed an extension of direct government participation in the economy principally through the nationalisation of Dutch-owned enterprises in consequence of the dispute over Irian, and, partly because of the dearth of suitably qualified Indonesian staff, this contributed to reductions in manufacturing output. Concurrently, other foreign concerns faced increasingly arduous restrictions and some, such as the General Motors assembly plant in Jakarta, were eventually closed.[28]

The subsequent Eight-year Overall Development Plan, scheduled to run from 1961 to 1968, incorporated even more grandiose proposals, but many of these were essentially political and were never seriously implemented. Based on a categorisation of projects whereby exploitation of natural resources with the aid of foreign capital would furnish the necessary foreign-exchange earnings, manufacturing industry was to receive almost a third of planned investment with the largest allocation designed to produce a greatly enlarged and more dispersed cotton-spinning industry. Although this plan was curtailed by the downfall of Sukarno, in the field of manufacturing it was not achievement but declining output that characterised the first half of the 1960s, and by mid-decade many state-owned enterprises were working well below installed capacity. Despite the plan's proposals, lack of foreign exchange continued to hamper imports of raw materials and spares, and years of inadequate maintenance and non-replacement of obsolete equipment were taking their toll. An arbitrary price control also hamstrung many industries; cotton yarns were controlled so that production was unprofitable, but woven cotton goods were not, so that neither section operated at capacity. Short of funds to cover running costs, manufacturing establishments also faced rising prices for domestic raw materials and for transport and power. There were also serious management problems which were exacerbated by the confiscation of British and American enterprises in 1964 at the time of confrontation with Malaysia and attention and finance were directed increasingly to non-economic objectives. 'For years', Soehoed remarks,

> manufacturing industries, like other sectors of the Indonesian economy, had suffered from shortage of managerial and technical skills in the individual enterprises and from a system of government controls which make it hard even for capable managers to run their plants efficiently.[29]

But the situation deteriorated in the early 1960s and when Sukarno was displaced, Indonesia inherited 'little but unfinished projects and unbearable debts' from the over-ambitious and largely ineffective Overall Development Plan.[30]

Suharto's New Order had to revitalise a ravaged economy. Rampant inflation, enormous foreign debts, a serious decline in productive capacity, and the merest trickle of foreign investment offered little hope of an immediate upswing in manufacturing. Essential prerequisites for any improvement were the rehabilitation of existing plants, the revival of international and domestic confidence to encourage investment, and a reversal of the serious rundown in the nation's infrastructure. At the time, Indonesia's total installed electricity-generating capacity was substantially smaller than West Malaysia's and within South-east Asia only Laos had a lower *per capita* electricity output. Even in 1968 over four-fifths of the country's roads were classed as 'bad' or 'very bad', railway track, rolling stock, bridges, and signals required urgent overhaul, and equipment and facilities for inter-island shipping were inadequate and out-of-date. But the new regime was realistic about the vast range of problems and it introduced a series of flexible, largely *ad hoc,* policies to stabilise the economy and initiate rehabilitation. With World Bank assistance, improvements began in transport facilities. Priorities were established in the allocation of scarce foreign exchange with manufacturing of essential goods such as cement, fertiliser, paper, and tyres receiving special consideration. Various other measures, including the reduction of interest rates and the temporary removal of import duties on raw materials, were introduced to encourage manufacturing. Perhaps the most revolutionary change from the days of Sukarno, however, was the adoption of a new attitude to overseas capital. The Foreign Investment Law of 1967 sought to attract foreign capital and terms were arranged for the restoration of confiscated foreign establishments, mostly British, to their owners, including industrial undertakings.

By 1969 stabilisation had proceeded sufficiently for the Suharto government to introduce its First Five-Year Plan (1969-73), known locally as *Repelita* I. Designed largely to engender an 'atmosphere of development' and permitting broad flexibility in implementation, this economically rational document so unlike its predecessors merely laid down the general objectives of what some called 'a strategy for action'; major structural changes in the economy were not envisaged and the plan was concerned with consolidating the rehabilitation process. Heavily reliant on foreign finance, especially overseas aid, it allotted 17.7 percent of total proposed expenditure to industrial development. Two groups of industries received priority: those serving the basic needs of the development programme, particularly in agriculture, including the production of fertiliser, cement, and agricultural and processing machinery; and those producing goods such as textiles, paper, tyres, and chemicals which were in seriously short supply and whose growth would result in significant import substitution. As one of the major areas of manufacturing employment, the textile industry was accorded special attention; substantial amounts of foreign capital were directed to the improvement of the industry's equipment and the quality of its product, a doubling of textile output was planned, and several large new mills were opened. Since Indonesia was importing about nine-tenths of its fertiliser requirements and these were expected to rise sharply with the extension of the rice improvement programme, the capacity of the urea plant at Palembang was trebled (an increase which it was estimated could save the country US $36 million in imports annually), and plans were prepared for a new fertiliser plant at Cirebon. Equally, there was an urgent need to expand cement production since national consumption had been rising annually for years and domestic production satisfied only a fraction of demand. To achieve this end, the new Tonasa cement factory was opened in 1968 at Pangkajene in South Sulawesi and the existing plants at Gresik and Padang were extended. Additionally, two new large cement plants were opened in 1975 in Cibinon, West Java, production from which is expected to rise rapidly, and factories at Cilacap (Central Java) and Baturaja (South Sumatra) are due to start production in 1977. Indonesia is therefore moving quickly towards a situation in which most of the enlarged demand for cement is met by domestic production.

In consequence of these and other developments there was an upsurge in manufacturing output in the early 1970s. This owed much to the rehabilitation and expansion of state-owned enterprises and the establishment of new plants by government, but it was also caused by a significant rise in overseas investment in the manufacturing sector. Having been excluded from Indonesia for so long, the prime objective of foreign investors in recent years was to gain a foothold in a potentially large, expanding market. While providing suitable incentives for this investment, the Indonesian government has been determined to increase local participation in manufacturing by encouraging the creation of joint ventures and by 1970 certain regions and fields of activity were closed to foreign capital except in this form. Moreover, under the new Second Five-Year Plan (1974-79), which is strongly concerned with the need to create employment and to achieve a more equitable division of the results of development, strenuous efforts will be made to increase domestic investment in industry, both through co-operation with overseas finance and through the provision of credit and other assistance to handicraft and small-scale establishments.

About four-fifths of the foreign capital invested in the country up to 1973 was in joint Indonesian-foreign enterprises. These carry the advantage of various concessions and provide a local partner who is often invaluable in dealing with the Indonesian bureaucracy. The main conditions applicable to this form of investment are that the undertaking must employ as many Indonesians as possible, and, where suitable local staff are unavailable, must provide training, and that the Indonesian counterpart, who must be 'indigenous', should move towards a majority shareholding. Yet despite vigorous efforts to ease the situation, the foreign investor faces many problems. The stultification of private industrial enterprise under Sukarno makes it difficult to find local partners with sufficient capital and experience, and, as Professor Mohammad Sadli, former Chairman of the Investment Board, has admitted, much frustration arises from processing of applications, the complicated regulations, the interference of local officials, excessive Customs inspection, and the general inadequacy of communication facilities. Nonetheless, since 1967 substantial amounts of overseas capital have moved into the manufacturing sector, particularly from the United States, Japan, and Europe; whereas in the early 1960s modern large-scale industry in Indonesia was essentially a government preserve, it now displays a balance between the *Perusahaan Negara,* or state-owned enterprises, concerned principally with such basic industries as fertilisers, cement, tyres, and paper, and the predominantly joint ventures in the light consumer-goods industries. Some of this foreign investment has gone into the production or assembly of goods for re-export with the entire operation confined within a bonded warehouse area, a pattern reminiscent of Taiwan and South Korea. In response to rising domestic demand, however, most of the joint private ventures are engaged in processing imported raw materials or in assembling imported components for the Indonesian market. In conjunction with the powerful local Salim group of companies, for instance, Volvo recently established an assembly plant for cars, trucks, and buses on a 10-hectare site at Ancol on the outskirts of Jakarta, for which initially all the parts are shipped from Sweden, although ultimately some components will be manufactured locally. Occasional joint manufacturing establishments have been set up in the Outer Islands, but the outstanding concentration of this development is in Jakarta and the other large urban centres of Java. Whether it has taken the form of joint private ventures or new state-owned plants, the recent growth of modern manufacturing industry has had similar effects on the urban format. Characteristically, sites have been selected on the urban fringe and, since this encourages the emergence of associated *kampung* housing, it exacerbates the process of peripheral expansion which has become so marked in Indonesia's largest cities.

One in every nine of the Indonesian workforce is now employed in manufacturing industry, which accounts for almost an eighth of Gross National Product. In recent years the country has acquired an enlarged, more diversified modern manufacturing sector with scope for substantial future expansion, but its industrial structure remains dominated by cottage and small-scale establishments. While growth has undoubtedly occurred, however, it has done relatively little to solve problems of employment and regional imbalances in development. For the most part, the new industries have been confined to areas of existing development and the broad spatial pattern of manufacturing activity resembles that of late colonial times. Today, over 80 percent of all manufacturing establishments are located in Java, with the capital alone containing as many as the whole of the Outer Islands; in consequence, under the Second Five-Year Plan efforts will be made to distribute new industrial investment projects throughout all the nation's provinces, to create, in the words of the Chairman of the Investment Co-ordination Board, 'more equal growth in the economic development in all regions'. In addition, the policy of encouraging private foreign investment has tended to promote more capital-intensive forms of manufacturing and the Governor of Jakarta has estimated that an investment of a million US dollars yields only 200 new jobs.[31] Essential as it was in view of earlier deficiencies, much of the development that has occurred is of a kind which leads to significant, and necessary, increases in production, but provides relatively few new employment opportunities for the burgeoning urban labour force and has marginal effects on the levels of living and purchasing power of the mass of urban dwellers. 'As a generator of employment', Soehoed observes, 'the manufacturing industries have disappointed earlier expectations'.[32] Herein lies one of Indonesia's major dilemmas. An expanded modern manufacturing sector, oriented to the local market, is expected to serve the nation's growth needs in terms of rising productivity and output and, at the same time, to absorb overabundant urban labour. Currently, there is scant prospect of industrialisation matching, let alone exceeding, anticipated rates of population growth in the largest cities.

NOTES

[1] Robert R. Reed, 'The Colonial Origins of Manila and Batavia: Desultory Notes on Nascent Metropolitan Primacy and Urban Systems in Southeast Asia', *Asian Studies,* vol.5, no. 3, 1967, 550.

[2] J.C. van Leur, *Indonesian Trade and Society,* The Hague, Van Hoeve, 1955, 137.

[3] T.G. McGee, *The Southeast Asian City,* London, Bell, 1967, 48.

[4] J.C.M. Warnsinck (ed.), *De reisen van Nicolaus de Graaff gedaan naar alle gewesten des werelds, beginnende 1639 tot 1687 incluis,* The Hague, 1930, 13 cited in B. Schrieke, *Indonesian Sociological Studies,* Part II, The Hague, Van Hoeve, 1957, 251.

[5] W.F. Wertheim, *Indonesian Society in Transition,* The Hague, Van Hoeve, 1956, 172-3.

[6] S.A. Reitsma, *Van Stockum's Travellers' Handbook for the Dutch East Indies,* The Hague, 1930, 236.

[7] J.C. Jackson, 'Post-Independence Developments and the Indonesian City: Preliminary Observations on the Spatial Structure of Palembang', *Sumatra Research Bulletin,* vol. 2, no. 2, 1973, 3-11.

[8] H. Lehmann, 'Das Antlitz der Stadt in Niederländisch-Indien' in H. Louis and W. Panzer (eds.), *Länderkundliche Forschung: Festschrift zur Vollendung des Sechzigsten Lebensjahres Norbert Krebs, Dargebracht von Seinen Schülern, Mitarbeitern Freunden und dem verlag,* Stuttgart, 1936, 120-1.

[9] R. Murphey, 'Urbanization in Asia', *Ekistics,* vol, 21, no. 122, 1966, 11.

[10] Purnaman Natakusumah, 'Bandung' in Aprodicio A. Laquian (ed.), *Rural-Urban Migrants and Metropolitan Development,* Toronto, 1971, 31.

[11] Hildred Geertz, 'Indonesian Cultures and Communities' in Ruth T. McVey (ed.), *Indonesia,* New Haven, 1963, 33-41.

[12] Hans-Dieter Evers, 'Urban Involution: the Social Development of South-east Asian Towns', *International Conference on Southeast Asian Studies,* Kuala Lumpur, February 1972 (mimeo).

[13] H.T. Chabot, 'Urbanization Problems in South East Asia', *Transactions of the Fifth World Congress of Sociology,* Louvain, 1964, vol. 3, pp. 125-31.

[14] Gavin Jones, 'The Recent Growth of Asian Cities', *Hemisphere,* vol. 8, no. 2, 1964, 12.

[15] E.M. Bruner, 'Urbanization and Ethnic Identity in North Sumatra', *American Anthropologist,* vol. 63, no. 3, 1961, 515.

[16] Richard Critchfield, 'The Plight of the Cities: Djakarta—the First to "Close"', *Columbia Journal of World Business,* vol. 6, 1971, 93.

[17] Edward M. Bruner, 'The Expression of Ethnicity in Indonesia' in Abner Cohen (ed.), *Urban Ethnicity,* A. S. A. Monographs no. 12, Tavistock Publications, London, 1974, 251-80.

[18] In his recent study of migration to Jakarta ('Migration to Jakarta', *Bulletin of Indonesian Economic Studies,* vol. XI, no. 1, 1975, 79), for instance, Gordon P. Temple concluded that migrants choose to move to the capital because they feel that it 'offers them the best hope of finding reliable employment opportunities'. Most move, in other words, in response to their perceptions of the availability of means of making a living.

[19] Critchfield, op.cit., 89.

[20] ibid., 92.

[21] S. Soekanto, 'Elites in Three Southeast Asian Countries: A Sociological Perspective', *The Indonesian Quarterly,* vol. 1, no. 2, 1973, 58.

[22] Purnaman Natakusumah, op.cit., 18.

[23] Critchfield, op.cit., 90.

[24] Wertheim, op.cit., 193.

[25] ibid., 110.

[26] W. van Warmelo, 'Ontstaan en groei van de handweefnijverheid in Madjalaja', *Koloniale Studien,* vol. XXIII, 1939, 5-25.

[27] A.R. Soehoed, 'Manufacturing in Indonesia', *Bulletin of Indonesian Economic Studies,* no. 8, 1967, 84.

[28] ibid., 68-72.

[29] ibid., 80.

[30] ibid., 65.

[31] Critchfield, op.cit., 89.

[32] Soehoed, op.cit., 75.

CHAPTER 8

Politics and Foreign Affairs

IN ALL COMMUNIST STATES, and in many states of the so-called Third World, the formal or legal structure of government as defined in a constitution, and the physical reality of the possession and exercise of power, are separated by a wide gulf. In Indonesia, not only is this contrast very marked, but the passage of time produces new kaleidoscopic patterns of form and substance in government. The viewer, nevertheless, sees largely what he wishes to see, and it is perhaps significant that most Western scholars of the Indonesian political scene have been more charitable than have their Indonesian counterparts. Indonesia's formal gyrations over the three decades since independence, from the hastily drafted and makeshift constitution of 1945, through parliamentary government and the court of Sukarno to the *Orba* of Suharto and its final array in the respectable legitimacy of 1945, might suggest that Indonesia has fulfilled its destiny. But the Indonesia of the 1970s is far removed from the youthful exuberance of that of 1945, and if some of the issues that confronted the infant republic have been resolved while its population has nearly doubled, at least as many have been set aside, and there is little to suggest that most Indonesians accept decisions of government as other than highly opportunistic.

The working of Indonesian political institutions often resembles the traditional *wayang kulit,* or shadow play, in which the audience sees only the projected silhouettes of puppets of gods and heroes of an epic of the *Mahabharata.* For Indonesians, who know the characters, the intricacies of plot, and the inordinate length of the performance, the play's the thing. But to those who have to interpret Indonesian political behaviour in models and terminology intelligible to Western society, distinguishing shadow from substance is essential, and even more necessary is determining just who is the *dalang* (puppet-master). While much is known about political life, there is also much that is unknown, and, given the Indonesian psyche and love of the Byzantine in politics, is perhaps unknowable to Westerners. Thus the *peristiwa 17 Oktober* (the 17 October incident of 1952), when armoured units surrounded the Presidential palace, has been closely analysed by political scientists, but no really convincing explanation of this celebrated climacteric in modern Indonesian history has yet appeared, although it is agreed that several pressing political issues were brought to a focus, and that the parties to the confrontation were the surrogates for a variety of political forces. Again some two decades later, the student riots of January 1974 already appeared by the end of the year as another major enigma; transmogrified into the *peristiwa Malari* (an acronym from *Malapetaka Januari,* or 'January disaster'), their apparent anti-Japanese character was for all politically conscious Indonesians buried under an avalanche of intriguing domestic issues and covert confrontations. Were the riots a PSI-*Masyumi*-inspired plot, as General Murtopo had charged? Was the army divided against itself, and what was the role of General Sumitro, then commander of *Kopkamtib,* the Command for the Restoration of Security and Order? Sumitro had shown evidence of taking the President's independence day address of 1973, which called for growing intercommunication between government and the people, at something like face value; his speeches may well have encouraged more trenchant criticism of governments by the students, some of whom felt that the army would protect them, just as it did during their campaigns against Sukarno. *Kopkamtib* had carried Suharto to the highest office; could it do the same for Sumitro, and was he using the same weapons against Suharto that the latter had used against Sukarno? Some saw an even more nefarious conspiracy, cooked up by the arch-fixer and manipulator Murtopo to destroy his rival. In this view, Murtopo urged on the students so that both they and Sumitro could be cut down together; *post hoc ergo propter hoc,* and Murtopo did survive with his powers and influence virtually intact, while Sumitro was removed from office. Some of these contentions seem highly dubious, but that all could gain some measure of credence was the inevitable price of a system in which government may say one thing but mean another, in which the press, if not totally shackled, has nevertheless to be very circumspect in any criticism of authority, and of a government which ceaselessly tries to manipulate opinion in support of a regime obsessed with the need for security and stability. Unanimity among Indonesia's leaders is, of course, no more to be expected than it is among those of the Politburo, and if the political commentator on Jakarta at times sounds like a Kremlinologist, it is because he has to compound a meagre diet of facts with a broad measure of hearsay, intuition, and the licence tacitly accorded the political scientist.

The Structure of Government

Sukarno's *konsepsi* of a return to the constitution of 1945, a move supported by the armed forces and the PKI, was an attempt to restore the strong Presidency implicit in that document. But as with most constitutions, it says nothing about the role of the military or of the parties; it vests supreme authority in the MPR *(Majelis Permusyawaratan Rakyat)* assembly, which selects the President and Vice President, although the manner in which this is to be done is not clear. The MPR consists of all members of the DPR *(Dewan Perwakilan Rakyat)*, or Parliament, together with an equivalent number of representatives from the *Daerah* (regions), and of other elements in the population unrepresented in Parliament. How the MPR removed the provisional element from its titular acronym has been related in Chapter 4; it exists primarily to approve of decisions taken by the President without prior reference to it, and to give the regime a cloak of legitimacy directly derived from the earliest days of the great Indonesian revolution. For the reality is that Indonesia has an authoritarian military administration, the modal form of government in the Third World. But, by the standards of that world, Indonesia's regime might be judged a relatively benign one. In comparison with other states of the Malay world such as Malaysia and Brunei, or perhaps even with the Philippines, government appears at times excruciatingly inefficient and corrupt, particularly in its dealings with the individual citizen. But all of these states possessed advantages at birth denied to Indonesia, not the least of which was that as independence was freely conceded and not fought for, their armed forces were never able to appropriate a position in society comparable with those of Indonesia.

A body with 920 members, far larger than the United States Congress, is clearly incapable of effective leadership, and with General Nasution as Speaker, the enigmatic former Army Chief of Staff whose prolonged apparent lack of resolution earned him the title of Indonesia's Hamlet from the influential Hong Kong *Far Eastern Economic Review*, the MPR appears unlikely ever to take forceful action. The government not only controls an overwhelming majority among the DPR members, but is even stronger among the 460 members drawn partly from the regional assemblies, all of which were won in the 1971 election by the government party *Golkar* (*Golongan Karya*, or functional groups), and partly from other organisations. The time has long passed since it was necessary for Suharto to move with great caution in establishing his own title to the Presidency, but since 1965 Suharto has repeatedly appeared before the MPR to obtain approval for his decisions, just as the Party Secretary in the Kremlin periodically parades the Supreme Soviet for some act of rubber-stamping, after which it is permitted to give its customary standing ovation to its master. Few Russians are taken in by these exercises, and, in all probability, few politically conscious Indonesians are either. Such ceremony reflects the Indonesian preference for symbolism and form, rather than function, in government; it confirms the principle of legitimacy revered in the Javanese *adat,* and, by appearing in civilian dress, the President camouflages the pervasive influence of the military and stresses national solidarity.

Unlike the MPR, which meets irregularly, Parliament is expected to sit for four sessions a year. As neither the President nor the cabinet is responsible to it, the DRP is as much a cipher as is the larger body, and its principal purpose is to pass as rapidly and with as little comment as possible legislation desired by the government. Highly contentious matters, such as the Marriage Law of 1973 and the Regional Government Law of 1974, about which it might be expected that in a national forum a great deal would be heard, were approved with great speed and without amendment, even although they generated a great deal of heated discussion outside. Through its committees, the DRP does have some other investigatory and review functions, but a legislative body without a vigorous and independent party life cannot command any great credibility or respect. The rumps of Indonesia's legally permitted parties, forcibly combined into unnatural groupings and confronted with what gives every appearance of constituting a built-in *Golkar* majority through apparently free but in reality highly manipulated elections, are cowed and dispirited. Nor have the representatives of *Golkar* itself, a non-party in that it has no mass base or permanent local or national organisation, any prospect of achieving positions of power or influence. Many of those nominated to stand for election were the relatives of senior local officials, retired civil servants, or veterans, and impressive though the government and military effort was on behalf of *Golkar* candidates, it was mounted specifically for the 1971 election and would need reactivating for any in the future. Least of all does Parliament exercise perhaps its most important function in real democracies, control of the public purse; but determining precisely where that power does reside in Suharto's *Orba* is almost as difficult as it was for the Sukarno era. Sukarno's illegal dismissal of Parliament cannot, however, be repeated; on the other hand, Parliament cannot censure the government.

Real power resides with the President, some members of the cabinet, commanders of the armed forces, with key members of non-departmental state agencies, or with some of all of these in concert. In general, power appears to have become more particulate, that is, less institutionalised and more attached to cliques and factions around particular individuals. Under the constitution the President is Supreme Commander of all the Armed Forces; but Suharto's authority also arises from his status as a soldier with substantial combat experience, whose professionalism the army as a whole respects. Crack commanders who come too much in the public eye, and virtually all Indonesian generals adopt a flamboyant and ostentatious life-style, are apt to find themselves suddenly posted to new jobs in more distant provinces or overseas, where they no longer command attention, and so far none of those removed have been able to generate enough support to make effective protest. Unfortunately for the generals, even the preservation of the privileges of the military necessitates a healthy and expanding economy if there is not to be social explosion, and of their incompetence to achieve this unaided, the experience of several developing countries provides eloquent testimony. The President thus carries the overriding responsibility for maintaining a working accommodation between the military, with its preoccupation with national cohesion, and the civilian arm of government, which must carry the main burden of implementing modernisation programmes.

In contrast with Sukarno's enormous final cabinets of a hundred, far too large to be effective, Suharto has retained a small cohesive organisation. In addition to the President and Vice President, the Second Development Cabinet of 1973 included 17 Departmental members, of whom but three (Home Affairs, Defence, and Industry) were from the armed forces, and 5 non-departmental Ministers of State. One important cabinet group was the so-called technocrats, around Ali Wardhana, Minister of Finance, and Widjojo Nitisastro, Minister of Economics and Head of the National Planning Board. These professional economists were given the task of restoring the devastated Indonesian economy, and of replenishing the country's almost non-existent foreign-exchange resources, after the Sukarno excesses. In the latter aim, at least, they succeeded far beyond their own or anybody else's expectations; Indonesia's foreign-exchange earnings for 1974 were $3,400 million and for 1975 were expected to reach nearly $4,000 million. Moreover, if not all the goals of *Repelita* I, the First Five-Year Plan, were achieved, the record of implementation was far higher than that of any previous plan, and preparations for *Repelita* II could proceed with modest optimism.

How cabinet or ministerial decisions are translated into action at the regional or local level, where the activities of all Departments have to be co-ordinated, is far from clear. The day-to-day work of government falls on the country's 1.67 million-strong bureaucracy, whose principal creative feat so far has perhaps been the coining of acronyms, more than 10,000 of which have appeared since independence; many of these fall into speedy disuse, but their numbers are always swollen by new issues. Indonesia in theory retains the working-day of Dutch times (7 a.m. to 2.30 p.m.), but in practice, most *pegawai* are part-time workers, and absenteeism is rife. Anyone of importance has usually left his office soon after midday, often to another job, for it is impossible to live on official salaries, even with other fringe benefits awarded to government servants. Low salaries are in large part a consequence of overstaffing; faced with the potential danger of a large unemployed mandarinate, government has always found it difficult to restrict recruitment of new graduates in a limited labour market. The low salaries are a powerful inducement to corruption, but the potential inflationary effect of any substantial increase is always advanced as a reason for government inaction; nevertheless, in 1971 a 100 percent across-the-board salary increase for all government employees was authorised. But it is common to find senior officials with salaries equivalent to less than $200 per month across the exchanges, with luxurious houses, large cars, and hill-station residences, and it is notorious that the life-style of the head of *Pertamina* requires a real income very many times his official salary.

Dissatisfaction with Indonesia's creaking ramshackle bureaucracy is intense, both among the populace, which is impotent to remedy it, and with the military, which can do a very great deal wherever it so chooses. The special privileges of the armed forces were not diminished with the reduction in their share of the budget from over 70 percent in the final years of Sukarno to the 30 percent or so of the early 1970s; on the contrary, their influence in national life has grown with *Orba*. The *dwifungsi*, or dual functions of the military as the guardian of national sovereignty and integrity from dangers both within and without, and which provides the theoretical underpinnings of army interference in social and economic life, derive from the earliest activities of the occupation-sponsored paramilitary forces, and, despite sporadic outbreaks of student protest at the appointment of senior officers to high civilian posts, have never seriously been challenged. In making these appointments the President clearly shows his commitment to this strong Indonesian political tradition, and it was also evident in the creation of a Council of Presidential Assistants (*Aspri*), whose four members, all generals, were in effect Executive Vice Presidents for political, economic, financial, and military affairs respectively, using their immediate access to the President to function, as many Indonesians saw it, both as cabinet overlords and as a supernumerary Parliament. The Council was wound up following the riots of January 1974, but it was promptly replaced by two new bodies, a Committee for Political Stabilisation and Security, and a Committee for Economic Stabilisation. Later, a third for Social and Cultural Stabilisation was added, and a committee to supervise all three and to act as an overlord for all economic development and planning was established in August. To the opposition parties and the students, these changes appeared merely window dressing. The ex-assistants appeared with their powers and influence undiminished, and continued their criticism of the cabinet technocrats, some of whom appeared in danger of losing their jobs by late 1974.

The very success of the technocrats in attracting massive foreign investment, in restoring Indonesia's credit worthiness and its standing in the world polity and economy, was always likely to provoke a reaction. If continued, it could well come to constitute the first real challenge to the military's privileged *dwifungsi*, for the armed forces were well aware that the important international agencies that Sukarno had defied in vain, particularly the World Bank and the International Monetary Fund, bodies with which the technocrats closely worked, regard all military regimes with distaste. The example of nearby Thailand, where these organisations had thrown the full weight of their support behind the civilian authorities in their efforts to deny the Thai generals access to the national exchequer and other levers of economic power, was too close for comfort, particularly in view of the sudden and unexpected collapse of the Thai military regime late in 1973. Nor did IGGI, the consortium of donor nations and another supporter of technocrat pragmatism, take a charitable view of the military establishment, for although obliged to accept the government as it found it, IGGI's main concern was to secure payment on Indonesia's enormous foreign debt, and as quickly as possible. In attacking the technocrats' alleged subservience to these international bodies, and, as they claimed, the overprivileged position of foreign enterprise that had resulted from it, ex-Presidential Assistant General Murtopo and his associates were ventilating problems that were very real to many Indonesians, not least the student population. Indigenous enterprise had apparently benefited very little from *Repelita* I and technocrat policies, and government assistance to the *peribumi* (indigenous) businessman, it was alleged, was far too limited to offer any real prospect of successful competition with the foreign enterprise, or even with the Indonesian Chinese.

In Indonesia, as in many other countries of the Third World, it has been the planners' misfortune that initially economic development creates not only greater inequality but also public awareness of it. Yet in their rejection of technocrat planning as a Western importation which cannot work in the totally different Indonesian social and institutional background, the large element of the generals' self-interest is obvious. There is little reason for believing that the greater free-for-all that would follow dismantling of the planners' system of controls and regulations would benefit the *peribumi* entrepreneur; the irrepressible Chinese would almost certainly be the principal beneficiaries, and indeed, the military did endeavour both during late 1973 and on earlier occasions to restrain attacks on Chinese property. Despite Murtopo's championing of the indigenous entrepreneur, few politically sophisticated Indonesians believe that a Chinese businessman has any great difficulty in buying a colonel, or even a general. Moreover, while it is scarcely possible that there can be anything else on the scale of *Pertamina*'s storehouse of riches, Indonesia's long-acclaimed but long-in-coming wealth of physical resources is a prize that the military cannot afford to allow to pass completely into the hands of the planners.

This implies a continued strong military influence in key regions with such resources, and opposition to the state entities that the planners would like to develop them. What the technocrats intend by the latter are state or joint ventures under civilian and cabinet control, which *Pertamina* before 1975 certainly was not. The complex international financial operations designed to save *Pertamina*, the largest such rescue endeavour ever mounted, have certainly increased the control of the Finance Ministry and the National Planning Board over its multifarious activities. But the military establishment can be expected to resist any reduction in its present massive representation in *Pertamina*'s key operating staff. Dr Ibnu Sutowo has perhaps been downgraded, but certainly not disgraced. To write off the future of this dynamic personality would seem to be unwise, particularly if, as has been rumoured, General Suharto gives up his office after the next scheduled election in 1977.

The brief history of independent Indonesia in Chapter 4 showed that throughout much of the archipelago, while Jakarta may propose, it is often the regions which dispose. One of the principal difficulties of the foreign enterprise in developing Indonesian resources is the treatment it will receive in its selected area of operation, and whether the local civil and military authorities will honour arrangements made in Jakarta. Accommodation, of course, is usually reached, but the expense and delay are major obstacles to planning. But the fact that the military and civil arms of government intertwine at every administrative level above the village makes life difficult for Indonesians as well as for foreign entrepreneurs. From the Ministry of Home Affairs in Jakarta the chain of local government runs through the *propinsi* (provinces, or first-level regions) and *kabupaten* (regencies, or second-level regions) to the *kecamatan* (sub-districts), and finally to the *kelurahan,* or village level. Village officials are elected, by time-hallowed tradition from among village residents; as some village land is set aside for the remuneration of the *pamong desa,* they tend to be persons of substance. Officials of the higher levels of local government *(pamong praja)* are all appointed, have staffs of professional civil servants, and exercise authority over officials in the lower tiers. The first- and second-level regions, however, have their own legislatures, the DPRD *(Dewan Perwakilan Rakyat Daerah),* which since 1971 have been firmly under the control of *Golkar,* the government quasi-party. The military, however, has its own parallel organisation, with an additional supra-provincial level. The local commander is the representative of a department charged with both defence and security, and the latter, together with the *dwifungsi* role, can provide many opportunities for engaging in activities elsewhere not permitted to the military, depending on the personal ambition and skill of the commander, and on his standing with both his superior officers and the civilian authorities. Influence with the latter can be secured through the regional assemblies, which contain many *Golkar* members whose candidature was sponsored by the local army command. Some commanders have been very active in promoting regional economic development, which has generally operated to enhance the status of the commander himself rather than that of the Ministry of Defence. If the local military and civilian arms of government appear at times in harmony, and at others in discord, important decisions, as always in Indonesia, are taken away from the public eye.

Conflict between the regions and the centre is a recurring theme in many countries, and it is through a series of historical accidents that Malaysia and Singapore are sovereign independent countries whereas Aceh and Maluku are not, for all their histories are closely intertwined. Perhaps the most crucial question facing Indonesia is whether a sense of national unity and cohesion can be created in a far-flung archipelago poorly equipped with transport and communication facilities, and beset with great ethnic, linguistic, religious, and cultural differences; more importantly still, can it be achieved by consensus, or has it to be imposed from above, in a *Diktat*? In the latter case, how can it ever be finally accepted? The experience of Mexico, Brazil, India, or even of China, to cite the other large countries of the Third World, shows how quickly old rivalries and passions can flare up when basic questions of food supply, employment, or other critical social and economic issues are concerned. Indonesia has had one bout of regional revolution, and the military is determined to see that national unity is preserved at all costs. But so was the military in Pakistan, and it led the country to disaster and the loss of more than half its population.

The desire for some measure of autonomy is strong in many parts of Indonesia, but it lost respectability through being used by the Dutch in the plan for a United States of Indonesia, and through the events of 1957-58; alleged continued support for regional separatism provides the government with a pretext for continuing the ban on the *Masyumi* and PSI (socialist) parties, imposed by Sukarno in 1960. But the division of Indonesia into regions for the purposes of self-government is provided for in the 1945 constitution, and was the subject of legislation in 1948 and 1957; in 1966 the need for a liberal measure of regional self-government was reaffirmed by the Provisional Consultative Assembly (MPRS). In broad outline, the system of local government in Java inherited from the colonial era has been simplified and extended to the whole country, but since 1957 movement towards meaningful autonomy in a 'revolution of rising expectations' has been reversed. Although there have been some improvements in the allocation of funds from the central government to regional authorities, a basic issue in the revolts, it is clear that the New Order is no more willing than the Old to allow the regions any powers other than implementing decisions and policies of the central government.

The law of 1957 provided for elected Regional Legislative Councils at both provincial and regency level, which in turn would elect the chief executive, or *kepala daerah*. But the responsibilities to be transferred were very imperfectly defined, and involved nothing of a policy-making nature. The imposition of martial law rendered the measure largely a dead letter, and, by a Presidential decree of 1959, provincial governors were made Presidential appointees, and regency chief executives were to be appointed by the Minister of Home Affairs. The regional chief, in fact as well as in law, thus became an agent of the central government responsible to the President, and his relationship with the local legislative body was never defined. In practice, regional government became a responsibility of the local army commander during the period of martial law, but generally in Central and East Java, the army and the civilian authorities worked amicably together.

Martial law ended in 1963 except in the provinces adjacent to Malaysia, and disappeared with the end of confrontation. Nevertheless, the army has continued to exert a substantial degree of influence in local government, and chafing at Jakarta control found expression in an MPRS resolution of 1966, calling for an autonomy 'as wide and as real as possible'.

Indonesia's 26 provinces vary very greatly in size and population; Irian Jaya's 412,000 square kilometres contain only a little over 900,000 people, whereas Jawa Timur (East Java) has 26 million packed into some 47,000 square kilometres. Seldom do provincial boundaries closely correspond with the physical realities of topography, climate, or biotic elements, but several possess a cultural unity which has endured over long periods; the three small provinces of Java, together with Bali, are in this category. In the vastness of the *Tanah Seberang* the pre-war unit of colonial government was the residency, but in 1938 a move was made to bring about a higher level of authority through the creation of the three 'governments' of Sumatra, Borneo, and the *Grote Oost* (Great East). Since independence the residency has been phased out as a unit of local government, and the provincial status previously only enjoyed by the three divisions of Java has been extended throughout the Outer Islands. Initially, regencies were amalgamated to form provinces, as in the three provinces of North, Central, and South Sumatra, and Kalimantan. Later, new provinces were created out of these larger units through conferring provincial status on the old regencies, whose boundaries have on the whole been subject to only minor changes. In this way the number of provinces grew from 10 in 1950 to 26 by 1964, but, although increasing population and enhanced economic development occasionally justify the creation of new units, the process of division has also served to reduce regional loyalties and cohesion. The division of Sumatra into 8 provinces (compared with 9 pre-war residencies) and of Sulawesi into 4 such units, clearly militates against the growth of a regional solidarity which made possible the 1957-58 revolts. The creation of additional regional units is, of course, an old device for enhancing the power of the centre, and the process has also been observed in Indonesia's neighbour, the Philippines. The scope for further division is clearly substantial; Maluku, Irian, and the Nusa Tenggara could all be parcelled up should this become necessary, but much will depend on the future implementation of the 1974 Regional Autonomy Act.

Yet even before this measure, the hold of the government on the provinces appeared solid enough. The government party controlled all the provincial assemblies, and no less than 19 of the 26 provincial governors in 1973 were military men. Nevertheless, the new act appeared to mark a major departure from the principle expressed in the MPRS resolution of 1966, which called for a wide and realistic measure of autonomy; efficiency and responsibility were claimed to be the new criteria, to which the democratic functioning of government in the regions would have to be subordinated. Provincial assemblies, moreover, have no voice in the selection of candidates for governor apart from choosing from a list drawn up by the Minister of Home Affairs, who may then confirm or reject the selection. This may be represented as merely legal confirmation of a practice that has been followed since 1957, but it met much criticism outside Parliament. Even more ominous to the critics was the government's stated intention of adopting the Regency as the main instrument of regional development in place of the Province, a device which many saw as an attempt to use parochialism as a counter to a sense of regional community.

Two provinces, however, do possess a substantial measure of autonomy. One is the *Daerah Istemewa* (Special Region) of Yogyakarta, which has retained the status originally bestowed on those parts of the country that continued to recognise a hereditary ruler. The only such to survive the revolution, however, was the Sultanate of Yogyakarta, which in 1948-49 was the heart of the Republic of Indonesia. But Yogyakarta's status also reflects the high personal standing of the Sultan himself, a revolutionary leader who has managed to keep aloof from the struggles of party politics. The other province with the status of Special Region is Aceh, the most militantly Islamic part of the country, which rejected the secular Indonesian Republic just as it had resisted the Dutch. For his part in the *Darul Islam* movement Daud Bereuh, the leader of the *uleebalang* (religious leaders), was jailed for many years, but the province was never completely pacified, and in 1963 the government relented. Daud Bereuh was released from jail, and the province was declared a *Daerah Istemewa,* subject to Islamic law. Aceh's status under the 1974 Regional Autonomy Act is not clear, but in practice it is likely that it will largely be left to run its own affairs, just as it had done for many years even before 1963.

Additionally, there is the *Daerah Khusus Ibukota* (Extra Special Metropolitan District) of Jakarta itself, with provincial status (other major cities have the rank of regency). Governor Ali Sadikin's administration of the national capital has demonstrated several flamboyant aspects, but, as governments in Indonesia have largely been made and unmade in Jakarta, it may be assumed that the central government takes every precaution to ensure that it remains in firm control of the city.

Nevertheless, the central problem of every military or quasi-military regime throughout history cannot be suppressed - *quis custodiet?* The Jakarta generals appear to present a united front, but from its very beginnings the army has never been a monolithic organisation. There is conflict between the professionals, genuine military men, unable to make fortunes, and those officers who are more interested in politics and the relations of the army with society, and who use their positions for personal gain; inter-arm and inter-unit rivalries are superimposed on the ethnic, religious and cultural differences common to the whole country, and a judicious policy of *penghijauan* (the green, a reference to the army's jungle-green uniforms, and hence, the appointment of senior officers to high civilian positions), in which all these rivalries are nicely balanced, helps to ensure loyalty. The Ambonese, who played so important a role in the Royal Netherlands Indies Army, are now of little military significance. But largely by virtue of the superior education they have long enjoyed through the Lutheran church schools, Bataks continue to provide a disproportionately large contribution to the officer and non-commissioned officer corps. After the collapse of the regional revolts, Sukarno courted safety through the appointment of more Javanese to key positions in the army, but the New Order has witnessed some relaxation of Javanese predominance, most notably in the appointment of General Panggabean, a Batak, first as Army Commander and in 1969 as Deputy Commander of the Armed Forces and Minister of Defence.

Divide and rule is thus imposed on the military as well as on the civil administration. Nevertheless, the danger of the sudden rise of a potential new pro-consul can never be discounted. With General Panggabean's 1969 appointment came a reshuffle of the armed forces top leadership to produce a more centralised High Command structure, greatly limiting the freedom of manoeuvre of the chiefs of staff and their commanders. New supra-regional commands embracing major islands and island groups were created, Java, Sumatra, and Sulawesi being assigned to the army, Kalimantan to the air force, and Maluku and Irian to the navy. These appointments have been rapidly turned over, in order to prevent any incumbent from attempting to build up a substantial power base. Demonstrably efficient commanders of crack units, whose activities and influence in local or even in national affairs bring frequent exposure to the public eye, are apt to find themselves posted to remoter provinces or to distant embassies. Since 1969 there has also been a substantial reduction in the country's over-large population of generals, but there are still too many for comfort or efficiency. Some of the removals from the active list, such as that of General Sutowo, appear to be window-dressing; but in 1971 there were rumours that even General Nasution, Indonesia's senior soldier, was about to be put out to grass. By surrounding himself with military aides with whom he had long worked, Suharto greatly increased the strength of his position. Yet in any military regime the question of the succession can never be put on one side; no one in Indonesia or outside it saw in 1965 the eventual successor to Sukarno, and in 1975 Suharto still has no clear heir, although Sutowo was beginning to appear as a possibility. But history, and the contemporary experience of the Third World, are eloquent that the choice of the leader is seldom confirmed by events. Anti-party, and anti-Islam, at least as a political force, the military in Indonesia is a powerful supporter of *immobilisme*. Yet all nations must somehow contrive to permit a measure of socio-political change and development if they are not to explode. Military regimes give an impression of stability over the short period, but in reality they are among the most unstable on earth.

Foreign Relations

Indonesia's long preoccupation with foreign affairs when it needed to conserve all its energies for grappling with its formidable internal problems, exacted heavy social and economic penalties. If this misuse of resources was inexcusable, the country's origins in a revolutionary war helped to create an Indonesian image of being menaced by hostile imperial states, opposed to the completion of the great Indonesian revolution. Indonesia's pugnacious confrontations, its formidable military strength, at least on paper, and its strong leftist orientation, generated great alarm among Indonesia's neighbours. Sukarno's famous *Peta Mas* (golden map) in the Merdeka Palace in Jakarta had received wide publicity; it showed a Greater Indonesia which included, in addition to the then still disputed territory of West New Guinea, the Sulu archipelago and the whole of Mindanao, the entire island of Borneo, the Malay peninsula and its extension into southern Thailand. *Indonesia Raya* was thus closely identified with the Islamic

Malay world, even if it did not embrace all the peoples of basically Malay stock, which would have permitted an extension over the whole of the Philippines and into parts of the western Pacific and Indian Oceans. Was Indonesia serving advance notice that, after it had disposed of the Dutch, Malaya, Thailand, and the Philippines would be called on to satisfy Indonesian claims? And where would these stop? Events down to 1965 certainly justified apprehension.

The fall of Sukarno dissolved these fears, at least for the foreseeable future, and the new regime hurried to re-establish good relations both with Indonesia's neighbours and with the Western creditor nations towards which Indonesia was obliged to turn for immediate economic assistance. The country resumed membership of the international organisations from which Sukarno had withdrawn it, such as the IMF, the IBRD, and the United Nations. In the latter body, and in great contrast to its earlier behaviour, Indonesia adopted an effacing posture, and, while it generally voted with the growing Third World bloc, it did so without enthusiasm. Thus support for the Arab states has been almost entirely nominal, and Indonesia did not participate in the Arab oil boycott of certain nations and in the production cutback of 1973-74. Pan-Islamism is unlikely to receive other than token support from the present regime, for its possible repercussions in Indonesia itself could be very damaging to the military establishment. Indonesia's principal accomplishment in this field was in helping to arrange a reconciliation of Pakistan and Bangladesh at the Lahore Islamic Conference of 1974.

The immediate losers in this diplomatic reorientation were the communist powers, which had provided Sukarno's Indonesia with substantial economic and military aid. In a speech in 1967 Suharto accused Peking of direct complicity in the *Gestapu* plot, and later in the year diplomatic relations were declared 'frozen'. Jakarta's continued iciness towards Peking began to appear highly anomalous in the early 1970s with the recognition of the Chinese People's Republic by both Malaysia and the Philippines, and its seating in the United Nations in place of Taiwan. However, the President's closest advisers, including General Murtopo, still appear resolutely opposed to any resumption of relations. As the China question inevitably involves the role of Indonesia's own Chinese population, an extended treatment of these issues is given below.

Nevertheless, relations with the other participants in Sukarno's Jakarta–Phnom Penh–Hanoi–Peking–Pyongyang axis survived the débâcle of the PKI, although there was a notable cooling of the unqualified support that Hanoi had always possessed in the days of Sukarno. With the USSR, however, relations were very strained. Work on the large Soviet-aided projects such as the Cilegon steelworks in West Java was terminated, although the USSR agreed to match the Western creditors in granting the country a moratorium to 1969 on its indebtedness. The USSR in fact had little choice, for refusal would not only have further inflamed anti-communist feeling in Indonesia but would have greatly prejudiced the standing of the USSR for many years to come. More immediately, it ran the risk of inviting a repetition of Sukarno's rejection of Indonesia's financial obligations to the Netherlands, in this case a repudiation of a debt of nearly $1,000 million, out of a total Indonesian foreign indebtedness of some $2,400 million. Such a possibility was made all the more likely by the understandable Western reluctance to provide any further financial assistance to Indonesia that was likely to be passed straight on to the USSR. In 1970, however, after an earlier Soviet economic mission to Jakarta had achieved nothing, an agreement virtually identical with that reached with Western creditors was concluded with the USSR over the debt question, and relations began gradually to improve. This development was clearly connected with the growing Soviet naval interest in the Indian Ocean (once renamed by Sukarno the Indonesian Ocean), and the Russian desire to create an Asian security system, which, notwithstanding protestations to the contrary, was clearly aimed against China. To such Russian overtures, Indonesia, together with most of the other nations sounded by the USSR, remained distinctly lukewarm. The Russians nevertheless undertook to complete their abandoned aid projects, including the Cilegon steelworks. But as if to save further national embarrassment over a long-deferred project which had featured in every Indonesian development plan, this undertaking had been redesignated the Krakatau steel complex, and had passed under the aegis of proliferating *Pertamina,* which declared its intention of completing the project by itself, in concert with other foreign interests. This inordinately expensive project was soon a major contributory reason for *Pertamina*'s acute financial haemorrhage, and its future in 1975 was still uncertain.

But even more remarkable was the rapid change in relations with Malaysia, so recently the object of an Indonesian armed confrontation. Indonesia's standing with much of the Malay population of the peninsula was always very high, even during confrontation, when Kuala Lumpur was dismayed to discover that many radios remained tuned to Radio Indonesia.[1] Malik, Suharto, and Panggabean in turn received lavish welcomes on their first visits to

Kuala Lumpur after confrontation, each stressing the kinship of blood and language uniting the two peoples. Apart from dropping support for the rebel Brunei leader Azahari's Kalimantan Utara republic, the Suharto regime promptly ended one of the irritants to the ruling Alliance government in Kuala Lumpur, the sanctuary Sukarno's Jakarta had provided to the xenophobic Muslim extremists of the opposition Pan Malay Islamic Party (later renamed *Partai Islam,* and, since 1972, a member with the Alliance in the National Front). These had long supported a merger of the old Federation of Malaya with Indonesia, as a means of keeping the peninsula's large Chinese population in permanent subjugation. It is doubtful, however, that such a superficially attractive goal ever had any appeal to the new Indonesian leaders, for the incorporation of the highly industrious and acquisitive Malaysian Chinese into an enlarged Indonesia could only exacerbate Indonesia's already difficult Chinese problem. Nevertheless, there was much evidence of Indonesian and Malaysian co-operation apart from that within the Association of South-east Asian Nations (ASEAN), a regional association founded in 1966 with both Singapore and Indonesia as founder members, together with those former members of the earlier Association of South-east Asian States (ASA), founded in 1961 by Thailand, Malaya, and the Philippines, and which had come to grief over the Sabah dispute between the two latter countries.

Certain aspects of this co-operation served to further the paramountcy of Malay interests in Malaysia, a major objective of Kuala Lumpur policy.[2] They could also hardly fail to increase the feeling of a community of interests with Indonesia in the peninsula, which was being steadily advanced by the brisk market for Indonesian books, magazines, and films among the Malay community. Thus Indonesia provided large numbers of Malay language teachers and other educational specialists capable of teaching sciences and humanities in Malay, in order to assist the Malaysian government in implementing its cherished aim of changing its entire educational system to teaching in the Malay medium. Malay students were also offered scholarships and inducements for further study in Indonesian universities, and in 1972 a common system of spelling was adopted for *Bahasa Indonesia* and *Bahasa Malaysia* in place of the separate transliteration systems inherited from the Dutch and British colonial regimes. In more practical matters, Indonesia's *Pertamina* provided the Malaysian government with advice on the setting-up of a similar organisation *(Petronas)* for Malaysia's own oil industry. Yet for many of the Malaysian intelligentsia, including even Malays, the obvious *camaraderie* between General Panggabean and the Malaysian generals, on the occasion of his first visit to Kuala Lumpur, was fraught with misgiving. There was no reason to doubt the loyalty of the Malaysian armed forces to the lawful government, and even if the senior army commanders were almost entirely Malay, non-Malays were prominent in the higher ranks of the navy and the air force. But the danger was obvious.

Yet few non-Malays appreciated that Indonesia had in fact cautioned the Malaysian government against any unnecessarily provocative or forceful action by the powerful security forces marshalled during the race riots in Kuala Lumpur following the May 1969 election, when several Western correspondents reported instances of flagrant discrimination by Malay units between Malay and Chinese rioters, giving rise to adverse comment in the West. This was, however, in keeping with Indonesia's earlier stated intention of avoiding involvement in any potential communal conflict in the Malay peninsula, a necessity which had provided an argument for earlier opposition to the establishment of Malaysia. Nevertheless, late in 1971 Indonesia and Malaysia jointly took action which, if also challenging to the wider world, appeared to many to be directed against the *Nanyang* (the 'South Seas', hence South-east Asia) Chinese through their principal economic and social focus of Singapore.

This was the declaration of the Strait of Malacca as the exclusive territorial waters of the two states. The funnel-shaped Strait opens to the Indian Ocean in a broad expanse of more than 500 nautical miles, but southwards it narrows rapidly to scarcely 30 nautical miles. For the powers traditionally committed to maintaining the freedom of the seas, the Strait was an international waterway; but in the world of the 1970s, the time-honoured 3-mile limit of territorial waters, or even a 6- or a 12-mile limit which had been the occasional alternatives, appeared lost in a general inflation. Sukarno, indeed, had been among the first to launch this trend, claiming in the early 1950s that all the seas between the Indonesian islands were territorial waters, a claim that was immediately rejected by Britain, the United States, and the USSR. But similar extravagant claims were increasingly made by other states, especially Latin American, and with increasingly valuable fishing, oil and gas, and other mineral resources at stake, to say nothing of the growing problem of pollution of the oceans, the tacit recognition of a 12-mile limit for territorial waters plus a 200-mile limit for exclusive economic exploitation seems more and more likely, especially since the indecisive international conference on the sea at Caracas in 1974 failed to heed the pleas of landlocked states and the traditional keepers of the freedom of the seas for the maximum internationalisation of the oceans.

The Malacca Strait is a major international shipping lane, and Singapore's lifeline. The island republic could never be expected to accept such a decision. Nor did the Great Powers, although the move did meet with some approval from a China alarmed at growing Soviet naval power in the Indian Ocean; as if in a test case almost immediately thereafter, a United States carrier task-force made the transit to the Indian Ocean without challenge. But there was a more immediate motive for the decision. The Strait is heavily congested, and traffic steadily increases, not only in the number of transits, now around a hundred per day, but also in the size of vessels. But although usually calm and unruffled, the Strait is also very shallow; supertankers of more than 300,000 deadweight tons moving from the Persian Gulf to Japan avoid it and make use of the Lombok Strait, and the future monsters of 500,000 or so tons will probably avoid Indonesian waters completely and travel south of Australia. However, giant tankers of 200,000 tons regularly use the route, and both countries dread that one of these behemoths may run aground or collide with another vessel during bad weather, and create a major environmental disaster.[3] The rapid development of the petroleum industry in the Strait itself through offshore drilling, and the development of the Dumai refinery and loading terminal on the East Sumatran coast, which will accommodate tankers of up to 300,000 tons, compound the potential dangers. A tanker of this class draws some 25 metres of water fully laden, but at certain times in the year even the main navigation channel possesses barely 30 metres, and over large parts of the Strait the depth is less than 20 metres. Clearly, the margin of safety is already very slender, and, with the development projects already in hand and projected, improvements are urgently necessary. The internationalisation of the Strait was thus seen by some as the preliminary to the establishment of an authority which would undertake the expensive navigational improvements deemed desirable, recouping itself through tolls levied on vessels making the transit. Put more bluntly, it could be seen as an attempt to extract the resources for the undertaking from others, and particularly from Japan.

Although linked with Singapore in ASEAN, the long-held view of most Indonesian leaders of South-east Asia's first port, financial centre, and principal emporium was that it was a parasite on the national economy, whose services were to be dispensed with as quickly as possible. As the major focus of the smuggling trade it had given succour to the rebels in 1957-58, and the blatant manner in which the trade was carried on was an affront to all patriotic Indonesians. Prime Minister Lee Kuan Yew's scarcely veiled contempt for the intellectual calibre of the leadership of the Malay world, and indeed for the unenterprising, as he saw it, outlook of all Malay peoples, were as insufferable as his presumed omniscience. Significantly, an offer of a loan of Malaysian $100 million in 1966 for the purchase from Singapore of essential consumer goods and raw materials for the stricken post-*Gestapu* Indonesia, came not from the government, but from a group of Singapore merchants. Nor were matters made any easier by the execution in 1968 of two Indonesian marines, condemned for causing bomb explosions in the city during confrontation when Singapore formed part of Malaysia, even though an appeal for clemency was made by Suharto himself. Yet, as always, the illegal barter trade continued because it was highly beneficial to both parties and there was no effective substitute; the new Indonesia, just like the old, found that providing for itself the services that it customarily sought in Singapore was a difficult and expensive undertaking, nor could it be accomplished in the short period. Gradually relations improved; Prime Minister Lee paid homage at the Hero's Monument, the memorial on the burial site of the executed Indonesians, during his visit to Jakarta in 1973, and Singapore relented sufficiently to recognise Indonesia in its official trade statistics, all reference to trade with the republic having been deliberately omitted since the separation of Singapore from Malaysia in 1965. Lee's 'rugged society' was perhaps beginning to feel vulnerable to Indonesian-Malaysian *rapprochement*.

Singapore at least proved one of the more active members of ASEAN, a body which some political scientists have hailed as an embryonic South-east Asian Common Market. But there was no intention on the part of its organisers that ASEAN should develop into a working equivalent of the EEC, still less that it should embrace the supranational ideals implicit in the Rome Treaty. ASEAN's miniscule secretariat is perhaps a fair indication of the relative standing of the organisation in the eyes of its members. Even within its limited goals of greater regional economic and social co-operation, Indonesia despite its size and population is in no position to play the equivalent of a West Germany. Moreover, the best prospects of a greater degree of economic co-operation in the immediate future appear to rest in the mainland, and any greater integration of the economies of mainland and archipelagic South-east Asia will have to await the attainment of a substantially higher level of economic development than that of the present.

But if ASEAN itself remained a moribund body, Indonesia did

provide one instance of practical economic co-operation, by undertaking during the world petroleum crisis of 1973-74 to meet the requirements of other ASEAN members, despite its commitments to Japan and other major customers. The crisis underlined the growing community between Indonesia and Malaysia, for both are oil-surplus states, and sharply separated them from the deficit countries of Thailand and the Philippines, a division that grew more marked with the general commodity boom. At a regional conference on Natural Resources and Economic Development held in October 1974 in Kuala Lumpur, the division between the haves and have-nots of South-east Asia was clearly defined, although, in fact, the Philippines was itself doing extremely well from the fantastic appreciation of sugar prices. The resource-rich group, with buoyant foreign-exchange reserve positions, took an optimistic view of regional development, whereas those faced with greatly swollen bills for oil imports looked gloomily at the future. The sharp fall in commodity prices, but not, unfortunately for the West, in oil, towards the end of the year, suggested that the latter group was perhaps the more realistic.

Indonesia's relations with its ASEAN partners were somewhat ambivalent. Preoccupied, and excessively so in the eyes of its critics, as the government was with security, it could not but help further the quest through foreign policy. If it did not like the large Chinese component in the populations of some of its neighbours, it was greatly to Indonesia's advantage that the *Nanyang* Chinese should not succumb to the siren-call of Peking. The advance of communism within the region was therefore something to be resisted. Yet Indonesia's revolutionary tradition stood squarely in the way of participation in the system of security pacts and defensive alliances that also had this goal, and the doctrine of non-alignment established at the Bandung conference precluded close association with the allies of the United States. One possible solution to the problem was that hinted by General Panggabean during his visits to Malaysia and Singapore in 1970-71, namely that Indonesia would come to the assistance of any neighbour menaced by communist attack. Foreign Minister Malik, however, gave no support to this army view, preferring to seek 'Asian solutions to Asian problems' through involving as many as possible of the states of the southern and eastern margins of Asia, together with Australia and New Zealand, in an international equivalent of the traditional *musyawarah-mufakat* on problems of common interests.

Foremost among these was the Vietnam War, and its potential aftermath. Ever apprehensive of a communist resurgence in

Indonesia itself, the government could not relish a major extension of communist power and influence on the South-east Asian mainland. Revolutionary tradition required that some token support at least be given to North Vietnam's struggle against 'imperialism'; nevertheless, the post of ambassador to Hanoi was left vacant for some two years, a qualified approval was even given to American bombing, and contacts with Saigon, ruptured since 1964, were re-established through the opening of a trade mission. With the extension of the war to the Khmer Republic (Cambodia) following the overthrow of Norodom Sihanouk by General Lon Nol in March 1970, Malik endeavoured to organise a major Asian conference on the Khmer question. In the event, the participants in the conference held in Jakarta in May 1970 consisted only of the nations of ASEAN and ASPAC (the Asia and Pacific Council, a grouping of Australia, Japan, South Korea, Malaysia, New Zealand, the Philippines, Taiwan, Thailand, and South Vietnam established at Seoul in 1966 for economic co-operation and resistance to communist infiltration and aggression) less Taiwan, and little was possible save the iteration of irrelevant platitudes. Indonesia, however, continued to interest itself in the Cambodian war (1970-75), and is believed to have given some military assistance to the Lon Nol regime. In 1974 it joined with Malaysia, Thailand, and several Arab countries in defeating an attempt to have Sihanouk's government-in-exile given the seat in the United Nations held by the Lon Nol regime, in a vote that surprisingly split the often monolithic Third World group in the General Assembly.

If relations with China and the problem of the overseas Chinese could never be long set on one side, the rise of the Japanese economic colossus and its remarkable penetration into the South-east Asian economy posed issues which were scarcely less controversial. As with all the nations of South-east Asia, Indonesia still retains bitter memories of the occupation, whose eradication is made more difficult by the fact that, unlike West Germany, Japan has never expressed any contrition for the ravages and devastation it caused during World War II, nor any morsel of sympathy for the victims of the often barbarous behaviour of its armed forces and secret police. Such insensitivity, in conjunction with the notorious aloofness of the Japanese businessman or government servant overseas and their almost complete isolation from the local community, go far to explain the image of the 'ugly Japanese' in South-east Asia. These social shortcomings, moreover, are buttressed by a hard-faced commercialism, which, if not actually extortionate, frequently involves what in the opinion of Western competitors is distinctly sharp practice. Japanese war reparations are thus transmogrified as development grants made for humanitarian reasons, but, as with Japanese loans, which are on very tough terms, are used for the rigorous promotion of Japanese exports.

Japan has steadily increased in importance as a trading partner of Indonesia in the post-war period. By the mid-1960s, when it had become Indonesia's chief non-communist creditor, it was also Indonesia's principal supplier and leading market, and by the early 1970s was accounting for close on 40 percent of Indonesia's total trade turnover (imports plus exports). Such a trade dependency on one partner was in the opinion of many potentially very dangerous; even the Netherlands Indies never approached such a figure in its trade pattern with the mother country. Moreover, massive Japanese investment, principally in extractive industries such as oil and gas, metalliferous minerals, and timber, seemed all too likely to confirm Indonesia's already strong trade orientation towards Japan.[4] As the balance of trade was already heavily in Indonesia's favour even before the great increase in oil prices of 1973-74, Indonesia will find it difficult to resist pressure to take yet more imports from Japan, which in 1972 were about equivalent in value to those provided by the EEC and the United States combined. As elsewhere in South-east Asia, fears were expressed that Japan might succeed in accomplishing through economic domination what it had failed to achieve through military adventure. Moreover, as with West Germany also, it appeared inevitable that sooner or later Japan would create for itself a political role consistent with its enormous economic strength.

The *peristiwa Malari*, the anti-Tanaka riots, forced a reassessment of Indonesia's Foreign Investment Law, and provisions were made to ensure a majority *peribumi* (indigenous) interest in new enterprises. It is doubtful how successful these changes will prove, for there are several loopholes in the regulations and enforcement will be difficult. But the oil crisis and the growing spectre of world economic depression profoundly shook Japanese confidence, and the economic Titan momentarily appeared to have feet of clay. More heavily dependent than any Western power on imported energy, Japan was peculiarly vulnerable to the pressure tactics of the Arab oil exporters, in which, however, Indonesia did not participate. The shock led to a rapid change in Japan's stand on the Middle East dispute between Israel and the Arab world, and to the seeking of long-term contracts for the supply of oil from Indonesia. As the world began to move towards recession as the astronomical magnitude of the prospective flow of resources to the oil exporters became apparent and as fears mounted for the future of the world monetary and financial system, Japan was forced to revise its investment programme in Indonesia. Its commitment to the development of oil and gas resources remained, but investment in mining and timber was sharply retrenched, and late in 1974 the consortium which had been assembled to support the Asahan multipurpose water utilisation scheme announced that it was withdrawing from participation. The origins of the Asahan project reach back before World War II, and for more than two decades it has been the cynosure of Indonesian development projects. Dutch, Swedes, Russians, and Japanese had examined in turn prospects for hydroelectricity generation from the Asahan river in its descent from the Toba highlands of North Sumatra to the Malacca Strait, and for associated electro-chemical and electrometallurgical industries based on nearby raw materials such as the bauxites of Batam island. But over and over again the costly project has been deferred, and preparatory work abandoned. Its development with Japanese assistance still remains a possibility, however.[5]

The creation of a tripartite economic and political relationship involving Indonesia with Japan and Australia is a major objective of the group around General Murtopo, which sees in the rise of an indigenous Japanese entrepreneurial class supremely competent in Western technology a model for Indonesian development. A strategy based on the cultivation of *peribumi* entrepreneurial skill is greatly preferable, it is argued, to one in which the Western multinational corporation is allowed to acquire a major role. Yet the unique historical and cultural factors that have shaped Japan's economic development have been stressed by many scholars, and it is highly questionable whether Japan's experience provides a model for any Third World country. Indonesian entrepreneurial ability, if it develops at all, will do so in a manner that is peculiarly Indonesian.

Many of the Indonesian élite hold Australia in high regard, a situation that owes much to the action of the Australian waterside workers in banning the loading of Dutch ships bound for the Netherlands Indies during the revolutionary war. In fact, however, the Liberal-Country Party coalition, which took office in 1949, itself had little sympathy with the Indonesian revolution, and strongly supported the Dutch on the West New Guinea issue. During the later 1950s and early 1960s the Dutch and Australian administrations in New Guinea worked increasingly closer together. Sukarno's bellicose foreign policy and the provocative violations of the Papua-New Guinea border by Indonesian forces after 1963 confirmed all the suspicions of the Menzies government, and there were fears not only for the integrity of the Australian-administered territories but for the safety of Australia itself. The potential menace of Indonesia's large and well-equipped armed forces prompted a re-examination of Australia's own defences, and led to the perhaps ill-advised acquisition of American F-111 supersonic aircraft. The fall of Sukarno was thus a great relief to Canberra, and the preservation of good relations with Jakarta has since been a major consideration in Australian foreign policy, under both the Liberal coalition and the Labour administration that succeeded it in 1972. A determination not to become embroiled with Indonesia over New Guinea was not the least of the reasons prompting the Whitlam government to accelerate the achievement of full independence in the Australian-administered territories by 1975.

Australia is, in fact, far more concerned about its highly populous neighbour than Indonesia is about Australia, and for obvious reasons. Indonesia has nothing to fear from Australia; but the reverse is not so certain. A resurgence of Indonesian aggressiveness does not appear likely in the foreseeable future, but in an unstable and uncertain military regime it can never be completely ruled out. Indonesian sailors and fishermen, periodically driven on to the coasts of northern Australia, have sometimes remained undetected for weeks, underlining both the emptiness and indefensibility of the tropical north. The 'White Australia' policy notwithstanding, the environment of northern Australia is so totally different from that of South-east Asia that the popularly held view of the north as a potential rice-bowl for Asia's teeming millions has no foundation in fact. Yet living with a large and powerful neighbour is a new experience for Australia, and will impose new demands on resources; *Bahasa Indonesia* is already taught in very many Australian High Schools, and many Australian universities have active programmes of Indonesian and Malay studies. No Indonesian university has a programme of Australian studies, although there is vigorous competition between senior Indonesian bureaucrats for fellowships and courses of study in Australia, provided under Australian government-aid schemes.

All this is in keeping with Australia's changing political orientation in the post-war period; no longer an outpost of Europe, the country increasingly regards itself as an extension of Asia, and has been generally successful in getting itself accepted as such in many Asian countries. This change in orientation is clearly visible in the direction of Australian trade, which is more and more conducted with Asian countries. Yet neither for Indonesia nor Australia is the other a major trading partner, and in several lines of raw material and mineral production they are competitors for the Japanese market; Indonesia is no longer, as was the Netherlands Indies, the major source of Australia's oil imports, and indeed Australia is fast approaching self-sufficiency in this key commodity. Australia, on the other hand, is one of the few really large regular food-surplus areas of the world, and if Indonesia's agricultural effort proves too little and too late, as may well be the case, a special relationship with Australia may be greatly to Indonesia's advantage in a world in which the large food surpluses of the past appear to have gone for ever. Certainly Indonesia finds investment by indigenous Australian companies a welcome alternative to that by the Western multinationals, or by the reconstituted Japanese *zaibatsu;* for Indonesians, as for most Asians, the Australian, with his traditional lack of respect for authority, absence of social stuffiness, and his egalitarian outlook, is free from many of the shortcomings of the European and American. Australia and Indonesia do, of course, have a common interest in the Indian Ocean, fast threatening to develop as another area of Great Power conflict with the growing strength of the Soviet navy. Australia has been among the staunchest of America's allies since 1945, but relations with the United States appear to have experienced some cooling-off under the Whitlam brand of Australian nationalism. Nevertheless, the ANZUS pact and the long support given by Canberra to American policy in Vietnam did not deter Foreign Minister Malik from hinting on occasions at a possible broadening of ASEAN to include Australia and New Zealand, although Whitlam's espousal of the cause of Peking on each visit to South-east Asia was coldly received in Jakarta. On the face of it, General Murtopo's scheme for an acceptable relationship between Indonesia and Australia, which would facilitate their respective economic development and which would promote political stability in South-east Asia and the adjacent Pacific, appears to involve a closer partnership of equals than would a similar relationship between Indonesia and Japan.

Indonesia's relations with the infant state of Papua-Niu Guini are problematic. The ex-Australian-administered territories have already demonstrated marked fissiparous tendencies, and with several hundred languages and a primitive economy are much less well equipped for self-government than was Indonesia in 1945. Refugees from Indonesian rule are now less welcome than was the case in Sukarno's time, and the newcomers' demands for land conflict with those of the indigenous population. While the growth of a Free Papua movement for the liberation of the Indonesian-occupied part of the island is possible, it would seem that the creation of some form of national cohesion within the Australian-administered territories themselves will tax all the resources of the new state, and that to add to its many problems would be highly unwise. Yet much the same was said of Indonesia itself in 1949, and all such advice it chose to ignore.

One entirely unexpected development in 1974, however, suggested that perhaps the boundaries of Indonesia were not finally determined. This was the overthrow of the ex-Salazar and Caetano regime in Portugal, and the decision of the new administration in Lisbon to allow all Portuguese possessions the right to determine their own futures. The almost 15,000 square kilometres of eastern Timur and the Ocussi-Ambeno enclave in the western, or Indonesian, portion of the island constituted with Macao the last remnants of the once extensive Portuguese empire in the eastern seas, and since the boundary settlement with the Dutch in 1859, under which the Portuguese gave up their claims to Flores and Sumbawa, contact with the rest of the archipelago had been slight. Sukarno repeatedly denied that he had any territorial claims in Timur, for unlike New Guinea, which most of the leaders of the revolution had known from their imprisonment, knowledge of the Portuguese half of the island was scanty. Portuguese rule sat lightly on the 600,000 inhabitants of eastern Timur, most of whom were shifting cultivators, and a more favourable man to land ratio than that of the smaller, but more populous, Indonesian portion of the island provided a living standard superior to that of most of eastern Indonesia. This disparity became more marked in the last years of Sukarno, when the shortages of many foods and essential commodities, such as soap and matches in Kupang, prompted a thriving smuggling trade from Dili, the capital of Portuguese Timur. Moreover, and as with other Portuguese overseas possessions in general, Portuguese Timur had made good progress with a realistic development plan, while the Indonesian economy was in a parlous condition.

Portugal envisaged terminating its rule in October 1978, but this date was to be subject to review by a Timur Popular Assembly to be elected in October 1976. But with the growing turmoil in Portugal itself, and the threat of civil war between the communists and other leftist groups on the one hand, and the socialists and their supporters on the other, it appeared likely that this date would be brought forward. The divisions in Portugal, moreover, were soon communicated to its possession, and the strong position in Lisbon of the communist-oriented higher levels of the Portuguese officer corps was paralleled by the rise of the leftist Revolutionary Front for Independent East Timur (*Fretilin; Frente Revolutionaria*

Timorensa de Libertação e Indepêndencia), which held out for immediate independence and the establishment of a socialist state. The principal opposition party, the Timur Democratic Union (*UDT; União Democratica Timorensa*), however, favoured a more gradual approach to independence, retaining some links with Portugal, while a third party, the Popular Democratic Association of Timur (*Apodeti; Associação Popularia de Democracia Timorensa*), stood for union with Indonesia. This was by far the smallest of the three, and was undoubtedly subsidised from Jakarta. In 1975 the situation in eastern Timur deteriorated rapidly. *Fretilin* acquired substantial quantities of modern arms, derived in part from the Portuguese armed forces, although Vietnam and even China were identified as suppliers. Early in August, amid charges and counter-charges of incipient *coups* from left and right, vicious fighting broke out. The governor and the remnants of the Portuguese administration fled to Atauro island to the north, and *Fretilin* established itself master of Dili and of much of the eastern half of the island, confining the supporters of the opposition UDT and *Apodeti* to a narrow strip along the Indonesian border.

Thus the tragic pattern of Angola, which Portugal had finally abandoned in November to a tripartite civil war, was repeated in Timur. The prospect of consolidation of *Fretilin* rule was, however, highly alarming with all that it implied both for the possibility of yet another resurrection of the PKI and for the growth of regional separatism. Indonesian warships patrolled the seas off the Timur coast to intercept supplies of arms and ammunition from other communist countries, and Indonesian 'volunteers' began to come to the aid of the anti-*Fretilin* forces. In mid-December *Fretilin* proclaimed the establishment of an independent Republic of East Timur, and Indonesian forces, still labelled 'volunteers' by Jakarta as in the days of confrontation, moved to the attack. Dili was speedily occupied, and Ocussi-Ambeno declared its union with Indonesia. *Fretilin* forces took to the hills, vowing to prosecute a Vietnam-type war, but in the absence of direct communist power intervention, a development that would be fraught with peril, an eventual Indonesian takeover appeared inevitable and indeed occurred. Communist supporters in the UN cranked out a resolution condemning Indonesian aggression, and Lisbon severed diplomatic relations with Jakarta; but Australia, deep in a constitutional and economic crisis, had little time for events in Timur, and both of its principal parties secretly welcomed the Indonesian action.

There remains also for an Australia determined to rid itself of the incubus of being the last colonial power the problem of two insignificant scraps of the Malay world, Christmas Island and the Cocos-Keeling group. Just 300 miles to the south of Java, Christmas Island was part of the Colony of Singapore, and was transferred by Britain to Australia just in time to prevent it passing to the new independent Singapore. For more than a century Cocos-Keeling was the property of the Clunies-Ross family, and its Malay inhabitants worked as servants of the family and on its coconut plantations in a mini-welfare state. But population growth outran the capacity of the paternal Clunies-Ross regime to provide employment, and those desiring to leave were resettled under agreement and at the family's expense in North Borneo (now Sabah); those leaving were not allowed to return. This superficially idyllic regime was increasingly out of place, and uneconomic, in the post-war world, and in the late 1950s the administration of the group was handed over to Australia, which brought the islands back into the world of affairs after their fleeting brush with Australian history through the sinking of the German raider *Emden* by the cruiser *Sydney* in 1914, developing the group as a staging-point in the trans-Indian Ocean air service between Sydney and Johannesburg. With the changing world conceptions of the territorial sea, the islands clearly have substantial importance if their maritime boundaries lie 200 miles offshore in all directions, both strategic and possibly economic. Neither Australia nor Indonesia has made any pronouncements about the future of the islands, although it is known also that the Jakarta generals are interested in their future, and could be expected to press an Indonesian claim should Australia express any intention of withdrawing.

NOTES

[1] While both were staying at the Tunku Abdul Rahman School (a residential High School for Malay boys) in Ipoh in 1962, one of the authors noticed an essay set for the Fourth Form on 'The man I most admire'. Of some 40 or so boys, all but 5 had selected Sukarno; not one had nominated a leader of the Federation of Malaya, as it was then.

[2] The Malaysian government did not, of course, express this quite so openly or so crudely. But the Second Malaysia Plan, in making special provisions for increasing Malay incomes and enlarging Malay participation in non-agricultural activities, was distinctly more communal than was its predecessor. Moreover, in its policy of allocating university scholarships, in appointments to the public service, and in numerous other ways, the supremacy of Malay interests is clearly visible.

[3] The 230,000-ton *Showa Maru* ran aground off Singapore early in 1975, holing three tanks and discharging oil that speedily destroyed valuable fishing grounds.

[4] In mid-1973 it was reported that the chairman of Mitsui had informed President Suharto that his company was prepared to invest some $1,000 million in Indonesia

during the Second Five-Year Plan, *Repelita* II; Prime Minister Tanaka had already pledged some $700 million for the development of Indonesian natural gas. 'Investment in Asia', *The Far Eastern Economic Review*, 24 June, 52, and 'Japan: 1974', 13 May, 1974, 28.

[5] In June 1975 a new agreement with a consortium of Japanese companies, led by Sumitomo, was signed by President Suharto in Tokyo during a state visit. Under the new agreement the Japanese government will provide some 70 percent of the capital cost of the more than $800 million project in the form of low-interest loans. Construction is scheduled to begin in 1976, and the aluminium reduction plant will commence operation in 1981. Yet there is much misgiving in the Japanese Ministry of Finance at the enormous cost of the undertaking, which bids fair to develop as Japan's largest and costliest overseas investment project, and its implementation could well be a hostage to the fortune of the world economy.

CHAPTER 9

The Chinese: An Indigestible Minority?

DESPITE THE OPTIMISM of the nation's motto, 'Unity in Diversity', the profusion of ethnic and cultural groups inhabiting the archipelago necessarily creates problems for Indonesia, and some of the most intractable of these concern the future of the large Chinese minority. There are Chinese in virtually every urban centre, but the major zone of Chinese settlement forms an arc around Singapore encompassing localities where economic development created opportunities attractive to large-scale immigration; these include the plantation area of North Sumatra, the Riau archipelago and the nearby 'tin islands' of Bangka and Belitung, the northern ports and larger inland centres of Java, and West Kalimantan. The total size of this minority cannot be given with precision. Chinese have not been enumerated separately in Indonesia's censuses since 1930 and, in any case, determination of what constitutes a 'Chinese' in Indonesia is not always easy. Through past intermarriage with Indonesians many 'Chinese' particularly in Java, have some non-Chinese ancestry. Moreover, without becoming Indonesians, a significant proportion have lost part of their 'Chinese' affinities. Many, for instance, can neither speak nor read any Chinese language, and, as with the nation's badminton ace Rudy Hartono (born Nio Hap Liang), substantial numbers have adopted Indonesian names. More recent estimates of the number of Chinese in Indonesia, however, vary between 2.5 and 3.5 million, representing over a fifth of all the Chinese in South-east Asia.

There are, therefore, nearly as many persons of Chinese descent in Indonesia as there are in Malaysia, but in two crucial respects their position in these two neighbours is different. Comprising 34 percent of Malaysia's population, the Chinese there are not greatly outnumbered by the largest indigenous element, the Malays; in Indonesia, on the other hand, the Chinese are a true minority forming only about 2.5 percent of the nation's inhabitants. Additionally, although almost all Chinese in Malaysia are now citizens of that country, probably less than half of the Chinese in Indonesia possess local citizenship. Indeed, according to an official assessment in 1968 1.5 million Chinese were Indonesian citizens, a quarter-million held Chinese passports, and a further 1.5 million were considered stateless since they did not hold local citizenship nor did they have documentary proof of, or regard themselves as possessors of, Chinese nationality. At present this last group is in the most difficult and anomalous position, a position which must be clarified before there can by any real progress towards a solution of Indonesia's 'Chinese problem'. There are suggestions that official use of the designation 'stateless' indicates that the Indonesian government is keeping the way open for these aliens eventually to acquire Indonesian citizenship, which most would probably welcome, but, because of long-held fears and prejudices, which are particularly strong in some indigenous quarters, successful moves in this direction will require patience and a more adroitly sensitive reaction to the opportunities by the authorities.

As elsewhere in South-east Asia, Indonesia's 'Chinese problem' is largely a compound of mutual lack of understanding, suspicion, and hostility. The tendency of the Chinese to regard themselves as different, if not superior in cultural heritage, energy, and ability, and to give the appearance of standing clannishly and exclusively aloof aggravates indigenous feelings of resentment and distrust strongly coloured by commonly accepted stereotypes. Notwithstanding contrary personal experience, in Indonesian eyes all Chinese seem to be the same and elicit similar reactions. The archetype is the wealthy, unscrupulous opportunist, a trader or middleman, prepared to do anything for a profit; tainted by jealousy, in this view the Chinese objective is 'to wax rich in this Indonesian paradise'. Like similar popular assertions, the myth that Chinese and trade are synonymous, that 'every Chinese is a shopkeeper', dies hard despite the absence of a sound factual basis.[1] Even in 1930 less than 37 percent of the employed Chinese in Indonesia were involved in trade; then, as now, very large numbers were engaged in agriculture, fishing, mining, industry, and in other non-commercial pursuits. Indeed, whatever the popular Indonesian conceptions may be, the fact remains that the Chinese minority is not monolithic, but extremely diverse; as Williams correctly observes, there is no value, and considerable danger, in simply regarding the Chinese, as many Indonesians still do, as 'a bloc of aliens with grasping economic ambitions and sinister political goals'.[2] Diversity is manifest, for example, in terms of language, ranging from those who still speak their several ancestral tongues to those who know no Chinese language; in degrees of acculturation, varying from the essentially traditional Chinese to the heavily Indonesianised; and in occupations, political inclinations, and attitudes towards their present situation. There can be no solutions to current problems until the range of these differences is recognised and Indonesian views of the Chinese move closer to individual realities.

In the scholarly literature it has long been common to recognise two socially and culturally distinct components in the Chinese population.[3] Firstly, there is what Skinner has termed 'the locally rooted society', a component comprising the locally born Chinese with little or no orientation to China and a sufficiently strong infusion of Indonesian cultural elements to make many aspects of their way of life strange to Chinese visitors from other parts of South-east Asia. Many members of this component have some Indonesian ancestry and because of their mixed origin and their hybrid culture they became known as *peranakan*. In contrast there are the *totok* or 'pure' Chinese. Comprising surviving immigrants and their offspring, the *totok* retain a distinctively Chinese way of life; they continue to speak their ancestral languages; and they are more oriented—at least in sentiment—to China. Broadly speaking, the majority of Chinese in Java, and especially in the eastern two-thirds of the island, are *peranakan;* somewhat similar Chinese communities exist in several other areas, for example in Bangka, West Kalimantan, and in West Sumatra, but for the most part the Chinese of the Outer Islands are predominantly *totok*. This contrast is a product of the history of Chinese settlement in Indonesia.

Although contacts between China and the archipelago are of far greater antiquity, the earliest permanent Chinese settlements in what is now Indonesia date from the late thirteenth century. When Europeans first arrived in the area three centuries later, Chinese trader-colonies existed in the ports of north Java and in selected localities elsewhere in the islands. The Dutch particularly encouraged Chinese to settle in and around Batavia, and the subsequent extension of their control in Java and the farming-out of various monopolies brought a deeper penetration of Chinese in that island. Indeed, despite the growing influx of Chinese in the eighteenth century to work the gold of western Borneo and the tin of Bangka, the larger towns of Java remained the prime foci of Chinese settlement in the Indies until the present century. Except for those moving into the mining areas, who were mostly Hakka, these early migrants were predominantly Hokkien from Amoy and its hinterland and by 1930 two-thirds of the Chinese in Java were of Hokkien origin. The migrants were also overwhelmingly male, and, as time passed, the progeny of their unions with local females produced an increasingly large mixed-blood population both in Java and in the main areas of Chinese settlement in the Outer Islands. In 1815, for instance, there were about a thousand Chinese children in Bangka, all presumably with non-Chinese mothers, and in 1858 only two-fifths of the Chinese at the mining settlements of Larah and Lumar in western Borneo had been born in China, the rest being apparently of mixed origin.[4] According to Duyvendak, in the case of Java, where nearly two-thirds of the Chinese were at least third generation by 1930 and most of these had one or more Indonesian ancestors, this 'mixed race' formed 'the backbone of the Chinese population'.[5]

This intermarriage, and the tendency in Java for urban Chinese families to employ a Javanese *babu*, or nursemaid, to care for their children, facilitated the transfer of elements of Indonesian culture to these growing *peranakan* communities to yield a hybrid culture which, in Java at least, was Hokkien-based and largely urban. Related partly to the lapse of time between the first Chinese settlement and the arrival of significant numbers of Chinese women, and partly to the differing nature of local cultures, there were noticeable variations in the degree of this acculturation. The Muslim *peranakan* known to have been present in late eighteenth-century Batavia, for example, seem subsequently to have been totally assimilated and this may have occurred on a small scale elsewhere.[6] Whereas in some parts of Java, such as the former *Vorstenlanden* of Yogyakarta and Surakarta and the Tanggerang area to the west of Jakarta, the degree of acculturation was marked, in other areas there was a stronger retention of Chinese characteristics. Typically, however, the result was the emergence of a community with a mixed culture which, partly because the Chinese were treated as a separate segment of the plural society by the Dutch, retained its own identity and interests. Generally, *peranakan* lost the ability to converse in their ancestral language and came to rely on either Indonesian, a local regional language (such as Javanese or Sundanese), or Dutch, or on a combination of these, and often in Java with a leavening of terms derived from Hokkien; thus, in a survey of Chinese high-school pupils in Semarang in 1954-55 Willmott discovered that in 81 percent of the cases where neither parent was born in China, Indonesian was the medium of daily conversation in the home.[7] Occasionally, however, retention of the ancestral tongue has produced peculiar mixtures and Skinner records that the language in use in north-east Bangka is 'an almost creolised Hakka dialect with heavy borrowings from Bangkanese Malay, and the influence of Malay norms is evident in the material culture, settlement patterns, family structure, and religious behavior'.[8] The *peranakan* cuisine shows particularly strong Indonesian influences; rice is usually cooked in the local manner and eaten in conjunction with similar ancillary dishes, and according to one observer 'there is little difference between the menu of lower-class Peranakans and that of lower-class Indonesians'.[9] Equally, although Western dress is usual among men and younger females, older *peranakan* women are still identifiable by their distinctive modified Indonesian dress style. The *peranakan* have also adopted many Indonesian manners and mannerisms, values, beliefs, customs, and ceremonies.

The growth of a *totok* community with a distinctively Chinese way of life and of sufficient size to produce, particularly in Java, 'two essentially separate social systems' within the Chinese population, occurred in the first thirty years of this century.[10] The spectacular development of export production from the late nineteenth century brought a dramatic acceleration in Chinese migration to the Indies both to Java and to the new enclaves of the developing colonial export economy in the Outer Islands. The total Chinese population of the archipelago rose from 221,400 in 1860 to 809,000 in 1920 and, with the peak immigration during the 1920s, this number had risen to 1.2 million by 1930. Even on its own this sudden intrusion of large numbers of new arrivals fresh from south China was sufficient to create a new strand in the Indies Chinese population, but it was accompanied by other forces working in the same direction; of particular importance were the composition of the new migrant stream and the emergence of conditions favourable to the preservation and transmission of Chinese culture.

The wave of migrants in the twentieth century differed in two significant respects from that in earlier times. Firstly, substantial numbers of Chinese females began to arrive after World War I, so that there was a rapid increase in the number of Chinese children with both parents born in China and these were, in consequence, raised in a purely Chinese family atmosphere. Secondly, the speech-group composition of the migrants changed. A large proportion of the new arrivals were not Hokkien but members of other groups, especially Cantonese, Hakka, and Tiechiu and, notably in Java, this 'retarded acculturation to the Hokkien flavored Peranakan way of life'.[11]

Concurrently, the emergence of a *totok* element accompanied, and was reinforced by, the growth of Chinese ethnocentrism associated with the development of what became known as the 'Chinese movement' in the Indies.[12] Originating at the start of this century, this partly reflected Chinese dissatisfaction with their current position under colonial rule. Their main grievances concerned the restrictions on the place of residence and movement of Chinese, the unequal administration of justice, discriminatory taxes, the absence of government schools for Chinese, and the institution of several measures such as the government takeover of the opium monopoly and the extension of its monopoly of pawnshops, which interfered with Chinese sources of income. It also derived much from the rapid increase in immigration from a reawakening homeland and growing influx of modernist and nationalist influences from China. Thus, K'ang Yu-wei, a leading Chinese reformist, went to Java in 1903, several Chinese naval vessels visited Semarang, a Chinese consul-general was established in Batavia in 1912, and, in combination with the development of a Chinese press, these events generated greatly increased interest in Chinese culture, history, and nationalism.

The movement began with the founding of the *Tiong Hoa Hwe Koan* (Chinese Association) in Batavia in 1900. This brought an immediate response and similar organisations were quickly established throughout the archipelago to promote Chinese culture on the basis of the teachings of Confucius, and thereby to encourage greater unity of the Indies Chinese through a resinification of the *peranakan*. To facilitate these ends schools were established which used Mandarin as the language of instruction, relying on textbooks and teachers imported from China. Chinese Chambers of Commerce were also set up in all the main cities and these became an important link between local Chinese and the government of China, collecting and forwarding contributions both for disaster relief in the homeland and for the government exchequer. After the success of the Chinese revolution in 1911 these various bodies became more concerned with political nationalism, organising support for the *Kuomintang* in addition to their propagation of a stronger Chinese consciousness, and in time branches of the *Kuomintang* were created throughout the country. But the 'Chinese movement' was dominated by the *totok*, and, partly through its success in gaining concessions from the Dutch, it did not eliminate the cleavage in the Chinese population. Restrictions on the place of residence and movement of Chinese, for example, were removed in Java in 1919 and in the Outer Islands in 1926, but the *peranakan* seem to have taken greatest advantage of the new freedom. Similarly, when the colonial authorities started in 1908 to establish the *Hollandsch-Chineesche Scholen* (Dutch-Chinese Schools), in which the language of instruction was Dutch and the curriculum paralleled that in elementary schools for

Dutch children, this emphasised the distinctiveness of the *peranakan* by exposing many to Dutch influences while *totok* children had their Chinese awareness heightened through their Chinese-language education.

Lumping all Chinese together as *orang Cina,* as did the Dutch colonialists, most Indonesians have either been unable or have chosen not to recognise the differences between *totok* and *peranakan.* Nonetheless, the differences are so far-reaching as to make nonsense of conceptions of the Chinese as a distinctive monolithic community interacting in predictable ways with indigenous society. At all levels social intercourse between *totok* and *peranakan* has been limited and the two groups have long regarded each other as different. Characteristically, *totok* have looked down on the partly acculturated *peranakan,* viewing them as *jip hoan* (persons who have become 'foreign' or 'barbarian'), an attitude prevalent even in the nineteenth century when, for example, *peranakan* in western Borneo were commonly seen as inferior and many of them joined small secret societies for self-protection against their immigrant 'superiors'.[13] Within the higher-income, more Westernised, elements, there has been more social contact between *peranakan* and Indonesians than between *peranakan* and *totok;* both have shown a strong preference for restricting the selection of marriage partners to their own group, and almost all Chinese social and political organisations have been essentially *peranakan* or *totok.* Several factors have reinforced this cleavage. Willmott's survey of Chinese high-school pupils in Semarang in 1954-55, for instance, revealed that while in most *peranakan* families Indonesian was the language of daily conversation in the home, a Chinese language performed this role in 96 percent of the cases where both parents were China-born.[14] Yet, although the social distance between the two groups owes much to this language-barrier, this is not the only cause, for there are also distinctions in cultural practices and in value orientations. *Totok* usually display all the 'traditional' attributes commonly associated with Chinese in South-east Asia; they attach great value to hard work and frugality, to self-reliance and independent entrepreneurial activity, to a willingness to speculate, and to the focal role of the family and social ties in business. *Peranakan,* in contrast, are both more Indonesianised and more Westernised, and they are more concerned with leisure, social status, and security. Arising partly for these reasons and partly because aliens have a much narrower range of opportunities, the differences are clearly apparent in terms of employment. *Peranakan* show a much greater diversification of occupations, a far higher association with paid employment, and a more marked preference for white-collar jobs and certain professions such as medicine, law, and engineering. *Totok,* on the other hand, are overwhelmingly concerned with entrepreneurial activity either as own-account workers or as employees in tiny family businesses. Thus, in 1957 in Sukabumi, West Java, while three-quarters of the alien Chinese, or *totok,* were engaged in trade, this was the case with only 44.6 percent of those who were citizens.[15] Finally, reflecting these social and occupational contrasts, the two groups tend to show different patterns of intra-urban residential location; the *totok* continue to concentrate principally in the shophouses of the old central Chinese quarters, but *peranakan* are more widely dispersed and occupy a greater variety of housing, ranging from dwellings in the urban *kampungs* to suburban villas.

It is true that by the mid-1950s some of these distinctions were becoming blurred. Migration from China virtually ceased with the Japanese invasion, and has not been renewed, and in consequence the proportion of the Chinese population born in Indonesia rose from nearly two-thirds in 1930 to over 70 percent in 1950, and it is now well in excess of four-fifths. Moreover, the rapid increase in the number of *peranakan* children attending Chinese-language schools in the 1940s and 1950s, and the forces promoting greater unity of the Chinese in this period, which included the common enemy of the occupying Japanese and the subsequent failure of the new Indonesian authorities to distinguish adequately between the different components of the Chinese minority when applying discriminatory measures, served to reduce some of the social distance. But the most critical change after independence was the emergence of a new division between those Chinese who became Indonesian citizens and those who did not. While almost all *totok* fall into the latter category, most, but not all, *peranakan* are now Indonesian citizens. Overlying the old social and cultural cleavage, this contrast in status has become progressively more significant during the last twenty years; it has placed the two groups in very different positions and has made possible sharp variations in their treatment. In sum, it lies at the heart of Indonesia's so-called 'Chinese problem'.

Immediately after the occupation Indonesia's nationalist leaders gave an assurance that locally born Chinese would be recognised as citizens of the new state. This led to the adoption in 1946 of a passive system whereby Chinese born in the country acquired Indonesian citizenship unless they specifically rejected it, while facilities were also provided for the naturalisation of those born in China. These measures were accepted in the 'Round Table

Agreements' between Indonesia and the Netherlands in 1949 which gave the local-born a two-year period to reject their Indonesian citizenship if they wished to be considered nationals of China. Despite its apparent liberality, this passive system caused considerable confusion about the status of Chinese in Indonesia, primarily because acceptors possessed no simple positive documentary proof of citizenship. In applying various regulations, officials generally assumed that all Chinese were aliens unless they could show otherwise, yet the only way to confirm Indonesian citizenship was to prove from court records that it had not been rejected, a lengthy and expensive process. In addition, the position of the Chinese remained equivocal because of China's longstanding adherence to the principle of *jus sanguinis*—that wherever they were born persons of Chinese descent were Chinese nationals—which meant that from the point of view of China even those who opted for Indonesian citizenship retained their Chinese nationality and were thus dual nationals.

Although diplomatic relations were established between Indonesia and the new Peking government in 1950 and the position of the Chinese in Indonesia was a problem to both, each was preoccupied with other matters in the early 1950s. By 1954, however, China had begun to develop a more active foreign policy and came to see the Overseas Chinese as a potential liability in its international affairs. In order to promote easier relations with Indonesia, its largest and most sympathetic South-east Asian neighbour, Peking deemed it necessary to resolve this question of dual nationality by abandoning the principle of *jus sanguinis* and so reducing the impediment the Indonesian Chinese represented to the advancement of its policies. Secret negotiations between Indonesia and China on dual nationality began in Peking towards the end of 1954 and were concluded in Indonesia during the Bandung conference the following year. After substantial opposition in Indonesia, the resulting Dual Nationality Treaty was ratified in 1957, its final form incorporating most of Indonesia's wishes, but its implementation was delayed until 1960.

From Peking's point of view, this treaty was 'a major propaganda achievement for the policy of peaceful co-existence'.[16] Links between Indonesia and China moved progressively closer as Sukarno's foreign policy built up its anti-Western neocolonialist stridency. He looked more and more to China as the only major power sympathetic to his militant foreign adventures in the early 1960s; the two nations signed a Treaty of Friendship in 1961, and Peking congratulated Sukarno on the Irian affair and gave strong verbal support, though not armaments, which were obtained from the Soviet Union, for the campaign to crush Malaysia. Indonesia recognised North Korea, North Vietnam, and the National Liberation Front in South Vietnam; with Foreign Minister Subandrio, Sukarno visited Peking and in 1965 announced the formation of an anti-imperialist, anti-colonialist Jakarta–Phnom Penh–Hanoi–Peking–Pyongyang axis.

Throughout this period there are good grounds for believing that Peking saw the Indonesian Chinese as a potentially embarrassing cause of discord in foreign relations. To avoid embroilment in disputes with the Indonesian government, Peking adopted a policy towards the Overseas Chinese which sought to detach them from China and to persuade them that their future lay in Indonesia. Peking thus abandoned all claims to those who did so; the Indonesian Chinese were encouraged to acquire local citizenship, to identify more fully with their country of residence, and to move towards greater integration in its society. Indeed, as Stephen FitzGerald, currently Australia's ambassador in Peking, has so ably shown, China's intentions towards the Overseas Chinese were the reverse of most popular Western, and many Indonesian, interpretations. Having quickly recognised that these Overseas Chinese were an unlikely instrument for successful subversion, Peking's major object was to reduce their potential for international friction; concern with their interests then declined sharply to the extent of ignoring most discriminatory measures introduced by the Indonesian government. In the eyes of Peking it was not the Overseas Chinese who offered the best prospect of revolutionary success in Indonesia, but the PKI, and this was overwhelmingly Indonesian in membership.

Yet, while the signing of the Dual Nationality Treaty was a significant move in relations between Indonesia and China, the long delay in its implementation and the concurrent introduction of more restrictive measures merely compounded the uncertainties and difficulties facing Chinese in Indonesia. As Willmott reports, 'officials took the signing of the treaty as an indication that Chinese of dual nationality might be regarded as foreigners' and discrimination against Chinese, including those who had previously opted for Indonesian citizenship, was widespread.[17] When the treaty was finally put into practice in 1960, it substituted an active system for the earlier passive procedures. Every adult Chinese with dual nationality who wished to retain Indonesian citizenship had two years in which to reject Chinese nationality before a court; those who were minors at the time would be required to make this choice on reaching 18 years of age. This process involved 'an impressive array of bureaucratic and legal obstacles', but those who failed to comply with it lost their Indonesian citizenship and became aliens.[18]

Although Chinese held the cabinet portfolios of Health and Finance in 1954 and Sukarno regularly voiced his opposition to racial discrimination, with worsening economic and political conditions in Indonesia in the later 1950s public and official antagonism towards the Chinese minority mounted. Vigorous efforts were made to curtail their economic role and to reduce their cultural distinctiveness. In the long term, many measures introduced at this time were no doubt desirable, but, largely because of the indiscriminate and unfeeling manner with which they were applied and especially of the general failure of officials, usually intentionally, to distinguish between citizens and aliens, their immediate effects were disruptive and the cause of much hardship.

As they became more concerned with Chinese nationalism and with the need to defend their interests, during the occupation and the early years of independence the Indonesian Chinese achieved a new degree of unity, which was enhanced by the lessening of distinctions between *totok* and *peranakan* as the latter experienced some measure of resinification. Apart from the establishment of community and political organisations, this trend was closely related to a rapid extension of Chinese-language education. The Japanese had closed the Dutch-Chinese schools in 1942. *Totok* children had always been educated in Chinese-language schools, but now a growing proportion of *peranakan* offspring went to these same institutions. By the early 1950s over half of all *peranakan* children were attending Chinese-language schools and, since most of the rest were enrolled in Christian establishments, this educational segregation of Chinese and Indonesians exacerbated the distinctiveness of the Chinese, citizens and aliens alike. This situation continued until 1957 when the Indonesian government closed the majority of 'alien' Chinese schools and ordered citizens to send their children to Indonesian-language schools, thus eliminating 'foreign-language, foreign-content education for citizens of Indonesia'.[19] This sudden change has had lasting effects since it effectively means that today every citizen of Chinese ancestry who is less than about 25 years of age has been educated in the Indonesian language.

Concurrently, the Chinese economic position came under growing pressure. Aliens were excluded from certain lines of business in which the Chinese had long been important, including rice-milling and textile wholesaling, and they were also forbidden to establish new enterprises or to expand or relocate existing businesses. A head tax was imposed on foreigners, remittances to China were stopped, and the amount of foreign exchange available to Chinese was severely restricted. In 1958 all *Kuomintang* organisations, including youth groups, were banned and, except for a select few which continued under close military supervision, the publication and circulation of Chinese-language newspapers and magazines were prohibited. The same year most types of small business were closed to aliens and the employment of foreign personnel by any enterprise was discouraged. Then in 1959, in an apparent move to undermine the Chinese role as middlemen in the national marketing system, a regulation was introduced which forbade retail trade by aliens outside designated larger urban centres. This regulation was implemented by the local military authorities and it was particularly strongly enforced in West Java, especially in the vicinity of Bandung and Bogor, where substantial numbers of rural Chinese were transferred into larger towns. Initially, China ignored this discriminatory measure as it had those noted earlier, but late in 1959 the resulting hardship provoked Peking to lodge a strong protest and to make arrangements to transport to China those Chinese who now wished to quit Indonesia. According to official counts, a total of 102,297 Chinese left the country during 1960. Thereafter, however, despite attacks on Chinese property in many towns in West Java in 1963, the diversion of attention in other directions brought a general reduction of pressures on the Chinese in the later years of Guided Democracy.

Not surprisingly, throughout this period of increasing pressure and uncertainty over their status, the Indonesian Chinese were intensely concerned with the protection of their interests. The strong desire of many *peranakan* to retain a distinctive identity while accepting Indonesian citizenship had brought the establishment of the *Persatuan Tionghoa* in 1948 to defend the status, position, and culture of the Chinese. Later this was transformed into a political party, the *Partai Demokrat Tionghoa Indonesia,* but since this achieved little in the way of success or support, in 1954 a group of young Western-educated *peranakan* formed a new political organisation known as *Baperki (Badan Permusyawaratan Kewarganegaraan Indonesia).* Although membership of *Baperki* was open to all citizens and it did gain some Indonesian and Eurasian members, it was essentially a Chinese organisation and its chief objectives were to protect the interests of the Chinese and to foster their incorporation into Indonesian society as equal and recognised partners. In its early years, *Baperki* was actively engaged in politics; it fielded candidates in the 1955 and 1957 elections, in some areas in alliance with the PKI, and it drew a substantial proportion of the Chinese vote. It also made its views felt in discussions on the Dual Nationality Treaty and other measures affecting the Chinese, frequently receiving backing from the PKI. Nevertheless, although it remained influential and adopted a political stance squarely behind the President, with the institution of increasingly rigorous measures against the Chinese in the late 1950s, *Baperki* became more concerned with community service. In particular, it did much to assist the Chinese by establishing schools with an Indonesian curriculum, to provide for those banned from attending Chinese-language institutions after 1957, since there were at the time insufficient places for them in government schools. But its close links with Sukarno, the support it received from and gave to the PKI, its favourable disposition to Peking, and its attraction for *peranakan* left-wing sympathisers aroused distrust in military circles, which were in any case suffused with suspicion of the Chinese. When the New Order assumed control, *Baperki* was banned and former membership became a distinct personal liability.

Most victims of the bloodbath and wave of detentions following the abortive 1965 *coup* were Indonesians. Nonetheless, as a result of Peking's alleged involvement and clandestine supply of arms, and of the popular tendency to equate Chinese and communism, which meant that Chinese were seen as actual or potential subversive agents and economic saboteurs in Peking's service, the new strength of public and official anti-communist feeling threw a cloak of suspicion over the entire Chinese minority. In actual fact there was scant evidence to show that Chinese were 'proportionately more involved in PKI/*Gestapu* activities than the Indonesians themselves or other minority groups' or that Chinese 'played an important role in making or executing policy during the *Gestapu*', and none of the *coup*'s leaders were Chinese,[20] but in the early years of the New Order Chinese were subjected to indiscriminate violence and increasingly restrictive official measures, and relations between Indonesia and China declined to a new low. Anti-Chinese riots against persons and property erupted in several towns towards the end of 1965 and were repeated in the subsequent two years. Meanwhile, there were vociferous demands, particularly from student activists and right-wing Muslim organisations, for the deportation of aliens, the seizure of Chinese-owned businesses, the ending of Chinese 'economic domination', and the rejection of all things Chinese by citizens. In 1966, for instance, alien Chinese forcibly expelled from Aceh were sent in army lorries to special camps in Medan to await deportation; and while some were transported to China in vessels sent by Peking, several thousand still remained in these camps in 1973. Military raids and searches in Jakarta in April 1967 brought regular reports of the discovery of evidence of Chinese subversion, and resulted in many arrests. Again, late in 1967, in retribution for the murder of villagers by guerrillas, Dayaks in interior West Kalimantan turned on the local Chinese who were predominantly rural agriculturalists, killing many and causing most of the remainder to shift to rudimentary camps in Pontianak, Singkawang, and Mampawah on the coast, a process of withdrawal and associated economic dislocation which was accelerated in 1971 when the authorities requested Chinese along the Sarawak border to move back to the Kapuas river.

Pressure on the Chinese reached a peak in 1967. The observance of Chinese religious ceremonies and festivals was severely circumscribed; Chinese were strongly urged to adopt Indonesian names; the use of Chinese characters in public (in shop signs for example) was prohibited; all 'alien' organisations except those concerned with health, religion, funerals, sports, and recreation, were declared unacceptable; in some areas at least the 1959 restrictions on trade were more tightly enforced; Chinese were subjected to various kinds of extortion; and all Chinese-language schools were closed, although since 1968 certain institutions have been permitted to teach Chinese as an additional subject within the national curriculum. Faced with these pressures, several thousand non-citizen Chinese, as many as 100,000 on one estimate, left Indonesia, some for China and some for other destinations principally in South-east Asia and Europe. Concurrently, relations with Peking, which protested against the tough treatment, even persecution, of the Indonesian Chinese, rapidly approached breaking-point. During 1966 scheduled Garuda flights to Canton were stopped and the Jakarta office of the New China News Agency was closed. Clashes before the Chinese embassy in the capital, and its subsequent sacking, followed in 1967. In September that year Indonesia suspended trade with China and a month later diplomatic relations between the two nations were 'frozen' and their respective diplomatic staffs were recalled. This was a serious setback to China's foreign policy in South-east Asia and, as Indonesia drew closer to Taiwan and openly courted Western support for its economic plans, China's attitude became increasingly acrimonious; the new Indonesian leaders were branded by Peking as 'Fascist suppressors of the masses' and Suharto's government was portrayed as 'the most reactionary and most decadent' in Indonesian history. Since Indonesia regards its diplomatic relations with China as merely 'frozen' and Peking has spoken only of their 'suspension', the process of re-establishing relations would be relatively simple. Yet, although indirect trade continues through Hong Kong and Singapore, in 1974 an early *rapprochement* seemed unlikely.

After 1967, the growing official Indonesian concern to afford the Chinese greater security in the interests of national development, caused the general situation to ease. In one important respect, however, the position of many Chinese was made more difficult when Indonesia unilaterally declared the Dual Nationality Treaty invalid in April 1969. By removing the right of minors to opt for Indonesian citizenship when they reached 18 years of age, the rescinding of the treaty means that all Chinese children, wherever they were born, automatically follow the nationality of their parents. Non-citizens can, of course, apply for naturalisation and Foreign Minister Adam Malik has declared that if resident Chinese nationals 'want to become Indonesians, then we will let them'. But while there has been an increase in successful applications in recent years, the procedure remains complex and is open to irregularity and delay. 'The Indonesian authorities', reports Munthe-Kaas, 'have so far shown no urge to speed up or facilitate the process of naturalisation for either Chinese nationals or the stateless Chinese in spite of their professed commitment to this goal'.[21]

By the late 1960s the 'Chinese problem' had become less explosive; although rioters ransacked Chinese shops in Menado in March 1970 and similar outbreaks occurred in Semarang in mid-1971, acts of anti-Chinese violence and discrimination have become less frequent and in the early 1970s a more tolerant atmosphere prevailed. To a large extent, this reflects a growing recognition of the need for co-operation and understanding by both the Indonesian authorities and the Chinese. Official policy has shown an increasing acceptance that the Chinese have a significant role to play in the rehabilitation and development of the economy and that their displacement, particularly from channels of internal and external trade, could produce severe disruption. The desperate need to mobilise domestic capital for developmental ends necessarily required the recognition that a substantial proportion lay in Chinese hands, and capital 'accumulated and expanded in the territory of Indonesia' by alien Chinese was now perceived as domestic foreign capital which could not be transferred abroad and, as 'national wealth in the hands of aliens', was to be employed in the interests of national economic development.

It was because of this situation that government became intolerant of popular excesses and student activities against this economically necessary minority. To encourage their investment and enterprise, efforts were made to give the Chinese greater protection and a greater sense of security. A special committee for Chinese affairs was established which sought to eliminate earlier attacks and formulated a 'Basic Policy for the Solution of the Chinese Problem', and there were official declarations, not always reflected in practice, that Chinese citizens possessed the same rights, privileges, and duties as all Indonesians. The measure of success of these moves has been the marked rise in investment in manufacturing by Chinese who are citizens, by resident alien Chinese, and by Chinese from Hong Kong, Singapore, Malaysia, and Taiwan. As evident in several Presidential pronouncements, at the same time government came to view assimilation as the only long-term solution to ethnic friction and calls have been made to the Chinese to abandon their exclusiveness to eradicate 'all obstacles which cause disharmony with native citizens'.

For their part, the Chinese, or at least those who are citizens or who aspire to this status, have begun to come to terms with their situations and, as might be expected, they have started to make appropriate adjustments. There are, for instance, signs of a general resignation to the need for at least the appearances of assimilation by those who were not previously enthusiastic largely, one suspects, because of a pragmatic recognition that there is no real alternative; in its present form, however, this is perhaps better termed 'accommodation' since it signifies a move towards, rather than a wholesale embracement of, the official concept of assimilation. Equally, a characteristic *modus vivendi* has emerged between Chinese business and the Indonesian military and officialdom, clearly manifest in the cementing of close business links between Chinese and highly placed Indonesians, a process mockingly known as *cukongism* (from *cukong* meaning 'grandfather' or 'boss'), and in the generous financial backing provided by Chinese businessmen, eager to keep Suharto in power because his stress on development promised wide possibilities of profit, for the government's *Golkar* in the 1971 elections. Nevertheless, on what is still an emotional and complex issue, two points may help to clarify perspectives. Firstly, as is apparent in the continued eruption of occasional anti-Chinese riots, the disquiet voiced in some quarters about Chinese commercial domination, and in the widespread prejudice against the financially successful, there is still a gap between official national policy on the one hand and popular Indonesian sentiment and the actions of local authorities on the other regarding the Chinese minority; moreover, despite high-level emphasis on the principles of equality, there are many areas in which Chinese, citizens and aliens alike, apparently lack the same access to benefits accorded to indigenous Indonesians.

Secondly, although the aliens are certainly in a difficult position and face many restrictions, the Chinese suffer fewer disabilities than might seem to be the case. Significantly small numbers of Chinese, for example, are unemployed. Chinese investment is rising, and students of Chinese ancestry continue to occupy a larger proportion of university places than their share of the population would suggest.

During the last decade and a half there have been two opposing views in Indonesia on the future of the Chinese minority. Firstly, what are sometimes known as the *participationists* have urged that the Chinese should be allowed to retain their identity and move towards integration *(integrasi)* in a context of cultural pluralism. Holding that any other approach would represent a betrayal of their heritage, and based on the firm belief that 'cultural diversity can exist within a framework of common striving for social progress',[22] the participationists argued that since the Chinese had as much right to their cultural distinctiveness as any other ethnic group, they were fully justified in seeking to protect their group interests. This view, which places the onus on Indonesians to accept the Chinese for what they are, was predominant in the Sukarno era. It was strongly favoured by *Baperki* and by its Indonesian supporters, particularly the PKI, and largely for this reason in recent years it has become less respectable. A very different attitude prevails among those who have favoured the absorption or assimilation *(assimilasi)* of the Chinese. These *assimilationists* hold that the Chinese must merge into, and conform with, the society of the nation's majority culture as rapidly as possible so that they will ultimately disappear as a distinct, easily recognisable, ethnic group. This approach places the burden on the Chinese to become more Indonesian and sees the loss of their distinctiveness as the price the Chinese must pay for ready acceptance. Its proponents maintain that the Chinese must stop setting themselves apart, by, for example, forming exclusively Chinese organisations or by specifically trying to protect Chinese interests, and some Chinese supporters of this line have openly backed official discriminatory or restrictive measures. The assimilationist viewpoint was propagated systematically by sections of the younger *peranakan* from about 1960; controversy with those supporting *integrasi* was marked in the later years of Sukarno, but in general the idea of assimilation was more sympathetically received among Chinese in Java than in the Outer Islands where there has been far less acculturation.

Since the advent of the New Order the assimilationists have received the weighty support of Indonesia's political and military leaders. In 1967, for example, when Suharto declared that a clear distinction must be made between aliens and citizens since the latter were in the same position as all other Indonesians, he also recommended that Chinese with citizenship should be actively encouraged to abandon their 'Chinese characteristics' and speed up 'their integration and assimilation with the native Indonesians'. Assimilation has, indeed, become the official goal and many of the measures introduced in the later 1960s were aimed at expediting the process. Yet, while assimilation is also now the stated objective of some prominent Chinese and seemingly creates relatively few apprehensions, or at least meets less resistance, among more acculturated *peranakan,* in the Outer Islands in particular private fears as to what exactly assimilation means are widespread. Most Chinese appear prepared to accept the inevitability of some change, or to compromise appropriately, but at heart many see no reason why they should have to jettison their culture to prove that they are worthy and loyal Indonesian citizens.

Undoubtedly, the ultimate solution of Indonesia's 'Chinese problem' will require a progressive diminution of 'the importance of the factor of economic competition',[23] together with substantial changes in the attitudes of both Chinese and Indonesians to mitigate their mutual feelings of prejudice, hostility, and apprehension. But the crux of the problem at present is the large number of essentially indigestible Chinese who are destined under current citizenship laws to remain perpetual aliens. Treated differently from citizens and subjected to what must seem to them to be consistent discrimination, these aliens could not shake off their separate identity even if they wished to, and there is scant prospect of a widening or acceleration of the officially desired process of assimilation while over half the Chinese population is in this nebulous position of insecurity and uncertainty. As Charles Coppel has suggested, perhaps the easiest way to remove this impediment would be by application of the principle of *jus soli,* giving all those born in Indonesia the right to citizenship; since the proportion of noncitizens born in China is already small and fast declining, within a generation this large alien component would thus disappear and the road would at least be open for the eventual assimilation of the entire Chinese population.[24] Such a liberalisation of access to citizenship would certainly meet strong opposition from Indonesians, but it does already have indigenous advocates. Since the process of changing attitudes is inevitably slow and stuttering and even loss of cultural exclusiveness does not remove differences of physical appearance, in some form Indonesia will have a 'Chinese problem' for years to come, but its eventual resolution will be much nearer once the government and people have fully accepted the reality that the non-citizen Chinese are there to stay and accord them an appropriate status. They can hardly be deported; regarding Indonesia as home, very few would wish to go to China; and they cannot be left for ever aliens in the land of their birth. Whatever the official goal, assimilation of the Chinese in Indonesia will remain a chimera so long as half of the Chinese minority is in this unenviable position.

NOTES

[1] Go Gien Tjwan, 'The Assimilation Problem of the Chinese in Indonesia', *Cultures et développement,* vol. I, no. 1, 1968, 53.

[2] Lea E. Williams, *The Future of the Overseas Chinese in Southeast Asia,* New York, McGraw-Hill Book Co., 1966, 17.

[3] e.g., G. William Skinner, 'The Chinese Minority' in Ruth T. McVey (ed.), *Indonesia,* New Haven, 1963.

[4] James C. Jackson, 'Mining in 18th Century Bangka: the Pre-European Exploitation of a "Tin Island"', *Pacific Viewpoint,* vol. 10, no. 2, 1969, 49, n.66, and *Chinese in the West Borneo Goldfields: a Study in Cultural Geography,* University of Hull Occasional Papers in Geography no. 15, Hull, 1970, 45.

[5] J.L.L. Duyvendak, 'Chinese in the Dutch East Indies', *The Chinese Social and Political Science Review,* vol. XI, no. 1, 1927, 6.

[6] Lance Castles, 'The Ethnic Profile of Djakarta', *Indonesia,* no. 3, April 1967, 162.

[7] Donald Earl Willmott, *The Chinese of Semarang: a Changing Minority Community in Indonesia,* Ithaca, Cornell University Press, 1960, 112.

[8] Skinner, op. cit., 104-5.

[9] Tan Giok-Lan, *The Chinese of Sukabumi: a Study in Social and Cultural Accommodation,* Monograph Series, Modern Indonesia Project, Ithaca, Cornell University Press, 1963, 41-2.

[10] Skinner, op. cit., 104.

[11] Skinner, op. cit., 105.

[12] For a Chinese view of *peranakan* culture and the early 'Chinese movement' see Kwee Tek Hoay, *The Origins of the Modern Chinese Movement in Indonesia,* Translation Series, Modern Indonesia Project, Ithaca, Cornell University Press, 1969.

[13] Jackson, *Chinese in the West Borneo Goldfields,* 45.

[14] Willmott, op. cit., 112.

[15] Tan Giok-Lan, op. cit., 30ff.

[16] Stephen FitzGerald, *China and the Overseas Chinese: a Study of Peking's Changing Policy, 1949-1970,* Cambridge, Cambridge University Press, 1972, 108.

[17] Donald E. Willmott, *The National Status of the Chinese in Indonesia, 1900-1958,* Monograph Series, Modern Indonesia Project, Ithaca, Cornell University Press, 1961, 31.

[18] Skinner, op. cit., 112.

[19] Willmott, *The National Status of the Chinese in Indonesia,* 87.

[20] Harald Munthe-Kaas, 'The Dragon's Seed', *Far Eastern Economic Review,* vol. LVIII, no. 6, 9 November 1967, 282.

[21] ibid., 285.

[22] Go Gien Tjwan, op. cit., 58.

[23] ibid., 59.

[24] Charles Coppel, 'The Position of the Chinese in the Philippines, Malaysia and Indonesia', in *The Chinese in Indonesia, the Philippines and Malaysia,* Minority Rights Group, Report no. 10, London, 1972, 16-28.

CHAPTER 10

Whither Indonesia?

A CASE COULD BE MADE out for the view that there are several newly independent countries of the Third World to whom the fates have been even harsher than they have to Indonesia. In comparison with its vastly more populous neighbour India, even Indonesia's disturbing demographic situation pales; Indonesia is not smitten with the deeply entrenched system of caste, nor except in very limited parts of its territory does it have to contend with one of the most basic and enduring causes of India's economic difficulties, a scanty and highly capricious rainfall.[1] Yet even by the standards of India, many of Indonesia's problems are formidable enough, and if Calcutta must be conceded its unenviable claim to be 'the worst city in the world', Jakarta in the late Sukarno period was surely in the worst half-dozen. This brief and selective survey of Indonesia has identified but a few of the country's many intractable problems, and, as with India, they raise issues which concern the fundamental organisation of society, and particularly of rural society. For Indonesia is, and will long continue to be, an agricultural society, and this is a matter that the Indonesian élite must come to terms with as rapidly as possible. In the last analysis, whether Indonesia can maintain itself as a single nation or achieve a modern society depends firstly on raising agricultural productivity by a substantial margin, and, secondly, on achieving a more socially equitable division of the produce of the soil. All other questions are subordinate. This is not, of course, to deny the desirability of pressing on with industrialisation as rapidly as possible; but, for reasons which emerged in the study of demographic movements and of the development of manufacturing industries, it is manifestly impossible to create more than a fraction of the new employment opportunities that will become necessary over the next two decades through the establishment of new, or modern, industries. Nor will a greater concentration on small-scale co-operative production, employing what has become known as 'intermediate technology', that is, the employment of obsolescent but still serviceable machinery or of other relatively high-labour-content methods of manufacturing, serve; most of the new employment opportunities, if they are to be created at all, must be found in agriculture.

This is the conclusion reached by the distinguished economist Myrdal and his collaborators in his monumental *Asian Drama*.[2] Although an excessive preoccupation with the Indian region and only the hastiest of glances at South-east Asia detract from the relevance of the analysis to the whole of the continent, Myrdal's conclusion is that, contrary to accepted belief, the prospects for creating new employment opportunities in agriculture on a massive scale and consistent with Asia's needs, are very favourable. Myrdal's prescription for securing this desirable end is basically simple: remove the disincentives and obstacles to the exercise of peasant initiative, so that it becomes both possible and financially attractive for him to make the extra investment to raise output. When the peasants of Asia can get 300 or more full working-days into the year instead of a little more than a hundred as at present, both the continent's food problems and the deplorably low living standards of its population will be well on the way to amelioration. The essential action to bring about this change, in Myrdal's view, is land reform.

Before pursuing the relevance of this analysis to Indonesia, it needs to be said that seldom is the agrarian situation made central in any prognosis of Indonesia, either within the country or outside it. *Repelita* I, as with so many other Asian national development plans, said a great deal about the necessity for achieving a large increase in food production; nevertheless, only some 30 percent of planned expenditure was allocated to the agricultural sector, the support of some 70 percent of the population. The agricultural proposals, indeed, stressed ways of economising in capital through *gotong-royong* schemes for irrigation and drainage, and through the *Bimas* and *Inmas* programmes. In themselves these are laudable enough; but so long as the greater part of the resources committed in development plans is pre-empted by ends whose principal benefits accrue to the limited urban sector and especially to the élite—power, transport, communications, manufacturing, mining, even indeed much of the very limited allocation for education—the claimed commitment to agriculture needs heavily discounting. Moreover, notwithstanding the pledges made by the estate companies for the rehabilitation of their properties, the disparity between agricultural and non-agricultural private investment is equally marked.

All foreign scholars of Indonesia, of course, concur that the agrarian situation gives rise to great concern. But Byzantine Jakarta politics and the turmoil of the struggle for and exercise of power distract attention from the agricultural round, in which the great bulk of the population gains, and that barely, a livelihood; it is, however, generally conceded that military regimes, even in the best of circumstances, are ill-adapted for the task of sustained economic development. Penny, however, concludes that 'unless the present constellation of political, social and cultural forces is changed, there is little chance of improvement in the economic situation in agriculture, or in the nation as a whole'.[3] The prospects of such a radical reorganisation of society seemed as remote in 1975 as they had a decade earlier.

What is particularly discouraging about government policies for food-producing agriculture is that in virtually every respect they are identical with those pursued without success for almost half a century by the Dutch colonial regime. It is as if it had been decided that the Dutch failed not because their strategy was defective, but because they did not push it vigorously enough. All that is needed is more of the same; more irrigation, more multi-cropping, and more transmigration, plus more high-yielding seeds and more fertiliser. This dismal reinforcing of failure has not worked and cannot possibly work, for it leaves unchanged the complex of economic and social relationships between those who own and those who use the land; indeed, this is precisely its intention and justification.

Unlike its near neighbour, the Philippines, Indonesia is not a country with a marked concentration of landownership; the large holdings of the Outer Islands are units of management producing mainly non-food export crops, not collections of tenancies. It is indeed probable in Java that the area owned by large landowners is larger than has generally been realised, and that there is a substantial area of land owned by the urban upper class and the senior levels of the bureaucracy. Nevertheless, this can only be a very small fraction of the total area of land under cultivation, so that the scope for conventional land reform through redistribution, with attendant back-up services in the form of improved credit and marketing facilities, appears limited. However, this does not mean that nothing can be done; land reform must be made to fit the actual conditions present, and needs to vary from country to country, and even among different regions of the same country.[4] It is clear from the earlier chapters that Java and the *Tanah Seberang* require different treatment, as do the three major divisions of Java itself, a situation recognised in the Basic Agrarian Law of 1960 with its varying stipulations on the legal maxima of landholdings.

Some redistribution is proceeding slowly under this legislation, but the whole question of land reform is tainted through its association with the PKI, and the mass killings of 1965-66, which in all probability were as much motivated by removing all troublemakers as well as communists, injected a poison into rural life which will inhibit all institutional change for some time to come. The land-reform programme does not disturb the traditional village inequality, which will be further enhanced by population growth, and as more and more of Java moves progressively from the cultivation of rice to that of maize and finally to tapioca, which, as Penny aptly remarks, 'is the end of the road'.[5]

There are basically two categories of problems in Java: farmers who possess some resources in land and capital, but who do not, or who cannot, perceive and take advantage of economic opportunities open to them, and the great and growing army of the landless who possess nothing but their own labour. Penny provides several examples of apparently irrational economic behaviour by farmers, but which, when viewed from within the cultural and institutional constraints under which farmers operate, nevertheless appear entirely logical. The new technologies are merely inserted within those constraints, and, as elsewhere in Asia, will further reinforce inequality. As was seen earlier, their employment is not the result of autonomous decisions by farmers themselves, but is imposed from above, sometimes under harsh conditions; in other words, the old Dutch policy of 'let me show you, let me help you, let me do it for you' continues unchanged. Somehow the scope for the exercise of peasant initiative must be enlarged, and conditions created under which farmers will be willing and able to make extra investment in improved technology. This must involve greater freedom for the operation of market forces; the official rice-procuring machinery, which is designed to serve the needs of the administration and not those of the people as a whole, supports Myrdal's contention that in Asia the 'extraction process is governed not by ordinary market forces but by custom and by economic and social power in the village'.[6] The operation of market forces would be enhanced by fiscal reform, replacing the present system of indirect taxation through price manipulation by direct taxes on farmers, from which at present they are almost entirely free, and which could be designed to promote the optimal use of land and irrigation water. But even if it were physically possible, it would not make much sense to divide up the cultivated area of Java so that the landless had a proportionate share; this would merely replace one kind of inequity with another. But something could usually be done even in the most congested parts of Java to implement Myrdal's suggestion of providing the landless with a plot of their own, however small, to increase their sense of dignity and self-respect and to encourage them to make investment of labour in it.[7] Certainly some land could, and should, be released, by eliminating the *lungguhs* of the village officials and placing them on salary. The abolition of this anachronistic feudal relic is long overdue; it would provide a powerful stimulus to a break-out from the cultural straitjacket in which village life is confined, and would help to promote greater agricultural efficiency by reducing the large class of cultivators who in fact do no cultivation at all, and whose total eradication should constitute a fundamental objective of policy.

Such a reform is highly unlikely, if only because it was urged by the PKI; in Java, ownership or control over land is the basis of social and economic power, and those who possess it were confirmed in their positions by the events of 1965-66. The complex process of dividing the economic pie into progressively smaller pieces through the elaborate work-making and work-sharing practices of traditional agricultural life, in which 'even the implements become smaller', will continue, as rural society endeavours to find a place at the barest level of subsistence for those who cannot be accommodated within the gainfully employed. Yet it is obvious that this process cannot proceed indefinitely. Even to keep it going at the present requires increasingly expensive external resources in the form of food imports, fertilisers, and of other farm inputs; Geertz has argued that Java's last trump, the new technologies, was having to be played when the cultural and political atmosphere was such that it would almost certainly be wasted, and that the result would be further paralysis.[8] Since Geertz wrote, Indonesia has produced another ace from its sleeve, oil and natural gas, and its command over external resources is greater than it has ever been. But by the 1990s most of Indonesia's petroleum resources will be gone, and even if more are discovered as they surely will be, Indonesia's population will be double that of 1970. It is, of course, possible that by then some new resource may have turned up, so that Java's rural paralysis can continue for a few more decades. But such a Micawberish consummation can only postpone the day of reckoning.

Thus one is driven again to consider the prospects for maintaining a national polity and economy in which the resources of the regions continue to be made available for Java's 'static development', the principal issue of 1957-58. The events of those years, it was seen, resulted in a marked increase in Javanese control of the armed forces, but although the effluxion of time has produced some modification of this paramountcy, it has not removed the apprehensions of the administration. In the regions, central government control appears complete; nevertheless, it continues to feel vulnerable and will permit of no truly independent expressions of opinion or discussion of national goals. It is not, of course, that the *daerah* are unwilling to allow a substantial part of their resources to be used for the benefit of Java, but they must be allowed scope for their own socio-political development. The analysis here strongly suggests that the instruments adopted by the military in its determination to preserve national unity must ultimately be self-defeating; the best way, surely, of ensuring a united and modestly prosperous Indonesia is to stimulate the exercise of local initiative throughout Java through greater economic and social freedom, so that the island can escape from its poverty trap and come to provide what Fisher calls 'true metropolitan functions' for the country as a whole.[9] The 'passivity of the masses', as Myrdal says, will prevent any spontaneous peasant revolt, to say nothing of the memories of 1965-66; if revolution comes to Indonesia, it can only come as it has elsewhere in Asia, and as it did after the Japanese occupation, through the forging of links between the intelligentsia and the peasantry. And events in South-east Asia in the early 1970s suggest that the student population, just as earlier in Russia and China, is rapidly moving in the direction of broadening its contacts with the *rakyat;* the speed of government reaction in Burma, Malaysia, and in Indonesia itself at the student protest is clear evidence that the danger was immediately perceived.

Nevertheless, there were grounds for the optimism of many Western politicians, government servants, and businessmen over Indonesia's prospects in 1975. The enormous debts that Suharto had incurred to resurrect the shattered Indonesian economy, and which were enhanced by the *Pertamina* crisis, did not appear an insuperable burden; the resources with which to pay them off were there, and moreover were being developed. Indonesia had retained its creditworthiness; indeed, a large segment of its indebtedness had arisen from the operations of importunate lenders. The runaway inflation of the 1960s had been brought under control, the rupiah was strong, and Indonesia's imports of food and raw materials did not depend entirely on Western charity as in India. The uncertainty that hung over the future of many cherished projects, including the long-deferred Asahan, was not of Indonesia's making, but arose from the incipient world depression. And although many thousands of communist sympathisers, or suspected sympathisers, were still incarcerated after years without trial, Indonesia is not a police state as that term is usually understood in the West. The administration is dominated by the military, but the presence of the army is seldom obtrusive, in marked contrast with the last years of Sukarno, when ill-disciplined bands of gun-waving troops levied toll almost everywhere, and made life hazardous, even in the centre of Jakarta. It would be going much too far to describe the country as within the Western camp, for Indonesia still regards itself as non-aligned, in the Bandung tradition. But it did not participate in the oil blackmail of 1973-74, and has declared that it will take no part in any future embargo. It has given no aid to the Muslim rebels of Sulu and Mindanao in the Philippines.

With the communist victories in Vietnam, Cambodia, and Laos, many will see Indonesia as the principal barrier to the further spread of communism in South-east Asia. There is little doubt that Indonesia will receive large quantities of American arms, although in all probability not to fight the large set-piece battles that the army of South Vietnam (ARV) was equipped to fight, and in the end so conspicuously failed to do. As many more, perhaps, will inveigh against this further American support for military regimes around the world, and prophesy catastrophe. It should be clear from this study that the Indonesian situation is entirely different from that in those other countries in the Third World where the communists have identified themselves with nationalism. The proto-armed forces of Indonesia were in the struggle for independence from the very beginning, and it is to this that the military administration traces its legitimacy. In contrast, it has been the communists who have betrayed the revolution, and imperilled national unity and independence again and again, as many Indonesians view their country.

There is, of course, much that is unattractive to the Western mind in the present regime; it is at least a matter of some doubt whether there has been any decline in the magnitude of corruption since the Sukarno regime, and it is a sad comment that the two industries which are regarded as having the most to contribute to national economic salvation, petroleum and timber, are generally thought of as the most corrupt. Malaysia earns much praise for the slick efficiency of its administration and the pace of its economic advance; the fact that its government respects the letter but not the spirit of Westminster receives less comment. But between 1968 and 1973 Indonesia's GNP increased by some 8 percent annually, a respectable performance even against that of economic high-flyers such as Japan. Its position as the only member of OPEC to receive large Western aid (Nigeria is not in the same class) is highly anomalous, but IGGI accepts the Indonesian arguments for its continuation, not surprisingly in view of the donor nations' own economic interests in the country. Indonesia should apply perhaps to its fellows in OPEC, or to the Arab petroleum producers, who have their own organisation for assistance. Apart from Bangladesh, there are few parts of the Muslim world where the need is greater, and perhaps none where the range of investment opportunities is greater. Indonesia's long-term future does indeed cast dark shadows; but that is an observation that can be made about very many countries of the modern world.

NOTES

[1] India and Indonesia are geographically closer than is often realised; Great Nicobar is only 90 nautical miles from the northern tip of Sumatra. In 1974 the two countries reached agreement on the delimitation of the boundary, and agreed to co-operate in the development of any oil-and gas-fields that might lie athwart it.

[2] New York, 1968. The argument is summarised and translated into a programme for action in the same author's *Challenge of World Poverty*, New York, 1970.

[3] D.H. Penny, 'The Economics of Peasant Agriculture: The Indonesian Case', *Bulletin of Indonesian Economic Studies*, no. 5, 1966, 42.

[4] Myrdal, *Challenge of World Poverty*, 123.

[5] Penny, op. cit., 25.

[6] Myrdal, *Challenge of World Poverty*, 130.

[7] ibid., 121.

[8] Clifford Geertz, *Agricultural Involution*, Berkeley and Los Angeles, 1963, 146.

[9] Charles A. Fisher, 'Economic Myth and Geographical Reality in Indonesia', *Modern Asian Studies*, vol. 1, 1967, 185.

Glossary of Indonesian terms and acronyms

abangan	The most important Javanese cultural tradition, only moderately Islamic
adat	Customary law
Ampera (Amanat Penderitaan Rakyat)	'Message of the people's suffering', a speech by Sukarno The Suharto cabinet of July 1966
ASA (Association of South-east Asian States)	A loose association, formed by the Federation of Malay, Thailand, and the Philippines in 1961
ASEAN (Association of South-east Asian Nations)	An association formed in 1967 by the former members of ASA, together with Indonesia and Singapore, for social and economic co-operation
ASPAC (Asia and Pacific Council)	A defensive anti-communist alliance, formed in 1966, by Japan, South Korea, Malaysia, the Philippines, Taiwan, Thailand, South Vietnam, Australia, and New Zealand
Aspri (Asisten Pribadi Presiden)	Presidential Assistant The Council of Assistants to President Suharto

Avros (Algemeene Vereeniging van Rubberplanters ter Oostkust van Sumatra)	General Association of Rubber Plantations of the East Coast of Sumatra
Baperki (Badan Permusyawaratan Kewarganegaraan Indonesia)	Consultative Body on Indonesian Citizenship, an organisation formed by Indonesian Chinese
Bappenas (Badan Perencanaan Pembangunan Nasional)	National Development Planning Council
barisan	Line, rank, lined-up formations, hence troops; also political front, and mountain range
bekel	Javanese steward or bailiff
belukar	Secondary forest
Berdikari (Berdiri di atas kaki sendiri)	'Standing on one's own feet', or self-sufficiency. A speech of Sukarno in April 1965
Bimas (Bimbingan Massal)	Mass guidance. An agricultural improvement programme, using university students
BPM (Bataafsche Petroleum Maatschappij)	The Netherlands Indies subsidiary of the Royal Dutch-Shell group
BPS (Badan Pendukung Sukarnoisme)	Body for the Promotion of Sukarnoism
BTI (Barisan Tani Indonesia)	Indonesian Peasants' Front, an organ of the PKI
Bulog (Badan Urusan Logistik)	Logistics Bureau

Conefo	Conference of New Emerging Forces, Sukarno's planned rival to the United Nations
daerah	Region (s); viewed from the capital, the provinces (*propinsi*), and from the provinces, the regencies
Darul Islam	'The home of Islam', a militant faction striving for a theocratic state
Dekon (Deklarasi Ekonomi)	Economic Declaration; Sukarno's speech of March 1963 heralding economic reforms
DI (Daerah Istimewa)	Special Region
DKI (Daerah Khusus Ibukota)	Extra Special Metropolitan District
DPA (Dewan Pertimbangan Agung)	Supreme Advisory Council
DPR (Dewan Perwakilan Rakyat)	People's Representative Council, or Parliament
DPRD (Dewan Perwakilan Rakyat Daerah)	Regional Representative Council
dwifungsi	Dual functions of the military as guardian of national sovereignty and integrity
dwitunggal	The dual unity of Sukarno and Hatta
EYD (Ejaan Yang Disempurnakan)	Improved spelling system

Gestapu (Gerakan September Tiga Puluh)	The 30 September Movement, the abortive communist *coup* of 1965
Golkar (Golongan Karya)	Functional Groups, reorganised as a government quasi-party for the elections of 1971
gotong-royong	Co-operation; mutual aid
IGGI	Inter-Governmental Group on Indonesia
Inmas (Intensifikasi Massal)	Mass Intensification (*Bimas*)
IPKI (Ikatan Pendukung Kemerdekaan Indonesia)	League of Supporters of Indonesian Independence, a small party mainly supported by army officers
Japerta (Jawatan Pertanian Rakyat)	Department of Public Agriculture
kabupaten	Regencies, or districts
Kami (Kesatuan Aksi Mahasiswa Indonesia)	Indonesian University Students' Action Front
kecamatan	Sub-districts
kelurahan	Administrative area of the village, the smallest unit of government
KNIP (Komite Nasional Indonesia Pusat)	Central National Committee of Indonesia, the first Parliament
Kopkamtib (Komando Operasi Pemulihan Keamanan dan Ketertiban)	Command for the Restoration of Security and Order

Kostrad (Komando (Cadangan) Strategi Angkatan Darat)	Army Strategic (Reserve) Command
KPM (Koninklijke Paketvaart Maatschappij)	The Dutch inter-island shipping line
LD (Liga Demokrasi)	Democratic League
Lemigas (Lembaga Minyak dan Gas)	Oil and Gas Board
lurah	Village headman
Malari (Malapetaka Januari; known to Indonesian students as Limabelas Januari)	15 January 1974, the student riots in Jakarta
Manipol (Manifesto Politik)	Sukarno's political manifesto of 1959; *see Usdek*
Maphilindo (Malaya, Philippines, Indonesia)	A loose federation of the three countries, proposed by Sukarno at Manila, 1963
Marhaen (isme)	A peasant name; Sukarno's cult of the 'little man'
Masyumi (Madjelis Sjuro Muslimin Indonesia)	Indonesian Muslim Advisory Council. An important political party until banned in 1960
MPR (S) (Majelis Permusyawaratan Rakyat) (Sementera)	(Provisional) People's Consultative Assembly
mufakat	consensus
Murba	Proletarian party, sometimes called 'national communist' party

musyawarah	Consultation and discussion, in order to reach a consensus
Nasakom (Nasionalisme, Agama dan Komunisme)	Sukarno's projected blend of nationalism, religion, and communism
Nekolim (Neokolonialisme, Kolonialisme dan Imperialisme)	Sukarno's acronymic epithet for the exploitations conducted by the capitalist Western World
NHM	Nederlandsche Handel-Maatschappij
NIAM (Nederlandsch-Indische Aardolie Maatschappij)	Netherlands Indies Oil Co., a joint venture of Shell with the Netherlands Indies government
NKPM (Nederlandsche Koloniale Petroleum Maatschappij)	Netherlands Colonial Petroleum Co., a subsidiary of Standard Oil of New Jersey (Exxon)
NPPM (Nederlandsche Pacific Petroleum Maatschappij)	Netherlands Pacific Petroleum Co., a subsidiary of Caltex
NU (Nahdatul Ulama)	Muslim Scholars' Party
Nusantara	Archipelago, hence Indonesia
Nusa Tenggara	South-east Islands; also Sunda Kecil, formerly the Lesser Sunda Islands
Oldefos	Old Established Forces, synonymous with capitalism and imperialism
Orba (Orde Baru)	New Order; the regime of President Suharto
Orla (Orde Lama)	Old Order; the Sukarno regime

pamong desa	Village officials
pamong praja	Government officials
Panca Sila	Sukarno's five principles of the Indonesian state. (Belief in God; nationalism; humanism; democracy; social justice)
panglima	Commanding Officer
Parkindo (Partai Keristen Indonesia)	Indonesian Christian Party (Protestant)
patih	Javanese Minister, or high official
PB (Peta Baru)	New Peta, the Indonesian name for the high-yielding Philippine IR rice varieties
PBP (Partai Pembangunan Persatuan)	United Development Party, a loose union of four Muslim parties, created in 1973
PDI (Partai Demokrasi Indonesia)	Indonesian Democratic Party, a grouping of five non-Muslim parties in 1973
pegawai	Government servant
peranakan	Indonesia-born, or assimilated, Chinese
Permesta (Perjuangan Semesta)	Universal Struggle, the Sulawesi revolt of 1957
Permigan (PN Pertambangan Minyak dan Gas Bumi Nasional)	National Oil and Gas Mining Company
Permina (Perusahaan Minyak Nasional)	State National Oil Mining Company, successor to TMSU, and reorganised as a state company in 1961

Permindo (Perusahaan Minyak Indonesia)	Indonesian Oil Enterprise, successor to NIAM
Pertamin (PN Pertambangan Minyak Indonesia)	Indonesian Oil Mining, successor to *Permindo*
Pertamina (Perusahaan Tambangan Minyak dan Gas Bumi Negara)	National Oil and Gas Mining, successor to PN *Pertamina* (PN *Pertambangan Minyak dan Gas Bumi Nasional*) formed in 1969 by a merger of *Permina* and *Pertamin*
Perti (Pergerakan Tabyah Islamyah)	Islamic Education Movement, a minor Muslim party based in Sumatra
Peta (Pembela Tanah Air)	Defenders of the Fatherland, the Japanese-sponsored volunteer corps
Peta	An Indonesian rice variety, and parent of the Philippine 'miracle rice' IR5
petani	Peasant
PKI	Indonesian Communist Party: (i) *Perserikatan Kommunist di India* (the 'old' PKI founded 1920); (ii) *Partai Kommunis Indonesia* (the 'new' PKI founded 1945)
PMI (Parmusi; Partai Muslimin Indonesia)	New Muslim Party, founded 1967, absorbed by PBP in 1973
PN (Perusahaan Negara)	State Enterprise
PNI (Partai Nasionalis Indonesia)	Indonesian Nationalist Party, a fusion in 1946 of several parties, including a wing of the old PNI founded in 1927 as Perserikatan Nasional Indonesia by Sukarno and others

PNT (PN *Timah*)	State Tin Corporation
PPN (B) (Pusat Perkebunan Negara (Baru))	(New) National Plantation Centre
priyayi	Nobility, or aristocracy
PRRI (Pemerintah Revolusioner Republik Indonesia)	Revolutionary Government of the Republic of Indonesia, the rebellious Sumatran government of 1957-58
PSI (Partai Sosialis Indonesia)	Indonesian Socialist Party, banned since 1960
PSII (Partai Serikat Islam Indonesia)	Indonesian Islamic Union Party, a minor party
PT (Perseroan Terbatas)	Limited Company
PTUS	Indonesian subsidiary of United States Rubber Co. Inc. (Uniroyal)
Repelita I	First Five-Year Development Plan (1969-73)
sandang pangan	Clothing and food (Javanese), the primary goal of the Sukarno cabinet of 1959
santri	The Muslim devout
Sarbupri (Sarekat Buruh Perkebunan Republik Indonesia)	Union of Plantation Workers of the Republic of Indonesia
sawah (an)	Ricefield (s)

Sobsi (Sentral Organisasi Buruh Seluruh Indonesia)	All Indonesia Central Organisation of Trade Unions, controlled by the PKI
tanah kering	Unirrigated land
Tavip (Tahun Vivere Pericoloso)	Year of Living Dangerously, Sukarno's Independence Day address of 1964
tegal (an)	Dry field (s)
TMSU (Tambang Minyak Sumatera Utara)	North Sumatra Oil Mining, replaced by *Permina*
totok	The China-born Indonesian Chinese
Usdek	Sukarno's acronymic Political Manifesto (*Manipol*) of 1959
(Undang-undang Dasar 1945	The Constitution of 1945
Socialisme à la Indonesia	Indonesian socialism
Demokrasi Terpimpin	Guided Democracy
Ekonomi Terpimpin	Guided Economy
Kepribadian Indonesia)	Indonesian Identity

Selected Bibliography

Admiralty, Naval Intelligence Division, *Netherlands Indies,* 2 vols., London, 1944.

Ide Anak Agung Gde Agung, *Twenty Years Indonesian Foreign Policy, 1945-1964,* Mouton, The Hague, 1973.

S. Takdir Alisjahbana, *Indonesia: Social and Cultural Revolution,* Oxford University Press, Kuala Lumpur, 1966.

G.C. Allen and A.G. Donnithorne, *Western Enterprise in Indonesia and Malaya: a study in economic development,* Allen and Unwin, London, 1957.

B.R.O'G. Anderson, *Java in a Time of Revolution: Occupation and Resistance, 1944-1946,* Cornell University Press, Ithaca, 1972.

A.G. Bartlett, *et al., Pertamina: Indonesian National Oil,* Amerasian Ltd., Djakarta, Singapore, and Tulsa, 1972.

P.T. Bauer, *The Rubber Industry: A Study in Competition and Monopoly,* Longman, London, 1948.

Howard W. Beers, editor, *Indonesia: resources and their technological development,* University Press of Kentucky, Lexington, 1970.

Don C. Bennet, 'The Basic Food Crops of Java and Madura', *Economic Geography,* vol. 37, 1961, 75-87.

C.C. Berg, 'De Sadeng-oorlog en de Mythe van Groot-Majapahit', *Indonesie,* vol. V, 1951, 385-422.

J.H. Boeke, *The Evolution of the Netherlands Indies Economy,* Institute of Pacific Relations, New York, 1946.

Ester Boserup, *The Conditions of Agricultural Growth,* Allen and Unwin, London, 1965.

J.O.M. Broek, *The Economic Development of the Netherlands Indies,* Institute of Pacific Relations, New York, 1942.

Edward M. Bruner, 'Urbanization and Ethnic Identity in North Sumatra', *American Anthropologist,* vol. 63, no. 3, 1961, 508-21.

Edward M. Bruner, 'The Expression of Ethnicity in Indonesia' in Abner Cohen, editor, *Urban Ethnicity,* A.S.A. Monographs no. 12, Tavistock Publications, London, 1974, 251-80.

Bulletin of Indonesian Economic Studies, Australian National University Press, Canberra.

Lance Castles, 'The Ethnic Profile of Djakarta', *Indonesia,* no. 3, 1967, 153-204.

W.J. Cater, *The Economic Position of the Chinese in the Netherlands Indies,* Blackwell and Mott, Oxford, 1936.

F. Cayrac-Blanchard, *Le Parti communiste indonésien,* Armand Colin, Paris, 1973.

H.T. Chabot, 'Urbanization Problems in South East Asia', *Transactions of the Fifth World Congress of Sociology,* Louvain, 1964, vol. 3, 125-31.

Chang Kwang-chih, 'Major Problems in the Culture History of Southeast Asia', *Bulletin of the Institute of Ethnology, Academia Sinica,* vol. 13, 1962, 1-26.

J.L. Cobban, 'Geographic Notes on the First Two Centuries of Djakarta', *Journal of the Malaysian Branch, Royal Asiatic Society,* vol. XLIV, pt 2, 1971, 108-50.

C.D. Cowan, 'Governor Bannerman and the Penang Tin Scheme, 1818-1819', *Journal of the Malayan Branch, Royal Asiatic Society,* vol. XXIII, pt 1, 1950, 52-83.

Richard Critchfield, 'The Plight of the Cities: Djakarta—the First to "Close"', *Columbia Journal of World Business,* vol. 6, 1971, 89-93.

Bernhard Dahm, *History of Indonesia in the Twentieth Century* (translated from the German by P.S. Falla), Pall Mall Press, London, 1971.

A.C.A. Dake, *In the Spirit of the Red Banteng: Indonesian Communists between Moscow and Peking, 1959-65,* Mouton, The Hague, 1973.

Alice Dewey, *Peasant Marketing in Java,* Free Press, Glencoe, Ill., 1962.

J.L.L. Duyvendak, 'Chinese in the Dutch East Indies', *The Chinese Social and Political Science Review,* vol. IX, no. 1, 1927, 1-13.

Hans-Dieter Evers, 'Urban Involution: the Social Development of South-east Asian Towns', *International Conference on South-east Asian Studies,* Kuala Lumpur, February 1972 (mimeo).

Herbert Feith, *The Decline of Constitutional Democracy in Indonesia,* Cornell University Press, Ithaca, 1962.

Herbert Feith and Lance Castles, editors, *Indonesian Political Thinking, 1945-65,* Cornell University Press, Ithaca, 1970.

Charles A. Fisher, *South-east Asia: a social, economic and political geography,* Methuen, London, 1964.

Charles A. Fisher, 'Economic Myth and Geographical Reality in Indonesia', *Modern Asian Studies,* vol. 1, 1967, 155-89.

Stephen FitzGerald, *China and the Overseas Chinese: A Study of Peking's Changing Policy, 1949-1970,* Cambridge University Press, Cambridge, 1972.

D.W. Fryer, 'Jogjakarta: Economic Development in an Indonesian City State', *Economic Development and Cultural Change,* vol. 7, 1957, 452-64.

D.W. Fryer, 'Recovery of the Sugar Industry in Java', *Economic*

Geography, vol. 33, 1957, 171-87.

D.W. Fryer, 'Economic Aspects of Indonesian Disunity', *Pacific Affairs,* vol. 30, 1957, 195-208.

D.W. Fryer, *Indonesia: The Economic Geography of an Under-developed Country,* unpublished Ph.D. thesis, University of London, 1958.

D.W. Fryer, *Emerging Southeast Asia: a study in growth and stagnation,* George Philip and Son, London, 1970.

J.S. Furnivall, *Netherlands India: a study of plural economy,* Cambridge University Press, Cambridge, 1944.

Clifford Geertz, *The Religion of Java,* Free Press, Glencoe, Ill., 1960.

Clifford Geertz, *Peddlers and Princes: social change and economic modernisation in two Indonesian towns,* The University of Chicago Press, Chicago. 1963.

Clifford Geertz, *Agricultural Involution: the process of ecological change in Indonesia,* University of California Press, Berkeley and Los Angeles, 1963.

Clifford Geertz, *The Social History of an Indonesian Town,* MIT Press, Cambridge, Mass., 1965.

Bruce Glassburner, 'Economic Policy Making in Indonesia, 1950-1957', *Economic Development and Cultural Change,* vol. 10, 1962, 113-33.

Bruce Glassburner, editor, *The Economy of Indonesia: selected readings,* Cornell University Press, Ithaca, 1971.

Go Gien Tjwan, 'The Assimilation Problem of the Chinese in Indonesia', *Cultures et développement,* vol. I, no. 1, 1968, 41-59.

J.W. Gould, *Americans in Sumatra,* Martinus Nijhoff, The Hague, 1961.

D.G.E. Hall, *A History of South-east Asia,* Macmillan, London, 1960.

C.J.J. van Hall, *Insulinde: De Inheemsche Landbouw,* W. van Hoeve, Deventer, n.d.

Willard A. Hanna, *Bung Karno's Indonesia,* American Universities Field Staff, no. 28, New York, 1961.

H.J. Heeren, 'The Urbanisation of Djakarta', *Ekonomi dan Keuangan Indonesia,* vol. 8, 1955, 696-736.

Karl Helbig, *Batavia. Eine tropische Stadtlandschaftskunde im Rahmen der Insel Java,* C.H. Wäsers Druckerei, Bad Segeberg, 1931.

Benjamin Higgins, *Indonesia's Economic Stabilisation and Development,* Institute of Pacific Relations, New York, 1957.

Benjamin and Jean Higgins, *Indonesia: the Crisis of the Millstones,* Van Nostrand, Princeton, 1963.

Claire Holt, editor, *Culture and Politics in Indonesia,* Cornell University Press, Ithaca, 1972.

P. Honig and F. Verdoorn, editors, *Science and Scientists in the Netherlands Indies,* Board for the Netherlands Indies, Surinam, and Curacao, New York, 1945.

James C. Jackson, 'Mining in 18th Century Bangka: the Pre-European Exploitation of a "Tin Island"', *Pacific Viewpoint,* vol. 10, no. 2, 1969, 28-54.

James C. Jackson, *Chinese in the West Borneo Goldfields: a Study in Cultural Geography,* University of Hull Occasional Papers in Geography no. 15, Hull, 1970.

James C. Jackson, 'Post-Independence Developments and the Indonesian City: Preliminary Observations on the Spatial Structure of Palembang', *Sumatra Research Bulletin,* vol. 2, no. 2, 1973, 3-11.

Russell Johnson, *et al., Business Environment in an Emerging Nation: profiles of the Indonesian economy,* Northwestern University Press, Evanston, 1966.

Gavin Jones, 'The Recent Growth of Asian Cities', *Hemisphere,* vol. 8, no. 2, 1964, 8-13.

Howard P. Jones, *Indonesia: the Possible Dream*, Harcourt Brace, New York, 1971.

G.McT. Kahin, *Nationalism and Revolution in Indonesia*, Cornell University Press, Ithaca, 1952.

Nathan Keyfitz, 'The Population of Indonesia', *Ekonomi dan Keuangan Indonesia*, vol. 6, no. 10, 1953, 641-55.

Nathan Keyfitz, 'The Ecology of Indonesian Cities', *American Journal of Sociology*, vol. 66, 1961, 348-54.

E.S. de Klerck, *History of the Netherlands East Indies*, 2 vols., Brusse, Rotterdam, 1938.

Koentjaraningrat, editor, *Villages in Indonesia*, Cornell University Press, Ithaca, 1967.

Justus M. van der Kroef, *Indonesia in the Modern World*, 2 vols., Masa Baru, Bandung, 1954 and 1956.

Justus M. van der Kroef, 'The Sino-Indonesian Rupture', *China Quarterly*, no. 33, 1968, 17-46.

Justus M. van der Kroef, *Indonesia since Sukarno*, Asia Pacific Press, Singapore, 1971.

Kwee Tek Hoay, *The Origins of the Modern Chinese Movement in Indonesia*, Translation Series, Modern Indonesia Project, Cornell University, Ithaca, 1969.

J.D. Legge, *Indonesia*, Prentice-Hall, Englewood Cliffs, 1965.

J.D. Legge, *Sukarno: a Political Biography*, Allen Lane, London, 1972.

H. Lehmann, 'Das Antlitz der Stadt in Niederländisch-Indien' in H. Louis and W. Panzer, editors, *Länderkundliche Forschung: Festschrift zur Vollendung des Sechzigsten Lebensjahres Norbert Krebs, Dargebracht van Seinen Schülern, Mitarbeitern, Freuden und dem verlag*, J. Englehorns Nachf., Stuttgart, 1936, 109-39.

J.C. van Leur, *Indonesian Trade and Society: essays in Asian social and economic history,* W. van Hoeve, The Hague and Bandung, 1955.

Daniel S. Lev, *The Transition to Guided Democracy,* Cornell University Press, Ithaca, 1966.

R. William Liddle, *Ethnicity, Party, and National Integration: an Indonesian case study,* Yale University Press, New Haven and London, 1970.

I.M.D. Little, Tibor Scitovsky, and Maurice Scott, *Industry and Trade in Some Developing Countries,* Oxford University Press, London, 1970.

Margo L. Lyon, *Bases of Conflict in Rural Java,* Research Monograph no. 3, Center for South and Southeast Asian Studies, University of California, Berkeley, 1970.

J.A.C. Mackie, 'Indonesia's Government Estates and their Masters', *Pacific Affairs,* vol. 34, 1961, 337-60.

J.A.C. Mackie, *Konfrontasi: The Indonesia-Malaysia Dispute, 1963-1966,* Oxford University Press, London, 1974.

T.G. McGee, *The Southeast Asian City,* Bell, London, 1967.

G. McNicoll, 'Internal Migration in Indonesia: Descriptive Notes', *Indonesia,* no. 5, 1968, 29-92.

Ruth T. McVey, editor, *Indonesia,* Southeast Asia Studies, Yale University, by arrangement with Human Relations Area Files Press, New Haven, 1963; rev. ed., 1967.

Ruth T. McVey, *The Rise of Indonesian Communism,* Cornell University Press, Ithaca, 1965.

M.A.P. Meilink-Roelofsz., *Asian Trade and European Influence in the Indonesian Archipelago between 1500 and about 1630,* Martinus Nijhoff, The Hague, 1962.

J.E. Metcalf, *The Agricultural Economy of Indonesia,* U.S. Department of Agriculture, Washington, 1952.

P.D. Milone, 'Contemporary Urbanization in Indonesia', *Asian Survey,* vol. 4, no. 8, 1964, 1000-12.

P.D. Milone, *Urban Areas in Indonesia: administrative and census concepts,* Research Series no. 10, Institute of International Studies, University of California, Berkeley, 1966.

G.J. Missen, *Viewpoint on Indonesia: A Geographical Study,* Nelson, Melbourne, 1972.

Rex Mortimer, *The Indonesian Communist Party and Land Reform 1959-1965,* Monash Papers on Southeast Asia no. 1, Centre of Southeast Asian Studies, Monash University, Clayton, Victoria, 1972.

Rex Mortimer, editor, *Showcase State: the illusion of Indonesia's 'accelerated modernisation',* Angus and Robertson, Sydney, 1973.

Rex Mortimer, *Indonesian Communism under Sukarno. Ideology and Politics, 1959-1965,* Cornell University Press, Ithaca, 1974.

G. Myrdal, *Asian Drama: an inquiry into the poverty of nations,* 3 vols., London, 1968.

Purnaman Natakusumah, 'Bandung' in Aprodicio A. Laquian, editor, *Rural-Urban Migrants and Metropolitan Development,* INTERMET Metropolitan Studies Series, Toronto, 1971, 11-31.

R. Van Niel, *The Emergence of the Modern Indonesian Elite,* W. van Hoeve, The Hague, 1960.

R. Van Niel, editor, *Economic Factors in Southeast Asian Social Change,* Asian Studies at Hawaii no. 2, University of Hawaii, Honolulu, 1968.

Oey Hong Lee, *Indonesian Government and Press During Guided Democracy,* Hull Monographs on South-East Asia no. 4, University of Hull, Hull, 1971.

Oey Hong Lee, editor, *Indonesia after the 1971 Elections,* Oxford University Press, London, 1974.

Oey Hong Lee, 'The Indonesian Chinese under the New Order', *Cultures et développement,* vol. VII, no. 1, 1975, 95-122.

Ingrid Palmer, *Textiles in Indonesia: Problems of Import Substitution,* Praeger, New York, 1972.

L.H. Palmier, *Indonesia and the Dutch,* Oxford University Press, London, 1962.

L.H. Palmier, *Communists in Indonesia,* Weidenfeld and Nicolson, London, 1973.

J. Panglaykim and H.W. Arndt, *The Indonesian Economy: Facing a New Era?,* Rotterdam University Press, Rotterdam, 1966.

Guy J. Pauker, 'Indonesia's Eight Year Development Plan',*Pacific Affairs,* vol. 34, 1961, 115-30.

James L. Peacock, *Indonesia: an anthropological perspective,* Goodyear, Pacific Palisades, 1973.

Karl J. Pelzer, *Pioneer Settlement in the Asiatic Tropics,* American Geographical Society, New York, 1948.

Karl J. Pelzer, 'The Agrarian Conflict in East Sumatra', *Pacific Affairs,* vol. 30, 1957, 151-59.

C.L.M. Penders, *The Life and Times of Sukarno,* Sidgwick and Jackson, London, 1974.

Bram Peper, 'Population Growth in Java in the 19th Century: A New Interpretation', *Population Studies,* vol. 24, 1970, 71-84.

J.M. Pluvier, *Confrontations. A Study in Indonesian Politics,* Oxford University Press, Kuala Lumpur, 1965.

Robert R. Reed, 'The Colonial Origins of Manila and Batavia: Desultory Notes on Nascent Metropolitan Primacy and Urban Systems in Southeast Asia', *Asian Studies,* vol. 5, no. 3, 1967, 543-62.

Anthony Reid, *The Indonesian National Revolution, 1945-1950,* Longman, London, 1974.

M.C. Ricklefs, *Jogjakarta under Sultan Mangkubumi 1749-1792: a History of the Division of Java,* Oxford University Press, London, 1974.

B. Schrieke, editor, *The Effect of Western Influence on Native Civilisations in the Malay Archipelago*, Royal Batavia Society of Arts and Sciences, Batavia, 1929.

B. Schrieke, *Indonesian Sociological Studies*, W. van Hoeve, The Hague and Bandung, Part I, 1955; Part II, 1957.

Selosoemardjan, *Social Changes in Jogjakarta*, Cornell University Press, Ithaca, 1962.

Allen M. Sievers, *The Mystical World of Indonesia: Culture and Economic Development in Conflict*, Johns Hopkins Press, Baltimore, 1974.

Sie Kwat Soen, *Prospects for Agricultural Development in Indonesia, with special reference to Java*, Centre for Agricultural Publishing and Documentation, Wageningen, 1968.

S. Soekanto, 'Elites in Three Southeast Asian Countries: a Sociological Perspective', *Indonesian Quarterly*, vol. 1, no. 2, 1973, 50-9.

Mary F. Somers, *Peranakan Chinese Politics in Indonesia*, Interim Reports Series, Modern Indonesia Project, Cornell University, Ithaca, 1964.

J.E. Spencer, 'The Migration of Rice from Mainland Southeast Asia into Indonesia', in J. Barrau, editor, *Plants and the Migrations of Pacific Peoples*, Bishop Museum Press, Honolulu, 1966, 83-9.

J.E. Spencer, *Shifting Cultivation in Southeastern Asia*, University of California Press, Berkeley and Los Angeles, 1966.

T.K. Tan, editor, *Sukarno's Guided Indonesia*, Jacaranda Press, Brisbane, 1967.

Tan Giok-Lan, *The Chinese of Sukabumi: a Study in Social and Cultural Accommodation*, Monograph Series, Modern Indonesia Project, Cornell University, Ithaca, 1963.

Tan Goantiang, 'Some Notes on Internal Migration in Indonesia', *International Migration*, vol. VI, nos. 1/2, 1968, 39-52.

A.L. Ter Braake, *Mining in the Netherlands East Indies,* Institute of Pacific Relations, New York, 1944.

G.J.A. Terra, 'Farm Systems in South-East Asia', *Netherlands Journal of Agricultural Science,* vol. 6, no. 3, 1958, 157-82.

The Chinese in Indonesia, the Philippines and Malaysia, Minority Rights Group Report no. 10, London, 1972.

The Siauw Giap, 'Urbanisatieproblemen in Indonesië', *Bijdragen tot de Taal-, Land- en Volkenkunde,* vol. 115, pt 3, 1959, 249-76.

K. van der Veer, *De Rijstcultuur in Indonesië,* W. van Hoeve, 's-Gravenhage, 1949.

T. Vittachi, *The Fall of Sukarno,* Praeger, New York, 1967.

B.H.M. Vlekke, *Nusantara: a History of Indonesia,* W. van Hoeve, The Hague, 1965.

W. van Warmelo, 'Ontstaan en groei van de handweefnijverheid in Madjalaja', *Koloniale Studiën,* vol. XXIII, 1939, 5-25.

Donald E. Weatherbee, 'Portuguese Timor: an Indonesian dilemma', *Asian Survey,* vol. 6, 1966, 683-95.

W.F. Wertheim, 'Sociological Aspects of Inter-island Migration in Indonesia', *Population Studies,* vol. 12, 1959, 184-201.

W.F. Wertheim, *Indonesian Society in Transition: a study of sociological change,* W. van Hoeve, The Hague, 1956.

Widjojo Nitisastro, *Population Trends in Indonesia,* Cornell University Press, Ithaca, 1970.

D.E. Willmott, *The Chinese of Semarang: a Changing Minority Community in Indonesia,* Cornell University Press, Ithaca, 1960.

D.E. Willmott, *The National Status of the Chinese in Indonesia, 1900-1958,* Monograph Series, Modern Indonesia Project, Cornell University, Ithaca, 1961.

Ronald A. Witton, 'The Development of Cities in Java: A Preliminary Empirical Analysis', *Southeast Asian Journal of Sociology,* vol. 2, 1969, 62-80.

O.W. Wolters, *Early Indonesian Commerce: a Study of the Origins of Srivijaya,* Cornell University Press, Ithaca, 1967.

Index

Printed in the United States of America
by Lithocrafters, Inc., Ann Arbor, Michigan